Malcolm X
and the Poetics of
Haki Madhubuti

Malcolm X and the Poetics of Haki Madhubuti

REGINA JENNINGS

McFarland & Company, Inc., Publishers
Jefferson, North Carolina, and London

"Malcolm X: An Autobiography" and excerpt from "Morning Raga for Malcolm" by Larry Neal are from *Hoodoo Hollerin' Bebop Ghosts*, copyright ©1968, 1974 by Larry Neal. Reprinted with the permission of Howard University Press. All rights reserved.

Excerpts from *Black Feeling, Black Talk, Black Judgment* by Nikki Giovanni are copyright ©1968, 1970 by Nikki Giovanni. Used by permission of HarperCollins Publishers, Inc.

Excerpt from *Black Art* by Amiri Baraka is copyright © by Amiri Baraka. Reprinted by permission of SLL/Sterling Lord Literistic, Inc.

Poems and excerpts from *The Poetical Works of Marcus Garvey*, compiled by Tony Martin, are used by permission of The Majority Press.

Excerpts from "Heritage," "Timid Lover," "The Shroud of Color," "Incident," and "Song of Praise" from *Color* by Countee Cullen, copyright ©1925 by Harper & Brothers, 1953 by Ida M. Cullen, are reprinted by permission of GRM Associates, Inc.

Excepts from *Blacks* and all books by Haki Madhubuti, copyright by Haki Madhubuti, are used and reprinted by permission of Haki Madhubuti and Third World Press, Inc., Chicago.

Excerpts from "Mulatto" by Claude McKay used courtesy of the Literary Representatives for the works of Claude McKay, Schomburg Center for Research in Black Culture, The New York Public Library, Astor, Lenox and Tilden Foundations.

Excerpts from "Good Morning, Revolution" and "Goodbye Christ" and other poems in *The Collected Poems of Langston Hughes* by Langston Hughes are copyright ©1994 by the Estate of Langston Hughes, and are used by permission of Alfred A. Knopf, a division of Random House, Inc., and by permission of Harold Ober Associates.

LIBRARY OF CONGRESS CATALOGUING-IN-PUBLICATION DATA

Jennings, Regina.
Malcolm X and the poetics of Haki Madhubuti / Regina Jennings.
p. cm.
Includes bibliographical references and index.

ISBN-13: 978-0-7864-2619-5
ISBN-10: 0-7864-2619-5
(softcover : 50# alkaline paper) ∞

1. Madhubuti, Haki R., 1942– — Criticism and interpretation.
2. X, Malcolm, 1925–1965 — Influence. 3. African Americans — Race identity.
4. African Americans — Intellectual life — 20th century.
5. American poetry — African American authors — History and criticism. I. Title.
PS3563.A3397Z73 2006   811'.54 — dc22   2006023508

British Library cataloguing data are available

©2006 Regina Jennings. All rights reserved

No part of this book may be reproduced or transmitted in any form or by any means, electronic or mechanical, including photocopying or recording, or by any information storage and retrieval system, without permission in writing from the publisher.

On the cover: Haki Madhubuti (photograph ©2006 Lynda Koolish); background: Malcolm X waits at Martin Luther King press conference, March 26, 1964 (Library of Congress)

Manufactured in the United States of America

McFarland & Company, Inc., Publishers
Box 611, Jefferson, North Carolina 28640
www.mcfarlandpub.com

To the spirit of the 1960s

Acknowledgments

I would like to thank Dr. Gayle T. Tate, scholar extraordinaire, for not only discussing the ideas of various chapters in this text but also for practicing academic, social, and political sisterhood. I would also like to thank the noted scholars Kariamu Welsh for her suggestions for the manuscript, Carolyn Karcher for always encouraging the significance of my point of view, and Daudi Ya Azibo for his close reading and constructive criticism.

Contents

Acknowledgments vi

Preface 1

Introduction: Malcolm Imagining the Black Arts Movement and Madhubuti 5

ONE. From Nigger to Negro: Dysfunctional Beginnings of Identity for New World Africans 29

TWO. How New Is the New Negro? 51

THREE. Africa as Motif in Pre-1960s Poetry: Selections of the Antebellum, the Reconstruction, and the Harlem Renaissance 60

FOUR. Early Influences of a Revolutionary Aesthetic in Black Poetry: Langston Hughes and Marcus Garvey 104

FIVE. W.E.B. Du Bois, Cheikh Anta Diop, Malcolm X, and Haki Madhubuti: Claiming and Containing Continuity in Black Language and Institutions 125

SIX. Issues of Memory and Maleness: Malcolm and Madhubuti: Institution Builders and Educators 135

SEVEN. Malcolm and Haki and Safisha Madhubuti on African-Centered Education and Africa in the Imagination ... 157

EIGHT. Malcolm X and Madhubuti: A Physical and Personal
  Merging 174
NINE. Communion: X, a Magnet for Madhubuti and Brooks ... 188
TEN. The X-Factor Influence: A Theoretical Frame for
  Resistance Poetry 199
ELEVEN. The X-Factor Influence on the Transformed Image
  of Africa in the Poetry of Haki Madhubuti: Issues of
  Re(re)naming and Inversion 220

Chapter Notes 257
Works Cited 271
Index 283

Preface

The image of Malcolm X remains a contentious one in mainstream media and the dominant culture. Recently a talk show host contrasted Martin Luther King with Malcolm X, urging her audience to accept King for his nonviolence and reject X for his violence. King is the prince of peace, and X the prince of darkness, Western inspired. Yet, Malcolm X has never led a posse of revenge-seeking Black people to physically harm anyone, and for many African Americans, his legacy is one of heroism. In *Malcolm X and the Poetics of Haki Madhubuti*, I seek to place a practical foundation under his heroics by comparing his oratory to the poetry of one of his listeners and disciples, the poet Don L. Lee/Haki Madhubuti. Many of the issues that were new and original that Malcolm X espoused during the 1960s are now living in American culture and my attempt in this writing is to reveal the manifestations of X's vision in contemporary culture. The uniqueness of his legacy as well as his continuation of Black Nationalism in America has to be showcased in order for his accomplishments, not simply his assassination, to be remembered. This methodology is vital in constructing an African-centered perspective that brings to light how Diaspora Africans view one another and the world. Such a worldview has only recently been considered important to scholarship because it deviates from the master narrative that claims universality when in reality it replicates an Anglo-American and Eurocentric worldview.

In *Malcolm X and the Poetics of Haki Madhubuti*, I trace the trajectory of imagery in poetry by African Americans to argue the significance of the 1960s Black Arts poetry. This is a poetry, like X's oratory, that is often thought unrelated to the development of ideology, art appreciation, and advancement in America. Yet major African American poets, Amiri Baraka, Sonia Sanchez, Haki Madhubuti, have all discussed X's profound influence on their artistic elevation and evolution. However, Madhubuti has not only continued to write from what I call a malcolmian perspective, but also, he has followed X's mandate to build independent institutions, and his enterprises are in existence today. They are Third World Press, the Institute of Positive Education, the Betty Shabazz International Charter School, and recently the Barbara Sizemore Campus.

Yet, despite his corpus of literature, over twenty-five books of poetry and essays, Madhubuti like X remains unpopular with key contemporary editors probably because of his successful and autonomous Black Nationalist voice. His independent institutions are remarkable for their stability and longevity. He literally listened to the pronouncements of X and others and dedicated his entire life to ensuring the grounding of African-centered ideology in publishing and educational units. The poet Madhubuti like other Black Arts artists decided to create art to undermine the assimilation tendencies in Negro behavior. In fact, one of the major purposes of the Black Arts was to shift linguistically and culturally the Negro from that racial appellation to one that identified with Africa. Malcolm X had preached the problems of the "so-called Negro" and his dubious phrase ignited the notion of change and difference within his listeners labeled Negro.

Haki Madhubuti created independent art that assisted in the Negro's need for name change after the assassination of Malcolm X. He lifted primary points from Malcolm's oratory and developed art around malcolmian themes, providing longevity to the legacy of X, offering him to present and future generations.

In this book, to highlight the significance of Madhubuti's continuation of the oratorical themes of Malcolm X, I trace the roots of the race name "Negro" and analyze its usage in literature written by Blacks during the 18th through the 20th centuries. This investigation shows how early American poets, autobiographers, and novelists consistently presented dislocated images of Africa that tangled the psychology of Negro America in only enslavement and assimilation. My investigative route enabled a contrasting and important beginning that prepares for the understanding of the art of war, the poetry written during the Age of Malcolm X. This literary war with America challenged previous art and stimulated imagery seeped in contemporary Pan-African humanism that forced the emergence of a new people, the African American people. This is the art and the oratory that caused the elimination of the synonym for slave, "Negro," and the acceptance of "African American." To examine artistry from this perspective provides African Americans with a history of self-

and race-inspired achievement instead of what Malcolm X referred to as "a history of losses."

Malcolm X and Haki Madhubuti are in this sense founders of a new American people because they are the destroyers of a race name that debased a people for over three hundred years.

Introduction: Malcolm Imagining the Black Arts Movement and Madhubuti

Before the Black Arts Movement manifested in the late 1960s, Malcolm X, the once fiery spokesman for the Nation of Islam, articulated an artistic possibility that would reinvent the "so-called Negro" into a reconfigured African-centered Black. He spoke specifically to Negro creative writers, encouraging them to design artistic products that would assist in reinventing a people complete with a new racial conception, appellation, and identity. Through the motion in this invention, X envisioned his people as a global unit, focused on the African Diaspora and in America behaving independently of White control. For Malcolm, culture was a transforming power that would center the psychology of the American Negro onto him and herself. He wrote about this in the "Statement of Basic Aims and Objectives" of the Organization of Afro-American Unity, his final organization before his assassination. Malcolm called for cultural centers with workshops for people of all ages that included creative writing, and this creativity was to unite Africans wherever they reside. It was also to connect the history of American Negroes especially to the glorious past in the land of Africa.[1] Through culture, Malcolm desired the transformation of the "so-called Negroes" into African and African American people, and the poets during the Age of Malcolm X not only listened to his message, but also orchestrated his song.

For example, responding to mandates of Malcolm X, 1960s poets combined and invented culture and revolution in art. After Malcolm's assassination, this energy coalesced into the Black Arts Movement, formalizing itself into the most significant aesthetics shift in the trajectory of Black American art.

Malcolm X and the Poetics of Haki Madhubuti explores how the activism and oratory of X specifically informs Haki Madhubuti's literary, aesthetic, and psychological viewpoints. In this study, Madhubuti represents Black Arts poets, but he is one with a crucial and unique difference worthy of investigation. Haki Madhubuti institutionalized "malcolmian" themes beyond his poetry: he built independent Black schools and founded Third World Press. All have been in operation since the 1960s. Madhubuti not only sought to change the intellectual activity of his listeners and readers. He also labored long in the study of institution building in order to assist in the development of young people for generations to come.

Haki Madhubuti, known as Don L. Lee in the 1960s, assumed a leadership mantel that brings much of X's dogma into the 21st century. This extraordinary accomplishment is understated in its lack of attention, especially since Madhubuti started from excruciatingly impoverished beginnings. He is not your average university professor, although he is one. He is not your average poet, although he is that. He is not your average essayist, although he writes essays. His dichotomous accomplishments in unity point to a contemporary Black Nationalism that in this age of multiculturalism requires focus for study. As such, *Malcolm X and the Poetics of Haki Madhubuti* examines why and how Madhubuti crafted racially transforming art independent of White America, and it documents his building autonomous institutions primarily for Black people. This kind of report retells the legacy of Malcolm X differently from that of a tragedy or that of a dead hero. Through the imaginative, visionary, and practical work of Madhubuti, Malcolm X is a living hero, making the term "role model" accessible and significant.

By examining oratory and poetry, *Malcolm X and the Poetics of Haki Madhubuti* tells the story of two diverse yet similar Black leaders using "location theory." This is a framework to scrutinize historical and cultural consciousness in literature, asserting an authenticity purposeful to those of the African Diaspora. Thus, according to the architect of location theory, Molefi Asante, in this text I deconstruct the language, attitude and direction of Malcolm X and Haki Madhubuti. Questions for consideration include whether or not the language of each man is oppressive or liberating. Does it express the beliefs and values of Black people? Does the language promote African agency or European cultural hegemony? I begin with the prominent theme of racial name change in order to establish how the

Negro turned into the African American. This was a major theme in the teachings of Elijah Muhammad, head of the Nation of Islam and X's personal mentor, and it became a prominent theme in Madhubuti's corpus of poetry. Today, African Americans assume this racial appellation without the necessary history behind how such a re(re)naming took place. X and Madhubuti deliberately spoke to and designed art around this issue. X was the teacher, Madhubuti an audience participant, an indirect willing pupil, who continued and concretized X's thought after his assassination.

To establish the problems with the word "Negro," I take a historical journey through various literatures that contain uses for the racial name. Afterwards the book concentrates on poetic imagery from the 18th to the 20th century that defines expressively the negative nature and connotations of the word and racial name "Negro." The second half of the text highlights X's pronouncements and Madhubuti's thematic transference of Malcolm's perspectives into art and institution building. Exploring the major themes in Malcolm X's oratory for comparison to images in early and contemporary poetry of Madhubuti illustrates the following: the origins of a revolutionary poetry movement, a revisiting of 1960s Black Nationalism, the contemporary identity of the Negro, and the rudiments of Afrocentricity and African-centered thought.

In order to examine poetry and political oratory arising during the 1960s, I use African-centered paradigms for clarification of Black culture and psychology. Such a methodology allows an understanding of the race-centered and transforming ideology of X and the consequent artistry that emerged because of his viewpoints. Additionally, analyzing the oratory and poetry from frames that relate to African thought and comprehension accomplishes what both X and Madhubuti determined in their oratory and poetry. They desired that the Negro people attach their consciousness to Africa, to discover origins and non-Western ways of interpreting phenomena. X, following the ideology of Elijah Muhammad, was determined to break the Eurocentric stronghold in the consciousness or psychology of the Negro. Similarly, Madhubuti in his poetry and essays sought to expand this disruption from solely American thought and consciousness in order to bring into being concepts that X envisioned.

X's approval of culture as a transforming tool suggests how important he considered its impact in redirecting the future of a people. Most think about Malcolm X as a political figure and leader of Black people. However, his insisting that cultural centers occupy Black communities also illustrates textually how urban culture affected him prior to his becoming a minister. Before Malcolm X became a political proponent and leader of African people worldwide, he demonstrated in the *Autobiography of Malcolm X* a respect and appreciation for Negro culture. This desire assisted in his later drafting a cultural component in his charter for the Organization of Afro-American Unity. Relying on book knowledge and personal experience, X conjoined the two, often repeating his biography in oratory, making the personal the political. Before his maturation, X found purpose, insight, and beauty in the nightlife of Boston and Harlem, enjoying the talent of his people. Once his criminal activities landed him in jail, he stepped into another cultural focus: oratory and its persuasive use to promote the historical wonder of the Negro, a misnamed African.

Malcolm Mastering Oratory

Karl Evanzz, in *The Judas Factor* (1992), emphasizes Malcolm's study of oratory while incarcerated. In this masterful work, Evanzz painstakingly provides evidence of FBI penetration in the Nation of Islam and X's social circle. He also argues a historical course of FBI interference in Black organizations, from Marcus Garvey's Universal Negro Improvement Association during the 1920s to the assassination of Patrice Lumumba in the Congo in the 1960s. As it pertains to Malcolm, he discloses facts about how, while in prison, X studied Paul Robeson's speaking style to win prison debates and to challenge debate leaders.[2] Evanzz says that X, by listening to Robeson's verbal discourse, prepared himself to alternate between stressed and unstressed syllables, "giving even the pauses rhythmic qualities."[3] Like young Malcolm Little once practiced his lindy-hop dance routines in cloistered apartments, he now in prison rehearsed the art of oratory in order to make public his verbal veracity.

Malcolm's study of effective oratory shows his understanding of public speech and its relationship to the Negro. Molefi Asante discusses this special relationship in *The Afrocentric Idea* (1987) where he illustrates the specific verbal play and fascination with *nommo*,[4] the word that stimulates Black language. He argues that because of the restrictions on literacy during slavery, a kind of verbal play permeated Black culture. Speech patterns that included the understated, the insinuated, the hidden and double-speech were features in Black talk. Similarly, Sterling Stuckey in his valuable text *Slave Culture* (1987) says that the enslavement of various African ethnic groups caused the variations to merge into a collective culture, history, and language.[5] This amalgamation fused multiple African verbal forms into English along with the underlying double-speak that combines the sacred and the secular. For when describing African verbal forms, one must include the living and the dead because of the importance of ancestral veneration in African societies,[6] and in the Americas, the enslaved continued a profound and complicated reliance on God. For example, Harriet Tubman sung and hummed spirituals to let her escapees from bondage know her exact whereabouts.

In this historical and traditional sphere of Negro/Black oratory, Malcolm X regenerated *nommo*, "the word," as he started his ministry in the Nation of Islam (NOI). In that mental preparation, he employed his culture's verbal techniques, and his oratory not only effected the listeners of his time period. Rather, as Michael Dyson reminds us, Malcolm's language usage has also inspired contemporary rap and hip hop artists. Dyson remarks in *Making Malcolm* (1995) that

> [Malcolm's] broad familiarity with the devices of African American oral culture—the saucy put-down, the feigned agreement turned to oppositional advantage, the hyperbolic expression generously employed to make a point, the fetish for powerful metaphor—marks his public rhetoric.[7]

Malcolm understood that his art of oratory had to revolutionize his people from subservience to autonomy. One notes how he had close relationships with Harlem hustlers *and* leaders of nations.[8] In language he could shift effortlessly between slang and political discourse, regularly speaking to Negroes of all classes. William Sales in *From Civil Rights to Black Liberation* (1994) provides a series of anecdotes that illustrate X's interaction with all kinds of folk.[9] Speaking in multiple modes, X established a broad influence, his purpose for entering the realm of public discourse, even beyond his membership in the Nation of Islam. For his art, Malcolm had what Asante calls a "functional objective." His art of oratory was to speak into existence transformation, renewal, and productivity, "the creative manifestation of *what [was] called to be*. That which is *called to be*, because of the mores and values of the society, becomes the created thing."[10] X's stimulating discourse attracted shifts in worldview and transforming events in society and the world such as deconstructing White racism, challenging the legitimacy of non-violent activism, centering the Negro in world history, and inspiring the founding of the discipline of Black studies.

Malcolm X's comments on culture in the Organization of Afro-American Unity document demanded that the Negro reconnect to Africa as a point of origin instead of America with a beginning in enslavement. He saw this reunification as a blow to White supremacy. A cultural connection to Africa, he also thought, would manifest healing for a people suffering historical wounds from centuries of bondage, racism, discrimination, and mockery undergone in America and abroad. One of X's main oratorical themes is a revisit to the institution of slavery whereby he argues from the point of view of the enslaved and isolates the behavior of enslavers for examination. Many scholars have written on the psychological damage of enslavement on American-Africans. This type of scholarship is useful in tracking the continuing beliefs that plague contemporary African Americans.

For example, psychologist Talmadge Anderson[11] compares enslaved Blacks with prisoners of war because war prisoners and Blacks were tortured for the same reasons, information, incrimination, indoctrination, intimidation, and isolation. They were tortured to get information about revolts and to incriminate and betray fellow slaves. Torture indoctrinated the slave with the values and desires of the slaveholders and it forced the abandonment of African beliefs and practices.[12] Thus, the enslaved African and his next generation Negro lived in states of perpetual terrorism, and Malcolm developed his oratory to break this monolith, urging:

> We must launch a cultural revolution to unbrainwash an entire people. Our cultural revolution must be the means of bringing us closer to our African brothers and sisters. It must begin in the community and be based on community participation.... Artists must ... depend on the Afro-American for inspiration.... The cultural revolution will be the journey to our recovery of ourselves.[13]

The selves Malcolm refers to are both African and human. The African and the human "selves" were to erase the commodity emphasis inherent in the renaming of the African to Negro.

Malcolm Manifesting New Cultural Exporters

Reading and critiquing the racism in America, Elijah Muhammad, leader of the Nation of Islam, provided Malcolm with the pretext and context for what X later embellished into his own ideology and source for solution. With speeches that were powerful textual events, X conflated history, nationalism, self-defense, current events, and revolution, inspiring not only Madhubuti and the Black Arts poets, but also most of the 1960s Black Power advocates: Huey P. Newton, Bobby Seale, Stokely Carmichael (Kwame Touré), H. Rap Brown (Jamil Al-Amin), Kathleen Cleaver, and Angela Davis.

Other than Madhubuti, two other prominent Black Arts poets were most effected by X, Leroi Jones and Larry Neal. In 1968, Neal authored the manifesto of Black Arts, "The Black Arts Movement," three years after X's assassination. Presenting the purpose and direction for Black art in this essay, he points out the marriage between activism (Black Power) and art. Unlike those of the Harlem Renaissance (1920–35), the 1960s artists were wedded to the Black masses. Novelist, dramatists, poets designed worlds in art based on their own terms, refusing to speak to White America for approval. Instead, this art spoke directly to Black people, representing their uniqueness. A new aesthetic seeped in an amorphous "blackness" projected a culture of self and racial determination. Neal wrote, "The Black Arts Movement represents a flowering of a cultural nationalism that has been suppressed since the 1920s."[14] For Neal and other writers such as Madhubuti and Etheridge Knight, who contributed to the essay, this original artistic route was rooted in the folk tradition and it linked to the revolutionary potential of Black people worldwide. Similarly Malcolm X's "cultural revolution" was a journey for the Negro or Black to recover group consciousness in order to neutralize the power of what X called "the common enemy."

Along with the artists, this pervasive and powerful artistic credo also informed and inspired political activists such as Huey Newton, Bobby Seale, Stokely Carmichael and H. Rap Brown. They too paraded folk artistry and poetry to advance their political objectives. For example, Huey P. Newton, co-founder of the Black Panther Party, wrote poetry for the Panthers' newspaper, *The Black Panther*. Bobby Seale, the other co-founder, regularly performed two of his favorite poems, "Stagolee" and "Uncle Sammy Called Me Full of Lucifer," on Oakland, Berkeley, and San Francisco streets.[15] Stokely Carmichael (Kwame Touré), Student Non-Violent Coordinating Committee leader and founder of the All Africans Peoples Party, led rallies with the chant "Black Power" in call and response, an African and African American verbal pattern. H. Rap Brown (Al-Amin), Black Power proponent, orator, and activist, rapped toasts modeled after the folk hero "Shine." His vernacular performances caused him to get the nickname "Rap." Kathleen Cleaver, communications secretary of the Panthers, wrote poetry for *The Black Panther* newspaper that metaphorically conflated Huey Newton and Malcolm X. Also, her attire, large afro, hoop earrings, mini-skirt, attracted a new revolutionary aesthetic in clothing for women in the Panthers and in Black communities throughout the nation and abroad. Kathleen Cleaver predated Elaine Brown in female leadership in the Panthers. Angela Davis, intellectual and activist, discusses the influence of Malcolm X in her autobiography, *Angela Davis* (1974). As a communist party leader, her Black cultural performance was in oratory, defiance, dress, and style: her large "fro" started a nationwide trend. Mainstream media promoted her face and photograph first for being a professor and a communist; next, for being on the FBI's most wanted list when she escaped capture for allegedly supplying guns to Jonathan Jackson, younger brother of the incarcerated Panther George Jackson.

Yet, X not only energized political activists. He also stimulated artists such as Barbara Chase-Riboud, who designed her *Monument to Malcolm X* (1969) which aimed to "embody the idea of Malcolm rather than to make monuments to a dead man."[16] Elizabeth Catlett's painting *Negro es Bello II (Black is Beautiful)* (1969) illustrates obviously African male and female faces surrounded by Black Panther buttons. On the buttons are prowling panthers and the Black Panther logo: Black is beautiful.[17] Newton and Seale in their respective autobiographies, *Revolutionary Suicide* (1973) and *A Lonely Rage* (1978), claim X's ideas as source material for the formation of the Black Panther Party.

Ironically, before the founding of the Black Panther organization, M.S. Handler's wife conflated Malcolm X with an image of an actual panther. M.S. Handler, author of the preface to the *Autobiography of Malcolm X*, used his wife's comments to capture a visit with Malcolm X. He writes:

> Mrs. Handler was quiet and thoughtful after Malcolm's departure. Looking up suddenly, she said: "You know, it was like having tea with a black panther." The description startled me. The black panther is an aristocrat in the animal kingdom. He is beautiful. He is dangerous.[18]

In the 1960s, Whites were unaccustomed to a persona like Malcolm X, one who was Muslim, anti–American in the traditional civil rights sense, a global thinker, a Black Nationalist, and a visionary. This may account for Mrs. Handler's inability to compare X to another male White or Black. For comparison, she retreats into the animal kingdom, a jungle where historically all Blacks have been designated and compared to animals beginning in the enslavement period.

In the *Autobiography* during Malcolm's hustling days he fed into this perspective that changed when he embellished the theology of Elijah Muhammad. His initial manichean view of reality from Muhammad, Whites evil, Blacks beautiful, not only impacted the new poets. It also forcefully pulled into its foment the budding and established Black literati of the post–World War II period: James Baldwin, the most prolific writer of this epoch, gained great respect for X, and they appeared in venues together. All of the leading Black Arts authors, Leroi Jones (Amiri Baraka), winner of the Obie for *The Dutchmen* in 1964, Don L. Lee (Haki Madhubuti), Carolyn Rodgers, Ronald Snellings (Askia Muhammad Toufe), and Larry Neal, acknowledge X's magnifying presence.

Larry Neal was at the Audubon Ballroom, February 25, 1965, when Malcolm was killed. He had come to sell issues of his paper, the *Black American*, the organ for a group that supported Malcolm after his split from the Nation of Islam. When Neal writes about the manner in which X spoke, he compares it to poetry and music. Listen to Neal: "What I liked most about Malcolm was his sense of poetry: his speech rhythms, and his cadences that seemed to spring from the universe of Black music ... that blues idiom music called jazz. Malcolm was like that music."[19]

Also like musicians, Black Arts poets performed their poetry like blues artists, soul singers, and Black ministers. Their audience was a congregation of sorts and the artists had a malcolmian message to deliver: (1) Black nationalism, (2) the relationship between Black America and the Third World, (3) the development of a Black cultural thrust, (4) the right of oppressed peoples to self-defense and armed struggle, (5) the necessity of maintaining a strong moral force in the Black community, (6) the building of autonomous Black institutions, (7) the need for a Black theory of social change,[20] and the necessity to discard the name Negro and to re(re)name.

Because of the raw, rough, urban slang and political coercion depicted in this poetry, members of the established literary tradition faulted the Black Arts poets' offerings. For example, during the 1970s, the acclaimed poet Robert Hayden insisted that Madhubuti was "unable to separate poetic technique from ideological ranting."[21] However, this art, similar to early American Black poetry, is a pastiche of "field hollers, work songs, vendors' shouts, chants, work songs, spirituals, blues, gospels, jazz, rhythm and blues, and soul music."[22]

The poet Amiri Baraka, then Leroi Jones in the early 1960s, an architect of the Black Arts Movement, sums up Malcolm's influence on him and others, saying, "Malcolm X had begun to reach us. I'd heard of the Nation of Islam and had even heard Malcolm speak on television and he charged me in a way no one else had ever done. He *reached* me. His media appearances made my head tingle with anticipation and new ideas."[23] X, now an image in Jones/Baraka's consciousness, generated inspiration for writing new texts. X as an act of speech stimulated Jones/Baraka to create a companion script, starting dialectics[24] specific to the founding of global group consciousness. The slogan "Nation Time" characterizes this stimulus as it represents a 1960s form of salutation.

Haki Madhubuti, then Don L. Lee, admits a similar narrative to Baraka's. He says, "Most people who know me and/or my work understand the significant influence that Malcolm X has had on my life. I've dedicated many of my books and published poems and essays in respect to his life. I've said many times in public and in private that of the men who emerged in the 1960s, I credit Malcolm X with liberating my voice and planting the seed of commitment to building independent Black institutions in me."[25]

In the documentary *Eyes on the Prize*, Sonia Sanchez recalls X's boldness in language projection. In *Revolutionary Suicide* (1973) Huey Newton talks about not only Malcolm's message but also his masculine style that attracted "the brothers."[26] Like Angela Davis, Kathleen Cleaver and the afro, the image of X transformed the culture of African American males. Newton and other males donned the loose fitting prison style of Malcolm X after seeing him perform oratory. Likewise, Malcolm X meant so much to Bobby Seale that he had a one man riot on hearing of X's assassination.

What the poets and the political activists represent is X's remarkable impact on a generation of intellectuals and innovators. Because of X's oratory, rhetoric and style, he generated a polyvocal vision among the vanguard who witnessed him on television, radio, live, or in print. Huey Newton and Bobby Seale founded the Black Panther Party. Baraka created and named Black Arts and then began the Black Arts Repertory Theatre. Madhubuti began his writing career in 1966 with the self-published book *Think Black* that he sold in the thousands from the back of his car across the nation.

The Black Arts Movement

The Black Arts Movement is the most profound artistic collective since the Harlem Renaissance, yet distinctively dissimilar in approach, perspective, and objective. It advanced social engagement, and it was a partner of Black Power, a radicalized phrase chanted by political activists. As a political phrase, Black Power had earlier been used by Richard Wright to describe the mid-1950s emergence of independent African nations. However, the Black Power presentation that represents the Black Arts rendition originated in 1966 with the Student Nonviolent Coordinating Committee's civil rights workers Stokely Carmichael and Willie Ricks. They turned the slogan into a concept of Black Nationalistic activism, particular to the turbulent 1960s. Because of the prominence of Stokely Carmichael/Kwame Touré as a great orator, he repeated and vitalized the phrase, becoming solely associated with the chant, activated in call and response. The phrase Black Power, quickly adopted in the North, was a transformational metaphor, combining "Black is beautiful" aesthetics, armed self-defense, and mental racial separation for the purpose of race and self discovery. These are major ideas from the oratory of Malcolm X.

Kalamu Ya Salaam explains Black Arts in an interview with Ishmael Reed:

> I think what Black Arts did was to inspire a whole lot of Black people to write. Moreover, there would be no multiculturalism movement without Black Arts. Latinos, Asian-Americans, and others all say they began writing as a result of the example of the 1960s. Blacks gave the example that you don't have to assimilate. You could do your own thing, get into your own

background, your own history, your own tradition and your own culture. I think the challenge is for cultural sovereignty and Black Arts struck a blow for that.[27]

Scholars consider Amiri Baraka's move to Harlem after the assassination of Malcolm X as the symbolic birth of the Black Arts Movement. Leroi Jones/Amiri Baraka was the most respected and widely published Black writer of his generation with *Preface to a Twenty-Volume Suicide Note* (1961), *The Dead Lecturer* (1964), and *Blues People* (1963), not to mention his plays. Baraka founded the Black Arts Repertory Theatre School in Harlem and came up with the term "Black Arts." In Neal's essay "The Black Arts Movement" Madhubuti describes this artistic movement as destruction of old ideas (Western ideology) and the birth of new ones (African and African American thinkers and thought). He says: "We must destroy Faulkner, dick, jane, and other perpetuators of evil. It's time for DuBois [sic], Nat Turner, and Kwame Nkrumah. As Frantz Fanon points out: destroy the culture and you destroy the people. This must not happen. Black artists are culture stabilizers; bringing back old values and introducing new ones. Black art will talk to the people."[28]

The roots of the Black Arts Movement however are in the Umbra Writing Workshop, founded by Tom Dent in the early 1960s in his apartment at 242 East Second Street on New York's Lower East Side. The Umbra Writing Workshop's guiding philosophy was "literary integrity" that would illumine "social and racial reality."[29] Umbra attracted a group of talented young writers who offered a unique combination of civil rights activism, artistic ambition, experience in community cultural development, and an interest in local and international politics. Several participants became prominent literary figures: Calvin C. Hernton, Askia Muhammad Toure, and Ishmael Reed.

Like Malcolm X in his pre–Nation of Islam period, the Umbra writers were close to jazz musicians such as Archie Shepp, Cecil Taylor, Marion Brown, and Sun Ra and to experimental artists of other nationalities. The *Umbra* magazine appearing sporadically between 1963 and 1975 illustrates techniques of poets ranging from T.S. Eliot and Ezra Pound to Langston Hughes and Sterling Brown. The poetry also demonstrates Black rhetorical traditions and experiments in visual arts and music — celebrating African American culture and critiquing mainstream values. The Umbra workshop provided some of the core membership and intellectual direction of the Black Arts Movement. This membership included the On Guard for Freedom group, the Congress of Racial Equality, and the Revolutionary Action Movement (RAM), where Larry Neal, Askia Toure, and Bobby Seale had been members. RAM and similar organizations contributed to the revolutionary emphasis in the Black Arts Movement.

Prior to its heavy FBI infiltration, RAM, a national organization with a strong presence in New York and Philadelphia, provided the initial political thrust to Black Arts ideology. Additionally, Maulana Karenga's US (opposed to "them") had influence along with Malcolm X and Elijah Muhammad's Nation of Islam and the Black Panther Party. Baraka in his seminal 1965 poem "Black Art" writes: "we want poems that kill." This was not exclusively personification. During the 1960s, the idea and performance of armed self-defense established a social climate that challenged the historical police brutality that plagued Black communities. Members of the Black Panther Party for Self-Defense chanted the slogan "off the pig" at Panther rallies. Armed struggle was legitimately viewed as an alternative means to non-violent activism to gain liberation. As Kalamu Ya Salaam writes: "Black Arts dynamism, impact, and effectiveness are a direct result of its partisan nature and advocacy of artistic and political freedom 'by any means necessary.'" America had never before experienced such a militant artistic movement.[30]

Images in Black Arts

Emerging from Black Power, the spiritual, rhythmic, and creative thrust of Malcolm X's oratory, the Black Arts authors developed a militaristic use of language. Nikki Giovanni's "The True Import of Present Dialogue, Black vs. Negro" presents this clearly:

> Nigger
> Can you kill
> Can you kill
> Can a nigger kill
> Can a nigger kill a honkie[31]

This metaphoric and figurative trope follows the theme in Leroi Jones's "Black Art," a poem that defies the separation of artist and audience. In its cerebral nature, it urges action. Resurrecting rage and resistance, this poem portrays a repeated inquiry, an early question that a warrior in formation would ask, particularly one previously enslaved and segregated. This conversational, prosaic piece from folk culture represents the "bad woman's" genre, the poem itself a revision of Jones's previous critique of American poetry that goes:

> Poems are bullshit unless they are
> teeth or trees or lemons piled
> on a step ...

> Fuck poems
> and they are useful, they shoot
> come at you, love what you are
>
> ...
>
> We want poems that kill.
> Assassin poems. Poems that shoot
> guns. Poems that wrestle cops into alleys
> and take their weapons leaving them dead...[32]

Both Giovanni and Jones write poems that expose the rage against historical police, Ku Klux Klan, and White male citizens' brutality against Blacks. Additionally, they simultaneously define new rhetoric and action to prevent future and current injustices. This is energy of resistance in art where rage and resistance are aspects of beauty. This is functional art, from a Black Nationalist point of view, providing solutions. As representatives of *nommo*, the poems generate vitality and dynamism within the listeners, critiquing and offering solutions to systematic abuse. They are alternatives to protest marches. Instead, the artist is a conduit of change, creating and continuing the revolutionary rhythm rarely articulated aloud in Black American discourse for obvious reasons. Portraying a major theme in Malcolm's rhetoric, the poems insist on Blacks practicing self-defense. Malcolm says:

> If you don't take this kind of stand, your little children will grow up and look at you and think "shame." If you don't take an uncompromising stand—I don't mean go out and get violent; but at the same time you should never be nonviolent unless you run into some nonviolence. I'm nonviolent with those who are nonviolent with me.[33]

The Black Arts poets took a "stand" in art, deliberately designing poetics to challenge, threaten, and stop the violence that characterized Black life and Black protests. Cities burned during the 1960s and the poets articulated why. Neither the poets nor X created the external violence. Since shipped to America, Blacks have been victims of violence and terror. And the rage, it has always already been there, just below the surface. The Black cultural revolution brought it to the forefront of expression. For the artists, Black people were inspiration, and for Black people, they valued this artistry because it spoke aloud their story. Additionally in the speaking aloud, the poets performed with rhythmic fluency, a verbal art part of Black culture. For Black Arts poets, self-defense and resistance focused their imaginations.

Language and delivery were not the only acts of war performed by the poets. They also wore attire that predicted a cultural and attitudinal shift. Many dressed in African clothing. This sartorial transformation accentuated X's urge for an African connection along with projecting within artist and observer a separation from traditional American attire. X, using the text of Elijah Muhammad's ideology, preached for a physical *and mental* separation from White America. X, however, intensified and expanded Muhammad's initial script and context because he himself physically wore a dashiki. There is a famous 1964 photograph of X in Ghana dressed in a dashiki, in a thoughtful pose, his finger to his head. Thus, he deviated from the standard male attire of the Nation of Islam — a suit and tie — and in doing so he set a precedent for his followers. He symbolically suggested the merging of Islam and traditional African attire.

In the 20th century X, like Elijah Muhammad, extended and merged some of the elements of 19th century Black Nationalism. Muhammad advocated separation of the races, the building of Black institutions imitative of White ones. He established schools and places of worship, and X founded the Nation of Islam's news organ *Muhammad Speaks*. The Nation of Islam also had roots in 19th century Ethiopianism, which spoke of the temporary rule of Whites and the elevation of Blacks. Black Nationalism in the 19th century was more critical of Europe than its 18th century counterpart, which revered European culture. However, the Victorian values of each century continued in the behavior and practices of members of the Nation of Islam. In contrast, X in his thinking and practices bridged both nationalism and Pan-Africanism, which in the 19th century was concerned with African uplift. During that time, the Haitian revolution informed the ideology of Pan-Africanism, as well as the African fighters known as the Maroons in Jamaica, many of whom resettled in Sierra Leone.[34] Pan-Africanism in the 1960s concerned the African nations seizing independence from European powers, and this perspective was not a factor in the ideology of Muhammad's organization. But it was for Malcolm X, who adopted this mode of thought, often mentioning current events from the continent in speeches he made in America. When he talked about the "trickery" of the media he used examples from the Congo, where African fighters were depicted as savages when responding to White aggression and violence.[35] X was not only affected by the political activities of Africans breaking the chains of colonialism. Malcolm was identifying psychologically with his continental brethren, physically conflating his American self with his original African source. As a result, his travels throughout Africa — Ghana, Egypt, Nigeria — caused him to dress in continental attire that in America inspired the poets to adorn African fabrics and a stylized African appearance.

Not all poets dressed this way, however. Some wore jeans, signaling the non-violent protestors' attire, and those in field jackets and jeans represented the Revolutionary Action Movement and the Black Panther Party. This uniform and identification derived from the Cuban and the Kenyan revolutions, and its acceptance symbolized the possibility of guerrilla warfare in America.

Not only did the clothing suggest radical transformation that activists inspired. Women and men stopped processing their hair to resemble the texture of European tresses. During the Age of Malcolm X, the afro was born and it was worn by both men and women, bringing together all of the various camps of political activists. The afro was a sign of a new radical emphasis among the changing Negro. This hairstyle rejected the close shaven and clean-cut look of traditional American males. For Black women, the afro disrupted the foundation of established feminine aesthetics, signaling extremism. Black women adopting this hairstyle challenged, transformed, and offered alternatives to the normal and accepted imitation of White female hair texture. For Black women, this took enormous courage, because self-esteem and beauty were (and are) associated specifically with hair. In X's autobiography he graphically describes his "conking" process in order to prove how much he wanted to resemble the White male. For the Black woman, this procedure is an integral part of her femininity and culture. African hair has been the bane of Black women, until recently. Because of the 1960s' Black is beautiful aesthetic inspired by X, the female poets Sonia Sanchez, Nikki Giovanni, Mari Evans, and others flaunted their raw hair as an image to fight the power, as rap star Chuck D might say. They let their hair "go natural," deliberately accepting and projecting an African appearance. Gwendolyn Brooks wrote a poem post-1960s saluting Black women who still wore the afro. Today, in Black America, people wear afros, dredlocks, locs, Nubian twists, Nubian braids and a host of other unprocessed, African inspired hair styles. During the 1960s, however, wearing an afro was an act of war.

Contemporary rap artists who don prison attire and urban street wear maintain this trend — based on the 1960s aesthetic. They wear African inspired hairstyles. However, most lack the progressive organizations and politics of the 1960s. Yet they do in lyrics normally critique the police, the government, and mainstream media apparatuses. Tricia Rose points that out in *Black Noise* (1994):

> For many poor and working-class African Americans, police and brutality are synonymous ... outside the territory of fighting street crime the police have played a key role in averting black freedom struggles, brutalizing protestors and intimidating activists. Police brutality, racism, and harassment form the political core of male rappers' social criticism and lyrics that effectively and cleverly address these issues.[36]

Influenced by Malcolm X, Chuck D of Public Enemy primarily addresses social issues in his artistry. Unlike other rap stars, Chuck D was born in 1960 to parents that represented the ethos of Black Power culture. His grandparents mourned the assassination of Malcolm X and he had young, radical parents in the 1960s. He writes, "My mother wore an Afro, and I remember wearing an Afro myself, as well as singing the "Free Huey Newton" song. My crucial developmental years took place right smack-dab in the middle of the Black Power movement. I witnessed my family, and Black people in general over a five-year span go from using the term 'Negro' in 1963–64, to using the term 'colored' in 1966–67, to using the term 'Black' and using it with pride by 1968."[37]

These are key racial areas where Malcolm X demanded change, transformation, and African-centered definitions that reached back into history. Michael Dyson offers more on this subject:

> Malcolm's unabashed love for black history, his relentless pedagogy of racial redemption through cultural consciousness and racial self-awareness, mesh effortlessly with black Americans' (especially black youths') recovery of their African roots. As rapper KRS-One summarized a crucial feature of Malcolm's legacy, black children will "come to know that they come from a long race and line of kings, queens, and warriors," a knowledge that will make them "have a better feeling of themselves."[38]

In this line of reasoning, the rap star Nas projects Black, royal imagery in his rap dedicated specifically to children. In "I Can" (2002),[39] he reminds a young chorus that they descend from African kings and queens. According to Chuck D, the killing off of the Black Power movement left his peers born in 1967 and afterwards without a politically conscious base from which to draft art. Nas, like Common and KRS1, are exceptions. Some of their funky beats penetrate politically conscious lyrics.

Key Racial Classifications for Study

Although the Black Arts Movement involves artists other than poets, *Malcolm X and the Poetics of Haki Madhubuti* comparatively analyzes poetry for causal effect from Malcolm X to Madhubuti. However, rhythm and blues, soul music, visual arts and drama all illustrate the fomentation of the 1960s Black Power revolt and are all a part of the Black Arts Movement. Other art forms, fiction and nonfiction, during this epoch echo what Giovanni implies in her poem entitled "Black vs. Negro," which W.E. Cross developed into a psychological model. Talmadge Anderson writes:

> Cross outlined five descriptive stages of change from a Negro (weak) to a strong Black state of being. Stages of the process are: 1) pre-encounter,

2) encounter, 3) immersion-emersion, 4) internalization and 5) internalization-commitment.[40]

In the pre-encounter the African American has no reference for race and acts other than Black. The encounter stage occurs when the person has a racist experience and becomes uncomfortable with or around Whites. The individual then discovers a Black identity. Once internalizing this new reality, she develops racial confidence. The individual may then advance to a cultural security and political commitment to eradicate injustices.

These various stages of cultural insecurity and security are reflected in the fiction of the Black Arts period. Joe William Trotter Jr. explains:

> Reinforcing the ideas of black poets were the works of black novelists, playwrights, and visual artists. Novelist John Oliver Killens succeeded his integrationist *Youngblood* (1954) with his militant *And Then We Heard the Thunder* (1968), which accented the need for black unity in the fight for social justice. Similarly, novelist William Melvin Kelley followed his *A Different Drummer* (1962), a treatment of black migration as a symbol of resistance to Jim Crow, with two condemnations of northern whites in *Dem* (1967) and *Dunsford Travels Everywheres* (1970)."[41]

In 1966 Romare Bearden organized the showing of "Art of the American Negro" in New York. In 1967, members of the Organization of Black American Culture painted *The Wall of Respect* on Chicago's South Side. "Outstanding muralists, including Eugene Eda, Dana Chandler, William Walker, and Mitchell Caton, painted striking, bold wall murals in Chicago, Boston, Detroit, St. Louis, and Washington D.C. In 1970 ... Eda produced in Chicago *The Wall of Meditation* which brilliantly portrays the 'Cross Road Blues'— Martin Luther King and Malcolm X pointing black people in opposite sociopolitical directions."[42]

Black Arts poets following Malcolm in poetry castigated racism, and dissected and deconstructed conforming (White) American perspectives and values. One of the main perspectives that the rhetoric of X and the poets elevated was the race name "Black." Following X, the poets reemphasized this word with a political as well as racially positive gradation. They were in fact reversing the sinister and evil meaning of the term in Western ideology. This strategy was to cause distance from the imposed race name Negro. About the term Negro, Malcolm said, "The worst trick of all is when he names us Negro and calls us Negro....We're not Negroes, and have never been until we were brought here and made into that. We were scientifically produced by the white man."[43]

Defining the term "Negro" as scientific, Malcolm's objectification forced his listeners (and the poets) to revisit history and the initial renaming, which became a repeated theme in Black Arts poetry. Establishing doubt about the word "Negro," Malcolm then moved his listeners to accept and adopt, among others, a reconstituted "Black." In *The End of White World Supremacy*, X's student Benjamin Goodman provides a Malcolm speech that speaks directly to the transformation of "Black" from negative to positive. X refers to the Black reversal as a "bragging about being black."[44] In 1966, Madhubuti wrote "Awareness," which chants this new identity in a form that Stephen Henderson (1973) would call "saturation."[45] Madhubuti writes:

> Black   People   Think
> People   Black   People
> Think   People   Think
> Black   People   Think —
> Think   Black[46]

Nikki Giovanni bumpily imitates this pattern and theme with "Poem (No Name No. 2)."

> Bitter   Black   Bitterness
> Black   Bitter   Bitterness
> Bitterness   Black   Brothers
> Bitter   Black   Get
> Blacker   Get Bitter
> Get   Black   Bitterness
>   Now.[47]

Beginnings and Endings

Scholars calculate the BAM as beginning in 1960–65 and ending in 1974-75. These dates confine the art of war to the 1960s and the 1970s, failing to consider the history of Black resistance writing. The BAM continued a resistance tradition in Black writing, which was unable to flourish in America because of White censure. Resistance writing and oratory have existed in America since Black bondage, but naturally, it stimulates White fear. Early Black writers were well aware of White repression and often their writing appealed to liberals and abolitionists. Therefore, because resistance writing had been historically invisible, when "Black Art" noisily appeared in the 20th century many labeled it an anomaly. Henry Louis Gates is an example, insisting that the BAM was "short lived," a movement that died.[48] Stanley Crouch in analyzing Larry Neal's legacy referred to his Black Arts works as "propaganda" and a "failure." He discovers no "aesthetic achievement" in Black Nationalist poetry.[49]

Each critic, however, overlooks the intended audience and the functionality and purpose of the poetry. This is the art that forced the Negro to look to Africa with acceptance, no small feat. It is also the literature that followed and fomented the rhetoric of Malcolm X. Themes, commentary, and conceptions from the 1960s are quite alive in contemporary "spoken word," "slam poetry," performance art, and literature. For example, rap artists Chuck D, KRS1, Common, Mos Def and others enliven the tradition of Black Arts, which changed for survival. X prioritized Black voices from the margins. This is a victory for African and Diaspora people. "Rap music brings together a tangle of some of the most complex social, cultural, and political issues in contemporary American society."[50] Rap music resists and challenges the status quo and the dominant culture in hidden and public critiques.[51] This genre continues and revitalizes the inversion tradition adopted and mastered by the enslaved and free Africans and later African Americans.

American Africans highlight the 1960s poets in performing the "slam" and "spoken word." *Def Jam* (2004), a Home Box Office poetry show, clarified that relationship when Mos Def introduced "The Last Poets," calling the Black Arts Movement members the "Godfathers of Rap." He added: "they were among the few to take poetry out of the shadow of academia directly to the street corner."[52] The Slam has revived the poetry genre and public performance, expanding the inclusion of "spoken word." "Slam" poetry is a competition where poets either free-style or act out edgy dramatic presentations. "Spoken word" is a contemporary term lifted from the aspects of performance of Black Arts writers. In the film *X*, Spike Lee captures a slam variation when he positions Denzil Washington (as Malcolm X) in an oral street corner competition with Al Sharpton and Bobby Seale. Sharpton and Seale portray circa-1950s street corner speakers who recruited pedestrians into New York Black organizations.

Also, in fiction, Toni Morrison from *The Bluest Eye* (1970) to *Beloved* (1987) encapsulates Black aesthetics. For example, in a scene from *The Bluest Eye*, Morrison uniquely deconstructs racism when having Pecola interact with a racist candy shop owner. Depicting an inner and outer window of racism, Morrison causes readers to experience the wilting powerlessness of a child subordinated to an overbearing, brutish adult. As well, she constructs humanity for a father who rapes his daughter, centering the novel on racism and his disjointed childhood, explaining his drift from innocence into horrific behavior. Exploring racism further and more complicatedly in *Beloved*, Morrison creates the first psycho-drama about slavery. As readers, we spend time inside of the characters' frightening perspectives, and in the end we visit the space time continuum before the American experience in an African sense and framework of chronology or spatial merging of the present, past, and future.

In *Meridian* (1976) Alice Walker presents a feminist protagonist who loves her people first, putting individualism in the background. Meridian is a civil rights activist, living through and attempting to understand the dynamics of gendered Black/White relationships. Her life is the antithesis of Celie's in the award winning *The Color Purple* (1987). Where Celie was beaten down but not broken by patriarchal and racist authority, in *The Color Purple*, her sister Nettie takes the novel right into the heart of Africa. Her character parallels American Christianity with the culture and religious practices of traditional Africans. Walker in factual fiction connected American Africans to brethren on the continent, one of the tenets of Malcolm X's ideology. Therefore, long after his assassination, Malcolm's inspiration for Black power transformed into cultural and textual variations traceable to Black Arts aesthetics. Yet, Black Art in the malcolmian sense does not begin in the 20th century. Rather, it begins in the 19th with Frederick Douglass, and it begins in fiction, not poetry.

The First Literary Resistor

In the 19th century when Frederick Douglass penned his first and only fiction, *The Heroic Slave*, he documented and celebrated the aesthetics of resistance in literature. His hero and protagonist Madison Washington, an escaped, enslaved male, commandeered the slave ship *Creole*, fought White males and won, forcing them to sail the ship to Nassau. Madison Washington escaped without a trace, disappearing into the obscurity of history. When Martin Delany, a Douglass contemporary, wrote *Blake or the Huts of America* (1861–62), his protagonist Henrico Blacus (Blake) became an international revolutionary from America to Cuba. Both Douglass and Delany interspersed their fiction with poetry, Black Nationalist poetry that insisted on freedom from enslavement by any and all means. In poetry, Phillis Wheatley begins this theme. Wheatley, the first Black American to publish a book of poetry, *Poems on Various Subjects, Religious and Moral* (1773), refers to slavery as "tyrannic sway." In talking about America's "freedom" from England in the poem "To the Right Honourable William, Earl of Dartmouth, His Majesty's Principal Secretary of State for North America, & c.," she writes:

> ...
> Should you, my lord, while you peruse my Song,
> Wonder from whence my love of *Freedom* sprung,
> Whence flow these wishes for the common good,
> By feeling hearts alone best understood,
> I, young in life, by seeming cruel fate
> Was snatch'd from *Afric's* fancy'd happy seat
> What pangs excruciating must molest,
> What sorrows labour in my parent's breast?
> Steel'd was that soul and by no misery moved
> That from a father seize'd his babe belov'd
> Such, such my case. And can I then but pray
> Others may never feel tyrannic sway...[53]

For the first Black poetry book published under the auspices of White editors and readers, her direction and memory in the above poem speak and mean a great deal. Most often Wheatley's poetry about accepting and blessing slavery is anthologized. In fact, she has been criticized for not writing more substantive poetry that realistically renders herself and her people, each in bondage. That critique is rather specious in its refusal to recognize the pressure that this delicate young woman lived with and under all of her life. She was a slave, owned by people who taught her literacy in English, as they demanded her abandonment of African religion and traditions.[54] She was regularly the only Black person at White events, because of her celebrity. She published her first poem (or at least her owner's parents published it) when she was fourteen years old. Because of the racism in America, her first book was published abroad. If Wheatley had written more poetry that spoke to the barbarity of slavery and her hatred of it, we might never have heard from her. Frances Ellen Watkins Harper, Wheatley's sister in poetry a century later, reintroduced "tyrannic sway." Harper wrote rousing poetry with an application traceable to the Black Arts poets' figurations and oratory. Harper wrote poetry to eradicate slavery, to free her people. All of these writers show that like in Africa, Black poetry (and literature) has been functional.

African art emerges from a God-centered culture with a hierarchical society that begins with the royalty and a council of elders. Poetry, music, dance are normally intertwined and they are avenues for the two-way relationship between the metaphysical and physical. Through voice, dance, and music one brings the Divine to earth. In this culture one may physically die, but death is mutable because the ancestors assist the living. In classical African culture the earliest poetry praised people and the Divine and portrayed the reality of earthly living. Whereas rationalism is the highest form of intelligence in Western culture, in African intellectual discourse it is the heart, as the Egyptians (Kemetic people) articulated, the intelligence of the heart.[55] Africans modeled drumbeats after heartbeats. Poetry was a form of incantation. Poetry was to make things happen.

Before the activism of the 1960s in art, a revolutionary resistance tradition existed among Black authors. The difference between then and the 1960s is a critical one. The four mentioned authors, Douglass, Delany, Wheatley, and Harper, wrote literature during enslavement. One must consider the racist and restrictive ethos of that period along with the mental disturbances that freighted the then Negro people. Black or Negro authors had not the luxury to organize and disseminate poetry as they would centuries later. However, those early offerings constitute the foundation for the Black Arts Movement, the artistic aim that Malcolm X during the 1960s *called to be*.

Malcolm X and the Poetics of Haki Madhubuti

This book is divided into eleven chapters. Chapter One, "From Nigger to Negro: Dysfunctional Beginnings of Identity for New World Africans," scrutinizes how the African transformed linguistically into a nigger and Negro. This chapter sets the foundation for the historical and literary journey into the transformed image of Africa, which signals the 1960s aesthetic. Chapter Two, "How New Is the New Negro?," discusses the trajectory of the concept and term "New Negro." Chapter Three, "Africa as Motif in Pre-1960s Poetry: Selections of the Antebellum, the Reconstruction, and the Harlem Renaissance," explicates poetry from Phillis Wheatley to Claude McKay, arguing a subhuman fragmentation in the image of Africa resulting from enslavement and discrimination. Chapter Four, "Early Influences of a Revolutionary Aesthetic in Black Poetry: Langston Hughes and Marcus Garvey," isolates for study imagery in Black poetry that dramatically inverts the symbolism found in the previous chapter's offerings. Concentrating on Hughes and Garvey, this chapter highlights the birth of a Harlem Renaissance revolutionary aesthetic, a precursor to the 1960s neo-aesthetic. Chapter Five, "W.E.B. Du Bois, Cheikh Anta Diop, Malcolm X, and Haki Madhubuti: Claiming and Containing Continuity in Black Language and Institutions," examines the intersections among all four men in action and in thought. Chapter Six, "Issues of Memory and Maleness: Malcolm and Madhubuti: Institution Builders and Educators," examines how Malcolm X influenced Haki Madhubuti to build independent institutions that remain intact today. Chapter Seven, "Malcolm and Haki and Safisha Madhubuti on African-Centered Education and Africa in the Imagination," focuses on Safisha Madhubuti's adherence to the X-factor influence and how she and Haki have maintained a personal relationship while building independent institutions. They each in gender complementary fusion envisioned and enacted a transformed image of Africa that X inspired. Chapter Eight, "Malcolm X and Madhubuti: A Physical and Personal Merging," discusses how Haki Madhubuti, along with Bobby Seale and Huey Newton, founders of the Black Panther Party, studied the physical and metaphysical aspects of Malcolm X in order to replicate parts of him long after his assassination. Chapter Nine, "Communion: X, a magnet for Madhubuti and Brooks," comparatively examines the biographies of Madhubuti and X specifically relationships between X and his sister Ella Collins and Madhubuti and his godmother Gwendolyn Brooks. Chapter Ten, "The X-Factor Influence: A Theoretical Frame for Resistance Poetry," explains Malcolm X's rhetorical narratives, issues, and themes that later became the primary images in the poetry of Haki Madhubuti. In this chapter, Madhubuti and Malcolm are interconnected by way of oratory and poetry. Chapter Eleven, "The X-Factor Influence on the Transformed Image of Africa in the Poetry of Haki Madhubuti: Issues of Re(re)naming and Inversion," explicates Madhubuti's poetry from the 1960s to the present, establishing Malcolm's thematic continuation.

ONE

From Nigger to Negro: Dysfunctional Beginnings of Identity for New World Africans

The poetry of the 1960s, sometimes referred to as "malcolmian poetry," came about largely because of the power and influence of the oratory of Malcolm X. What is known today as the Black Arts Movement, which Don L. Lee (Haki Madhubuti) helped architect, started with artists who created art deliberately to attack racism and to shift the attitude, culture, and identity of the "so-called Negro," a term from Elijah Muhammad, to something human. In this activist art, as a motif, the poets presented the problems inherent in the name "negro." Seeking to influence the Negro people to consider a process and identity shift that I call re(re)naming, the Black Arts artists encouraged the elimination of the name "negro" to clear the way for something else. In this artistic vortex of racial persuasion, the Black Arts artists promoted a prominent issue in the oratory of Malcolm X, after his assassination. Don L. Lee from his first book, *Think Black* (1966), to his second one, *Black Pride* (1968), wrote poems that directed his readers and listeners to reexamine the racial name "Negro" in order to disqualify its acceptance. Consider the following entitled "The New Integrationist":

> I
> seek
> integration
> of
> negroes
> with
> black
> people[1]

Notice the obvious play on and reversal of integration that characterizes the members of the non-violent camp during the Civil Rights Movement. Madhubuti disregards the present meaning of integration, writing poetry that derives from the cultural vibration of Marcus Garvey. He writes to design a specialized future. This art from the ideology of Elijah Muhammad, head of the Nation of Islam, uproots the subordinate racial foundation in preparation for a focus beyond America. Elijah Muhammad's platform converted American middle-class values, Black Nationalism, and Victorian mores specific to the Negro. Malcolm expanded this perspective to include Pan-African thought. Not beginning with 20th century definitions, Elijah Muhammad taught Malcolm X about the origins of the word Negro. Teaching the etymology and psychological damage of the term, he encouraged its demise because it connoted infantile thinking and producing. Muhammad taught about the synonym status between the Negro and the enslaved, and he was not alone in this observation. Albert Memmi in *The Colonizer and the Colonized* (1965) includes the American Negro with global colonized people.[2] Memmi explains the myths that the colonizer creates about the colonized and how through circumstances the oppressed people act out expectations of the powerful. Carter G. Woodson in *The Mis-education of the Negro* (1933) similarly refers to the racially devastating effects of the Negroes imitation of White America, and David Walker in *The Appeal* (1829) literally begins this theme and tradition in American literature. Revisiting the origins and derivatives of the appellation Negro will tell us how a name choreographed servitude subconsciously and why Muhammad, X, and later Don L. Lee insisted on the death of the term.

Backdrop: A Flawed Approach of Scholars

Some scholars on slavery once studied the enslaved in the New World as if they were unrelated to the African continent. Kenneth Stampp's important work *The Peculiar Institution* (1956) suffers from a focus on Negroes from the perspectives of slaveholders and on how they and those enslaved managed in bondage and responded to this peculiar set of circumstances. Stampp's study is extremely useful, but it lacks African-centered historical continuity, evident in a statement the author writes in his preface. He says: "I have assumed that the slaves were merely ordinary human beings that innately Negroes *are* only white men with black skins, nothing more, nothing less."[3] Although revolutionary for the 1950s, this unsatisfactory comparison denies an African cultural connection, as it denies the Negro's unique culture and history.

In fact, it affirms what David De Camp reminds us of and refutes in his introduction to Lorenzo Turner's *Africanisms in the Gullah Dialect* (1949), a linguistic text that overturned the general thinking that "Negroes" lost any African retention, turning into a blank slate. De Camp writes to refute the idea "that whatever language and culture the slaves had brought with them from Africa had been totally obliterated on the plantations and that the entire black race had had to start over again from scratch, this time under the tutelage of the white masters."[4] Although De Camp goes on to explode that conception, more recently, Kwame Appiah argues that 19th and 20th century thinkers, primarily Alexander Crummell, Edward Blyden, and W.E.B. Du Bois, were carbon copies of racist White intellectuals.[5] He arrives at this provocative conclusion after analyzing their remarks about continental Africans. Although there are divisions that Du Bois, Crummell and Blyden present in characterizing Africans, Appiah is not completely correct. Intrinsic or extrinsic racism is not a conception that any of the above intellectuals had the power to proliferate in the sense of our contemporary comprehension of racists and racism. In other words, they certainly lacked the power and the intent to establish institutions based on the detriment of the African, and they did not deliberately canonize a literature seeped in the epistemology and scientific proof of African inferiority. Appiah has concluded that Crummell, Blyden, and Du Bois were racists like some White intellectuals because he discounts the complete transformation of the enslaved African into the Negro.

For Stampp, he signals the environment of segregation when Martin Luther King and others were forcing the historical and racist separatism in America to end. During and prior to that time, equality with White Americans was the prima facie focus for Negro leaders of various ideological persuasions. What Appiah does not consider enough in his analysis is the Eurocentric breach between the African on the continent and the one transformed into the Negro in America. However, Crummell and Blyden did make troubling comments about the African, specifically reducing African spirituality to the emotions of "heathens." Yet, Appiah has to weigh in with the onslaught of Eurocentric education and nationalism that still leads the world as it did years ago. Negro intellectuals upheld the ideology of Whites, and this racist historical model caused the dehumanization of the African continent. The "Negro," made in America, fought to obtain the special privileges and human dignity accorded to Whites concentrated on winning that monolithic war. In religion and social structure, the Whites were in power, therefore, the Negroes reaching to obtain equality imitated those in control, and this includes accepting White ideology and prejudices.

Once the African accepted the name "Negro" an identity shift simultaneously occurred. Du Bois explains this change as he responds to a young man in 1928 who wrote to him about using the word "Negro" in *The Crisis*, the official organ of the NAACP, of which Du Bois was editor for twenty-five years. A section of that letter reads, "the word, 'Negro' or 'nigger,' is a white man's word to make us feel inferior. I hope to be a worker for my race, that is why I wrote this letter. I hope that by the time I become a man, that this word 'Negro,' will be abolished."[6] Du Bois responds with an insightfully long letter, quoted in sections here. Du Bois begins:

> Do not at the outset of your career make the all too common error of mistaking names for things. Names are only conventional signs for identifying things. Things are the reality that counts. If a thing is despised either because of ignorance or because it is despicable, you will not alter matters by changing its name.... But why seek to change the name? "Negro" is a fine word. Etymologically and phonetically it is much better and more logical than "African" or "colored." ... The feeling of inferiority is in you, not in any name.[7]

Du Bois blames the victim, the writer, for his discomfort with the word "Negro." This excerpt also demonstrates the confusion surrounding the term and other racial designators even among proponents. Du Bois was an important member of the National Association for the Advancement of Colored People and he says in his letter that "colored" has problems too. In fact, in this same missive he explains the climate and racial terminology during the young man's grandfather's era, saying that then, "colored people were mulattoes. The mulattoes hated and despised the blacks and were insulted if called 'Negroes.'"[8] Du Bois goes on to say, "But we are not insulted—not you and I. We are quite as proud of our black ancestors as of our white." Yet, this Black and White combination in "Negro" seems to omit the African. A "Negro" in Du Bois's thinking at that time is in the Stampp consensus.

That Du Bois's opinions and thinking were already in flux is a reflection of the complexity of being (re)named, which separated the Black in America from the African on the continent. The (re)naming process, the dehumanization of slavery and then the racism of segregation and limited opportunity, together damaged the self esteem of the transformed African who started identifying with Eurocentric perceptions. This is evident in the literary images written by Negro authors discussed later in this chapter. Emerging from a defeated "dark" and "savage" people (according to this thought) prepared the "Negro," transformed into a brute (a person of mentally repressed ideas and emotions) under slavery, to accept White superiority and Black or Negro inferiority. This is why Stampp would compare himself and his people to Whites. Negroes strove to be White in physical attributes, culture, and intellect in order to escape the prefigures of the "dark" continent and the dumb Negro.

Lorenzo Turner in *Africanisms in the Gullah Dialect* (1973)[9] was the first Black scholar to challenge and prove the falsity of what Sidney Mintz called the "blank slate" theory, that Negroes had no identifiable African cultural patterns.[10] Turner, along with Melville Herskovits who earlier wrote *The Myth of the Negro Past* (1941), pioneered the cultural bridge between the Negro and the African. Turner collected four thousand Gullah words (a language from the Georgia Sea Islands) and reconnected them to African etymology. Herskovits recovered Africanisms in religious and secular life in America. The enormous significance of both texts is their reversal of a host of myths that includes the feminization of Black men. Black men were debarred from fighting in American wars because of this conception, and up until the demand in the 1960s, it was commonplace to believe that Blacks had no history worthy of study.

Current scholarship on Africa and the Diaspora disproves those lingering falsities. However, to expose the trauma of (re)naming provides reasons that until the 1960s the American African, (re)named "Negro" aggressively tried to become what Stampp says above: White men in black skin. The break between Africans in America and those on the continent caused an abyss that enlarged over centuries due in part to distance and to (re)naming. New World Africans transformed into "Negroes" suffered an inadequacy that exposed itself in their written literature and certainly in social practices. Such comes to the forefront when examining the roots and revisions of the word "Negro."

A Step Back into History

During the 15th century, when Portuguese explorers seized African lands and enslaved African people, they simultaneously (re)named indigenous African groups. Disregarding the indigenous peoples' appellations, the

Portuguese explorers (re)named Africans in derogatory terms which transformed a people into a collective symbol of slavery. Since the practice of (re)naming linguistically and psychologically stripped land and point of origin from the various ethnic groups on the western tip of the continent, a once identifiably African people became a New World commodity, a degraded and dehumanized group of people. This New World African, transformed into the "Negro," was debated and legislated outside of the human family.

During that same 15th century epoch, prior to the enslavement of West African people, the word "negro" in Portuguese and Spanish refers to "black," a color description. However, once the explorers expanded the enslaving process, the terms "negro" and "black" altered in semantics, changing from a color to a derogatory category that means "slave."[11]

This divergence in literature and popular culture left "Negro" no longer an adjective but a noun, absorbing all of the baggage of bondage. During the epoch of the transatlantic slave trade, added meanings include stupid, coward, heathen, ugly, lascivious, savage, evil — general inferiority concepts and descriptors. With the proliferation of slavery, other Europeans besides the Portuguese then sailed into Africa, mentally carrying the multifarious degrees of African inferiority. In fact, the word "Negro" as a linguistic symbol not only transformed the New World African into a commodity, but also influenced how Whites developed beliefs about all people of African descent.

When Shakespeare created his masterpiece *Othello*, for example, the protagonist's internal figurations and characterization reveal degenerative qualities of the transformed "Negro." *Othello* is not just about an interracial tragedy but also about racial beliefs during the Elizabethan period. As Winthrop Jordan explains in *White over Black* (1977), "Shakespeare was writing both about and to his countrymen's feelings concerning physical distinctions between kinds of people; the play is shot through with the language of blackness and sex."[12] The Moor is "lusty" and the Moor himself considers his own complexion "begrime'd and black." Othello has assimilated a European version of the African and this acceptance intensifies in Iago's commentary on the newlyweds. Iago describes sexual intercourse between Othello and Desdemona as bestial. In fact, Jordan conflates the psychology and common beliefs that give meaning to the language. He states: "This was not merely the language of (as we say) a 'dirty' mind: It was the integrated imagery of blackness and whiteness, of Africa, of the sexuality of beasts and the bestiality of sex."[13] Eurocentric interpretations of African people cast the collective group as the inverse of the European and the White American. Exploiting distinctions in physical appearance, social practices, and spirituality, English and White American authors crafted the Negro people bereft of civilization. In fact, the African was debated out of historical progress.[14]

Other tales of bestiality were not confined to England; they also lived in the New World. For instance, the English belief that Africans had sexual liaisons with apes traveled in the imaginative pornography of the colonists who took for granted the lustiness and so-called large genitalia of Black women.[15] This largeness was thought to result from copulation between African females and orangutans. In fact, one of the premiere intellectuals of 18th century America, Thomas Jefferson, includes this line of thought in his essay on emancipation in *Notes on the State of Virginia*. His racial divisions and his "Negro" comprehension articulate this New World pattern of thought that expunged the African from the human family and into an array of perversions. Jefferson writes:

> The first difference which strikes us is that of color. Whether the black of the negro resides in the reticular membrane between the skin and scarf-skin, or in the scarf-skin itself: whether it proceeds from the color of the blood, the color of the bile, or from that of some other secretion, the difference is fixed in nature, and is as real as if its seat and cause were better known to us. And is this difference of no importance? Is it not the foundation of a greater or less share of beauty in the two races? Are not the fine mixtures of red and white, the expressions of every passion by greater or less suffusions of color and the one, preferable to that eternal monotony, which reigns in the countenances, that immovable veil of black which covers the emotions of the other race? Add to these, flowing hair, a more elegant symmetry of form, their own judgement and favor of the whites, declared by their preference of them, as uniformly as is the preference of *the Oranootan for the black woman* over those of his own species[16] [emphasis mine].

Jefferson's commentary displays the supposed norm of bestiality among Africans and most specifically African women as emblems of perversion. Additionally, he believes that Negroes prefer the company of Whites over their own. Our hero Othello certainly projects this isolationist behavior. He is a great general in Venice, often the only Black or Moor among a sea of Whites. Jefferson is a great American leader and his fathering biracial children shows the double standard and the complex hypocrisy of early American thought versus practice. His bipolar attitude that secretly merges represents the interconnected and isolated relationships that Whites formed with Blacks. Early American authors and statesmen together created slave populations that lacked venues of defense against external and internal racism. Trapped in America, surrounded by racist attitudes and linguistic transformation, the Negro emerged carrying a plexus of psychological trauma about the self and the group.

In the trauma of the "Negro" this new people attempted to project White ideals and identity, recalling Jefferson's reference to a "favor[ing] of the whites." Although some still called themselves African during the early centuries, their selected literature indicates that shame, uncertainty, inferiority, and distance disturbed the disrupted relationship from the continent. Functioning under the name "Negro," the transformed African, thinking Africa savage, started a new history that began in enslavement and progressed to second-class citizenship. Molefi K. Asante further explains why "Negro" as racial designator causes substantial confusion:

> There is no ethnic group in Africa that calls itself negro. The term is preeminently a creation of the European mind to refer to any African group or people who correspond to a certain negative image of culture.... Ethiopians (Shoa, Amhara, Galla, etc.) are one branch of the African people as Egyptians and Zulu and Yoruba are branches of the African people. "Negro" on the other hand is introduced to *obscure* the Africanness of classical Pharaonic civilizations.[17]

David Walker, the 19th century author of *The Appeal,* emphasized this identical point as he argued for the enslaved people to resist the tyranny of bondage. Making an Afrocentric parallel, comparing the genealogical relationship between the negro slave and the ancients in Egypt, Walker reminded 19th century Blacks of once owning historical greatness. Walker, as did Malcolm X a century later, believed that history would awaken the potential lying dormant in the Negro. This is the identical potential that X sought to highlight. John Henrik Clarke writes: "Malcolm X clearly understood that history is an instrument of both enslavement and liberation, and he was trying to tell his people, especially the young, how to use history affirmatively."[18] Plus, Malcolm X not only claimed a historical connection between the "so-called Negro" and the ancient Egyptian. He also discussed ancient African strongholds in Carthage, Sumer, Songhai, Mali and other geographies on the continent, before advocates of Black Studies imposed the discipline in the academy. Cheikh Anta Diop (1991) further elucidates why the reconnection of Africa and the Diaspora African were crucial to racial development, basing his insights on what he terms "historical conscience" and "historical continuity." He writes:

> The historical factor is the cultural cement that unifies the disparate elements of a people to make them into a whole, by the particular slant of the feeling of historical continuity lived by the totality of the collective.... The historical conscience, through the feeling of cohesion that it creates constitutes the safest and the most solid shield of cultural security for a people. This is why every people seeks only to know and to live their true history well, to transmit its memory to their descendants.[19]

This lack of cohesion and cultural shield left the stripped African — the Negro — without the proper armaments to prevent the absorption of subhumanity. African-centered psychologists agree that the mental health of Negroes suffered because of the dislocation from Africa and the distortion of African civilization and culture (Akbar 1991; Nobles 1986; Wright 1984). Although Sterling Stuckey in *Slave Culture*[20] brilliantly argues the formation of a collective Black culture when different groups of Africans found themselves together in America, the reverse happened as well. Africa in the imagination became a memory that had to refigure itself for sustenance in a new and hostile environment. If no sustaining were possible, the memory either dimmed or died. If on the other hand reconfiguration were possible, the combination of law, religion, custom, and education disadvantageous to the Negro forged a negating transformation. In this sphere, the Negro dangled between Africa and America, and both were sites of distortion and hostility. For the Negro such a disconnection between absence and presence eroded a collective sense of self, a continuity desperately required during the institution of slavery (and beyond). With this absence/ presence simultaneously existing, the gap or the dialectics between the two transmitted conflicting and defaming messages.

Racial (re)naming exposes dissonance when analyzing shifts in nomenclature enforced on people of African descent. The harm of linguistic dismemberment emerges further when examining two synonyms for "Negro," "guinea" and "nigger."

Literary Images of Synonyms for Negro

During the 18th and 19th century, Blacks wrote literature where "guinea" appears, suggesting its regularity in England and America. In differing contexts, Olaudah Equiano and Francis Harper employ the term "guinea" in their respective literatures. Beginning with Equiano in *Equiano's Travels* (1789), he uses the term to stand for legal currency. Considering that Guinea is the area of Olaudah Equiano's birth suggests a paradox in his acceptance of his personal geography as one representing currency. His use implies his accommodation to language that (re)formed him outside of the human family. The currency transformation of his geographic birthplace shows up in four different situations in his text. In the first example, he writes, "I had about nine guineas which during my long seafaring life, I had scraped together."[21] In the second, he writes, "A sailor on board took a guinea from me on pretence of getting me a boat."[22] And then he says, "I had thirty-seven guineas which would support me for a time."[23] And lastly,

"My captain once said he could get more than one hundred guineas for me in Carolina."[24] In this sampling, Equiano converts himself (a man from Guinea) into capital. He is a Guinea trading with guineas, psychologically merging himself with currency.

The natural tone of each excerpt implies his acceptance of the equivalence of place, body and currency. This multifarious blend into one had a history a century before his birth. "The Guinea Company" then existed, and it specialized in enslaving procedures.[25] Therefore, Equiano was born into a history where his people, the Guineas, served the capitalistic ventures of foreigners. In the English language, at that time, Africa was a topology of capital.

In America, Frances Harper presents another version of "guinea" in the novel *Iola Leroy* (1892). Harper writes a monologue of a fictional character, Uncle Daniel, who narrates the story of a defiant "Guinea man." Uncle Daniel says:

> We used to hab on our place a *real Guinea man*, an' once he made ole Marse mad, an' he had him whipped. Ol Marse war trying to break him in, but dat fellow war spunk to de backbone, an' when he 'gin talkin' to him 'bout savin' his soul an' gittin' to hebbin, he tole him ef he went to hebbin an' foun' he war dare, he wouldn't go in[26] [emphasis mine].

Harper's "Guinea man" is a resistor, standing for challenge and "spunk to de backbone." This Guinea man has a "real"-ness that separates him from other Africans, American born. Uncle Daniel, full of pride, speaks in a manner that suggests a separation or difference between the Guinea man and American born Negroes. This Guinea man does not suffer the historical discontinuity of his American brethren. Perhaps this is why he fights back.

In the above quote, the Guinea man does not assimilate the concept of heaven in the Christian sense of the metaphysical. It is probable that he recalls a function of freedom and cosmology from Africa that would compel him to doubt the idea of heaven provided by the oppressive master. Additionally, this Guinea man thought of himself as a man, not a horse for "breaking in."

In the *Narrative of Frederick Douglass* (1845), Douglass intimately explains the practice of "breaking in" as a function of social order within plantation life. Masters attempted to "break" the spirit and manhood (and womanhood) of those enslaved, and White men were trained to accomplish this specific purpose. Mr. Covey in the *Narrative* almost succeeded in debilitating young Frederick, until the enslaved man fought back and soon after escaped bondage. Yet Douglass, similar to the spunky "Guinea man," could operate only within the parameters of White privilege and supremacy. For example, even though the "Guinea man" challenged his master, his owner still had the power to sell or to kill him. The world of bondage as revealed in Harper's novel includes the enslavers' omnipresent power. In this same text Negro men, women, and children are sold as animals; one is "called a contraband"[27] and a "colored" daughter sells for a piano.[28] Therefore, this Guinea man who represents spunk still has shackles that restrict and restrain him. Orlando Patterson in *Slavery and Social Death* (1982) would say that those restrictions no matter his disposition caused him to have an absence of power.[29]

Within Harper's imagination, she illustrates an Afrocentric power of resistance along with psychological compartments and multiple voices that bespeak racial variations. This man from Guinea does not suffer the psychoses of the American Negro because of cultural factors. He did not have the disturbances in human relationships that the Negro slave experienced.[30] Heroically, the "real" Guinea man represents Africa, for example. He challenges slavery and expresses anger because of his forced removal from his homeland. Harper values this characterization because she capitalizes "Guinea," as she lowercases "negro." Therefore, in fiction, Harper gives more respect to the Guinea man with a direct African connection than she does to his American counterpart — the Negro, the slave, dislocated from Africa. Most importantly, Harper accents the power of resistance adjacent to accommodating and assimilating figures.

To augment Harper and Equiano's nimble maneuver of "guinea" the *Oxford English Dictionary* (1985) proves useful, beginning with the following sequence: "gennie," "gynny," and "ginnie." "The geographical name appears first in Pg. [Portuguese] as Guine (hence Sp. [Spanish] *Guiné*, F. [French] *Guinée*); its origin is unknown.... The European name of a portion of the West Coast of Africa, extending from Sierra Leone to Benin ... (in several instances the name is used *loosely* for *West Africa* or for *some far off or unknown country*)"[31] (my emphasis).

There is a phonetic resemblance in the loose usage of "gennie," "guinea," and "guinee." Before European expansionism extended its power internationally during the 13th and 14th centuries, a West African city known for its wealth and scholarship existed. This territory was called Jenne (pronounced Gen-nay) and it advanced education to the world. Jenne in Mali, not far from Guinea in pronunciation, sounds similar to the above derivatives. John G. Jackson tells us more about this ancient West African territory:

> Jenne was a valuable prize ... it was a prosperous trading center containing buildings of attractive design, and surrounded by great scenic beauty. It was also the home of advanced culture, being the seat of a noted university,

which employed a staff of thousands of teachers who gave courses of lectures and conducted researches on a variety of subjects.[32]

The possibility that Guinea and Jenne represent similar topologies is an intrigue that emphasizes the obscurity of African history and the result of (re)naming. During the time of Equiano and Harper, European scholars were actively degrading and dismissing any possibility of Africa's contribution to civilization. As Henry Louis Gates points out, Hegel with ideas from Kant and Hume insisted that Africa lacked writing, and therefore was a land of perpetual childhood.[33] Jenne refutes this falsity, with "a staff of thousands of teachers."

On the other hand, Equiano puts forward another image of "guinea" combining slavery and economics: He calls a slave ship a "Guinea" ship. In the following scene, Equiano, reflecting on his youth, describes when he and his sister were herded across strange African terrain to be enslaved. They were exchanged within a series of African ethnic groups, until finally his sister was torn from him, forever. Although he is eleven years old when this occurs, his anguish never dissolves. Emotionally, he recalls this incident, years after growing up in England and the Indies. He writes:

> To that Heaven which protects the weak from the strong I commit the care of your innocence and virtues, if they have not already received their full reward and if your youth and delicacy have not long since fallen victims to the African trader, the pestilential stench of a *Guinea ship*, the seasoning in the European colonies, or the lash and lust of a brutal and unrelenting overseer[34] [my emphasis].

In addition to currency, the man from Guinea is now a slave ship. The Guinea ship en route to enslaving topologies anchored in the West Indies (another (re)named island) in order to "season" the Guineas to ready them for American slavery. Seasoning is a part of the Middle Passage journey from Africa to the Americas. Before Africans were sailed to the New World, the traffickers stopped off in the islands. In order to strike fear in the captives, the enslavers selected a few Africans for killing, whipping or both. This procedural cruelty terrified the surviving Africans, causing an unspeakable dread and defeat on their arrival to America. This psychological terror assists the transformation of a human into a slave.

The *OED* compounds the objectification when listing the following metaphor that resonates and replicates Equiano's earlier "Guinea ship." The *OED* reports that "a guinea-***man*** is a slave ship" (my emphasis). This metaphor has two opposing directions. It both is and is not a (re)presentation of Harper's heroic Guinea man and the floating near image of Equiano's "Guinea ship."

The enslaving enterprise so ingrained the Western mind because of its preponderance that the victims became metaphors of the institution. Thus, the interior world of Equiano stretched to accommodate a dense disfigurement where his people were not only people but also vessels of capitalism. This psychological pull becomes more problematic when considering the first chapter of his autobiography. There, Equiano gives an authentic description and explanation of his life in Guinea before his capture, and scholars have authenticated his rendition. His group membership, eyewitness account, and participation in pre-colonial life and culture provide exceptional detail and special significance. However, in later sections of the autobiography, his accommodation to English life, aesthetics, and linguistics are quite notable. He thinks of himself as a "negro" complete with the lowercase "n."

In this system of enslavement and the maintenance of slavery, the idea of defeat hindered both the slave and the nominally free Negro. For example, Equiano, no matter how skillful and industrious, was never able to exercise total freedom. Even after self-purchase, he still lacked the power to protect himself from unscrupulous Whites. Equiano writes, "We told his worship of the [White] man's villainous tricks, and begged that he would be kind enough to see us redressed: but being negroes, although free, we could not get any remedy; and our ship being then just upon the point of sailing..."[35] White males controlled Negroes, whether enslaved or supposedly free.

Asante asserts that "location is determined by the signposts."[36] W.E.B. Du Bois articulates in his response to the student that "Names are nothing but little guideposts along the Way."[37] Equiano's language expresses signs and the ideology of enslavers that would necessarily cause him to mentally adjust to inferiority for self-survival, and his personality complies with forces that interplay.[38]

Self-survival reveals itself in still another popular phrase from the enslavement period that again indicates the person as capital: "put in the master's pocket." To be "put in the master's pocket" is to be sold by the master who receives the money. For the enslaved to participate, voluntarily or involuntarily, in this conceptual activity forthrightly states the acceptance of the self as a commodity or object. This phrase, in the same text where Harper shows admiration for the "Guinea man," in this first example explains parental differences. Alfred Lorraine, a slaveholder, says: "[my father] was very squeamish about selling his servants but [my mother] would have put every one of them in her pocket before permitting them to eat her out of house and home."[39] In *Incidents in the Life of a Slave Girl* by Harriet Jacobs (1861), we find "put in the pocket" again. When describing the selling of two enslaved people, a married couple, Brent/Jacobs says: "The guilty man put their value into his pocket, and had the satisfaction of knowing that they were out of sight and hearing."[40] Linda Brent/Harriet Jacobs explains her personal plight in this same terminology. She says, "it was very natural that he should make an effort to put me into his pocket."[41] Unquestionably Brent/Jacobs and the others acknowledge the transformation from human to currency. On the surface, this phrase indicates bipolar possibilities for the enslaved and the slaveholder. The Whites gain financial security and the Blacks gain uncertainty and removal. However, with the multi-play of thoughts and emotions that the Negro employed to adapt and bend to his circumstances, Prince Johnson, an enslaved man, explains, reverses, and combines a unique variation on the phrase:

> The rule was if a nigger wouldn't work, he would be sold. Another rule on that place was that if a man got dissatisfied, he was to go to Old Master and ask him to "put him in his pocket." That meant he wanted to be sold, and the money he brought to be put in the [master's] pocket. I ain't never known of but two asking to be *put in the master's pocket*, and both of them *was put in*[42] [my emphasis].

Enslaved people understood the nature of American society and they switched mental and social situations to function under legalized racism, terror, and inferiority. Literally and figuratively, to be placed in the "master's pocket" is a tragic sleight of hand causing the disappearance of an African. This phrase points to the dramatic influence of slavery on linguistics and the American imagination. Its informality also suggests that it may have resulted or originated from those in bondage.

Yet, no matter its origins, to be put in the master's pocket demonstrates the reality and the language response to an American condition. Conversely, in the above quote, the enslaved men reversed the disadvantage of the phrase to challenge the master's power. Like Linda Brent's Uncle Benjamin refused to acquiesce to his master's desires, the enslaved men showed their courage (and equality) as well. Brent's Uncle Benjamin committed the crime of acting equal to his owner, and thus was jailed. Brent/Jacobs writes:

> Three months elapsed and there was no prospect of release or of a purchaser. One day he was heard to sing and laugh. This piece of indecorum was told to the master, and the overseer was ordered to re-chain him. He was now confined in an apartment with other prisoners, who were covered with filthy rags. Benjamin was chained near them, and was soon covered with vermin. He worked at his chains till he succeeded in getting out of them. He passed them through the bars of the window, with a request that they should be taken to his master.[43]

Both Benjamin and the males in the previous excerpt permit their "will" to test the authority of the men who own them. They accept the challenge of being "put in the master's pocket," juggling their value as commodity and their human determination. When possible, Black people modified the messages sent from the people in charge, creating new aspects of realism and reality. They resisted, and resistance turned into a factor in early Black culture. Resistance was not antithetical to religion among those enslaved, for as V.P. Franklin writes in *Black Self-Determination: A Cultural History of African American Resistance* (1992),

> the religious teachings of the plantation missionaries endorsed accommodation and resignation to the powers of this world, the religion of the slaves sanctioned all forms of mental and physical resistance against the brutal and dehumanizing forces of evil inherent in the antebellum slave regime."[44]

However, those unable to resist or maneuver assumed a self and race preordination of inferiority. For example, when examining the "guinea" synonym, "nigger," the linguistic guideposts heighten into hell.

Nigger

The term "nigger" debases more than "guinea." An assaulting epithet more crass than "guinea" or "Negro," it attacks and insults the nature, quality, and capability of the American African, Guinea means currency, vessel, and subhuman. Nigger compounds the foulest sense of language usage. In the *OED*, "nigger" has another form — "niggar." Both are supposedly unrelated to "Niger," which precedes them in the dictionary. Yet, "Niger" equals Neger and Negro. Further along, the listing for "Nigger" equals Neger, Negro, and niggar. Therefore, "nigger" is not unrelated to the placename, "Niger." Nor of course is it unrelated to Negro.

Examine the following eighteenth century religious use of "nigger": "1786 Burns, *Ordination iv*, How graceless Ham leugh at his Dad, Which made Canaan a nigger."[45] In the Christianity professed to enslaved Africans in America, Ham, as the above directly claims, is a "nigger," and all of his progeny are "niggers." This religious belief fostered the argument for the perpetual enslavement of the African. There are several interpretations of the statement: either Ham laughed at his father's nakedness, or during the flood he disobeyed his father and had conjugal sex. In either event, God disfavored Ham, the originator of the African according to the Bible. The biblical scholar Cain Hope Felder of Howard University disclaims any legitimacy in the "curse" of Ham, pointing out the impossibility of Noah and his wife producing sons of various ethnic persuasions.

Yet in the thinking and acceptance of the curse of Ham, in society, to starkly separate the Whites from Ham's descendants, those in power linguistically put together "nigger" combinations that show its entrenchment in common culture. Examine the following: nigger-driver, nigger-hair, nigger-jockeys, niggerdom (niggers collectively), niggerisms, nigger-fish, niggerlings, nigger-dogs. The training of "nigger-dogs" exposes an inhumanity that needs more attention.

These dogs were trained to hunt escaping enslaved people; they were taught to rip the flesh from Blacks. Their training consisted of starvation and then the devouring of a human size figure resembling a Negro with fresh meat stuffed in the abdomen. Not a sport that originated in America, it appears in 15th century Europe from an event called "bear-baiting." The sport of "bear-baiting" involved chaining a bear to a tree, with his or her feet unrestrained. Once fastened, the bear was at the mercy of vicious and starved dogs.[46]

In this transported worldview, dogs, niggers, and bears are similarly treated. Such an ethos blunted the sensitivity of enslavers when inflicting cruelty to "niggers." Consider lynchings, public whippings, and burning people alive. Richard Moore (1992) unlike Du Bois believes that names become the things so named. Just as combining "nigger" with "dog" separated this particular canine from others, (re)naming the African "Negro" or "nigger" isolated a people from other humans. Thus, the transformed African equated with animals was negatively distinguished based on caste, class, color, and physical features. This psychological assault on the "nigger/negro remains unnamed in literature and in life. For some terrors, words are inadequate.

The following *OED* monologue exposes color distinctions that Du Bois earlier attempted to articulate. The *OED* reads, "When I say colored, I mean one thing respectfully; and when I say 'niggerish' I mean another thing disgustedly." The consequent generation of biracial people in America created another New World formation, "coloureds," often (but not always) superior to darker Blacks.[47] Although Randall Kennedy in his book titled *nigger* (2002) reports that nigger is no longer restricted to African Americans,[48] because of its historical usage, one expects a Black person when hearing the obscenity, even today. The nigger in the imagination is the African, the very dark, "real" one. Harper's Guinea man had that "real" quality, troped by Gwendolyn Brooks much later in her poem "The Life of Lincoln West."[49] This dark, real one is in the pre-1960s American artifacts of Sambo, coon, Jolly Nigger Bank, Mammy and other offensively playful objects manufactured in America at the expense of the Negro.

Further meanings for the term nigger includes drudgery, "char[ring]," and "burn[ing]." An analysis of the phrase "to nigger out land" explains possible associations between "nigger," "char[ing]," and "burn[ing]." "To nigger out land signifies ... to exhaust land by the mode of tilling without fertilization pursued in the slave states" (OED 1985). An image of "exhausted" land excludes but foreshadows exhausted people working the land. The profiteers from "nigger[ing] out" would envision the land and the people as one, just as enslavers envisioned the ship, the geography, the people, and the business as a unified one, the guinea. The origin of "to nigger out land" may stem from the sun-up to sun-down drudgery enforced on enslaved people. This image of an "exhausted people" and "exhausted land" suggests brute labor, not to mention a careless concern for the land and the environment.

Even more, the relationship between "nigger" and "char" reveals a quality of being black or blackened. In Western ideology, "black" represents among other attributes evil and dirt. The *OED* tells us: "Having an extremely *dark* skin; strictly applied to negroes and negritos, and other dark-skinned races"[50] (my emphasis). Next, it says: "Having *dark* or *deadly* purposes, *malignant*, pertaining to or involving *death*...; *baneful, disastrous, sinister.*" Hence, any association of blackness in this perspective constructs terrible consequences as well as fear. This reminds us of the character Othello again. He may have been the great general but his persona implicitly signals a foreboding that suggests tragedy. In the first part of the drama, he is in authority, strong and noble similar to the opening of and the character *King Lear*. However, the difference resides in Othello's race. Being "begrime'd" and "black" indicates a current and coming evil absent in King Lear's persona.

Forthright in his character, Othello turns into the language and behavior of pure evil. After all, Moors are niggers. No matter how noble, they must be separated from Whites. This bipolar component — White and Black division: niggers are one thing and Whites another — still occupies some American behavior. In June 1997, Mr. G.P. Garnet, the only Black at an all White party in Grayson County, Virginia, was certainly considered a "thing." He was found burned alive and decapitated once the party ended.[51] "Char" and "burn" may possibly allude to the fate of G.P. Garnet. Since American enslavement of Africans, niggers have been burnt alive for punishment and sport (Fedo 1979; Ginzburg 1992; NAACP 1919; Zangrando 1980).

The derivative "nig" offers less barbaric but more sinister denotations. "Niggard" means the following: miserly, parsimonious, mean, "narrowness of soul," etc. "Niggle" means handwriting but it also means "to haue to do with a woman carnaily.... How long has she been here? Long enough to be

... nigled."[52] A popular reason for the continuance of slavery is the access to legal rape of the Black woman.[53] Deborah Gray White explains why the Black woman's sexuality was recorded as lascivious and abnormal, and certainly long before her Thomas Jefferson had uttered his fantasies about Black women. In *Ar'nt I a Woman* (1985), Gray White historically discusses the images of Black women, writing: "One of the most prevalent images of black women in antebellum America was of a person governed almost entirely by her libido, a Jezebel character. In every way Jezebel was the counterimage of the mid-nineteenth-century ideal of the Victorian lady."[54] The image of the African female, she argues, emerges in part from the Englishmen's accounts when first seeing African women. She writes that "Unaccustomed to the requirements of a tropical climate, Europeans mistook seminudity for lewdness. Similarly, they misinterpreted African cultural traditions, so that polygamy was attributed to the Africans' uncontrolled lust, tribal dances were reduced to the level of orgy, and African religions lost the sacredness that had sustained generations of ancestral worshippers."[55] Gray White traces the multiple reasons and myths that surround the Black woman's pre-distorted sexuality. She further adds this important insight concerning the rape of the Black woman: "Rather than fault themselves, some Southern spokesmen blamed black women."[56] In sum, "niggling" and carnality seem suspiciously related to the customary violation of Black women.

To "niggle" also means to work in a trifling way. A classic stereotype about Black people is that they are both lazy and stupid, therefore, "trifling." Sometimes enslavers misread such stereotypes because as John Hope Franklin observes, the enslaved people often feigned ignorance in order to withhold labor[57] and Robin Kelley in *Race Rebels* (1996) points out this behavior today. His pioneering analysis elucidates the particular and to the dominant culture unusual responses of Black workers to economic situations. He writes that:

> For a worker to accept reformist trade union strategies while stealing from work, to fight streetcar conductors while voting down strike action in one's local, to leave work early in order to participate in religious revival meetings or rendezvous with one's lover, or to choose to attend a dance rather than a CIO mass meeting is not necessarily a sign of an "immature" class consciousness, but reflects the multiple ways working people live, experience, and interpret the world around them.[58]

Such cultural responses provide a fresh way to examine how Blacks seize power and validate their lives, neutralizing racism. Yet, examples from literature and folklore suggest that many Negroes since slavery thought themselves less industrious and intelligent than Whites. From the Federal Writers'

Project, we sample some self-negating examples. Between 1934 and 1941, members of the Federal Writers' Project interviewed formerly enslaved people. Some of the responses reflect Eurocentric stereotypes, beginning with the personal wisdom of Charles Grandy who says that, "White people is King over niggers."[59] And next, Nelson Dickerson: "All de black men seem to be lazy, an' I is one uf dem."[60] And finally, Jane Johnson: "De nigger come from Africa and other hot places when he come here, de white man made him work, and he didn't like dat. He is natchally lazy."[61]

The "lazy negro" is a characterization I have heard my entire life. Recently, some young women echoed related sentiments of dysfunction and inferiority on the #10 trolley in a Black working class area of West Philadelphia. I overheard two teenaged girls chatting about boys, parental restrictions, and school. One said to the other, "I am not as smart as the White kids. You know they have the gift of knowledge." When the other agreed, I interrupted their conversation. These young women were expressing the ideology of defeatism intrinsic in American customs and in literature. Consider the placement of "negro" in an early 20th century grammar book:

> Some nouns ending in o preceded by a consonant form the plural by adding **es** to the singular: **echo, echoes, veto, vetoes; cargo, cargoes; negro, negroes;**....[62]

"Negroes" follows "cargoes" and displays the transportability of a people and the transferred combination of commodity and beast that caused the teenaged girls to consider themselves inferior to Whites. In the grammar book, a race of people appears among foods, transportable objects and official exercises, and all begin with a lowercase letter. This 20th century grammar book reflects attitudes and American customs similar to those in 18th and 19th century literature, including *Equiano*, *Iola Leroy*, and *Incidents*. Accordingly, the only people in America are White.

Lowercasing the "n" in negro was the accepted literary style of early American literature. Negro writers of the 18th through 20th centuries who adhered to this format were writing correctly according to the standard literary format. In fact, during the early twentieth century, Marcus Garvey mounted a protest campaign to demand the capitalization of the negro "N."[63]

Richard B. Moore, chairman of a committee to expose the "evil" truth about the term "Negro," traces it in *The Name "Negro": Its Origin and Evil Use*. Citing records from Portuguese enslavers, he explains how "Ethiopian" and "African" once described peoples of the entire continent. This changed however when the Portuguese and others internationally expanded enslaving to solely West African people. At this juncture, the African and the

Ethiopian transformed into negroes. Even more, enslaving started early in Africa. Richard Moore cites Fernando Ortiz, a professor of ethnology, who discusses slavery prior to its exploitation in West Africa:

> this institution [slavery] continued into the Middle Ages and later times in some nations of Europe and ... the Saracenic domination of the Iberian peninsula (from 711 to 1492) along with the mercantile relations which were established between it and Africa, brought black slaves in abundance to Spain and Portugal many centuries before the Portuguese discoveries on the west coast of Africa.[64]

Historians John G. Jackson, *Introduction to African Civilizations* (1980), and Chancellor Williams, *The Destruction of Black Civilizations* (1976), both discuss the enslaving practices of the Moors and the Arabs. The Moors and Arabs collaborated with the Portuguese in order to purchase Africans of darker hue. Fernando Ortiz continues:

> In colonial countries the word "Negro" had a specific meaning beyond the simple connotation of color or skin. The expression "He is a Negro" was equivalent to saying "he is a slave" since almost all the slaves in certain countries and epochs were "Negroes." "Negro" came to be synonymous with slave; just as in other geographical and historical situations ... "Slav" was the synonym for slave.... So degrading among the Hispanic peoples, not excepting Spain itself, were the words *negro* and *mulatto*, that their use became limited to slaves, because they implicitly signified slavery or social vileness...[65] [my emphasis].

According to H.H. Fairchild, group labels determine how outsiders see the group.[66] They also, however, determine how insiders view themselves. With the Moors and the Arabs first selling other Africans based on skin-color, they set a foundation for pigment distinctions that were exploited under colonial slavery. Walter Rodney in *How Europe Underdeveloped Africa* (1982) presents an earlier mentioned hue differentiation with results that assisted the enslaving enterprise in Africa. Some Africans with European fathers helped maintain and manage the trade, and selection was based on skin color.[67] With West Africa as the prime geography for exploitation, the (re)naming caused and prompted the world to systematically persecute and degrade West African people. Moore says, it was like shouting "mad dog" and then waiting for the world to kill it. Traveling from g/Guinea to nigger to Negro to b/Black represents a journey where people of African descent attempted to juggle, repress, or escape enforced nomenclatures and meanings. Richard Moore insists that like "negro," "kaffir" and "native" are prejudicial words that release hate and "murderous deeds." He describes the Sharpeville attack when "hundreds of Africans, even mothers with babies on their backs" were "shot down in the back by those illustrious examples of Christian apartheid."[68]

Very often people say, "what's in a name?" We have all heard that sticks and stones will break our bones but names will never hurt us. The practice of (re)naming a people already named kills off historical memory, and in this linguistic rupture avenues of defeat, inferiority, and sub-humanity find fields for repetition and proliferation. Names do hurt.

This is the historical backdrop that Elijah Muhammad, teaching Malcolm X, intended to overturn. After X's assassination, Haki Madhubuti advanced poetry that persuaded the Negro to enter a cleared field of racial inclusion.

Summary

In the 15th century when Portuguese explorers expanded the enslaving process, they renamed the African "negro," which became a synonym for slave. Negro has other synonyms, guinea and nigger. With the combining of g/Guinea as an African area, a people, and also currency, the enslaved "guineas" linguistically and mentally thought of themselves as outside of humanity. This psychological distortion encouraged the enslaved Negroes to internalize inferiority prevalent throughout the New World in religion, institutions, literature, and society at large. Particularly in literature, the character Othello in Shakespeare's masterpiece displays more about Elizabethan beliefs about race than the tragedy of an interracial marriage.

The Blacks were not the only ones who internalized a racially scripted inferiority. The Whites created and projected racism and barbarity on all levels within the peculiar institution. New World Africans, renamed negro, were legally restricted from White American opportunities as they were legally forced to perform free labor for centuries. This accepted and expected American practice infiltrated the language in a myriad of ways, documented in the Oxford English Dictionary. Overwork, overworked people, exhausted labor, and burning associate the negro or nigger with serious manifestations that suggests overt cruelty and human rights violations. The literature written by American Negroes in the 18th and 19th centuries demonstrates a merging of currency and commodity that divides humanity. The enslaved when sold would say that they were "put in the master's pocket." To be put in the master's pocket meant turning into coinage or paper, not a people.

With the renamed Negroes relating only to America for existence, psychology, aesthetics, and philosophy, they inherited generations of inferiority. In fact, the selected literature suggests that Negro sub-humanity was normalized and expected.

The following chapter shows this dislocation and the results of being (re)named "Negro" in the modern age and why whether referring to this racial concept as the "new Negro" or the "so-called Negro" never solved the primary underlying problem.

TWO

How New Is the New Negro?

>have you ever
>heard Tonto say
>>"I'm part negro."

Don L. Lee poses this question in his 1960s poem "Wake Up Niggers (you ain't part Indian)" to illustrate the compounded and historical problems with the race name Negro, and to show a negative meaning inherent in the racial name. The way he presents the term signals an inherent problem. His deliberate non-capitalization of Negro prepares the reader to seek something other than this racial appellation. His presentation revisits the style of 19th-century authors such as Frances Harper who lowercased the Negro "n." Harper was following the demeaning format of the dominant culture.

During slavery, the personality of the American-born Negro contained disturbing human contrasts. All humans have contrasting personality elements; however, the enslaved African and the freeborn one in slavery had to make psychological accommodations that distorted perspectives. Their self image included an ontology of objectification, subhumanity, and currency. This explains why Lee/Madhubuti lowercased the "n" in "negro" to illustrate its historical ineffectiveness and improper use as a name that reflected his racial collective.

Generally, among the Black Arts poets, discarding "Negro" is an obvious strategy for collective and conscious transformation. The term is altogether missing in the Black Arts manifesto in 1968. Thus, the re(re)naming has already occurred, the Negroes/Blacks redefining themselves, with no one claiming a particular appellation. This nonselection suggests that at least the rejection of "Negro" as a racial identifier has entered the active consciousness of the Black Arts artists.

Larry Neal's African-centered direction in the Black Arts essay brings to light several of Malcolm X's repeated themes, rejection of Whites and the White aesthetic.[1] In the Black Arts essay, the following racial appellations appear: "African American" once, "Afro-American" ten times and "Black" more than twenty times, indicating a racial vortex of change. Yet, before the 1960s the term "Negro" had undergone alterations relative to racial advancement. For example, Alain Locke edited an important text titled *The New Negro* (1925) that shepherded in a definitive break from previous Negro meanings as it signaled a plausible independence from Eurocentric or White definitions. These fresh and humanistic meanings in the "new Negro" defined the artistic and political activities of the 1920s, specifically the Harlem Renaissance. The purpose of Locke's text was to refute the prevailing racist notion that African American people, who were Negroes then, were incapable of writing literature.

In this chapter, beginning with Elijah Muhammad, we will examine the various shifts of the term Negro. When Muhammad headed the Nation of Islam, he taught Malcolm and other Muslims about erasing the term:

> One of the first and most important truths that must be established in this day is our identity.... All nations of the earth are recognized by the name by which they are called. By stating one's name, one is able to associate an entire order of a particular civilization simply by name alone.... How can a so-called Negro say that his name is "Sam Jones," a white man's name with roots in Europe, when "Sam Jones" (Black man) comes from Africa or Asia?[2]

Malcolm X took Muhammad's instructions and replicated the theme rooted in urban culture, signifying and rebirthing the defiant masculine perspective that codified resistance in America. X speaks in the badman perspective, that is the renegade Black male viewpoint that developed during the enslavement of Blacks. X says:

> Yes, I think there is a new so-called Negro. We don't recognize the term Negro but I really believe that there's a new so-called Negro here in America. He not only is impatient. Not only is he dissatisfied, not only is he disillusioned, but he's getting very angry. And whereas the so-called Negro in the past was willing to sit around and wait for someone else to

change his condition or correct his condition, there's a growing tendency on the part of a vast number of so-called Negroes today to take action themselves.[3]

X actively transforms "Sam Jones," the so-called Negro, into an action figure, placing this invention within the badman tradition. During the enslavement of Blacks, a folk heroic tradition started where tales about defiant people assumed mythic proportions. Because the badman was one who normally defeated capture after escaping, harming, or killing Whites, the stories about such figures were seeped in supernatural tensions. Similar to Native American literary characters, the badman could often shapeshift. Bras Coupe, who lived in Louisiana in the 1830s, and Railroad Bill in Alabama during the 1890s are two such figures.[4] Malcolm X places the compressed resistance and tension of the "so-called" Negro in energy that implicitly hints of resistance. This suggestion stirs apprehension in Whites and triumph in Blacks.

Dissimilarly, Muhammad's method of discourse related the identity problem of the Negro through geography and psychological crossovers from Europe to Africa or Asia. In the Socratic method, Muhammad asks a question, whereas X provides the answer. In the declarative mode, X brings forward another idea of the "so-called Negro" one with anger and action on his mind.

This revisits the enslaved negro male who revised his circumstances, who demanded to be put in the master's pocket, to meet his own needs. Malcolm's modern new Negro though is more dangerous than the one "put in the master's pocket" because of the chronological difference from the one enslaved. This new Negro has more opportunities than his predecessors held in bondage. The modern new Negro could activate his willingness to take mental or physical action in order to rectify his subservient position in America. This is not the Negro in *Equiano's Travels*, who had to have White males intercede for him to address injustices by Whites.

Malcolm was speaking about the "so-called Negro" before television cameras in 1961. Therefore, his response is forged for a broader, more diverse audience than Elijah Muhammad's. Malcolm has entered his "so-called Negro" into the political arena, an unpopular topography for the religiously based Nation of Islam. Always aware of his audience, X implicitly threatens the established order with the concept of Negroes, so-called or otherwise, assuming agency. Malcolm displayed rhetorical imagery in this country that exacerbated what educator and theorist Andrew Hacker (1992) calls the underlying guilt and culpability that Whites acknowledge about the plight of Black people. Hacker puts it like this: "all white Americans, regardless of their political persuasions, are well aware of how black people have suffered due to inequities imposed upon them by white America."⁵

The concept of "the new Negro," however, did not begin with either Malcolm or Muhammad. That new Negro appeared in the mind of Alain Locke (1886–1954) back in 1925 when he edited a book of that title. Locke is an important figure in early 20th century intellectual life of the Negro. Alain Locke's new Negro found value for the first time in his own beauty and aesthetics, closely related to W.E.B. Du Bois's ideas of the talented tenth. Yet, that new Negro as Locke formulated him was working to integrate his talents into White society and to participate fully in American democracy. Additionally, that Negro was absolutely male. As Locke says, "The Negro mind reaches out as yet to nothing but American wants, American ideas. But this forced attempt to build his Americanism on race values is a unique social experiment, and its ultimate success is impossible except through the fullest sharing of American culture and institutions.... Only the steadying and sobering effect of a truly characteristic gentleness of spirit prevents the rapid rise of a definite cynicism and counter-hate and a defiant superiority feeling. *Human as this action would be,* the majority still deprecate its advent"⁶ [my emphasis].

Locke's new Negro still represses the human emotion of anger, rage, and reaction to the onslaught that Africans have suffered since first contact with Whites. Locke speaks in monolithic terms, disregarding the vibrations and images of another type of "new Negro," the one that Marcus Garvey initiated.

From 1917 to 1921 Marcus Garvey gave America a separate new Negro from Locke's version. Garvey's new Negro conception antecedes and paves the way for the 1960s model. Garvey's new Negro dressed up in military fashion, prepared to separate from White America, and to reclaim Africa from the colonizers. Garvey had a Black army complete with military uniforms and swords, also organizing a female military arm as well as the Black Cross Nurses. All of his divisions paraded through Harlem and raised the ire of the American government. This new Negro truly participated in a concept of nation building never undergone before by American Blacks. With the incarceration and then exile of Marcus Garvey, his new Negro submerged but did not die. That new Negro surfaced again during the 1960s.

The 1960s activists represented an original threat and seemingly self-focused confidence that consumes Black Power poetry. In opposition to Locke's new Negro that represses vital rage, the 1960s one walks and writes with a wail of revolution. That one also has a "definite cynicism" and "a defiant superiority feeling." Elijah Muhammad and Malcolm encouraged that conception.

Dissimilarly, Locke speaks in biological determinist terms of "gentleness of spirit." This emotion is certainly erased (and added to) from images of radicalism during the 1960s. For example, Don L. Lee, H. Rap Brown, Huey Newton and Bobby Seale will not be remembered for such a descriptor. Because they are resistors to injustices, they are aberrations to racism, capitalism, and White supremacy, breaking the illusion of omnipotence of White Western power. Additionally, in contemporary popular culture the notion of a Negro's "gentleness of spirit" nullifies in rap and hip hop culture and performance, which often glorifies the gangster ("gangsta"). With the exception of Martin Luther King's portrayal, America is not a culture that appreciates, respects, or replicates any male with a "gentleness of spirit." In patriarchal America, the cowboy, gangster, soldier, killer, and sportsman are often heroes.

In literary history, Marcus Garvey's poetry is an archetype for the 1960s verses, because his lyrics present many of the same issues that distinguish Black Power poetry. Nevertheless, Alain Locke sought to validate the collective racial self of his time period, not as independent and radicalized as that of Garvey, but an elevated reconfiguration of the Negro. Locke was an intellectual within the academy and he spoke that language and posed his arguments for that audience (and others as well). Garvey on the other hand was a leader of the grassroots. His audience was the general populace. Each man provided lively and precedent setting avenues for the transformation of the "new Negro." Each reconstructed the expansiveness of the Negro people.

For one, Alain Locke attacked the Eurocentric term "primitive" as a descriptor of African art, because he sought to connect the African influence on Negro art in America. This link is an Afrocentric qualification before the 1960s. This means that during the 1920s, Locke with all of his Harvard training and American idealism and understanding still sought a commonality, a genealogical and geographical uniting, with the continent. Locke became a leading critic and collector of African and African American art, and he insisted on documenting the proficiency of Negro and African art. He extended this same commonality in his examination of Negro music, becoming a scholar on Black folk music and pointing out African influences. He is one of the earliest to argue that Negro or Black music is the closest that America has to folk music, considering this folk music a source for classical and serious song. Locke wrote critical essays that respected and appreciated differences within races and cultures and he certainly thought, wrote, and spoke dimensionally about the significance of the Negro in art.

In contrast, Marcus Garvey's contribution to world thought concerns a concentration on his version of the new Negro as completely devoid of

White interference. He thinks and writes in dichotomous modalities, his roughhewn poetry emphasizes separation from White hegemony. Listen to "The Tragedy of White Injustice":

> Lying and stealing is the whiteman's game;
> For rights of God nor man he has no shame
> (A practice of his throughout the whole world)
> At all, great thunderbolts he has hurled;
> He has stolen everywhere — land and sea;
> A buccaneer and pirate he must be,
> Killing all, as he roams from place to place,
> Leaving disease, mongrels — moral disgrace.[7]

Despite the lack of concentration on craft, one clearly observes Garvey's dichotomous view of the "whiteman." Splitting the "whiteman" in isolation for review, Garvey, like Malcolm, builds a historic narrative to make his point. All of the Black Arts poets held up unflattering images of the "whiteman." They wanted to impress resistance to assimilation and to persuade the lost Negro to find himself and herself in the energy of (re)creation.

For Neal and Madhubuti to articulate neo-Black art with a separate symbolism, mythology, and critique repeats and extends the ideas of another significant intellectual, Langston Hughes. Hughes discusses literary and cultural perspectives in "The Negro and the Racial Mountain" (1926). In this essay, Hughes reasons that individual artists should respond to the group collective for material. His mountain is a metaphor. It is the Black middle-class desire to be White and to disdain low culture. Hughes, like the Black Arts poets, found sustenance and pleasure in Black culture: music, dance, mores, situations: the ways of Black folk. Hughes eloquently portrayed sentimental, realistic versions of Black life that anticipated a search for a new mythology. However, unlike the Black Arts poets, Hughes quietly created a communist inspired revolutionary poetry that he never publicly read.[8]

Madhubuti separates and deconstructs "black" and "white" conceptions extensively in *Enemies: the Clash of Races*. In 1978, Madhubuti critiques Black Liberation and White supremacy in a malcolmian manner, without euphemisms or creolization. While indicting collective White power, he exposes the disingenuous leadership among Blacks. This text demonstrates that Madhubuti never left the music of Malcolm X. Larry Neal by this time had abandoned some of the discordance in the manifesto, struggling to interpret what Ralph Ellison earlier called "the blackness of black." Amiri Baraka had embraced Marxism, which tilted his singular attention on race. But, Madhubuti never abandoned the Black Nationalist-/Pan-Africanist ideology of X that initially originated in his art.

What Time Is It? Nation Time

The title question refers to the secular Black Nationalist precepts that generally require Blacks to develop networks for economic growth and cultural affirmation. The title is a call and response mantra heard throughout the 1960s era, among activists, sympathizers, and nonaffiliated Black people. Nationalism is largely a result of and a reaction to the onslaught of racial exclusivity that has hindered Black people since American enslavement. The sloganeering of "Nation Time" was an aspect of the death of the Negro. In *Enemies: The Clash of Races* Madhubuti expands the arguments that Harold Cruse launched against the Communist Party in *Crisis of the Negro Intellectual* (1967). Cruse analyzes the failure of Black leadership to form a political, economic, and cultural autonomy for Blacks. Madhubuti takes this further by stating methods that he believed would solve inequities specific to Black people. His critique of White consciousness and proliferation is uncanny. He moves from Elijah Muhammad's dichotomous mythological version of the difference between the races to a secular one from factual behavior and global dominance. He writes:

> *White people have never come in peace.* Their move toward global dominance is not accidental, but is a crucial and well thought-out part of their foreign policy. The question whether they are Communists, Capitalists, Christians, etc. in the final analysis speaks mainly to strategy and tactics within the political and cultural frame of reference of their choice. The problem is not, actually, a Black problem. It is a white one.[9]

Madhubuti is a result of intellectuals such as Marcus Garvey, Paul Robeson, W.E.B. Du Bois and X. He is a part of the academy forced to widen its doors because of the revolutionary spirit of the 1960s. Earlier, in *Enemies*, he discusses his personal Black/Whiteness, his split American identity often at war, like Du Bois's double consciousness, trying to be Negro and American. In the above quote, the surreal, italicized first line, "White people have never come in peace," is lethal without threat, allowing what Blacks normally repress to surface. This non-integration perspective isolates the relationship between the races from the position of a thinker with a sober anger and intelligence. He is not writing for the comfort or inclusion of Whites, a difficult decision for authors of color. Writing specifically for the Black reader, he states his reasons:

> (1) For the total, uncompromising Liberation of Black people. (2) For the creation of a just world-order where each and every person is able to reach his or her highest potential and in doing so not violate the cultural or human rights of his or her neighbors as we all strive to live and develop

in an atmosphere of productive peace. (3) Writing is the most lasting and the major (yet limiting) form of communication that I have access to that reaches a good number of Black people. (4) Writing is a cleansing, dialectical, meditative and communicative process that helps keep me honest and committed to struggle. Keeps me open minded and active among those I dearly care for, many of whom I do not have daily contact with. (5) I love my people and know the greatness we have in us and know that that greatness, at this time in our lives, must be continuously pushed and forced out of us if we are to survive and develop as a people. Writing is one of the enforcers that I use.[10]

Madhubuti, like Malcolm X and his oratory, has committed himself to writing bravely to critique White America in order to *push the greatness out of his people*. This racially conscious perspective is dissimilar to Locke and even Hughes even though all are representative of variations within racial love. Where Locke and Madhubuti and X most differ is in Locke's universal appeal and the latter's comprehension of the importance of the specific as a fount for the general. Nation building was a core theme in X and Madhubuti's oratory and writing. Democratic pluralism to the point of racial neutrality that muffles distinctions is in Locke's.

Throughout X's entire life, no matter his wavering perceptions, he always worked for Black independence. Whether or not a Sunni or Elijah Muhammad Muslim, Malcolm X extends a Black Nationalist resistance tradition, American born. And Haki Madhubuti, stepped inside of that energy, found a home and built several mansions.

Summary

The concept and idea of the "New Negro" begins with the writing of Alain Locke during the 1920s. This great intellectual edited the text *The New Negro* in 1925 and it set a standard that let the world recognize the writing ability of the then Negro people. Locke also claimed a relationship between artistry in Africa and the creativity produced by the new Negro. During this same time period, Marcus Garvey had another idea about a new Negro. His was more racially exclusive than Locke's version that favored complete entry into American institutions. Garvey's Negro image was one that worked to build a nation within America and to assist in African development.

This Garvey notion of the new Negro is the archetype for the 1960s model that Don L. Lee/Haki Madhubuti and other Black Arts artists scripted in poetry. This ideology, a central focus in the teachings of Elijah Muhammad, prepared the metaphysical space for a change from the race name "Negro" altogether. To establish this erasure, Don L. Lee wrote in dichotomous terms about the relationship between Whites and Blacks in his text *Enemies: The Clash of Races* (1978). This critique was a sober intellectual comprehension of the defeatism of the Black that had occurred since interaction with Whites. It secularized racial difference and opened the channels for a regrouping of a people once enslaved.

In the following chapter, we will explore the racial images in poetry that contrast vividly with the literature of war that Don L. Lee and the 1960s Black Arts poets aimed at White America. We step back in time to capture the essentials of the Negro in poetry by Negro artists, beginning with Phillis Wheatley, the first to publish a volume of poetry in America.

THREE

Africa as Motif in Pre–1960s Poetry: Selections of the Antebellum, the Reconstruction, and the Harlem Renaissance

Focusing on the linguistics and context of racial appellations enforced on New World Africans, chapter one revealed the trauma of (re)naming on literate and nonliterate people of African descent. Chapter two discussed the variations in thinking from the phrase "New Negro." This chapter, in another direction, examines the imagery of Africa in early Negro or African poetry, which includes a range of self and race defeating modifications. It shows the results of racist (re)naming in the literary imagination of early American and Harlem Renaissance poets. The seminal inquiry here explores how the image of Africa prefigures itself in selected Black poetry before the 1960s. An image of Africa includes all racial references to people of African heritage in poetry. This investigation isolates multiple, dislocated, negative tropes, a motif that existed prior to the 1960s. Examining this particular motif explores how the literary imagination of early Black writers pictured the topology of Africa and how they imagined their relationship to the continent. To employ these ends, my range of analyses includes an examination of racist assumptions beginning in the antebellum and a projection of history to give context and clarity to the perspectives of each author. According to Richard Scholes (2000), history should be attended to more seriously when teaching literature because history situates texts in the cultural context that gives the work its original meaning.¹ By connecting the past to the present, this method enables an investigation of how we arrived at our current destination and more specifically how and why the artistic upheaval occurred in the 1960s. That upheaval largely emerged from the oratory of Malcolm X, who preached that the Negro was not a Negro — that he was "scientifically designed" for that purpose. Don L. Lee/Haki Madhubuti gained direction from this pronouncement and wrote malcolmian poetry such as:

> negro leaderships share more than a need for greed
> most have rusty knees, purple tongues, & dry lips
> ...
> they are trained at the best divinity schools
> do not spit verbs, read secular materials or
> ponder too deeply about the negro problem...²

In the above poem, Lee/Madhubuti isolates for study the problematic nature and behavior of what X called the "scientifically produced" Negro. Clearly in this poem, "negro" leaders are not visionary or doers. This malcolmian content stands in stark contrast to the lyrics that historically preceded it. In Madhubuti's offering, he seeks to force a new generation of thinkers to look critically at the race name Negro in order to accept something else. Differently, in the poetry of Phillis Wheatley and others following her, that poetry was to prove to an often disapproving audience that the Negro or African was human and had imagination.

To discuss this poetry through a frame of reference that joins the Pan-African thought of X and Cheikh Anta Diop, I have selected the ancient philosophical system from the ascendancy to Ma'at. This filter will enable commentary about the features of each African image. Ma'at, from the Kemetic (Egyptian) system of philosophy and divinity, is one of the nine Ntru (pronounced "Neturu") that compose the Ennead from which the Greeks millennia later shaped their muses. This research promises to yield literary tendencies affecting later poetry, introducing a new paradigm for uniting African and African American thought with an African-centered critique.

When employing an African-centered mode of analysis, one searches for historical substance and truth in order to piece together the fractured and fragmented history, philosophy, ethos, and culture of African people. Since the dispersal throughout the Diaspora, a historical, philosophical, and cultural loss plagued many intellectuals of African lineage, including Malcolm X and Haki Madhubuti. Using investigative methods long conquered and forced underground assists in the journey to rediscover a deeper understanding and acceptation of Black poetry. This chapter stands to contrast the transforming image of Africa in the poetry of the 1960s, posing questions that connect "the past to our present cultural situation."[3] My purpose then is to establish a continuum of dislocated images in art that foreground and maintain the psychological fracture experienced by the Negro to prepare for the later war poetry that Madhubuti wrote during the 1960s.

Ma'at: A Symbol of Justice and Balance

In the ascendancy to Ma'at outlined by Molefi K. Asante in *Kemet, Afrocentricity and Knowledge* (1990), there are three purposeful concepts for literary interpretation: (1) the unity of occasion and situation; (2) the elimination of chaos; and (3) the elevation of peace among disparate voices.[4] My schema works in the following way: The unity of occasion prefigures how the poet imagines Africa and the self as an African in America before the actual writing of the poem. The theory of elimination of chaos determines if the African poet in the New World has in small or large measure lessened the intensity of racism with the artistic production. Or, it evaluates if the expression extends the chaos inherent in the American experience. The elevation of peace among disparate voices concludes the results of the poets' creations. This principle can determine if the poet attempted to synthesize the African experience in America to build a kind of harmony. It will judge if the particular poetic voice presents a uniqueness of thought, culture, or behavior in the American-African experience.

In the 18th century Phillis Wheatley, the mother of African literature in America, begins the examination of African imagery in poetry. Frances Ellen Watkins Harper's expressions cover the 19th century and Claude McKay and Countee Cullen, the 20th. After Wheatley, the subsequent authors offer historical continuity for this specific motif. In Wheatley's poetry, the African and non-African sentiment have been points of contention where critics fault her for not agitating for social justice or rendering Negro sorrow. On issues of race, she has been called dispassionate and coldly objective.[5] However, this objectivity more probably concerns the intersections among racism, racist thought, and existence under the racial appellation "negro."

Phillis Wheatley

Phillis Wheatley (1753?–1784) wrote poetry during the American epoch when this country was in the process of self-creation. She published her first and only volume of poetry, *Poems on Various Subjects Religious and Moral*, in 1773. American leaders during that time compared fighting with Great Britain to the war between Anglo-Saxons and the Normans. Wheatley breathed in this revolutionary fervor. With the notion of "Black literature" nonexistent, she wrote as a Negro presuming the history, literature, religion, and custom of this epoch. Three years after her book's publication, Thomas Jefferson designed the Declaration of Independence, relying on Anglo-Saxon mythology. He writes:

> Hengist and Horsa, the Saxon chiefs from whom we claim the honor of being descended [had the] political principles and form of government we have assumed.[6]

Thus, Anglo-Saxon ideals provided a foundation for the new American government. The danger here for Africans and other peoples of color is in the inherent racism of this worldview. For example, in Wheatley's world, Native Americans were conscripted as non-people, either slaughtered or removed to reserves, and most of Wheatley's brethren were enslaved.[7] The Whites with omnipotent power over everything dark and female turned into human gods as scientific advances assisted in expanding their superiority and arrogance. Projecting superiority over the darker races, in America and abroad, American leaders shaped the law and religious ideology to sanction slavery.

All of this affected the literary imagination of Wheatley. Kidnapped in Africa before the age of six, she experienced the entire horror of global enslavement: the trek across Africa, the exchange among various ethnic groups and enslavers, the Middle Passage, the auction block, and finally bondage. However, before reviewing her ownership in America, an examination of slavery in Africa deserves attention in order to discover difference and commonality.

Scholars differ on the extent of African involvement in the slave trade. In *The History of Slavery* (1860) W.O. Blake states that the Portuguese were the earliest to seize African people. In *Equiano's Travels* (1789) we learn that the Spanish had African allies that aided in kidnapping victims. Similarly, Walter Rodney in *How Europe Underdeveloped Africa* (1982) discusses the biracial Africans, Portuguese fathers and African mothers, who maintained the trade. In Blake's massive text *The History of Slavery*, the Portuguese's linguistic dominance is obvious. Blake himself refers to West Africa as "negroland" or "Nigritia," and he offers the following summation about how "negro" turned into a synonym for slave:

> It is upon Ethiopia in an especial manner that the curse of slavery has fallen. At first, it bore *but a share* of the burden; Britons and Scythians were the fellow-slaves of the Ethiopian: but at last all the other nations of the earth

seemed to conspire against the *negro* race, agreeing never to *enslave each other*, but to make the blacks the slaves of all alike⁸ [my emphasis].

The designation "Ethiopia" during the 19th century included more geographical space than now. Blake details the advent of slavery from ancient times to his present day, and he shows the methodology for securing and transforming Africans into slaves. The significance in the above quote is the obvious conspiracy among the European nations to stop enslaving one another and to singly enslave the negro. In the above Blake capitalizes the Britons, Scythians, and Ethiopians, but not the "negro." He says more:

> So universal is the instinct for barter that the immediate effect of the new and great demand for slaves was to create its own supply. Slavery, as we have said, existed in *Negroland* from time immemorial, but on a comparatively limited scale⁹ [my emphasis].

Blake compares the growing business of the European and African slave trade, concluding that in Africa its scale was comparatively minimal. John Hope Franklin (1974) writes that "the Egyptians enslaved whatever peoples they captured."¹⁰ The Muslims also contributed greatly to institutionalizing slavery "by seizing Negro women for their harems and Negro men for military and menial service."¹¹ Basil Davidson (1990) discusses slavery in three ways. He says that it began by "piracy," "warlike alliance, and by more or less peaceful partnership."¹² Like Blake, he explains the differences between African and European slavery, stating that in Africa captives had more rights. However, he adds the following to erase a common notion about the peculiar institution:

> It is important to establish this point. For it was the ground of departure on which the whole connection between Europe and Africa was firmly set. Out of this common acceptance of bondage in a given situation there would flow ... a common acceptance of the slave trade between the two continents.¹³

Chancellor Williams (1976) expands the "common acceptance ... between the two continents" when analyzing the state of Kongo from the perspective of African leaders. Because slavery was a factor in African society, he says this about the participation of Africans:

> Up to the sixteenth century the people we are calling slaves were not slaves in the modern sense, but laborers either captured as prisoners of war or persons imprisoned for various offenses. So during the first stages of the slave trade many African chiefs and Kings actually thought they were supplying workers needed abroad — and at great profit to themselves.¹⁴

This scholar also exposes the avaricious kings who after learning the truth never ceased participating in the European-African slave trade. Yet, not all figures of authority assisted in enslaving. Queen Nzingha and King Shyyam for example fought courageously and against great odds (European technology) to ensure independence for Africans. Although Nzingha has been called a slave trader herself, Chancellor Williams believes that sometimes she made controversial decisions based on principles of war and war strategies. For instance, to outwit the Portuguese she at times acted as an enemy collaborator. During the 17th century, Nzingha fought the Portuguese for well over twenty years. To engage in battle for this length of time, it seems probable that she would factor masquerade into her knowledge of war and winning. However, the business of bondage went on for centuries for patriarchal reasons and exploitation. Chancellor Williams highlights this provocative point:

> For let this truth emerge from the many facts which are buried — and let it stand out clearly: One of the main attractions of slavery, and the magnet that drew thousands of white men on, was their sexual freedom unlimited with all the Black girls and women who were enslaved and helpless in the power of their masters.[15]

Sexual freedom and religious hypocrisy played twin roles in the operation of the peculiar institution. Historian John G. Jackson points out the hypocrisy of religious institutions that approved slavery. In fact, quoting Chapman Cohen, Jackson states the culpability and complicity of the church in the enslaving of Africans:

> The peculiar and damning fact in the history of slavery ... so far as the Christian Church is concerned, is this ... It was created by Christians, it was continued by Christians, it was in some respects more barbarous than anything the world had yet seen, and its worst features were to be witnessed in countries that were most ostentatious in their parade of Christianity. It is this that provides the final unanswerable indictment of the Christian Church.[16]

However, Christians were not the only religious group involved. The Arabs or Muslims also saw skin variation and lack of weaponry as preludes for enslaving in order to make profits. Richard B. Moore in *The Name "Negro": Its Origin and Evil Use* (1992) contends that after 1441 the Portuguese sailed below the Senegal River, and the river existed as a dividing line between "people" and "difference." Those above the Senegal River were known as "Moors" or "Azenegues." The darker people south of the river were a more easy prey, unequal contenders against Portuguese "crossbows and firearms."[17]

This easy conquest was well known prior to the fifteenth century. The distinction of "color" and the sophistication of "technology" together shape the conquistadors' advantage. Not perceiving the Africans as another people with an idea of humanity, the Portuguese instead concluded "easy conquest" and slavery. W.O. Blake reasons that this objectifying of a people had long been in operation. According to him, in 1412 Prince Henry urged the Portuguese to sail beyond the "Canaries, past the Cape Verds, along the coast of Guinea, through the Bight of Biafra, down that long unnamed extent of coast."[18] Three generations had been exploring this area and in 1434, "Antonio Gonzales, a Portuguese captain ... carried away with him some negro boys, whom he sold to one or two Moorish families in the south of Spain."[19]

The Moors who owned other Africans recognized cultural difference as inferior and participated in the slave trade. Thus, this African people who ruled Spain from the 8th to the 10th century helped coordinate the newly named "negroes" into the caste of enslavement. In the above quote, the substantial disregard for the ideas and language of the people isolated for capture is again relative to the issue of naming. Blake not only refers to the stretch of land as "unnamed," he later says it is "untamed." His employ of language implies that Europeans are the language bearers and domesticators of the world. A thing does not exist until they name it and claim it indicating that the (re)named (the indigenous) have no history or lineage worthy of regard.

This portends disappearance of the individuals denied authority in their own language based on whether or not the conquerors (re)name. In another part of the world, this identical linguistic conquest reduced the humanity of the indigenous nations (misnamed "Indians").

Phillis Wheatley survived the brutality of the Middle Passage to arrive in Boston. In fragile health, her frailties remained a constant burden throughout her short life. Young Phillis (seven or eight on arrival wrapped in a ragged piece of carpet), an African child, became a negro in America. After her purchase, her owners taught her literacy skills and she read European American literature that described and explained African images as inferior: "negro," "Nubian," "Egyptian," "African," "nigger," "black." This artistic and gifted child made decisions about her people and her world based on this imagery of Black in the Western literary imagination. According to Reginald Horsman, when she arrived and lived in America, she would have found a "confident, arrogant people ... fed by success."[20]

This success comes from voyages that yielded human labor and land. The English proudly carrying the banner of Cristobal Colon (Christopher Columbus) were a new people turning into a new nation.[21] Those who were not White were incidental to the dream of boundless empire. To ensure the dream, the legislators sentenced the providers of perpetual labor to chattel slavery. The negro was designated a commodity for life. Scientists, scholars, theologians, and philosophers rallied together to fabricate the negroes' nonhuman status, while Wheatley read and experienced the results. In addition, to strengthen the ethos of White superiority, Anglo-Americans compared themselves to those enslaved. Toni Morrison writes appropriately about this racial disparity that lingers largely in the contemporary moment in literary discourse but has historical origins. She explains the silences concerning issues of race in White literature and how ignoring race removes this anxiety from the dominant class. This silence also removes the material reality from Black people assisting in a marginal existence in discourse.[22] However, this absence is not really absent, and it is not an empty space. Morrison emphasizes in *Playing in the Dark* (1992) that

> Black slavery enriched the country's creative possibilities. For in that construction of blackness *and* enslavement could be found not only the not-free but also, with the dramatic polarity created by skin color, the projection of the not-me. The result was a playground for the imagination. What rose up out of collective needs to allay internal fears and to rationalize external exploitation was an American Africanism — a fabricated brew of darkness, otherness, alarm, and desire that is uniquely American[23] [my emphasis].

In the dominant culture during the epoch of enslavement, White becomes the exalted image, and this exaltation is a priori in the work of German philosopher Christoph Meiners: "He divided mankind into the white and the beautiful, and the black and the ugly."[24] Charles White, an English surgeon, aesthetically duplicates Meiners' ideology. First, he describes the brain mass of the European, suggesting intelligence above all others, and then he praises "that variety of features, and fullness of expression; those long, flowing, graceful ringlets; that majestic beard, those rosy cheeks and coral lips? ... In what other quarter of the globe shall we find the blush that overspreads the soft features of the beautiful women of Europe, that emblem of modesty, of delicate feelings, and of sense?"[25]

This sublime and beautiful tone rings disingenuous when reviewing the extensive rape of the Black woman during slavery. However, the quote's significance rests in the language that intersects literature and life. How then can we interpret the aesthetics and poetics of Wheatley and Frances Harper if such ideology and aesthetics represent the dominant culture's point of view? Because Negro poets, without any other examples, imitated the White literati, they subjectively created images of Africa that signaled self and race negation, obscurity, fright, and inferiority. Representatives of the Enlightenment influenced by romanticism held Negro poets in bondage. White people were architects of Whiteness because they were not Black:

enslaved, inferior, cowardly, and ugly. Early American Whites developed a language system with concepts and words such as "innocence," "individualism," and "freedom." They came to the New World to escape Old World restrictions to start over to fill in the "blank slate," yet they brutally held Africans.[26] When June Jordan calls Phillis Wheatley "Phillis Miracle," she thoughtfully considers the mountainous range of 18th century racism.[27] For Wheatley to have created at all is a miracle because White America never imagined a Negro who could write and certainly not one establishing a Negro literary tradition. The purpose for the Negro in America was quite clear. Vernon Loggins (1931) reminds us that

> The Negro, as all the world admits, was received into America for one reason only, and that was for labor. Snatched from Africa and thrust into the most afflicting of manual work, into the degradation of a slavery that was often accompanied by the harshest cruelty and that was at its best attended by crushing monotony, he was forced to forget his native traditions, or to remember them only in a subconscious way.[28]

Phillis Wheatley may have remembered themes from Africa in a subconscious way. Mostly, her poetry is rooted in Christianity, 18th century conventions and sentiments: She writes about nature, the imagination, memory, and death. Although born in Africa, a Eurocentric emphasis informs her axiology. Brought to America as a child, by twenty she writes lyrics reflecting a Christian missionary's sensibility.[29] Perhaps she unintentionally recalled her country, or she murdered such imagery in order to survive in the country of her purchase. Wheatley writes:

> Twas mercy brought me from my *Pagan land*,
> Taught my benighted soul to understand
> That there's a God, that there's a *Savior* too:
> Once I redemption neither sought nor knew,
> Some view our sable race with scornful eye,
> "Their colour is a diabolic die."
> Remember, *Christians, Negroes* black as *Cain*,
> May be refin'd, and join th' angelic train[30] [my emphasis].

Purchased at the age of seven or eight, Wheatley learned to read and write in English within a year after arriving in America. At thirteen, she knew English, Latin, and the Bible. Wheatley then mastered the heroic couplet popularized by Alexander Pope. She imitated Pope, a man who believed strongly in Negro inferiority.[31] Albertha Sistrunk (1982) documents the many similarities between Wheatley and Pope in subject matter, line structure, parallelism, diction, and tone. Of course, differences arise when one considers the content of the above poem. Alexander Pope never had to plead for his humanity. Wheatley's imagination and inspiration forged the art and ideology of enslavers.

Therefore, she presents a negative image of Africa in the above; the doubling within the poem implies African savagery and celebratory Christianity as a cure for the curse inherently Negro. Such words as "benighted," "black," and "Cain" unify the under-image of negative darkness because the biblical and mythological "Cain" represents evil. This particular image of Africa linguistically assaults the Negro, African and Black psyche. The assaulting diction goes as follows: (1) a "pagan land" assumes an African inability to understand abstract thought and knowledge; it thoroughly displays ignorance of African culture intertwined with spirituality and divinity; (2) "Twas mercy brought" asserts enslavement as just. This African imagery is both dysfunctional and disjointed. It shows that Wheatley's "unity of occasion," her prefiguring of Africa prior to writing the poem, was disturbing.

Yet, Wheatley does identify with Negroes, the transformed Africans in America. This identification is in the line: "Some view *our* race with scornful eye." Such identification indicates that although Wheatley rejects her motherland and although "black" or "dark" is negative, she, herself, is a part of this negative sequence. In her solidarity with other Negroes, she does attempt to eliminate a modicum of "chaos" by developing a way for her people to become quietly empowered. She accepts being black as "Cain" and she promotes Christianity as a transformer or medicinal for this curse and disease. Indirectly, she addresses the withholding of Christian training from Negroes and the idea that learning Christianity often involves gaining literacy. Her promoting a route to victory suggests that she attempts in this poem to "elevate peace among disparate voices," and that the poem's creation tries to build harmony among Blacks. She also capitalizes "Negro," asserting equality with the Whites, and in this capitalization she implies value in her Negro status. Another beneficial attribute and synonym for "Negro" is her selection of "sable," which tenderly describes her people.

However, as a whole, this unified image of Africa demonstrates a "(dis)unity of occasion." It prefigures "Africa" like European expansionists and it reflects the notion that Christianity can change the naturally afflicted Negroes, thus indicating that the Negroes must alter themselves to gain acceptance into Whiteness. Similarly, *Oroonoko* (1688), the African character by Aphra Behn, must resemble Whites more than Blacks for acceptance.[32] Another case in point is *Huckleberry Finn*, where Mark Twain showcases Jim's enormously unselfish allegiance to enslavers. This makes him agreeable to Whites. Different from and similar to the earlier and later novelists, Wheatley writes to bring her image of Africa closer to White America by way of religion. In her view, Christianity or becoming Christian eliminates racial deficiencies such as color. In this improbable dimension, Wheatley forecasts the tolerance of racism and the belief in Negro inferiority.

Wheatley probably understood well her role as spokeswoman.[33] As the first Negro to publish a volume of poetry, subsequent authors Jupiter Hammon and George Moses Horton mention her influence.[34] Yet, although Wheatley was not owned in the deep South, she still suffered the trauma of racism and bondage. For instance, in order to get her volume published, she and her owner Nathaniel left America for England. Publishers in England and America did not initially believe that an "African barbarian" could write such verse. On arrival back to the United States, Phillis had to face eighteen men who interrogated her to determine if she had the ability to write verse. Before signing the preface, they questioned her for an unknown length of time. Their signatures gave the book a required authenticity. Yet, even though vetted by distinguished White males, the skeptics remained. Thomas Jefferson, her most notable critic, denounced her talent, writing that

> Misery is often the parent of the most affecting touches in poetry. Among the blacks is misery enough, God knows, but no poetry. Love is the peculiar oestrum of the poet. Their love is ardent, but it kindles the senses only, not the imagination. Religion indeed, has produced a Phyllis Whately [sic]; but it could not produce a poet. The compositions published under her name are below the dignity of criticism.[35]

Jefferson, the brilliant statesman, divides Wheatley into animal separations. She cannot be human to him, lacking imagination and being unable to sensitively "love." His hypocrisy is evident but unworthy of any more attention. Such enslavers as Thomas Jefferson helped to create and proliferate the inherent racism that encompassed American society.[36] Nonetheless, because of the eighteen men who signed Wheatley's preface she almost reaches the human rung:

> We whose Names are under-written, do assure the World, that the Poems specified in the following Page[s] were (as we verily believe) written by PHILLIS a young Negro Girl, who was but a few Years since, brought an uncultivated Barbarian from Africa, and has ever since been, and now is, under the Disadvantage of serving as a Slave in a Family in this Town. She has been examined by some of the best Judges, and is thought qualified to write them.[37]

Henry Louis Gates (1987) explains the conditions in America during the 18th century as those that constantly assaulted the mind and body of the African.[38] Wheatley heard and read about herself as an "uncultivated Barbarian from Africa." She must have experienced dramatically the dual consciousness that W.E.B. Du Bois articulates two centuries later: "It is a peculiar sensation, this double-consciousness, this sense of always looking at one's self through the eyes of others.... One ever feels his two-ness,— An American, a Negro; two souls, two thoughts, two unreconciled strivings...."[39] Inherent in this Du Boisian quote, however, is a dislocated image of Africa because the racial classification "Negro" literally and figuratively means inferiority.

Yet, Wheatley secretly rejected inferiority when she first arrived in Boston. According to Shirley Graham Du Bois (1972) and John Shields (1988), Wheatley did remember and practice African customs and culture. She sun-worshipped. In the diary of one of Wheatley's owners, Mary Wheatley, she writes about young Phillis paying homage to the sun at a secret, predawn ceremony. But Mary catches her. This material was fictionalized by Shirley Graham Du Bois, and in the following scene Wheatley has just been caught practicing her religion:

> The child ... burst into tears and ran through the kitchen door into the house.... She had slipped out of the soggy, wet gown and sat huddled in the corner, her arms wrapped about her naked body. Mary did not see her on the slave auction block but Mrs. Wheatley would have recognized the same body position, the same shrinking away into herself.[40]

In Du Bois's imagination, Wheatley shrinks "away from herself." In this line of imaginative reasoning, it is possible that Wheatley slipped into the interior of her mind, submerging African customs in order to successfully negotiate her new environment. John Shields, a Wheatley scholar and editor of her *Collected Works*, confirms that West African people were sun worshippers. No one knows how often little Phillis escaped to the garden during predawn hours where she replayed her homeland, planting images of Africa in America. However, growing up "owned" in a Christian household would confuse and force underground direct images of Africa because in Boston, America, that religion and those customs were consistently negated. In Western ideology, Wheatley was a barbarian and a heathen, thus absent of God. The following poem suggests that as Wheatley matured, she believed all of the racially inspired deficiencies that relate to color. In "To The University of Cambridge, in New-England," she writes:

> While an intrinsic ardor prompts to write,
> The muses promise to assist my pen;
> 'Twas not long since I left my native shore
> The land of errors, and *Egyptian* gloom:
> Father of mercy, 'twas thy gracious hand
> Brought me in safety from those *dark* abodes[41] [my emphasis].

Wheatley in the age of individualism and the social transition to capitalism presents a creative expression that illustrates her (re)presentation of Africa that reflects the mindset of enslavers. In her imagination, Africa is a mistake. With the Greek muses guiding her "pen," she disintegrates or omits (from a lack of knowledge), the customs, beliefs, culture, and people of Africa. They are not even people: they are "errors." Indirectly, identifying a relationship to Egypt, she discounts it as source of awe or pride. Egypt is the biblically rendered public enemy. "Dark" in this traditional sense reveals dreariness and obscurity. It is an unnamed expanse, not approved by the Europeans. Paying homage to the Greeks, "muses" and "ardor," she discounts Africa because it emanates a personal gloom. Thus, in Wheatley's "unity of occasion" she negatively prefigures Africa. She even devalues its people, grateful for being enslaved in America. Africa and Egypt are remote, obscure, and gloomy. It is a gothic place one should escape.

This depressing tone anticipates the arrival of death obvious in the later poetry of Emily Dickinson. Draping melancholia over Africa, Wheatley implies that she is an error too. Her image of and association with Africa pay homage to the British and German philosophers David Hume and George W.F. Hegel who both claimed that Africa was dark, dumb, and savage.[42] Also, with the "muses" assisting her "pen," she equates writing with civilization (America) and non-writing with barbarity (Africa), not realizing that hieroglyphs or mdu ntr (sacred writings) began in Africa. Thousands of years before her muses, classical writing was happening in her "land of errors."[43] Consequently, in the above poem, Wheatley does not "elevate peace" or lessen racism, she extends it, and there is little unique about her versification. This poetry features prominently in the corpus of Western ideology.

However, in the next poem, "To The Right Honourable William, Earl of Dartmouth," Wheatley takes a different turn. Her image of Africa is not frightening or limiting. It is a topology of joy. Beginning in the fourth stanza, she presents Africa anew.

> ...
> I, young in life, by seeming cruel fate
> Was snatch'd from Afric's fancy'd happy seat:
> What pangs excruciating must molest,
> What sorrows labour in my parent's breast?
> Steel'd was that soul and by no misery mov'd
> That from a father seiz'd his babe belov'd:
> Such, such my case. And can I then but pray
> Others may never feel tyrannic sway?

Wheatley, known for being impersonal in her poems and totally mute on her private life,[44] offers sympathy for her African parents and for her brethren. The sway of tyrants metaphorically refers to America's enslavement of African people, thus demonstrating a racially inspired concern. Here, Wheatley attempts to "bring order out of chaos" by recalling a special racial and familial memory. Arguably, the focus of the entire poem is not Negro freedom. She indirectly compares the colonists' desire for freedom with a plea for her own people in America and in Africa. However, these intersections operate to illustrate Negro agency. In an age when Negro sub- or non-humanity was debated from pulpit to political podium, Wheatley asserts her parents' humanity. In remembering her father, through wishful thinking or actual flashback, she sympathizes with Africa.

"Fancy'd happy seat," a valuable image, designates a joyful birthplace and origination point. She prefigures Africa as mentally and physically healthy, eliminating some self-defeating thinking, finding pleasure in an African remembrance. Inner peace enlivens this poem. She shares a common joy and sorrow that Africans in bondage everywhere would understand and welcome. Overall, this stanza suggests that Wheatley imagined Africa in multiple combinations, moving from "gloom" to "errors" to "happy seat." Her imagination swings through a Western consumption of uncertainty, distance, and most privately her own human recollections. And despite Thomas Jefferson's declarations, this poet reflects "love," not just sensory but in the mind. This emotional fanning revisits the mental compartments of Equiano, Harper, and Jacobs discussed in chapter one. Olaudah Equiano, Frances Ellen Watkins Harper, and Harriet Jacobs had to psychologically balance concepts of bestiality, currency, and commodity. This marks the imaginative world of the enslaved African, and this line of reasoning infiltrated and often represented important institutions in America. Wheatley's "consciousness of synthesis" is demonstrated in her "unity of occasion." In the poem, she pushes her voice into print, manipulating the rhetoric of enslavers who desire emancipation while she pleads for her own. In this image of Africa, she prefigures the continent as a treasure, remembering her family, specifically her father.

Wheatley was not in a position to largely eliminate the chaos of racism in the modern or postmodern sense. However, she continued to write throughout her life and that act alone provides evidence for the African's humanity and ability. The above poem does clip the racism inherent in America because it projects Africans as people with emotions and social structures. Additionally, by comparing Africans with Europeans, she attempts to position her people in harmony or equality with Whites in England and America.

Because "Phillis Miracle" in general wrote poetry to prove her capability as a human being, her work is imitative in form, and for the most part in content. In my view, Wheatley does not share her in-the-midnight-hour voice that speaks from her own, true, sun-worshipping self.[45] She is a special Negro: literate, sometimes petted, owned and reared by Whites in an all White area. This miracle struggled to prove her elevation from barbarity. As such, her poetry overall is a versification in white-face. It is poetry aesthetically opposite to the later minstrel tradition whereby Whites donned black facial make-up to publicly perform. Wheatley powdered her poetics in white make-up in order to perform publicly during a brutal epoch in American history. Her expressions could not be otherwise. They begin lyrics, "decapitated" and "lynched,"[46] based on the results of racism, defeatism, imitation, and mockery. Thus, her poetry lacks knowledge of an African literary corpus or American-African spoken-word performance, particularly secular. It is dismembered from the continent, "strung up" with tropes of White America. Her poetry speaks more of 18th century conventions where she escapes into the Greek classics and the melancholia of elegy. While in the background, the Negro is purchased for labor that benefits the lives of others, not the slaves themselves. How else could a young, sensitive artist who correctly read her landscape get into print unless she projected the tropes of those who owned her and others like her? A "real" part of Phillis Miracle remains forever lost.

Frances Ellen Watkins Harper persists in the Christian poetics begun by Wheatley, but her motif of Africa is not as prominent. Harper's African motif rarely mentions the continent, presenting the Negro repeatedly and literally in white-face.

Frances Ellen Watkins Harper

Frances Ellen Watkins Harper (1825-1911) was an activist and poet, beginning this tradition picked up by Langston Hughes during the Harlem Renaissance and later Haki Madhubuti and others during the 1960s. Activist poets use art to construct and inspire social change. Unlike Wheatley, Harper was not enslaved. She was freeborn to nominal independence in America, but "orphaned at an early age, and raised and educated in a small school administered by an uncle."[47] In later years, as a dissatisfied teacher, she left the classroom for the abolitionist cause. At the age of twenty-nine, she published *Poems on Miscellaneous Subjects*, reprinted five times between 1854 and 1871. More than the actual writing, her poetry performance received much praise.[48]

In her work, critics found a lack in metrical unity and originality, but her books sold well. William Still, abolitionist and author of *The Underground Railroad*, claims her first book sold 50,000 copies. Combining art with activism, she may have been the first Black woman to receive a salary from the abolitionist movement.[49] Harper is a nationalist, exposed in the following excerpt where she says:

> Having been placed by a dominant race in circumstances over which we have had no control, we have been the butt of ridicule and the mark of oppression. Identified with a people over whom weary ages of degradation have passed, *whatever concerns them, as a race, concerns me*[50] [my emphasis].

Dedicating her life to lecturing, writing, and organizing for emancipation, when the physical shackles from slavery disappeared, she lectured and agitated for complete enfranchisement. Although an extraordinary race leader, ironically, selections from *Poems on Miscellaneous Subjects* (1895), *Idylls of the Bible* (1901), and *Atlanta Offering: Poems* (1885) replicate images imitative of Anglo-American aesthetics that obscure Negro humanity. With Christianity informing her aesthetic, she is similar to Wheatley, though she is fond of the four-line stanza: with a b a b scansion of near or exact rhyme. This causes Harper's work to read easily. In "Bible Defence [sic] of Slavery," the final stanza illustrates how she prefigures Africa.

> Oh! when ye pray for *heathen lands*,
> And plead for their *dark* shores,
> Remember Slavery's cruel hands
> Make *heathens at your doors!*[51] [my emphasis].

Personifying "Slavery," she like Wheatley argues for baptism and education for Africans on the continent and in America. Attacking the hypocrisy of missionaries teaching abroad but not missionaries at home, she reveals in diction how she prefigures Africa. She reduces the continent to the metonyms "heathen lands" and "dark shores." Simultaneously, the personification of slavery intrudes to eliminate some measure of chaotic racism, because Harper knows that literacy is a route into and out of Christian teaching. Normally, the missionaries built schools for the converts. Here Harper lays the foundation for later female activists. As Gayle Tate articulates in *Unknown Tongues* (2004), Harper uses her literary and labor will to insist upon and enact the education of her people. She views literacy as a foil to capitalism and a challenge to enslavement. However, there is no "elevation of peace" here. Her image of Africa predicts the adoption of both the religion and behavior of those who hold the "heathen" in bondage. In "The Dismissal of Tyng," she maintains this line of thinking:

> 'Tis right to plead for heathen lands,
> To send the bible to their shores,
> And then to make, for power and self,
> A race of heathens at our doors.[52]

The heart of the two poems exposes an argument earlier heard in David Walker's *Appeal* (1829). Activists like Walker and Harper manipulated and projected the ironic tension and source of hypocrisy among Christian devotees participating in the slave trade. Like Wheatley, Harper appealed to the inherent moral nature of Christian theology. Envisioning it the religion of cultivation, education, and enlightenment, she recognized that along with science, it sparked the American experiment. Therefore with missionary zeal, Harper molded Christian aesthetics into poetics. Additionally, she projected in literature imagery of God resembling American Whites. She probably had no knowledge of African spirituality and if she did, she dismissed it as inferior to Christianity. Still, the educational activist motif arises in this poem. She wants baptism and education for those enslaved. However, this multi-dimensional poem does not ascribe comforting or nurturing qualities to Africa, or portray it as equal to other continents. It is interracial poetry displaying harmony and inequality between Whites and Blacks. Impacted with Western celestial iconography, Harper's poetics clearly show the strong urge and desire for the Negro to be either near or all White.

Whiteness determined the standards of beauty established in America. The Negro woman normally strove to look like the Anglo woman. Dark, kinky-haired people were junctures of dysfunction and dislocation that assisted the turmoil and rupture in the personal aesthetics of Negro Americans. Negroes did not wish to be African. Harper, receiving signals from the White literati, chose American culture and language to depict her people. Her selection of the terms "pale" and "blanch" seems misplaced and Eurocentric when describing Negroes. Yet they overwhelm her poetry. "The Slave Mother" is a case in point. It goes, "She is a mother, *pale* with fear"[53] [my emphasis]. One might argue that Harper here refers to a mulatto, quadroon, or octoroon woman. That reasoning weakens, however, because Harper pens these descriptors, "pale" and "bright," religiously throughout her work. Such consistent usage foreshadows her tendency to imagine the enslaved Negro woman as White. The poem "Saved by Faith" illustrates this consistent choice of misplaced colors.

> Life to her no brightness brought,
> Pale and stricken was her brow,
> Till a bright and joyous thought
> Lit the darkness of her woe.[54]

"Brightness," "pale," and "bright" joyfully combine, while "darkness" describes "woe." This opposite imagery directly relates to the aesthetics of Meiners: The white is the beautiful, the black the ugly. To clarify a point, the idea that "darkness" equals trouble is also in how Africans comprehend the world, normally environmentally inspired. However, in traditional Western thinking, people are placed in this category. Early American White authors, as Toni Morrison argues, placed the "Africanist presence" in European derived anxiety, angst, and fear. Harper absorbs this gothic construction and murders the Africanist presence by omission. Therefore Harper, a woman of African ancestry, puts forward poetics far removed from herself and the Negroes' reality. Again in "Saved by Faith" only a certain class of Negro women have brows fairer than fair. In fact, to bring back the eloquence of Jefferson on race, he found displeasure in the "monotony" of color that hides the Negro's emotional state. Harper follows his lead and forwards the denial and monotony of color in "The Contrast."

> Before him rose a vision,
> A maid of beauty rare;
> Then a pale, heart-broken woman,
> The image of despair.[55]

The theme concerns the double standard between the sexes. A man may sully a woman's purity, and marry another, while the world reproaches the sullied woman. Yet, again, the adjectives suggest a woman, White. In fact, one might think a White author penned these ditties. The following lines from the same poem reaffirm this aesthetic: "He was leading to the altar / A fair and lovely bride." For Negro listeners and readers, the words assist and reinforce escape into Anglo aesthetics. Harper is not an elitist; she fights for the rights of those enslaved and at great and grave personal danger. She is not therefore picturing only Negro women like those in the novels of William Wells Brown. Although she is a freedom fighter, she cannot pull away from the aesthetics of the oppressor class. Although she speaks for all Negro people, she in her imagination thinks beauty and femininity only as White. She sisters with Sojourner Truth in this sense because Truth said publicly that White women are smarter (and therefore better) than Black women. With African or Negro absence in Harper's repeated and literal white-face poetry, she enlarges her identity crisis and tension. Houston Baker provocatively and incorrectly explains this attraction to White aesthetics as Black women somehow welcoming White male rape: the result a biracial offspring.[56] This is his interpretation of why 19th century Negro female authors glorify the aesthetics of biracial women. His male-centered patriarchal conclusion omits the textured horror and violence of the masculine brutality of rape. Harper because of the depths of racism deified the female of the dominant culture probably subconsciously, and this signals how entrenched White supremacy seeps. Because of the decapitation of the Black woman's worth and aesthetics, she escaped that shame and humiliation by idealizing and imitating the White female other. This other had full control over the Black woman similar to the patriarchal power of the White male. White women then and now have been projected as the most beautiful primarily because of the power of the White male. This power elevates his female counterpart, and what Baker does not mention is the glorification of this same ideal by Negro male authors. Enslaved people have acted similarly under White domination and Negro males have desired those closest to this image for marriage, celebration, and companionship.

During the 19th century, there were no cherished images of Black females, although the mammy and the breeder were appreciated. Harper was neither. She was a Black female, a freedom-fighter intellectual, a warrior woman in a country that had conquered her people and transformed the African into a Negro.

Therefore it seems logical that she imitate the images of power, and she does not restrict the use of such a visual as "pale" to Negro women. In the poem "Lines" she personifies a fair and lovely abstraction where we find the "Future Pale and trembling / Though her cheek was pale and anxious, / Yet, with look and brow sublime, / By the pale and trembling Future / Stood the Crisis of our time."[57] In an apocalyptic sense, this poem predicts the next century of Negro authors who extend the exaltation of the White ideal. The personification of time indicates the ideology, aesthetic dominance and hegemony of Whites over Blacks. This is Negro art in white-face. Phillis Wheatley begins this tradition during the antebellum and subsequently Harper multiplies it. Harper's repetitious, Eurocentric terminology, "bright," "light," "blush," "fair," enforces and approves the erasure of Negro people.

This pattern, therefore, fails to eliminate chaos, to lessen the degree of racism in society. In fact, it illustrates a result of racism — the victim desires the oppressor's appearance and identity. The victim imitates the oppressor. As such, little or no originality exists here.

In *Poems*, published in 1895, this technique persists. With the outlawing of enslavement, Harper's themes turn to temperance, sexism, faith, and familial relationships, specifically between mothers and children. She now writes more about ethics and morality. One knows that she writes about Negro people, but her terminology "brightly" shines a Western light. Good children, parents, relationships, and the Savior are all "fair" and "bright." Her poetry echoes complete assimilation: White features and Christianity.

Harper, a Christian enthusiast, adopted the biblical theme of Pharoah's idolatrous cruelty against the Children of Israel. In *Idylls of the Bible*, in blank verse, she retells the story of Moses. In her image of Africa, Moses is heroic and Pharoah is cruel, heartless, rich, vain, and murderous. She mentions Osirus and Isis (Asr and Ast, Ausar and Auset, Wasiri and Assata) in a balanced and controlled way, but the God of the Israelites is the favored deity. Under Christianity, enslaved Blacks drew analogies between themselves and the Children of Israel because the Bible speaks of Jewish enslavement in Egypt. Many enslaved Negroes knew biblical stories, whether literate or not. Consequently, the impact of the Bible caused Harper to see Africa as enemy:

> "I have decreed that every man child of that
> Hated race shall die. The oracles have said
> The pyramids shall wane before their shadow,
> And from them a star shall rise whose light shall
> Spread over earth a baleful glow; and this is why
> I root them from the land; their strength is weakness
> To my throne..."[58]
> The love of Moses for his race soon found
> A stern expression. Pharoah was building
> A pyramid; ambitious, cold and proud,
> ...
> He wished to hand his name and memory
> Down unto the distant ages, and instead
> Of laying that memory with the precious
> Fragrance of the kindest deeds and words, he
> Essayed to write it out in stone, as cold
> And hard, and heartless as himself...[59]

In the above poem, Israel represents pain and sorrow, and Egypt pomp and pride. In Christianity, God punishes Egypt (Africa) and curses the children of Noah's son Ham (an African). When Percy Bysshe Shelley wrote "Ozymandias" with lines about the Pharoah that read "wrinkled lip, and sneer of cold command"... "Look on my words, ye Mighty and despair!" the images enforce a Western trope of Egypt. For the African artist to develop the same portends something all together detrimental to the psychology of the artist. Egypt is, as Wheatley reveals, a synecdoche of Africa. To view it as enemy in light of the great memory lost — the dislocation from Africa — of those enslaved is to reject an African identification — a rejection of origins and of self. Critics of early Negro literature understandably seem so enthused that Negroes managed to write and to publish that they overlook the psychological displacement obvious in this American aesthetic. Dorothy Porter (1971) is such a critic. In the introduction to *Early Negro Writing*, she makes the following claims:

The remarkable thing is that these early black expressions were genuine, sometimes moving, and often pleasing specimens of narrative writing or poetry describing the condition, the aspirations, or the sufferings of black genius.... But it may be enough to realize that here we have the beginnings of the Afro-American's *artistic consciousness*—indeed, the first articulations of the *appeal of beauty and the moral sense*[60] [my emphasis].

From the above selections, the appeal of beauty and the moral sense relate more to the ethos and religion of another people, other than African. These images demonstrate that the racial divisions earlier defined—the white is the beautiful; the black is the ugly—made headway from generation to generation. In Wheatley and Harper's images, impersonating incorporates assimilation. The African is almost excoriated from the psychology of the Negro made in America. Therefore, this "unity of occasion and situation" displays an absentee Africa because Harper does not examine herself or her people for inspiration. Although her intention is noble, she parrots Anglo-American aesthetics, copying so completely that she fits squarely in the aesthetics of white-face. These decapitated lyrics are void of any even remotely African or inherently Negro affectation. Therefore, they fail to eliminate chaos on any level, lacking the paint and the promise of her people. This motif of absence signals profound internal dysfunction, so much so that Harper dismisses the obvious visual and hurt of African colors. Malcolm later called this paradox the chain of color, which restricted Harper until she abandoned it, like the soul leaving the body at death.

However, the reason why Harper writes poetry brings a measure of "peace among disparate voices." Harper projects her poetry as a vehicle to express activism and agitation for the rights of the Negro. Critic and scholar Maryemma Graham informs us that Harper was "known for her professional activism in the cause of human rights for black people, women, and the poor."[61] Thus, Harper is a pioneer in the tradition of protest and resistance literature, and in *Sketches of Southern Life*, she creates a narrator, Aunt Chloe, who does celebrate Black life prior to the Civil War and afterwards. Critics from Jean Sherman (1974) to Maryemma Graham (1988) applaud the Aunt Chloe persona as one of Harper's finest achievements. With this character, she captures the essence of Black vernacular, Ebonics, as Asante (1987) might say, a tendency which anticipates the poetry of Langston Hughes. In the following, "Aunt Chloe" narrates her personal authenticity in America:

> I remember, well remember,
> That dark and dreadful day,
> When they whispered to me, "Chloe,
> Your children's sold away!"
> ...

> And I heard poor Jakey saying,
> "Oh, mammy, don't you cry!"
> And I felt my children kiss me
> And bid me, both, good-bye[62]

In this image of Africa, Aunt Chloe, in a genuine, homespun voice, paints a picture of Negro life. From a mother's perspective, Harper smoothly expresses an economic benefit to enslavers and to the enslaved a textured trauma. Harper exposes the psychology of loss and the resilience of Negro survival under "tyrannic sway." Here, she synthesizes the African experience in America through a unique woman's voice and this woman is neither "pale" nor "bright." Narrating an American history pertinent to the Negro, from Aunt Chloe's point of view, she displays the destruction of family love, a process to maintain chattel slavery. Materializing the agony of family break-up, she advocates and renders the sorrowful sensations of people in bondage. Multi-dimensional Aunt Chloe not only evokes Black humanity, but also critiques the political society that legalized the peculiar institution.

> Of course, I don't know very much
>   About these politics,
> But I think that some who run 'em,
>   Do mighty ugly tricks.
>
> I've seen 'em honey-fugle round,
>   And talk so awful sweet,
> That you'd think them full of kindness
>   As an egg is full of meat.[63]

"Aunt Chloe" is a precursor to the folk tradition of Paul Lawrence Dunbar (1872-1906). Additionally, this character anticipates Jesse B. "Simple," a Langston Hughes character. The speaker "Aunt Chloe" has "honey-fugel" originality and wonderful sarcasm. Honey-fugel is a play on parade and masquerade in the context of political posturing. The narrative poem's force and fun merge in its incredulity "as an egg is full of meat." By presenting an authentic sound and circumstance of the people themselves, this poem's "unity of occasion" prefigures Africa (represented by the Negro) as good. This is an intelligent, ironic, and witty female African image. Warning against trusting those in control, Aunt Chloe is a critical commentator. Through Aunt Chloe, Harper found inspiration and richness in one of her own, so there is a measure of "peace among disparate voices." The poem and persona build harmony and reciprocal jocularity between the poet and the public. Additionally, Aunt Chloe's freshness in thought and behavior identifies a cultural verbal practice among Negro people, the term "aunt." Culture in Africa recognizes non-biological family as family. Similarly, in

America during slavery, when the enslaved were sold away, they adopted new family.

Aunt Chloe, a mainstay and product of slavery in poetry, confronts and eliminates a "degree of chaos" because she critiques racism and economics. Yet, with all of her folksy rhythm and wisdom, questions of aesthetics return to the following omission or oversight: her creator never describes her. Harper, as many American-African women of her day, and this one, had trouble depicting a Black female image in English. In my opinion, she may have either disliked or hated the Negroes' aesthetics, visualizing the Negro through the eyes of the dominant culture — the W.E.B. Du Boisian dual consciousness. And the complicated confusion in this double-consciousness eradicates self-appreciation. Status in America influenced the aesthetics of the Negro because to be Negro in America equaled an ontology of ugliness. When one considers the many operations and the pasty white complexion of Michael Jackson, the contemporary rock star, Harper's misplaced colors seem to pale in the outcome.

On the other hand, some of Harper's didactic poems present a dignity in the image of Africa. Because of her concern for the humanity of her people, she does sometimes display a nationalism and respect for Africa and Africans on the continent. Consider the dignity of Harper's "The Dying Bondsman":

> ...
> He had been an Afric chieftain,
> Worn his manhood as a crown;
> But upon the field of battle
> Had been fiercely stricken down.
> "For the spirits of my fathers
> Would shrink back from me in pride,
> If I told them at our greeting
> I a slave had lived and died"[64]

Showing the pride of the African male, Harper illustrates his abhorrence of bondage. In this image, the chief does not wish to meet his ancestors in chains, a condition of enslavement that diminishes him before his people. This character could be the prototype for the "Guinea Man" in *Iola Leroy* (1893), the one with spunk to de backbone, discussed in chapter one. Harper in showing respect for African culture presents a connected and historical relationship as the persona recalls a continental memory. As such, this is not a decapitated poem because it displays clearly a desirable historical and cultural connection. Readers experience a "unity of occasion" because in this African picture, she eliminates a measure of chaotic racism, and she prefigures worth in Africa. When an African persona relates to his own circumstance and not that of his oppressor, this challenges the commodity aspect of being Negro. Harper also illustrates "peace among disparate voices," because she reminds us of the autonomous African who comes from a place with its own history, culture, and cosmology. Bringing this African experience to America, she figures it equally with Western religion. Still, however, a problem remains. It is unclear from reading her poetry if Harper herself can articulate a relationship to the chieftain. However, it is clear that she admires him.

In addition, we are clear about her race love and concern, her nationalism. In "The Martyr of Alabama," Harper writes in the tradition of postmodern revolutionary poets.

"The following news item appeared in the newspapers throughout the country, issue of December 27th, 1894:
  'Tim Thompson, a little negro boy, was asked to dance for the amusement of some white toughs. He refused, saying he was a church member. One of the men knocked him down with a club and then danced upon his prostrate form. He then shot the boy in the hip. The boy is dead; his murderer is still at large.'"[65]

> He lifted up his pleading eyes,
> And scanned each cruel face,
> Where cold and brutal cowardice
> Had left its evil trace.
>
> ...
>
> A dark-browed boy had drawn anear
> A band of savage men,
> Just as a hapless lamb might stray
> Into a tiger's den.
>
> ...
>
> Through every fane send forth a cry,
> Of sorrow and regret,
> Nor in an hour of careless ease
> Thy brother's wrongs forget.
>
> Veil not thine eyes, nor close thy lips,
> Nor speak with bated breath;
> This evil shall not always last,—
> The end of it is death...

We have a revolutionary ending, not unlike the subsequent poetry of Marcus M. Garvey (Martin 1983). Harper calls for war, just as Ralph Ellison fashions the grandfather character in *Invisible Man* to warn his grandchildren that in America "life is a war." Harper wants the death of this "dark-browed" boy avenged. Similarly, seventy-five years later, Haki

Madhubuti immortalized Fred Hampton and Mark Clark, two Panther officials murdered by the Chicago police. Wanting injustices addressed, when Harper writes, "Veil not thine eyes, nor close thy lips," she desires reader-response, a call into action.

In a different direction, she sharpens her poem with language reversal, employing a term normally associated with Africans, "savage," to depict the "white toughs." This language twist flags Harper's attempt to challenge the enemies of Blacks at their own game, using their own language. This confrontation therefore demonstrates Negro equality, igniting the resistance tradition in African American literature. It revisits Benjamin Jacobs in *Incidents in the Life of a Slave Girl*, who unchained himself and sent the chains to his master, and it brings back the enslaved men who told their masters to "put [them] in his pocket." They so much hated the master that they demanded to be sold.

In the above poem, however, the orthography of "negro," the "n" in lowercase, demonstrates the paradox. Harper views the self and her people through lenses of linguistic racism. The negative understanding of one's ontology relative to language clarifies why Harper would not necessarily interconnect her relationship to the Afric chief. The chief gets a capital "A" to signal his relationship to other groups of people. The "negro" gets a lowercase "n" because it means negative, other, currency, beast, commodity, and slave. Human may or may not be in the mix.

Yet, while juggling her personal humanity, she, despite the gender (and racial) restrictions of her epoch, amazingly lived on her own terms. With admirable race love and nationalism for a woman of her time and circumstance, she exhibits extraordinary courage. Although she may have fantasized the prototype of another's aesthetics, she never accepted the conception of the woman as meek, weak, or only a helpmate to man. For example, as she agitated for social justice, she often traveled alone. Her woman warrior persona and attitude reveals itself in the following letter written while she journeyed to a speaking engagement. She writes: "Last week I ... got in conversation with a former slave dealer, and we had rather an exciting time. I was traveling alone, but it is not worth while to show any signs of fear.... I am in Darlington, and spoke yesterday, but my congregation was so large, that I stood near the door of the church, so that I might be heard both inside and out.... In Darlington, about two years ago, a girl was hung for making a[n] ... indiscreet speech."[66]

Although Harper recognized danger, White racism, and cruelty, she carried her mission forward, transcending it, like she rose outside of her appearance. Even though a "girl was hung for making" an "indiscreet speech," Harper adds to the indiscretion, believing in liberty or death, like Harriet Tubman.

In general, the selected poetry of F.E.W. Harper demonstrates the complexities of being a Negro writer and activist in America during the 19th and early 20th centuries. Although her literary legacy provides themes and motifs adopted by later poets, her white-face aesthetics derives from and produces the Negro reflection. Harper absorbed the horror of this symbol.

Yet, in some poems, she has a motif of resistance, which suggests a dichotomous and synthesizing pattern in her poetry. This variation emphasizes the becoming of the Negro people burdened with centuries of enslavement, attempting to call themselves into being. Harper's motifs mark the confusion and conflict in 20th century literature, replete with evidences of repressed psychological trauma.

Harper died in the 20th century when the term Negro and the abandonment of Africa as reference point were commonplace, except for in the works of Marcus Garvey. Asante (1990) says that peace is "not the absence of struggle."[67] Harper struggled for the "elevation of peace" as she confronted the assaults against her race. In doing so, she fought to "eliminate the chaos of racism," even though her poetics demonstrates the unresolved internal identity deficiencies of the Negro. The Harlem Renaissance, an important literary movement among Blacks, was subsequent to Harper's career. Yet, even during this prolific epoch of Black writing, the disturbing wounds of the Negro still rupture.

Claude McKay and Countee Cullen

Claude McKay and Countee Cullen developed motifs of Africa during the Harlem Renaissance, extending the disfigurement of the Negro. The Harlem Renaissance, beginning in the 1920s, marks the first time in America that Negro artists collectively created art that emerged out of their specific cultural experience. Some of this work indeed begins a homeward look back to Africa. During the Renaissance, W.E.B. Du Bois and Jessie Redmon Fauset edited the *Crisis*; Marcus M. Garvey headed the Universal Negro Improvement Association. White patrons and publishing houses welcomed and encouraged Negro writing. Zora Neale Hurston, Jean Toomer, and Langston Hughes become famous because of this epoch as well as the painters Aaron Douglass, Palmer Hayden, and Henry O. Tanner.

The Harlem Renaissance marks the first great migration of Negroes from the South to the North. The Northern industrials needed laborers and because of World War I and the European immigrants' inability to travel, they hired Negroes. From the North to the South, the word traveled until droves of men and women came north — mostly to escape the oppression and the overused land of the South. From the South and the West Indies they converged in Harlem, New York City.⁶⁸ Scholar and patron Alain Locke thoughtfully adds more about this migration, writing that

> The tide of Negro migration, northward and city-ward, is not to be fully explained as a blind flood started by the demands of war industry coupled with the shutting off of foreign migration, or by the pressure of poor crops.... The wash and the rush of this human tide on the beach line of the northern city centers is to be explained primarily in terms of a new vision of opportunity, of social and economic freedom, of a spirit to seize ... a chance for the improvement of conditions.... In the very process of being transplanted, the Negro is being transformed.⁶⁹

The transplanting of the Negro from the South to the North enlivened the new physical and mental geography with promise and possibility. Alain Locke (1925) in *The New Negro* tells us that the "aunties," "uncles" and "mammies" were gone. The new Negro looked inward for cultural validation and substance. The southern Negro now had the opportunity to become a northern sophisticate. With intellectuals such as Du Bois and Garvey stimulating ideas about equality, the transplanted Negro indeed transformed. However, the new Negro, still wearing a racial designator of defeat, continued to write a myriad of dislocated African images. In that transplanting and transformation, the Negro writers wrote new questions about themselves and their relationship to Africa. Africa became a symbol of interest to many of the Harlem artists in fresh ways. Largely, Garvey's "Back to Africa Movement" placed the image of Africa on the minds of Harlem artists. Still, some of this period's poetry reveals contiguous Negro distortions. Segregation nurtured this never changing line of thought. The shame of segregation added enormously to the Negroes' existing inferiority complex. Plus, the issue of the name "Negro" still emitted the connotations of commodity and beast. This troubling term even caused Du Bois difficulty when attempting to articulate its dimensions. Du Bois writes:

> In North America a Negro may be seven-eights white, since the term refers to any person of Negro descent. In sharp contrast ... "Negro" in Africa has been more and more restricted until some scientists, late in the last century, declared that the great masses of the black and brown people of Africa were not Negroes at all.⁷⁰

Scholar, historian, critic, sociologist, and activist W.E.B. Du Bois cannot clarify the meaning of "Negro." In *The Negro*, he uses "Egyptian," "Negro," and African synonymously. Further, he puts together combinations that do more to obscure than to elucidate. For example, how do you explain this blending: "Negro Africa" (27)? Molefi Asante (1990) offers more reasons for the problems with the term "Negro."

There is no ethnic group in Africa that calls itself negro or its language negro. The term is ... a creation of the European mind to refer to an African group or people who correspond to a certain negative image of culture.... The European writers often translated the ancient texts to the light of their political realities. No ancient African text mentions the word "negro." It simply does not exist.[71]

The term "Negro" then is outside of Africa, and Africa is the controlling image of one of Countee Cullen's masterpieces, titled "Heritage." Much of Countee Cullen's poetry contains identity themes that rival the dark, hauntingly beautiful and psychologically dysfunctional characters in Jean Toomer's *Cane*. Cullen, a major poet during the Harlem Renaissance, sought intellectual growth only in America, not Africa. He explains his deliberate erasure of Africa this way. "As heretical as it may sound, there is the probability that Negro poets, dependent as they are on the English language, may have more to gain from the rich background of English and American poetry than from any nebulous atavistic yearnings toward an African inheritance."[72]

Countee Cullen (1903-1946) selects terminology that perfectly describes his comprehension of Africa and that of Claude McKay: He is after all a Negro filled with the baggage of bondage. In 1970, Madhubuti (then Don L. Lee) says of the "negro," "a negro ... [is] some weird imitation of an inhuman.... The production and manufacture of negroes in this country has been systematically planned to bring about the best results possible.... In essence, negroes have been mass-produced in this country for the last 400 years."[73] Haki Madhubuti's "best results possible" are poetics and aesthetics that copy the master American narrative that erases everyone non-White. In Countee Cullen's absorption of White American ideology and literature, his poetry reveals a desperate desire for the love of his birth country, and this formidable desperation tricks his talent and genius in terrible ways. It takes him on a life long journey yearning for equality that White America refused to give. Therefore, Countee Cullen produced a series of dislocated images that mirror his inner torment, his angst.

He spent his childhood with a maternal grandmother who died when he was eleven years old. Then the Reverend Frederick A. Cullen, a Harlem minister, adopted him. Cullen later received an M.A. from Harvard in 1926, and during his life wrote eight books of poetry between 1925 and 1947. He won numerous literary accolades and prizes from high school to college including a Guggenheim fellowship in 1928 (Baker 1974; Davis 1981; Early 1991). Cullen is one of the finest poets of the Harlem Renaissance, especially in his skill in developing sensory, lyrical language. However, his psychic dualism reveals a Negro struggling with the symbolism and terror of racial inferiority. He never found peace, not in religion, not in art, not in America, and not in Europe. When examining his masterpiece "Heritage" we sample his wrenching confusion encased in seductive lyrics, a deceptively lovely poem that begins in African-centered emotive inquiry:

> What is Africa to me:
> Copper sun or scarlet sea,
> Jungle star or jungle track,
> Strong bronzed men or regal black
> Women from whose loins I sprang
> When the birds of eden sang?[74]

This lyrical seduction portrays a vision of Africa metrically written in tetrameter with an aa bb cc rhyme scheme. The colors, the lush foliage, the hearty, healthy people, the edenic splendor all compose a wonder for the senses. Printed widely as epigraphs, this stanza heads many Black literature chapters. Initially, one would not realize that this long poem is fraught with tension because of the picturesque opening and Cullen establishing his (and his race's) relationship to the continent. "Women from whose loins I sprang." Yet the persona never satisfies the repeated inquiry, "What is Africa to me?" However, unlike Nathan Huggins, author of *Harlem Renaissance* (1981), who believes Cullen's rhetorical question is disingenuous,[75] I think his refrain is genuine. The poem moves forward to reveal that for him, Africa represents a spectral presence and he struggles to figure out his relationship to it.

> One three centuries removed
> from the scenes his fathers loved.
> Spicy grove, cinnamon tree,
> What is Africa to me?

A sweet melancholy starts here with the centuries old removal and the African, masculine love of country. In "Spicy grove, cinnamon tree" he provides the reader with sight, taste, and fragrance. The narrator yearns for Africa the beautiful. He hints at the continent's gifts and great age, the place where life begins. Throughout the poem, his vision attempts to reconcile *what* and *how* he feels about this personal but distant geography. In the initial stanzas, the colors, memories, and people unify in a gorgeous bounty. This Africa in the mind initially prefigures a beauty based on truthful, "strong bronzed men" and admirable colors, "regal black." However, his slope into another direction urges the reader to rethink the original (re)presentation. This deviation occurs when Cullen shifts geography from the continent to the scholar's American life, referring to Africa not as metonym but as metaphor, Africa "a book one thumbs / Listlessly, till slumber comes." This slope foreshadows a deeper picture of the continent that Cullen prepares for engagement. For example, if his African topology comes from a "book" by a Eurocentric author, fear, shame, pity, and disgust portends a seriously flawed revision of his former "dream" of the "spicy grove and cinnamon tree."

Further on, in another direction, his sensory language suggests something more robust. Cullen, the son of a minister, connects sexually with Africa. A sense of sexual repression stimulates him to create an African image, which is a release of sexual tension. His language connotes a "wild" orgiastic freedom enfolded in traditional African customs. He writes: "Dripping mingled rain and sweat, / Tread the *savage* measure of / Jungle boys and girls in love" (my emphasis). "Savage" signals Europe or White American linguistics about Africa, along with the notion of rampant and wanton group sex, "dripping mingled rain and sweat." It seems that his unity of occasion, therefore, contains a prefiguring of Africa as a place to transplant sexual tensions and repressions. From its lush landscape and naked bodies, birth, young love, and copulation, all factor in his acceptance of Africa. His personal sexuality and sensuality projects onto the space of Africa.

"Ever must I twist and squirm, / Writhing like a baited worm, / While its primal measures drip / Through my body, crying Strip!" Here, Africa stands for wanton freedom that attracts and seduces the narrator. Rhythm and movement, a kind of dance, is devoid of custom or divinity, compounded with the Western notion of orgy. The terms "twist" and "squirm" intersect America in relationship to clothing and "strip." One strips in America; in Africa these "primal measures" may already lack clothing.

The words "primal" and "savage" are former anthropological terms for African people. They are not indigenous descriptors. In fact, Cullen's African inner picture resembles those of missionary zealots. The near naked bodies of Africans disturbed the missionaries carrying the word of God. Sex and Christianity are poles of sexual tension, particularly same-sex persuasions. Not surprisingly after his "crying Strip," the next stanza presents a gorge of guilt.

> I belong to Jesus Christ,
> Preacher of humility,
> Heathen gods are naught to me.

The projected sexual guilt encourages the narrator to elevate, advance, rely, and fall back on his Christian religion. His sexual connotations for and association with Africa cause revelation and confusion. He has gone too far into an ambiguous absurdity and he needs to make meaning of his revelation and confusion. To do that, he leaps into faith, a Christian existentialist. In knowing God he momentarily shakes off guilt, anxiety, and isolation. In fact, his leap of faith propels him into the dogmatic secularism of Christianity whereby he now believes that he is better than the Africans because of his religion. This is evident in the line: "Heathen gods are naught to me." This quells the previous sexual urges.

The sign "Heathen" recalls F.E.W. Harper's poetry, and its missionary abolitionism. His parallel placement of "Jesus Christ" and "Heathen gods" rings disingenuous, however, when one considers the preceding stanzas. The narrator retreats from incomprehension or meaninglessness to the arms of his adopted father's religion. Ideas of sex, nakedness, rising tension both holy and sexual conjoin and the poet reveals a transformation of God. Through this transformation he seeks transcendence. What he requests however seems impossible or is it possible. The poet follows with the idea to make the image of his God, Jesus the Christ, "dark."

>All day long and all night through,
>One thing only must I do:
>Quench my pride and cool my blood,
>Lest I perish in the flood
>...
>Not yet has my heart or head
>In the least way realized
>They and I are civilized.

The poet, like the Negro, straddles two worlds, and both are alarming. "Dark despairing features" and "dark rebellious hair" are earlier linguistic references to his shame about Africa. Countee Cullen suffers as he searches for meaning in life, a quest to "cool [his] blood." He attributes sexual behavior in his vision of Africa (and of himself) as uncivilized, and he doesn't wish to sin: "Less I perish in the flood." In this poem, his intellect "head" and his emotions "heart" both fail him. In this vision, Africa remains in nebulous, conflicting, and complicated territory. Cullen is incapable of transcending his present dilemma. What does Africa mean to him? It is an "atavistic" place in the imagination that sorrowfully cannot save him from American angst. What was Cullen facing in the real world of the Harlem Renaissance? What occurred in society that would call a man to question his racial origins, his emotions, and his God?

In Countee Cullen's society, Black males were lynched and the men (and women) who lynched were never punished. This American sport killed Black men (and some women) and it was designed in part to humiliate and cause fear in other Blacks, not lynched. In addition to this cruelty occurring regularly across the country, every day Countee Cullen faced segregation. Perhaps this reality of American life caused him to locate a release from torment in an imagined Africa, failing that he had nowhere to run or to hide. Therefore, Cullen, homeless on earth, could not transcend segregation based on biology, and possibly his (hidden) homosexuality complicated further his personal situation.

Cullen's chaos then derives from his reach for Western aesthetics and beliefs to determine the nature of his ontology. Little order comes out of the chaos here, and certainly no peace, a mental image of Africa dense with disorder. This is especially revealing in his closing lines when he decides that emotionally and intellectually neither he nor his African counterpart is "civilized." He dangles between two self-negating and self- (race-) defeating worlds. This is a tragic example of a sensitive artist's response to assaulting American language and laws that deteriorate his equality and humanity. His stifled ability to find value in himself and his race spurred his desire to resemble White America in order to create art. He exalted the White, that he was not, and this decision slowly poisoned his soul.

This metaphysical death is vividly portrayed in *Copper Sun* (1927) where he collaborates with his brother Charles. Charles Cullen sketched black and white drawings that augment some of the poetry. In the sketch that follows "The Litany of the Dark People," Charles Cullen sketches God as White. The psychologist Na'im Akbar explains this stark and obvious disconnection from the source of origin:

> The most obvious problem that comes from the experience of seeing God in an image of somebody other than yourself, is that it creates an idea that that image, that person, is superior and you are inferior. Once you have a concept that begins to make you believe that you are not as good as other people ... your actions follow your mind.[76]

In Cullen's mind, God and the oppressor are White. Since he is not a part of this portrait, then he must be in the opposite camp, just as white is the opposite of black. Hence, the opposite of God is Satan. Cullen not wanting to be in that sinful element carved another route: vulgar falsification. The artwork in *Copper Sun* exhibits a profound acceptance of the art of another race. Artificially, Cullen aids the arrogant superiority of White people by spreading their "unity of occasion" where the prefiguring of Africa is either vilified or absent. The very structure of the book itself sketches of White images for a Negro's poetry capitalizes the effects of racism. Cullen made the deliberate decision not to reach for any "atavistic yearning towards Africa," and to rely, for inspiration, on his American heritage. His American heritage pushed him up the hill with Sisyphus. His poetry, generally speaking, then is both lynched and decapitated (from an African or Negro source), a motif in "Timid Lover."

> I who employ a poet's tongue,
> Would tell you how
> You are a golden damson hung
> Upon a silver bough.[77]

This work is decapitated because it does not relate even remotely to the poet's own history and culture. The work is also lynched because it is "strung up with the tropes and figures of the dominating culture." This art in white-face forwards the poetics initiated by Harper. There is an important difference though. Harper was a deliberate political poet and Black Nationalist. Cullen is neither. "Song of the Rejected Lover" repeats his reliance on and preference for tales and legends of Western culture. He writes about Queen Guinevere and Lancelot and Camelot.[78]

Cullen assumes the legends and myths of England and America. Detailing the legend of "Camelot," Cullen reflects an American topology, which White people would applaud and promote. His complete dependence on an English literary tradition displays his belief that his own had nothing to offer. Such a conclusion extends the powerful double consciousness that Du Bois observed. Earlier when Harper crafted her imagery, her activism and the Aunt Chloe persona assured some measure of value in her people. This is not the case with Cullen. Du Bois writes:

> This history of the American Negro is the history of ... strife, — this longing to attain self-conscious manhood, to merge his double self into a better and truer self.[79]

Notice also that Du Bois discusses the merge of the "Negro" self with the "American" self. Such a merger will not satisfy the necessity to reach for one's African heritage. This conflation complements two divisions of assimilation, the Negro into the American. An American in the Du Boisian sense is a White person, and a Negro in this same reasoning is one who wants to be a White person. I recognize the trail blazing scholarship that Du Bois has conducted on behalf of the Negro. Such seminal works as *Black Reconstruction*, *Souls of Black Folk*, and *The Philadelphia Negro* record and analyze uniquely, and through a race-centered filter, Black American culture and history in the 19th and early 20th century. My pinpointing Du Bois in the context of racial renaming is to show that some of our best thinkers adhered to the tradition of linguistically separating the continental African from his American counterpart. Du Bois may have meant for his use of Negro to be a synonym for African or African American or Black, and the problem is in the uncertainty. The Negro as synonym for slave carries associations of commodity, currency, and bestiality. It also, once slavery physically ended, isolated the former slave from his and her African roots. Thus, during the early career of the great sage W.E.B. Du Bois, he was naturally most concerned about and identified with the Negroes in American society. This is the land of his birth. Additionally, most educated Negroes such as Cullen and Du Bois in school exclusively studied White intellectuals. This was the nature of the Western curriculum. How Cullen fashioned one of his books shows his excessive American consumption. In the above quote, therefore, Cullen's sense of a "better" or "truer self" would be a (re)creation of a combined White and Negro body, unequal creolization or hybridity.

Further, in *Copper Sun*, Cullen upholds his heroes, John Keats and Percy Bysshe Shelley, the romantic poets who, as scholar and critic Arthur Davis says, were never called "Nigger."[80] Issues of race so distorted the metaphysical and physical world of Countee Cullen that he stopped writing about race at all and contemplates suicide in "The Shroud of Color."

> "Lord, being, *dark*" I said, "I cannot bear
> The further touch of earth, the scented air
>   Lord being *dark* forewilled to that *despair*
>   My color shrouds me in, I am as *dirt*
>   Beneath my brother's heel; there is a hurt
>   ...
>   I strangle in this yoke drawn tighter than
>   The worth of bearing it, just to be a man[81] [my emphasis].

Cullen creates an unbearable burden of color, a "yoke" not "worth" bearing, defining his relationship to America, to Africa, and to himself. Earlier in the poem, Cullen reduces the self and recalls the "dirt" element factored into the Negro and the "begrim'd black" of Othello. At least Othello was a noble, military leader with status, and respected by the Whites (before Desdemona). In the above image, Cullen's persona is beneath the heels of his White brothers. In fact, his application of "dark" is more insidious than Phillis Wheatley's presentation. Wheatley's poetic "dark" certainly meant evil, but his rings with death. Arthur Davis believes that Cullen probably stopped writing about race because it bored him. I disagree. I believe that the pressure of race in Cullen's imagination and in American life slowly strangled his soul, forcing him to consider death at an early age.

The sheer pain of humiliation cannot be overlooked in the above poem. White America has tormented Blacks in ways that still remain unwritten because language cannot accommodate some tragic moments. Wordlessly, language does not speak a complete reality.

Ironically, one does not experience his conflicts about race when examining his book titles and selected poetry themes. His titles include *Color*,

Copper Sun, The Ballad of the Brown Girl, and *The Black Christ*. And consider this next poem:

> Once riding in old Baltimore,
> Heart-filled, head-filled with glee,
> I saw a Baltimorean
> Keep looking straight at me.
> Now I was eight and very small,
> And he was no whit bigger,
> And so I smiled, but he poked out
> His tongue, and called me, "Nigger."
> I saw the whole of Baltimore
> From May until December;
> Of all the things that happened there
> That's all that I remember.[82]

Cullen captures the enormous anguish and insult of being a "nigger" in this image of Africa. In his "unity of occasion" here, he prefigures himself as colorless because he does not expect the possibility of insult. The persona is innocence compounded by youth. Yet, the non-expectation of trouble or tension between the "Baltimorean" and the "other" demonstrates another form of racial escape. The other does not want to be a nigger/Negro; it is too painful, too confining, too degrading. Wearing that badge or "shroud" of color is all that he remembers. Therefore, in this above image of Africa, the other imagines America as good, before cruelly being reminded of his quasi-slave status in the racial hierarchy of this country. The closing line finalizes defeat. What a pity it is to be a Negro: powerless, inferior, lost, and confused, a thing to be insulted and kicked. This poem presents the compacted pain of racial insults, but I am unsure if it eliminates any of the chaos of race or racism. Cullen announces the pain of racism but offers no solutions. Because racism is clearly an American custom, nothing unique rests in the heart of the poem, although the imagery is both powerful and poignant. In "Song of Praise," Cullen opens still another side of himself:

> ...
> My love is dark as yours is fair,
> Yet lovelier I hold her
> Than listless maids with pallid hair,
> And blood that's thin and colder.[83]

Cullen equally competes with a White counterpart in the above. Although the language reflects formal English and imagery, Cullen signifies in the African American sense. In fact, he plays the dozens. Here is a moment when Cullen's image of Africa feels good to him, finding beauty in darkness. Signifying on the "love" of segregationists, he gives a "unity of occasion and situation" that suggests equality not generally found in his imagery of Africa. Prefiguring the dark woman's beauty, he elevates her above the "fair" woman. This image of Africa speaks a confident cockiness unaccustomed in his corpus of poetry.

As such, he does eliminate a small measure of chaos or racism because he celebrates the women of his race. Because this is a point of departure from his normal themes, however, I cannot say that it synthesizes the African American experience, causing a kind of harmonic trend. It does show a conflation within Cullen's image of Africa and in this poem, the Black is not the loser. Yet, even in his unflattering descriptors of the "fair" woman, he *is* able to describe her. His own love interest is not described; therefore descriptions of Negroes as in Harper's poetry stay buried. The overwhelming power of Western living kills off easy word-paintings for people of color. In America when one thinks of beauty, one normally thinks, White. Therefore, most often Cullen's poetry celebrates and promotes Western aesthetics just as he does so indirectly in the poem above. In Cullen's literary imagination, he wants to integrate to the point of non-distinction. Therefore, Cullen's poetry does not in general eliminate the chaos of racism — it reflects it. In fact, it provides evidence for the ocean deep damage racism has caused. In the imagination of the Negro artist, the bones of slavery bury (and rattle) the memory of African culture and humanity. Additionally, in the imagination of this Negro artist, he sees himself an ugly, tormented beast.

In total, Cullen serves up the beauty of White aesthetics as he strives to become one of its greatest recipients. His poetry furthers the sway of supremacy because in a contiguous reality it idealizes and idolizes Whiteness.

Claude McKay also developed images of Africa that bespeak a poet searching for a fusion of split alliances. However, his combine Jamaica, Britain, America, and Africa.

Claude McKay

Claude McKay (1889–1948) was already an accomplished poet with *Songs of Jamaica* and *Constab Ballads* when he arrived in America in 1912. Both poetry books depicted the joy and sorrow of the Black peasantry. His best known American volume, *Harlem Shadows*, was published in 1922. Although he spent a great deal of time abroad during the critical years of the Harlem Renaissance (1922–1934), McKay is a major force in that literary movement. Scholar and critic Arthur Davis sums up his influence this way: "His militant sonnets inaugurated a new era in black protest writing;

his poetry presented for the first time several themes which were to be used later by New Negro poets ... (33)."[84]

Davis is correct and along with his "militant sonnets" McKay renders a "nebulous" portrait of African imagery that bespeaks what Tyrone Tillery (1992) characterizes as McKay's forever-changing ethos. McKay traveled from communist sympathies, to anti-communist declarations, to Catholicism. Along the way, he publicly vituperated Marcus Garvey, regarding class as more significant than race, and he later blamed Negroes, themselves, for segregation and inequality in America.[85] McKay loathed the Negro literati so intently that he sought the companionship of White intellectuals. Shortly before his death, he refused to allow an African American to preface a new edition of *Harlem Shadows*, writing that: "'I don't want any American Negro hand to soil my work.... There isn't one who is fit.' McKay preferred to have his poems introduced by Dr. John Dewey, a white Englishman."[86] Like Countee Cullen, McKay suffered from high blood pressure (hypertension) and this abnormality, sharpened by and based on stress, factored into each poet's death.

McKay shaped the sonnet to give several impressionistic motifs of Africa revealing a poet's search for ancestral understanding. His image of Africa portrays a "dimness" that strongly suggests the deceitful power of the great omission of African history. McKay's imagery displays his Western idea of Africa and in this shadowy knowledge that appears as a "dimness," an emerging spark unsettles him. Thus, his "unity of occasion" prefigures Africa with Cullen's term, "nebulous." The selected images for this explication reveal a lynched and decapitated combination. In the following, the anxiety of this influence, this dislocation from Africa, is especially apparent. With Percy Bysshe Shelley as his model, McKay writes:

> ...
> When all the world was young in pregnant night
> *Thy slaves* toiled at thy monumental best.
> Thou ancient treasure-land, thou modern prize
> ...
> Cradle of Power! Yet all things were in vain!
> Honor and Glory, Arrogance and Fame!
> They went. The *darkness swallowed* thee again...[87] [my emphasis].

The "pregnant night" bespeaks the darkness earlier rendered by Wheatley. The history of Egypt seems unknown, mysterious, in "darkness." It is the enemy just as depicted in the Harper poem about the Israelites. With Christianity informing McKay's literary imagination, he supped from his literary foremothers Harper and Wheatley. His White forefathers help as well. "Africa" is very similar in imagery and theme to Shelley's earlier poem

"Ozymandias." Both address the vainglorious power of ancient Egypt and its drop from power, and both poems omit what Chancellor Williams (1976) calls the destruction of African civilizations. The poet's unawareness of Egypt bespeaks the limitations of the traditional Western education. The first line of the poem signals that the history of Egypt is unavailable at least to him and what follows therefore slips into obscurity. With McKay's education not very different from his predecessors, his image of Africa certainly fits a "land of errors." Implicit in this conception is his distance from this place, in geography and in the imagination. This also connects to Harper's blindness about her relationship to the African chieftain. She saw him apart from her. For the Negro, Egypt represents another group that enslaves. Chancellor Williams provides historical information that these early writers may not have known. Europeans and Asians, through women, destabilized the "land of the Blacks." Williams writes:

> [A] ruthless sexual traffic in Black women ... gave rise to a new breed of Afro-Asians. These were classed as Caucasians or Asians. They themselves bitterly objected to being identified with their mothers — African. When these later became known as Egyptians in Egypt, Moors in Morocco and Mauritanians or Carthaginians in Carthage (Tunis) great care was taken to distinguish them from Africans in daily intercourse, in paintings and in documentary literature. This "New Breed," half-African, was to join with their Asian fathers and forefathers in the wars and enslaving raids against the blacks that went on century after century until all North Africa was eventually taken.[88]

Williams' conclusion explains the cultural hybridity that Walter Rodney discusses in *How Europe Underdeveloped Africa*, where he provides information on biracial Africans and the important separation from full-bloodied people on the continent. According to Rodney, identifying more with the non-African parent, normally the father, some biracial Africans readily assisted in the enslaving of darker Blacks. This creolization of cultures may bring clarity to why the Moors enslaved other Africans, a practice based on what a Kenyan scholar calls "shadism." The process of enslavement destabilized Africa along with historical invasions from outsiders. The losing of African history is a factor of conquest because once invaders invade, they normally rename. For example, Egypt is a Greek renaming of "Kemet." The invasions of Egypt have been repeated and aggressive for two thousand years to the present. The Hyksos, Assyrians, Persians, Greeks, Romans, Turks, British, and French invaded Kemet. Additionally, with the transposing of power, hybridity, and white-skinned privilege, some scholars have suggested that Egypt is not a section of Africa. Thus, when McKay writes his poetry describing his version of "Egypt," the topology is like smoke in the poet's imagination because outsiders have transformed the legacy of Kemet, land of the Blacks.

Historian Anthony Browder (1992) explains the devastation that the Greek invasion perpetrated, beginning with the Library of Alexandria. This library held over 700,000 papyrus scrolls translated from Mdu/Ntr (sacred symbols). Julius Caesar accidentally destroyed a wing of the library during his conquest, "but it was later rebuilt by his successor Mark Antony around 40 B.C.E. In 391 A.C.E the Christian emperor Theodosius altered the restoration when he decreed: 'all that was ancient was pagan and therefore sinful.'" Christian fanatics burned the library to the ground.[89]

> As the knowledge of this ancient library faded from the memories of later generations, so too, did the recollection of the Africans who founded the earliest civilization in the ancient land that is now called Egypt.[90]

McKay's Egyptian-African image fades into and because of a Western aggression that transformed into ideology, aesthetics, poetics, and perspective. Identifying no relationship to or memory of the continent in the above poem, the narrator derides its effect on the world. From Wheatley to McKay in poetry the projection of Egypt is one dimensional—the implacable, vicious presence of pharaoh. Browder's assertion of memory loss opens the terrain for the accumulation of information that displaces African people, and the Negro is a displaced African.

The (re)naming of the African to Negro cleared a route to chattel status. Similarly, the renaming of Kemet to Egypt, a Greek word, detached it, in some respects, from the African continent. When conquerors (re)name, they cause the ideology of the original people to disappear. When Europeans conquered Black civilizations, they altered and subtracted African patterns of thought, culture, and history. This decapitated merging resulted in a severe absence, which affects and explains why McKay cannot imagine the continent. In "Outcast," because he admittedly lacks knowledge of the "words" or "songs," he cannot retell or recall the continent.[91] About this mental disappearance, he writes that:

> ... the great western world holds me in fee,
> And I may never hope for full release
> While to its *alien* gods I bend my knee.
> *Something in me is lost, forever lost,*
> Some *vital* thing has gone out of my heart,
> And I must walk the way of life a ghost
> Among the sons of earth, a thing apart [my emphasis].

Bending his knees to alien gods, he is split like Cullen in "Heritage," struggling with a discomforting uncertainty that religion does not satisfy.

This is the song of a broken man. In fact, he is not even human, his body held "in fee." He is a commodity and "a ghost," a "thing apart" from other men. This complex and paradoxical trauma of slavery explains a dislocation from Africa, and the promotion of Eurocentric aesthetics. Severed from a regenerative force (African "ntu"; see Kariamu Welsh Asante's *The African Aethetic*, page 11, for her aesthetics theory) the persona suffers homelessness, and a heavy-weighted mental void. Something stole his soul and this theft blinds him as tragically as Oedipus cutting out his eyes. The poet taps around sightlessly for fragments of his own people's worldview, axiology, and culture. As such, McKay's unity of occasion prefigures a remote, troubling picture of Africa, so it fails to eliminate any chaos of racism. He cannot synthesize his American experience to build any balance because his body (brute, commodity, currency) holds his soul in bondage. This poem is a tragedy, paying homage to a respected Eurocentric genre. There is no victory in struggle here.

> For I was born, far from my native clime,
> Under the white man's menace, *out of time*[92] [my emphasis].

This artificial closure "out of time" represents the "dangling negro," a false image because history tells us when "the negro" emerged. The African's *time* does not begin around the birth date of Christ. That date is a temporal shift that assisted in the decimation of the African. It signifies that there is no significant chronology, no spatial perpetual forever external to the Western worldview. McKay therefore conjures an image that insinuates not so much being outside of rhythm, but outside of civilization. This "time" as a spatial realm is Western and those outside of that worldview are objectified objects for hire. In his suffering despair from lacking knowledge, he provides no evidence of exercising free will. He is disconnected, disjointed, and dysfunctional, a man (persona) without a past (darkness) or a future. To Africans, this is disembodied, valueless imagery: "those under the influence of the alien image feel that they have no claim on any resources. The consequence is a persisting dependency."[93]

From internalized dependency, McKay made art. This art with a controlling image of disembodiment serves to confuse and to obscure. We visit this again in "Enslaved" where McKay says, "My heart grows sick with hate, becomes as lead / For this my race that has no home on earth."[94] If his "race" "has no home on earth," where can Black people go? I offer three avenues: they can forever drift, die, or commit mass suicide. Bobby Wright explains this particular angst in a formula he calls mentacide: the societal destruction of the ontology of Black people.[95] Edward Blyden explains how religion and geography influence the Negro's reflection of mentacide:

Wherever the Negro is found in Christian land, his leading trait is not docility, instead it is servility. He is slow and unprogressive. Individuals here and there may be found of extraordinary intelligence, enterprise and energy, but, there is no Christian community of Negroes anywhere which is self-reliant and independent.[96]

Accordingly, McKay, suffering from machinations of mentacide, accepts his guilt, victimization, and oppression as God's will; therefore and unsurprisingly, he vacillates between hating and loving America. This obvious shuttle appears in the next poem, "America."

> Although she feeds me bread of bitterness,
> And sinks into my throat her tiger's tooth,
> Stealing my breath of life, I will confess
> I love this cultured hell that tests my youth![97]

This upbeat confession gives the speaker a questionable confidence as it simultaneously exposes multiplicity in his relationship with America. Consider the oxymoron "cultured hell." A tiger's tooth, an African metonym, confuses or fuses places of origin. Personifying America to steal his "breath of life" positions it as killer of a people, mentally (mentacide). In fact, much of McKay's imagery portends his people's death. Yet, the narrator adores America's sadism. "I love this cultured hell that tests my youth!" The vitality to fight ("tests my youth") breaks through his anxiety, but what is he fighting for?

> Because I am the white man's son — his own,
> Bearing his bastard birth-mark on my face,
> I will dispute his title to his throne,
> Forever fight him for my rightful place.
>
> Because I am my cruel father's child,
> My love of justice stirs me up to hate,
> ...
> When falls the hour I shall not hesitate
> Into my father's heart to plunge the knife
> To gain the utmost freedom that is life.[98]

In "Mulatto," the narrator imagines killing off his father as a method to gain "freedom." This methodology is similar to the ideas of Harold Bloom where the past is fraught with tensions that burden contemporary authors along with Freud's Oedipal complex. The word "Negro" could replace the title "Mulatto" without removing any of the passion and meaning that McKay desired. "Mulatto" is a cry of revenge. The negative image of Africa is jealous of his White father, wanting the White male's privileges. Having a love/hate relationship with his father (as he does with America) the persona credits him with his "love of justice" that insists on killing. In other words, as a biracial child, his unleashed passion "stirs" his want to kill. Or his White half stimulates his instinct to kill, to experience "freedom." This prefiguring of Africa is hostile and erratic, similar to Bigger Thomas's emotions in *Native Son,* where killing provides a mental construct of "freedom." Moreover, the suggestion that his White half causes his ability to assassinate implies that the Negro half lacks courage. During this time period, the Negro was considered the lady of the races.

In sum, the selected poetry of Claude McKay does little to eliminate the chaos in Negro life. His poems reflect and yield to the potency of racism. From an Afrocentric perspective no peace is achieved. McKay's poetic choices are a systematically troubling reaction to racism, as they drench in the aesthetics of domination. Even if we examine his famous "If We Must Die," which is a passionate, fighting expression, it does not reference his own people. It is so race neutral that White speakers such as Winston Churchill recited the lyrics. This colorblindness is not a negative; however, when collectively reviewing images of Africa in Diaspora poets the presentation and issue of race releases a peculiarity that stems from enslavement. Franz Fanon in *Black Skin, White Masks* articulates McKay and Cullen's perplexity:

> every people in whose soul an inferiority complex has been created by the death and burial of its local cultural originality—finds itself face to face with the language of the civilizing nation; that is the culture of the mother country. The colonized is elevated above the jungle status in proportion to his adoption of the mother country's cultural standards. He becomes whiter as he renounces his blackness, his jungle.[99]

Part of McKay's renunciation resides in his inability to locate "his jungle," with his "dim" knowledge of Africa, his soul in bondage, and his bend to foreign gods. McKay seeks a "peace" in "darkness," one without language or sound. Darkness bothers McKay and for Countee Cullen his notion of "dark" brought him enormous "despair." Beginning with Phillis Wheatley, the idea of the "dark" compounded evil, mystery, remoteness, and foreboding, the gothic. From a dictionary of symbols, we find the following meaning of darkness:

> *Darkness* Equated with matter, with the *maternal* and germinant, but it pre-exists the differentiation of matter.... The darkness introduced into the world, after the advent of light, is *regressive*; hence, too, the fact that it is traditionally associated with the principle of *evil* and with the base, unsublimated forces[100] [my emphasis].

The "Darkness" that equates with the mother symbol is not the absence of light that beguiles Cullen and McKay. That darkness existed before anything else, transforming after "light" enters the world. With the coming of light that particular darkness associates or shifts to evil. Cullen and McKay as Negroes are within that shift; therefore, with Negro equated with darkness, dark is a synonym for Negro.

> The image of the Negro always alludes to the baser part of man — to the *substrata* of the passions. This psychological fact, empirically proven by psychoanalysis, finds its parallel — or its origin — in *traditional* symbolic doctrine, according to which *coloured* people are the children of *darkness*[101] [my emphasis].

During slavery (and beyond) symbolic appellations for Negroes include "boy" for a grown man and "girl" for adult females, thus, "children." "Coloured people are the children of darkness." This is the stream of thought that crafted segregation into the fabric of American society. No people want to merge with evil, knowingly. This is a premise of irrational "White fear" that led to lynching and to police murders of the dark.

Yet, American Blacks have spent decades trying to prove that they are equal to Whites, misunderstanding the dense and deeply interior set of impulses that inform the collective White mind. Blacks have been tragically running up against the symbolic meaning of a severely imposed racial appellation, the (re)naming. This imposition caused within the Negro gross, vulgar, and dangerous subservience:

> One of the persisting difficulties facing African American people is the difficulty to think independently. We are constrained by the perception that thinking and ideas are the exclusive privilege of those who are similar to the image of divinity. Our scholars are limited to imitating the scholarship of independent Caucasian thinkers. We analyze our situation and the nature of the world in general, exclusively from the frame of reference of Euro-Americans.[102]

Bobby Wright argues that this complex dependency stems from racism and the denial of opportunity. Like Talmadge Anderson in "Black Psychology and Psychological Concepts,"[103] Wright compares Blacks with prisoners of war, both suffering from psychological attacks. This identical discussion goes on today about the scandalous use of torture on Iraqi soldiers and how this proliferation may result in like treatment accorded to American soldiers. Thousands of returnees from Vietnam still suffer trauma as many now return from Iraq smelling the bodies of the dead. Bobby Wright charges the United States with genocide because this country for centuries kept "a people from developing life-sustaining options."[104]

The selected work from the above poets spanning the antebellum through the Harlem Renaissance strongly indicates that the literary visions of American artists of African descent lacked "life-sustaining options." For the most part, this particular versification reflects a disunity of occasion whereby the image of Africa reflects disembodiment, obscurity, and inferiority, all an understandable reaction to "independent Caucasian thinkers." Thus, the elimination of chaotic racism remains minuscule. They could not establish a harmonic trend when they could not articulate fully how they interpreted a world, which so abhorred and abused the African. In this monolith of racism and the legality of murder, such artists exposed how the monolith spawned their talent and materiality for creation.

This study also illustrates that prior to the 1960s, when African American artists considered themselves "Negroes," selected images of Africa advanced to confuse issues of race. Functioning under nomenclatures that the dominant society imposed, these artists poetically rendered a defamation and damnation of a people. These specific pictures of Africa demonstrate why Haki Madhubuti, influenced by Malcolm X, subsequently created poetry to overturn the hegemonic dominance of Anglo-American aesthetics in art.

Because of the 1960s Black aesthetic, American Africans progressed in physical aesthetics and linguistic poetics. This mode of progress illuminates our current decade. Examine the style and coiffures of contemporary Blacks. Many dress in African inspired clothing and others wear hairstyles derived from the continent. When Negro artists re-identified, re(re)named the race, and wrote war poetry, they inspired Blacks in general to adopt an African-centered perspective. Elijah Muhammad, Malcolm X and Haki Madhubuti in large part began this linguistic progression when they insisted that Negroes redefine the language and choose new racial appellations. However, in poetry prior to the 1960s, two authors refined the images of Africa in versification. Beginning this process, the versification of Langston Hughes and Marcus Garvey is precursor to the 1960s "malcolmian poetry."

FOUR

Early Influences of a Revolutionary Aesthetic in Black Poetry: Langston Hughes and Marcus Garvey

Langston Hughes (1902–1967) and Marcus Garvey (1887–1940) produced images of Africa that contrasted with the selected poetics of previous major Negro authors under discussion. Langston Hughes and Marcus Garvey are predecessors of the revolutionary poetics that reappeared during the Age of Malcolm X. Therefore, the art of Hughes and Garvey is a prototype to the creativity of Don L. Lee/Haki Madhubuti of the 1960s. Evaluating the poetry of Langston Hughes and Marcus Garvey from this perspective begins a "resistance to oppression [and] liberation from stereotypes."[1] This art eliminates the chaos of racism because it does not totally pantomime Western aesthetics and poetics. Viewing this art using the ascendancy to Ma'at, the ancient philosophical system of Kemet, will determine its unity of occasion and situation: which means how the author thought about Africa and himself as an African prior to writing the poem. The next filter is the elimination of chaos, which evaluates whether or not the art lessens or extends racism. The final tenet, the elevation of peace among disparate voices, judges the results of the poet's creation, teasing out if the poet synthesized the African experience to architect harmony. It also tests whether or not the poem is unique in thought, culture, or in general the American

African experience. To use an ancient African philosophical system for literary investigation is a methodology to piece together the fractured and fragmented history, philosophy, ethos, and culture of African people.

Langston Hughes and Marcus Garvey have images of Africa, all references to those of African descent, that are Black Nationalist, class conscious and sometimes race neutral. In the selected motifs of Langston Hughes, there is a class-conscious and race-neutral persona. Marcus Garvey on the other hand composes lines that idealize Black leadership in the now and in the future. This chapter examines such specific motifs, beginning with a brief comparison of the motivations behind each writer.

Marcus Garvey, a race leader during the Harlem Renaissance, was not primarily a writer. His poetry propagated his ideology, denouncing White injustices, celebrating local and national racial pride while espousing the significance of ethics. Dissimilarly, Langston Hughes made writing his career. In poetry, he wrote to present and condense issues of equality that concern Negro people, and he like no other poet of his period honored Black culture, designing memorable characterizations in verse. More privately, Hughes crafted revolutionary verses, which subdue race issues to highlight solidarity based on class.

Both Hughes and Garvey are Harlem Renaissance (1920-1935) writers appearing in New York when Negro art, novels, paintings, music, dance, visuals caused an artistic explosion. In addition to that vital and vivid urban aesthetic, White patrons and publishing houses embraced Alain Locke's "New Negro." Harlem became the Mecca, representing the epoch when people of African descent came from the South, the Caribbean, and Africa to converge in one place. This migration presented the artists a unique opportunity to observe Black cultural crossings as it allowed the Negro to function for the first time in an urban environment.[2]

According to Tony Martin, editor of *The Poetical Works of Marcus Garvey* (1983), Marcus Garvey wrote revolutionary poetry from 1927 to 1934. Faith Berry (1973), the Hughes scholar, says Hughes' revolutionary poetry starts in 1925 and ends in 1957.[3] Marcus Garvey, founder of the Universal Negro Improvement Association (UNIA), built an independent, activist organization that Hughes may have envied because UNIA members financially supported Garvey. For his livelihood, Hughes depended on White mainstream assistance, which as biographer Arnold Rampersad explains came with gross concessions. Because America before World War II (and afterwards) denied talented Negro artists access to media jobs, Hughes, like Zora Neale Hurston, relied on White philanthropy, which turned into censoring.[4]

Garvey never experienced such restrictions, publishing his own poetry and reading it before adoring audiences. According to historians Nathan Huggins and Arna Bontemps, Marcus Garvey had an impact on Claude McKay, Countee Cullen, and Langston Hughes. Yet, none ever credited Garvey with any possible importance. This isolation suggests the complicated dissonance in Negro psychology relative to the image of Africa. It also displays the dialectics that occurred during the Renaissance among the masses, the artists, and the new intellectuals. Hughes' dependency on Whites would prevent him from outwardly supporting the ostentatious Garvey, already engaging in debates with W.E.B. Du Bois. For one, Garvey in poetry and oratory loudly and proudly glorified the image of Africa, and such sloganeering as "Africa for the Africans" probably insulted White patrons accustomed to Negro subordination. Garvey put the issue and image of Africa in the imaginations of Harlem artists, inspiring better poetry than he produced, according to Tony Martin, editor of the *Poetical Works*. Garvey primarily a race leader and a man of the people who

> in a spellbinding West Indian cadence, gave voice to dreams that literally blew the minds of a large segment of his impoverished generation of black humanity in the New World. In all seriousness he "declared" the Republic of Africa and designated himself provisional president, while visitors from the West Indies, Africa, Europe, Central America, and Canada jammed Liberty Hall, as his large barnlike building in Harlem was called, and listened with a kind of awe.... *Nothing quite comparable had ever occurred before in the New World experience of black people*[5] [my emphasis].

Garvey's nationalism was unique and formidable, rejecting the ideology of interracial groups and the designs of the dominant society. For him, poetry was a vehicle for the promotion of racial unity. Hughes adopted another perspective, balancing and negotiating the security of White sympathy and support. In fact, he never read his revolutionary verse in public, publishing it in small leftist magazines. Before the public, he recited poetry portraying and explaining the "social, cultural, spiritual, and emotional experiences of Black America."[6]

Garvey, an outstanding organizer, seemed to galvanize the emotional experiences of his Harlem followers, who showcased their commitment by marching in self-promoting parades. They dressed as soldiers, nurses, and other occupations, all for the onlooker Negroes to review, idealize, and enact. Garvey's militant and military imagination induced him to write functional poetics dogmatic in nature, although a few of his poems are flights into whimsy where he promenades "joy," "music," and a "happy soul."[7] But mostly, his versification addresses disciplined behavior and highlights Pan-African thought.

Hughes' expressions in this period highlight a global unity and an affinity to communism. With early twentieth century communism downplaying Pan-African solidarity, Hughes' work focuses more on global revolution. His workers of the world unite to destroy oppression. Where Garvey wrote poetry to inspire Negroes to create a Black destiny, Hughes wrote to unite all races. Where Garvey's sense of the international involves Diaspora Africans, Hughes' incorporates nations throughout the entire world.

In a deliberate decision to alter racial appellations, both men redefine the term "black" without distancing themselves from the word "Negro." Marcus Garvey, in fact, demanded the capitalization of the "n" in "Negro," initially uncomfortable with "black" because of its history of horrifying associations.[8] Neither however encouraged a re(re)naming to go from Negro to Afro or African American.[9] Yet, each aggressively altered the aesthetics and poetics of the term "Black" and Black culture. John Henrik Clarke speaks to Marcus Garvey's redefinition of "black":

Garvey tried to change the images that influence the minds of African people, e.g., he taught respect for the color *black* ... by taking pride in things of this color. He founded the *Black* Star Line ... and the *Black* Cross Nurses as opposed to Red Cross Nurses. Some number of his members began to open factories to produce *black* dolls[10] [my emphasis].

As Garvey's "black" inversion was loud and proud, Hughes's was mellow, bringing subtle attention to changes in meaning and tone. For example, in "Island" he refers to Blacks and Whites in the same sound, under-emphasizing racial distinctions. He writes: "Black and white / Gold and brown — Chocolate-custard / Pie of a town."[11]

In "Freedom's Plan," through a revisionist history, Hughes demonstrates racial harmony, a black-white equity and unity in making America. In his unity of occasion, in that poem, Hughes visualizes himself as "black" and he is comfortable with the term, as he makes it equal to "white." Without a "white" aggressor or oppressor in the poem, he designs a romantic notion that allows him to create racial equality as he narrates a cultural crossing in the making of America. His belief in integration inspires a mysterious interracial brotherhood. In light of the segregation and racism gripping America during the Renaissance, his brotherhood image in "Freedom's Plan" expresses an ideal.

This particular theme contrasts with revisits to the Communist Party through *Native Son* (1940), *American Hunger* (1977), and *Invisible Man* (1945), where the narratives of Wright and Ellison rip any notion of sublimity prior to and after the Renaissance. Probably, like the character Todd Clifton in *Invisible Man*, Hughes holds onto the ideal and the philosophy pushing away racism. The text *Jubilee* (1967) provides another example of the historical schisms that Hughes overlooks between Black and White in "Freedom's Plan." In Margaret Walker's account of Vyry's narrative (her great grandmother), she delineates the color hierarchy that shaped the plantation system and experience. Often, not always, a huge hostility existed between the poor White laborers and the enslaved people. The poor Whites envied the slaveholding class and clung to the shared investment in Whiteness that included despising the Blacks. To reciprocate, the enslaved people mocked and resented poor Whites for not being wealthy. Hughes opts to smooth over historical trenches and tensions, presenting a softer side of Black and White relations. He elevates peace among disparate voices because he seeks interracial harmony. However, this is not a unique line of thought because previous poets sought such harmony because of Christianity. Hughes, though, found this desire within a secular system of belief. In "Good Morning Revolution," this neutral equality takes on an international focus:

> Good morning, Revolution:
>   You're the best friend
>   I ever had
> We gonna pal around together from now on.
> ...
> Listen, Revolution,
> ...
> We can take everything:
>   Factories, arsenals, houses, ships,
>   Railroads, forests, fields, orchards,
>   Bus lines, telegraphs, radios,
> ...
> And turn 'em over to the people who work.
> Rule and run 'em for us people who work.
> ...
> And we'll sign it: Germany
> Sign it: China
> Sign it: Africa
> Sign it: Poland
> Sign it: Italy
> Sign it: America
> Sign it with my one name: Worker...[12]

With global revolution the personifying subject, the African continent is one among other countries. In this long poem, Hughes begins as an American worker explicating the vast breach between labor and management. In a familiar and gossipy manner he discusses class separations. The "boss" in the poem does well while a fired worker starves. The poem then shifts to revolution in a wider context, internationalizing the worker. However, where is the Negro? Is the Negro in Africa or America or both? No matter where Negroes reside in the above, they are equal to everyone else. In this poem,

Hughes' unity of occasion and situation prior to the writing reveals equality within himself and the peoples of the world. There is no African distinction here. All of the nations have the identical problem. As such, there is a hint of the disappearing Negro here, similar to the poetics of Frances Harper.

This impression reduces the importance and the uniqueness of the Negroes' creation and situation because of the multiple foci. Basil Davidson (1995) provides African history that sheds light on this interpretation. He points out that during the 19th century, the European continent organized to invade and to carve up Africa for personal pleasure and profit:

> The colonial partition was the sharing out of Africa among strong empire building powers such as Britain, France and Germany; and several weaker ones such as Portugal, Italy, Belgium and Spain. For a long time during the nineteenth century, these powers quarrelled over the shares of Africa that each wanted to get. But in 1884–85, at a conference in Berlin (then capital of a German empire) they agreed to invade and take Africa without fighting each other. They marked out "spheres of interest." Then each invaded the continent within its own "sphere."[13]

The Africans fought aggressively against the invaders, but lost the war because of the Europeans' sophisticated weaponry. This is a repeat of how the original enslavers invaded the continent a century before the 1800s, and decided similarly only to make slaves of Africans, not anyone else. Yet, in the poem above, the European ownership of Africa is omitted. Additionally, Hughes positions Africa and Italy as friends despite the war threat that existed between Italy and Ethiopia when the poem was published in 1933. It seems that Hughes subdues the uneven power play between these countries in order to isolate the peasant class in each, hoping to encourage a rainbow coalition. With Mussolini invading Ethiopia two years later, Hughes's intention suggests obscuring realism for a futuristic dream. Before that, Italy had seized what it called Eritrea and attempted to claim Ethiopia, but with Emperor Menelik's resistance, in 1896, he and his soldiers defeated the invaders. "However, early in the 1930s, Italy's fascist government under its leader Benito Mussolini began shouting for revenge for the defeat of 1896. Claiming that Italy must also have her 'place in the African sun,' Mussolini prepared for war."[14] Although the African leaders petitioned the world court for help, none came, and this time the Italians defeated the Ethiopians. For Hughes then to position Africa the continent with European powers that have consistently oppressed African people and pilfered their resources troubles. It does not eliminate the chaos of racism, and by omission, it extends it. The "sign it" refrain further endorses his motif of sameness, projected throughout the poem.

From another perspective, if I consider the inflexible definition of

American, I could argue that no Negroes are in the above poem. Rarely treated as Americans, Negroes after slavery faced vulgar segregation. In fact, later generations had to protest for the rights that all "Americans" have by birth. In 1857 when Justice Roger Taney ruled that Dred Scott and all other Blacks were not citizens because they were a subordinate and inferior class of beings, he placed the Negro outside of citizenry. Ian Lopez (1996) writes that the "basic law of citizenship that a person born here is a citizen here, did not include all racial minorities until 1940."[15] Yet, two decades beyond the 1940s, Negroes had to organize, demonstrate, and fight for voting rights. Either de facto or de jure the law did not allow the Negro to experience the privileges of citizenship. Lopez argues the notion of race as a cultural and social construct, pointing out the trap of predicating Black and White divisions as natural. The racial category "White" occurred because of non-White classifications: Native Americans, Asians, Latinos, and Blacks. In legal and social classifications, Whites are above all others with Blacks holding the bottom. In order to banner a better future, Hughes dismisses this disparity.

However, in "Good Morning Revolution," he reverses an African image away from the stereotype, making the African a world citizen along with others who resists oppression. If we stretch Africa or America to include the Negro, than the Negro image merges into an international frame, with such eliminating a measure of racial chaos. In "Good Morning Revolution," he broadens the Negro, elevating peace in the uniqueness of the African Negro joining forces to fight. Compare this to Countee Cullen's "Shroud of Color," where the image of Africa prefers death to living in his own skin. Differently, in "White Man," Hughes pursues another direction, with a local emphasis. He creates an angry persona who verbally fights back against economic oppression.

> Sure, I know you!
> You're a White Man.
> I'm a Negro.
> You take all the best jobs
> And leave us the garbage cans to empty and
> The halls to clean
> ...
> You enjoy Rome—
> And **take** Ethiopia.
> ...
> I hear your name ain't really White Man.
> I hear it's something
> Marx wrote down
> Fifty years ago-
> ...
> C-A-P-I-T-A-L-I-S-T:..[16]

The closure is opposite the beginning. As in "Good Morning Revolution," he closes with the culpability of capitalism. Indirectly the poem hints that the racial divide would disappear if not for economic disparity. Additionally, Italy is included in the White man's image because it "took Ethiopia" while the superpowers failed to intervene. Hughes' "situation" of occasion prior to writing the poem is one of "Negro." Therefore, confusion exists that seems to melt in the following lines where he mentions "Ethiopia." The connection is between the African (Ethiopian) and the Diaspora African (Negro). There is a budding relationship that does not reach its full potential, but it is importantly in the poem. Still, Hughes opts for interracial brotherhood when he subordinates or omits intra-racial grievances, hanging onto the Party line. However, this poem, devoid of a cultural connection, does ease into the rights of workers. There is the harmony. Harold Cruse deconstructs this communist embrace in *The Crisis of the Negro Intellectual* (1967). There, he argues that Harlem intellectuals had no political program to offer the Negroes outside of communism, which restricted the race's autonomy. At least Garvey had a program solely for the Negroes, although according to Martin sometimes his nationalism bordered on fascism.[17]

This next poem, however, is written mostly for the Negroes. "Black Seed" delights in the metaphorical beauty of being dark:

> World-wide dusk
> Of dear dark faces
> Driven before an alien wind,
> Scattered like seed
> From far-off places
> Growing in soil
> That's strange and thin,
> Hybrid plants
> In another's garden,
> Flowers
> In a land
> That's not your own,
> Cut by the shears
> Of the white-faced gardeners —
> Tell them to leave you alone![18]

Beginning in the second line, Hughes architects a "dark" appreciation through alliteration, "dear dark." He crumbles or inverts the symbolic meaning of "darkness." Comparatively, "faces," "seeds," and "plants" further a fragile, natural, and delicate image. The metaphorical language parallels the divisions between Black and White Americans. However, he begins his first line with "world-wide" signaling the international. He then shifts this expansion into a singular focus that leads into American problems. The African in America becomes subject because "Scattered" and "seed" represent Black people shipped throughout the Americas to perform free labor. This African is now a "hybrid." The image of the "white-faced gardeners" alludes to the power of master over slave. This slave expanding into "worker," though, has revolutionary potential, which impacts the closure. Hughes' "unity of occasion and situation" clearly emphasizes the enslaved African. He links with that voice, sound, person and people before crafting the art. It certainly eliminates the chaos of racism because he fights against the "white-faced gardeners." And it elevates peace among disparate voices because it synthesizes the American Africans' experience.

Berry tells us that Hughes had to testify before Joseph McCarthy's Senate Committee on Government Operations in March 1953 and afterwards he suffered immeasurably. His books were banned from USIA libraries throughout the world, and the agency that acquired his readings dropped him. Hughes as he did on many occasions suffered a lost of prestige and revenue. This indicates that earlier when he carefully published his revolutionary verse in small leftist magazines, he was protecting himself. When he refused to publicly read his revolutionary poetry, he was reacting to his correct reading of the American climate. Langston Hughes had lived and understood the losses attached to being Negro:

> All over America we know what it is to be refused admittance to schools and colleges, to theatres and concert halls, to hotels and restaurants. We know Jim Crow cars, race riots, lynchings, we know the sorrows of the nine Scottsboro boys, innocent young Negroes imprisoned some six years now for a crime that even the trial judge declared them not guilty of having committed, and for which some of them have not yet come to trial. Yes, we Negroes in America do not have to be told what Fascism is in action. We know. Its theories of Nordic supremacy and economic suppression have long been realities to us.[19]

This 1937 speech given in Paris before the International Writers' Congress articulates a history of the Negro. As a brilliant intellectual, poet, and writer, Hughes could not elevate his American status because of race. His charge of White supremacy is a springboard to revisit the conspiring among Whites to misuse African people. It hails back to the conspiracy to only enslave Africans, to the Berlin Conference where powers sliced up Africa, to the discrimination Negroes faced in employment. In fact, a major part of Hughes' revolutionary conception presents the horrors perpetrated against his people. Placing Negro challenges in a larger context marks a rhetorical method of discourse. Hughes clarifies Jim Crow in this same worldwide stretch, evident in the following 1949 excerpt: "What is happening in China is important to Negroes, in fact, to people of color all around the world, because each time an old bastion of white supremacy crumbles its falling weakens the whole Jim Crow system everywhere.... I do not like Jim Crow in either Chicago or China."[20]

Hughes as an internationalist recognizes what Malcolm X later referred to as people of color globally having the same "enemy." And in America, White supremacy shaped Hughes' personality, causing him to repudiate "Goodbye, Christ" to satisfy a displeased patron. Choosing writing as a career, Hughes depended on his patrons; therefore, this next poem nearly caused him literal hunger.

> Listen, Christ,
> You did alright in your day, I reckon —
> But that day's gone now.
> They ghosted you up a swell story, too,
> Called it Bible —
> But it's dead now.
> The popes and the preachers've
> Made too much money from it.
> They've sold you to too many
> Kings, generals, robbers, and killers —
> Even to the Tzar and the Cossacks,
> Even to Rockefeller's Church,
> ...[21]

In Ebonics, "Goodbye, Christ" anticipates understanding by the masses. In this voice, Langston Hughes reformulates Christianity, stripping away the sublime, making it modern. Urbanizing Christ and the Bible, he decentralizes God. Hughes reverses the loftiness of Christianity made familiar by earlier Negro poets from Phillis Wheatley to Marcus Garvey. Thus, Hughes brings a new realism to Negro art, a gritty, crusty one. By denouncing religion, he extends the modernist tradition in poetry and indirectly suggests a new point of direction for the Negro.

"Goodbye, Christ" inverts Christian mythology, demonstrating a unity of occasion by prefiguring problematic deep structures that control Negro psychology. The psychologist Na'im Akbar (1991) tells us that in Christian countries where Negroes reside, they normally lack independent thought and action.[22] Therefore, the poem eliminates a measure of chaotic racism because it reminds the Negro of his only association with the master class, suggested later in the selling of religion in "Rockefeller's Church." Through religion the Negro shares with Rockefeller, but not in economics, point of view, or culture. Such indicates a new review of the metaphysical that profits a Rockefeller and oppresses a people. Deconstructing the Negroes' reliance on religion, Hughes makes it political. His later association to the *Saturday Evening Post* critiques the value of the dominant culture's social icons, demonstrating how one molds and folds into another. This concept of religion buys and sells reality. This poem eliminates racism because it empowers the urban Black to speak with authority about his reality. With most American Negroes adopting the principles and theology of Christianity, this poem indeed elevates peace among disparate voices because it deviates from the mainstream mode of thought. It is unique.

"Goodbye, Christ" offended both Negroes and Whites, prompting Hughes's later rejection. He referred to it as a youthful mistake. His dance for the money upholds and reveals a doubly racist intention: deny the Negro both opportunity and independent thought.

In contrast, Hughes never had to apologize for or retract his lyricism praising his people's culture. His jazz aesthetic pictured in "Dream Boogie" or "Harlem" with the famous line "what ever happens to a dream deferred" promotes his affection for music and for composers. Next, in a redefined association of "black" he transforms Africa. The slogan and rallying cry "Black is beautiful" became a descriptor of the 1960s decade. This phrase influenced the aesthetics, activism, and collective consciousness of the transforming Negro people.

Hughes inverts the symbols of black and white. Night, which is normally a symbol of fear and distrust, repeats in gentle and inviting terminology that warmly folds the speaker. Historically, the enslaved African would welcome the "dark" because the dark belonged to him and her. That is when she could tend to her own family and to herself without the pervasive and intruding eyes of either master or overseer. Hughes captures that lovely and attractive night appreciation in the Black imagination. Such also highlights the later rhythm and blues song "Night Time Is the Right Time." Inverting the symbols, he eliminates the chaos of racism because he, like Elijah Muhammad, strips adulation from the image of "white." Inverting the symbols also causes an easy readability close to song. In fact, in concerts, the female a cappella group *Sweet Honey in the Rock* sing the lyrics of the poem "My People." In the African American experience, he elevates peace among disparate voices because he begins a body of language and thought that neuters the omnipotent power of "white," which Madhubuti echoes in the 1960s. This unique inversion carries forward the resistance seculars spoken by those enslaved.

Hughes as poet spokesman for his people fought racism, presenting Black culture and people poignantly in art. Hughes' sway with language personal to the people prepared later writers to appreciate Blacks as source material. His technique therefore abandons the decapitated lyrics of pre–and post–antebellum. Hughes's direct unity of occasion figures Africa as a whole place unique in its geography, not a continent of currency, or one fraught with tension or dimness. Hughes welcomes the continent.

Hughes, like Marcus Garvey, desires Africa as a romantic vision that stimulates the Negro imagination. Marcus Garvey first came to America to meet his hero Booker T. Washington even though he was more of an internationalist. As a pragmatist, however, Garvey admired Washington's genius for elevating the Negro through education and economics. Washington died before they could meet and Garvey went on to design an independent organization that never practiced subservience. Instead, Garvey set a standard for Negroes to reach, treating his people as a nation with ties to Africa. He said:

> Any sane man, race or nation that desires freedom must first of all think in terms of blood. Why, even the Heavenly Father tells us that "without the shedding of blood there can be no remission of sins?" Then how in the name of God, with history before us, do we expect to redeem Africa without preparing ourselves — some of us to die.[23]

Marcus Garvey speaks in revolutionary fervor, boldly challenging the Negro to take up arms if necessary to erase substandard citizenship in America and around the world. This is the energy that invigorated Earl Little, the father of Malcolm X and a Garveyite. Marcus Garvey put together a program and built an organization to fight White supremacy and to begin liaisons between continental and American Africans. Preaching the Garvey doctrine assisted in Earl Little's assassination. Additionally, Elijah Muhammad, head of the Nation of Islam, stayed with the UNIA until Marcus Garvey's exile.

The Jamaican born Garvey started the Universal Negro Improvement Association (UNIA) in New York on July 15, 1914, and in four short years he amassed branches throughout the country and the world. In 1919, he launched his Black Star Line, a fleet of ships to begin trade with Africa. 25,000 people in Madison Square Garden celebrated this remarkable accomplishment.

As an advocate for Negro rights, Garvey sought various ways to share his vision. In addition to starting the *Negro World* newspaper, he wrote poetry to advance his message and in this creativity, he envisions an African image unlike any other:

> Africa's sun is shining above the horizon clear,
> The day for us is rising, for black men far and near;
> Our God is in the front line, the heav'nly battalion leads
> Onward, make your banners shine, ye men of noble deeds.
>   There's a flag we love so well
>   The red, the black and green,
>   Greatest emblem tongues can tell.
>   The brightest ever seen.[24]

In heroic stanzas, Garvey prefigures a unity of occasion by creating a nationalist poem. In his African image, the Negro is "inside of time" with territory, army, flag, creed, and God. The poem's upbeat tone is proud, patriotic, and visionary. Garvey creates a sense of peace among disparate voices because he presents disciplined African-centered behavior that brings autonomous results. This is the autonomy that Hughes yearned for in his Paris speech where he articulates the pain of dependency, denied human rights, and oppression in America. In the above, the diction liberates Black or Negro men from "lazy" and "shiftless" stereotypes. These actors are "men of noble deeds." Their nobility is reflected in the African "sun" motif that Hughes has projected in selected poetry as well as the "sun" reference to Africa that Mussolini employed. "Sun" is a concept and a metonym that relates directly to Africa because of climate and ancient religious beliefs and practices. In light of this, Garvey's use of "brightest" differs from Harper's. This brightness comes from being blessed by God, whose advancing soldiers present another version of Christianity. This God conception displays his wrath against the people's enemies as opposed to a portrayal of meekness and forgiveness. Patriotism and divinity combine in the "tongues" synecdoche, which promotes the flag as symbol of independence from colonial rule. Negroes in America have represented an internal colony. This image of Africa is so powerful that it eliminates the chaos of racism because when Blacks are potent, the emanation lessens racism. Also, such vital emanation can bring out White hatred, which can then be fought directly.

Garvey, in this transformed African image, makes "black" an acceptable race indicator. "The day for us is rising, for black men far and near." Like Hughes, he inverts the meaning of "black" from fright to splendor. This "day," a metaphor for the sun, also provides the image of "black" with fighting potential, not unlike the "hybrid" slave worker in Hughes' "Black Seed," who harbors revolutionary reaction. The next line, "our God is in the front line, the heavenly battalion leads," furthers and displays the idea of resistance with soldiers leading the battle.

This is a new Negro in a welcoming category of "black." However, the "Negro" name at this time still presented problems that even confused the editors of the *Negro World*, Garvey's newspaper. The editors intuited the urge to re(re)name, to abandon Negro for something else. One *Negro World* editor, William H. Ferris, thought up the improbable "Negrosaxon" as a possibility for re(re)naming.[25] The question of whether or not the racial appellation "Negro" should remain bothered the intellectuals.

This befuddlement largely demonstrates the discomfort that collectively Africans in America experienced over the term "Negro," intuiting its origination from enslavers. Garvey through poetry attempted to elevate the artificially created Negro into a conception of equality, not necessarily with Whites but within the Negro self. Garvey was not pushing for integration, except with other Blacks. Simultaneously Whites clung to the very Whiteness that they structurally and culturally created, as George Lipsitz (1998) argues in *The Possessive Investment in Whiteness*. Being White paid tremendous dividends to European descendants.

The troubling naming issue illustrates one phase of absorbing the "investment of whiteness." Struggling, juggling, and still wondering in the 20th century what to racially call one's self or group — Negrosaxon, colored, Negro — illustrates the vortex of White supremacy. As Lipsitz and others elaborate, America has created this investment in supremacy by providing opportunities for Whites and disadvantages for Blacks. For centuries, housing, legislation, employment, education, and opportunity enormously benefited Whites, leaving all others with so little that their circumstances mirrored and progressed the inferiority myth (Lipsitz 1995; Lopez 1998). This possessive investment includes and ignites pantomiming and believing in the aesthetics of domination.

The aesthetics of domination filtered deeply into the masculine, patriarchal imagination. This is evident when we examine how Marcus Garvey internally visualizes females. Garvey's imagination yields a "hybrid" that hails ideals of White and Black aesthetics. This cultural crossing is in the following lines from "The Black Woman" and "The Black Mother":

> Black queen of beauty, thou hast given color to the world!
> Among other women thou art royal and the fairest!
> Like the brightest of jewels in the regal diadem,
> Shin'st thou, Goddess of Africa Nature's purest emblem!
> Black men worship at thy virginal shrine of truest love,
> Because in thine eyes are virtue's steady and holy mark,
> As we see in no other, clothed in silk or fine linen,
> From ancient Venus, the Goddess, to mythical Helen.[26]
> Where can I find love that never changes
>
> ...
>
> This I find at home, only with Mother,
>
> ...
>
> My Mother is black, loveliest of all.[27]

The above poems written in 1927 show Garvey's newness at the craft. As any beginning poet, his language is bumpy and telling of a combination of Negro and White aesthetics. Garvey has not found his own voice and he has given little thought to structure. These poems actually illustrate the profundity and the depth of White aesthetics sifted through the Negro imagination. The above poems though about Black women present language relative to predominately Western influences. Garvey has an interracial unity of occasion. Even though he inverts the symbol of "black" from ugly to upright, his mention of "fairest" reveals a White ideal. Mirror, mirror on the wall, who's the fairest of us all? Fairy tales occupy Garvey's imagination along with a Western, classical version of history. At that time and up until the 1960s, the only narrative taught was the master one of Western perspective; hence, Garvey knows Helen of Troy, not Yaa Asantewaa.

Susan Gubar in *Racechanges* (1997) displays the drawings of Richard Bruce Nugent of the Harlem Renaissance period from a series entitled "Drawings for Mulattoes." In them merge a split and joined Black/White female image that somewhat contains the complex and conflicting (re)forming aesthetics in Negroes. The drawings are vital. In some the merged Black/White female dances. In another, Black/White heads join. Analyzing the psychology of Nugent and the social climate of the Renaissance, Gubar comments and questions. "Taken as a whole, Nugent's series of prints questions whether the move from the African landscape to the Broadway stage or Harlem club is one of evolution or devolution, progress or decline and for whom."[28] Although Garvey preaches nationalism, his aesthetics indicates a Western allure.

Yet, in spite of this diction, Garvey praises pigmentation. His black woman gives "color" to the world, a glorifying contribution. Thus, he does elevate peace among disparate voices because he bumpily extends Hughes's beauty in black, and his harmony is in the cultural pride he exhibits because of his hue. His finding "worth" in "color" (or pigmentation) contrasts dramatically with other motifs found in the Renaissance fiction of novelists Nella Larsen, Jessie Fauset, and Zora Neale Hurston. All have quadroon protagonists. Larsen's heroine Irene Redfield in *Passing* (1929) suffers tragic mulatto confusions, and in *Plum Bun*, Mattie and her daughter Angela pass for White for excitement. Janie Crawford however cares little about color and finds joy in her own people. Yet the above female authors share the plotting of biracialism, which separates by color gradation the protagonists from the masses of Negro people. In fact, they together upscale the woman Negro closest to White in physical attributes. This demonstrates the Blacks investing in whiteness.

Garvey's general notion of color, however, is vastly different. He aims poetry to attack Negro practices of physical self-denial: "My mother is black, loveliest of all." However, he picks from the common language of his peers resembling the patriarchs to paint forms of beauty. As such, his comparisons are to the women of the privileged race, such as "Venus," as he gears his poetry to everyday people. He has not developed a wellspring of beauty from a condensed "black" perspective. But, he wakes up a desire ancient in Africans to pay homage to the female, prefiguring the Black woman as Queen. Hybrid combinations animate action while reflecting on and presenting an African continuity.

In the next poem, he concentrates on all members of the race, as he simultaneously illustrates more attention to the craft of writing poetry.

> Believe in God
> Lift yourself
> Lift your family
> Lift your clan
> Lift your race
> Lift your country
> Lift your nation
> And be
> An imperial whole.[29]

"Your Duty" repeatedly pulses with the need for racial responsibility. Here, Garvey inserts a religious impulse that sanctions royal behavior on earth. As an example of instructional poetry, it urges the reader and listener to make the ideal a reality. Nation building language — family, clan, race — unite reader and listener to the personal, private, and public spheres of interconnected relationships. All culminate to build up and on African thinking, his unity of occasion. The persona, the people, in the poem must relate ethically to and actively in the world. They are the doers who must cause the "right" thing to happen. This poem eliminates the chaos of racism because it concentrates on Black people taking care of themselves. It elevates peace among disparate voices because it synthesizes the American experience, Black. "Family" and "clan" are words out of an African lexicon. Pre-colonial African civilizations organized around clans.

The brevity of "Your Duty" makes memorization easy. Thus, his listeners or readers could quickly recall on demand his list of instructions for racial unity and success. Also, beginning with belief in God and next the self, he makes the Creator the only concept worth projecting on high. After this Force, the individual, family and others unfold in an ethical succession that sets the foundation for the beginning work of building. In "Your Duty" Marcus Garvey invigorates an ancient African category of poetry writing. The Kemets (Egyptians) often recited instructional verses as teaching formulas, because art was functional in all African societies. Art served a purpose. It did not exist without a reason wedded in the culture.

Garvey uses reason in the next poem, "Win the Fray," to urge his male listeners and readers to transform into the ideal. He travels from the upbeat uplift in "Your Duty" to the downbeat of lament. The temporality suggests a potential, future reward:

> O! when the Negro makes himself a man.
>   The wicked world will see a new parade;
>   The blacks will march in one tremendous clan—
>   A great phalanx of noble fighting braves.
> The day that Africa awakes, in deed,
>   And black men cease to dream away the time,
> The scoffing tribes of other men will heed,
>   The race's claims of sober righteousness.
> It's then for you to think and act to-day,
>   And show of what good mettle you are made
> It's not what other men may do or say,
>   But just how game you are to win the stake.

Garvey attempts the sonnet form with exact and near rhyme endings. His pentameter is a mix of iambs and trochees. "The wicked world will see a new parade" an example of iambic pentameter. "It's then for you to think and act to-day," trochaic throughout with the exception of "and act" equaling an iamb. The above poem is different from Garvey's usual verses that relinquish figurative diction for the sake of the message. Here he conflates his desire to merge message with language music. Beginning in a lament, he then proceeds with self-assurance and faith that his people will progress visually before the world. His unity of occasion and situation is consistently "his people" or "race first." He visualizes himself as only African and from that center he starts his message. He eliminates racism because it is not his focus. He has consumed much of the history and experiences of Black people and he seeks to create a harmony within the race. He hopes to give the Negro a new reputation.

From the general to the specific, his articles objectify "the Negro" in order to reclassify exactly what this concept can become: "a man." "Wicked" and "righteousness," religiously inspired words, show that Garvey believed in the holy metaphysical affecting his mission on earth. He (re)forms gender formations that whittle away racist stereotypes as they prompt leadership behavior and responsibility. Yet, this is not an obligation to the world or one to an employer. This is a call to assume accountability to one's self, family, and community, a transformational prayer with the hoped for result: Negro males traveling from "boyz to men." His closure reinforces faith in the "mettle" of his people.

Garvey signifies with the term "tribe." In a derogatory (and traditional) sense, "tribe" normally means a classification for African or Native American people. In fact, his placement of "braves" joins the Native American and African. However, Garvey's "tribe" refers to other racial groups. Such usage suggests two possibilities: Garvey deliberately reduces others to a debased level, or Garvey inverts the meaning of tribe. He signifies with tribe. Additionally, his new presentation of racial terminology resurfaces the conflicting issue of racial identity. This entangling manifests in the intermix of "Negro," "black," and "Africa," indirectly setting in motion the need for re(re)naming.

> Hail! United States of Africa — free!
> Hail! Motherland most bright, divinely fair!
> State in perfect sisterhood united.
> Born of truth; mighty thou shalt ever be.[30]

This bumpy stanza speaks of a significant unification that will give Africa the continent a needed agency. Although clothed in White aesthetics, the poem celebrates the unification of Africa probably based on territories prior to the European invasion. Kwame Nkrumah, the first leader in independent Ghana in 1957, espoused this idea of a United States of Africa. John Henrik Clarke (1991) says that Nkrumah's greatest achievement was in making Ghana an inspiration of independence throughout the African world. Clarke calls him "the first universal hero of this century."[31] Nkrumah certainly knew of Garvey's UNIA and the "Back to Africa" movement. Before heading his own country, he studied in the United States and lived in Harlem, struggling with a methodology that would ensure an African independence. Garvey, imagining Nkrumah's United States of Africa, recreates a feminine African image "motherland" for persuasion, acceptance, and appreciation. His make-up of the "motherland" mixes fairy tale, biblical, and traditional language, which again recalls Harper's "bright" poetics. However, Garvey clearly challenges racism and the myth of inferiority. He eliminates the chaos of racism, pointing to a solid African relationship. In the above, Africa is a dream with open arms. For his readers and listeners, Africa is where they belong. To augment this point, Garvey does not question what Africa means to him. On the contrary, he knows that it is his original birthplace and he boasts about that association. In fact, the continent is not a spectral presence but one of greatness, although the greatness remains undefined.

In the above, Garvey is not a Negro; he has "Africa on the mind" and his vision generates an enthusiasm for a future reunification of the continent. Because of such imagery, his readers could look beyond the injustices in America to find their own source of sustenance. Next, in "Africa for the Africans" he ends in a dictum later asserted by Malcolm X:

> Say! Africa for the Africans,
> Like America for the Americans:
> This the rallying cry for a nation,
> Be it in peace or revolution.

His closure indicates seizing freedom either peacefully or forcefully. This is not an integrationist or assimilationist poem. Garvey talks about revolution and the fight for territory. His "situation" prior to the writing is in an African warrior's pose. He speaks equality between the races, African and American, which means White. He lessens the sting of racism because if Africans control the continent then European racism and colonialism would not be a factor. His elevation of peace speaks for the reclamation of African authority. Putting his life on the line, Garvey's slogan resembles the "give me liberty or death" rallying cry of the American colonists.

In the first line, the exclamation point starts a rousing tempo, itself a "rallying cry." The colon in the second line prepares the comparison of the American Revolution with the Negroes' fight against White America. It anticipates the African countries' claiming independence decades later in the 1960s as it exposes how Garvey understands the American identity. In the above, only the Whites are Americans, and the poem pursues racial separation.

A contemporary view of race suggests a democratic hierarchy throughout the nation. Merit is supposed to be the measuring tool, not race-based set-asides or opportunities of inclusion. This blindfold of history underscores how many Whites fail to think of themselves in terms of racial category in the way that others have assumed. With their image of Whiteness projected as the prevailing dominant force in governance, culture, and aesthetics, they depict themselves much differently than do people of color. Lopez writes about surveys where Whites and Blacks were asked to define their respective identities. The Blacks identified themselves in terms of race. Most of the Whites did not.[32] Calling this "Transparency," he writes: "Transparency is due in part to positional privilege. 'White supremacy makes whiteness the normative model. Being the norm allows whites to ignore race, except when they perceive race (usually someone else's) as intruding on their lives.' Existing at the center of racial relations, Whites very rarely find themselves burdened by race in a manner that draws this aspect of identity into view."[33] For Marcus Garvey, the issue of race is central. He views America as the land of the Whites and to him to halt his people's dependency and pantomime, he wants them to work towards going "back to Africa." Their return of course includes assisting in the overthrow of non-African rulers. The tone predicts a fighting people, who remain the motif in the following poem:

Blacks are men, no longer cringing fools;
They demand a place, not like weak tools;
But among the world of nations great
They demand a free self-governing state.³⁴

In this weak heroic stanza, Garvey again pays more attention to message than craft. He parallels opposite images in the first two lines, shedding the tired stereotypes "cringing fools" and "weak tools." His visual before the writing of the poem, he signifies on White America. He is their worst fear, which Malcolm X later articulates. Garvey prefigures a Black male who will destroy segregation and inequality while desiring his own "state." Stepping up the idea of a New Negro demanding his own patriarchal destiny, he presents a people active in transformation. This is the ideology of the becoming Honorable Elijah Muhammad, who demanded that men be obligatory to themselves, their families, and nation: their own. Racism is eliminated if Blacks build a nation. This is also the foundation and philosophy of the Republic of New Africa, a 1960s activist group that argued for a portion of United States territory to be set aside for Black people. The final line is the dream, not deferred but realized. Negro America desires nationhood. The quieting of disparate voices emerges because of the singular focus.

In America, nationalism and male writing begins with David Walker. Nationalism that demands seizing of territory and authority has been qualified as male activity. Garvey is no different from most male writers of his epoch. He excludes women from roles historically designed for males. Therefore, when he writes of action he writes of and for men using masculine nouns and pronouns. Garvey as with all writers assumed much of the dogma of his human experience, growing out of the Western one where sexism and racism intersect and unite. Not surprisingly, Garvey imagined women as mothers and lovers. Even though he knew Ida B. Wells and other take-charge females, his imagination still relegated women to roles dependent upon male leadership. Yet, Marcus Garvey was motivated to write because of race love.

Summary

The motivation of race love inspired Marcus Garvey to write poetry in order to instruct, direct, guide, and transform "the Negro" into a complete human being capable of leading his people to greatness. Garvey unlike Hughes and other Renaissance authors did not desire writing as a profession. Instead, it was a vehicle to leave a lyrical and instructional legacy. Through poetry, readers and listeners could recall or learn his philosophy, thoughts, principles, and most importantly his practice. Garvey wanted his words to leap off the page and into Negro psychology; his poetry illustrates a revolutionary, transformed image of Africa.

Langston Hughes developed poetry with a transformed image that emphasized global revolution. Langston Hughes had the courage and racial love to depict his people as subjects in most of his writing. Like Garvey, Hughes understood the powerful images that undermined and attempted to destroy the natural beauty of his people. So, he transformed his image of Africa specifically to make black beautiful. The major difference between these two artists is in activism and academics. The powerful similarity is in the desire to reconfigure a subhuman species into a people. Garvey dedicated his life to activism and art that would institutionalize Afrocentric principles among the African, African American, and American publics. Hughes, on the other hand, dedicated his life to the craft of writing, and to advocating for the rights of his people. Together, they give impetus in literature for the sixties poets such as Haki Madhubuti to wage a more contemporary, Malcolm X inspired war with words. In the next chapter, we examine not only Malcolm's linguistic, oratorical war but also Cheikh Anta Diop's theorems and Haki Madhubuti's use of each that has produced lasting institutions and literature often censored in mainstream anthologies.

FIVE

W.E.B. Du Bois, Cheikh Anta Diop, Malcolm X, and Haki Madhubuti: Claiming and Containing Continuity in Black Language and Institutions

In *YellowBlack: The First Twenty-One Years of a Poet's Life* (2005) Haki Madhubuti discusses the influences that W.E.B. Du Bois, Paul Robeson, and Malcolm X contributed to his life and artistry. In reviewing his political thought, the writings of Cheikh Anta Diop also affected his thinking. In fact, Madhubuti in 1986 wrote a poem to Diop that appears on the back cover of the journal *Great African Thinkers*, edited by Ivan Van Sertima. All of these men share an interest and activism in proving the commonality among African people. In the perspectives of X and Madhubuti, this line of thought is the foundation for implementing Black Nationalism, primarily racial responsibility for the collective success of African people throughout the Diaspora. Cheikh Anta Diop's major theory and contribution reconstruct the history of the Diaspora and his vision filters throughout the ideology of X and Madhubuti. Diop scientifically proved and promoted that all African history emerges out of its prototype, ancient Kemet, more familiarly known as Egypt, a Greek renaming. In this chapter, we visit the threads that bind these men together, and because most know about the major writings of the great sage W.E.B. Du Bois, I will begin by introducing the significance of Cheikh Anta Diop, the African-centered physicist.

Cheikh Anta Diop (1925–1989), a Senegalese physicist, upset and challenged the traditional scholarship and conclusions concerning Egypt (Kemet) when he argued its Blackness and scientifically measured the melanin content in mummies.[1] The University of Paris rejected his findings and it took three attempts before he received the doctorate degree. His three controversial theses were published as *Black Nations and Culture*, which earned him international recognition, *The Cultural Unity of Africa* (1959) and *Pre-Colonial Black Africa* (1960). His conclusion that the peoples of ancient Egypt, hereafter Kemet, were Black and that the Kemetic language is the mother of African tongues stripped bare and defied a long held assumption. Most in the academic world had argued that the original people of Kemet were White, and that this geographic region was of the Middle East, not Africa. In recognizing the "Blackness" of Kemet, which literally means "land of the Blacks," Diop put together a theory to foster and buttress a vital African unity. About the term "Kemet" Diop writes:

> The Egyptians had only one term to designate themselves: kmt.... This is the strongest term existing in the Pharoaonic tongue to indicate blackness; it is accordingly written with a hieroglyph representing a length of wood charred at the end and not crocodile scales. The word is the etymological origin of the well-known root *Kamit* which has proliferated in modern anthropological literature. The biblical root *kam* is probably derived from it and it has therefore been necessary to distort the facts to enable this root today to mean "white" in Egyptological terms whereas, in the Pharaonic mother tongue which gave it birth, it meant "coal black."[2]

Advancing the value of being Black, Diop, a brilliant scholar from the tradition of Muslim savants,[3] extends and inverts the traditional meaning of the term. Using science and linguistics, he set the stage for determining a cultural unity and consciousness among Africans worldwide. Predating and preempting the 1960s call for continuity in the study of Africa, Diop strove to uncover an African purity, not hybridity or dual heritage with Whites. Putting forward such premises during the 1940s and 1950s, he deconstructed Africans at home and abroad who proudly mimicked European values and standards. In *Nations negres et culture*, he argues the importance of historical continuity:

> If only our traditional historians, ethnologists, and sociologists had full realized, as one has a right to expect of them, that the essential need of a people is not so much to be able to glory in a more or less great past but rather to discover and realize the continuity of their past.[4]

Discovering cultural continuity when comparing his Wolof language to Kemetic terms "dazzled" Diop, finding the obvious similarities. Here are a few from mathematical concepts: Egyptian = k(a)w = height, Wolof = kaw = height; Egyptian = seked = a slope, Wolof = segg = to lean, and seggay = a slope; Egyptian nb = basket, a half-sphere, Wolof ndab = calabash, a half-sphere.[5] In linguistics and language the similarities continued. Soon after such discoveries, Diop urged all African scholars to connect the history and culture of the Diaspora to this ancient civilization, one that originated the arts and sciences (Hancock, 1996; Jackson, 1980; West, 1993; Williams, 1976). Such a link would organize a reconstruction of Africa, torn asunder since the European invasion of the continent. That disruption particularly in West Africa created a memory loss or dormancy that haunts Africans worldwide. The renaming of Africans as Negroes is a major example of murdering history. Katherine Bankole (2001) provides a list of at least eighteen definitions of the word, Negro, and its demeaning meanings. She writes that

> The "Negro," deemed as inherently inferior, ugly, and subhuman, had low identity-self-esteem. Most of all the Negro had no history, or at least no history worth knowing beyond the Holocaust of Enslavement. ... The Negro is the metaphor for Black-self hatred.[6]

Against this backdrop of Negro self hatred, Diop argued for Africans worldwide to accept, validate, and investigate ancient African culture and history and compare it to populations throughout the Diaspora. Similarly, Malcolm X publicly spoke to bring the "so-called Negro" back to Africa, because all communities of people connect to a classical civilization. In Diop's reasoning, Kemet is a sensible choice. Greece is not the foundation for ancient African civilizations. Greece begins the ancient origins of Europeans (James, 1976; Poe, 1997). In *Civilization or Barbarism* (1991), Diop's formula for study of ancient Africa in comparison with other geographies of color involves a psychic, historic, and linguistic approach. Similarly, W.E.B. Du Bois wrote scientific volumes to share the Negro in world history. Additionally his use of literature and language emphasizes Diop's theory and his corpus unlocked the visionary, poetic voice of Don L. Lee.

W.E.B. Du Bois (1868–1963), writer, social scientist, critic, and co-founder of the National Association for the Advancement of Colored People, wrote fiction and poetry as well as social science texts that impacted the imagination and the direction of Don L. Lee. In *YellowBlack: The First Twenty-One Years of a Poet's Life* (2005), Madhubuti quotes Du Bois where the great sage likened the Negro's bloodline to the pharaohs in Egypt. Du Bois saw this bloodline connection as one that effected Kemetic art. Here is a short excerpt:

> The Negro is primarily an artist. The usual way of putting this is to speak disdainfully of his "sensuous" nature.... [He has] a sense of beauty, particularly for sound and color, which characterizes the race. The Negro blood which flowed in the veins of many of the mightiest of the Pharaohs accounts for much of Egyptian art, and indeed Egyptian civilization.[7]

Diop agrees with this premise but also points out how racist writers used this "Negro-African" trait to belittle the ability of the "Negro-African" to reason. Particularly in *Civilization or Barbarism* (1991), Diop writes understandingly of the Negritude poets who adopted the ideology of the "ideological ancestor of the Nazis, Joseph Gobineau, who insists that the African must ally himself with the White (gifted) race in order to develop his intellect."[8] Without scientific refutations at that time the Francophone intellectuals and poets allowed this one-dimensional focus to inform their imaginations. For example, Aimè Cèsaire wrote this lyric about the African: "'Those who explored neither the seas nor the sky,' and Leopold S. Senghor [followed with]: 'Emotion is Negro and reason is Greek.'"[9] Even the term that Diop uses, "Negro-African," suggests the effect of colonization and racism, because Africa is a continent of color.

Color gradations confused young Don L. Lee, born on the exact day as W.E.B. Du Bois, February 23rd, but a different year in 1942. He related passionately to Du Bois because of the great man's intellectual acumen, his clarifications of race, and his similar pigmentation. Both are fair-skinned Black males. Du Bois assisted in young Don L. Lee's reconciling his varying "selves." Lee/Madhubuti writes about this after reading *The Souls of Black Folk*: "Color and psychology, color and history, color and enslavement, color and politics, color and economics, color and culture, color and rage, took on new meanings for me." In Du Bois, he found a needed "authenticity" lacking from growing up in racist America. Lee/Madhubuti, in search of masculinity in a culture where his likeness was often inferior to the dominant figurations, located validation in Du Bois's poetry. He particularly admires "The Riddle of the Sphinx," which forthrightly expresses anger at White world domination. In fact, he compares the content and tone to contemporary public intellectuals with discourse too "timid" to actively speak against the global oppression of Blacks and other people. Yet, his favorite poem by Du Bois is "The Horizon," published in 1899. Its motif resembles that of the 1960s Black Arts. The poem contains the refrain "I am black," and Du Bois uses it to celebrate being Black and male. Madhubuti analyzes this poem as not only a predecessor to the revolutionary 1960s poetics, but also to the poetry of the Harlem Renaissance. Madhubuti writes, "We bring to language its beat, it[s] cadences, its walking rhythms, its stops and goes, its skips and its balances; we add style and substance to whatever language in which we communicate, dance, or sing. There is an African or Black side of most languages. Language is cultural. Our language is our name."

This is also how he heard Malcolm X (1925–1965) accentuating African-centered history, celebrating the Black and releasing his rage against racism. During his incarceration (1946–1952), Malcolm reeducated himself under the guidance of the Honorable Elijah Muhammad, head of the Nation of Islam (NOI), and he studied Robeson's speaking style for emphasis. X brings Diop and Du Bois's powerful messages to light. On his prison release, he quickly became Muhammad's top minister and in much of his oratory, he addressed the memory loss or dormancy in what Muhammad's Muslims coined the "so-called negro."[10] Such casting of the word "Negro" immediately spreads doubt about its credibility. Malcolm's usage of the "so-called negro" urges the people so named to desire another appellation, and this is his purpose. He says this about the renaming in a broader context:

> Negro History Week ... doesn't remind us of past achievements. It reminds us only of the achievements we made in the Western Hemisphere under the tutelage of the white man. So that whatever achievement that was made in the Western Hemisphere that the spot light is put upon, this is the white man's shrewd way of taking credit for whatever we have accomplished. But he never lets us know of an accomplishment that we made prior to being born here. This is another trick. The worst trick of all is when he names us Negro and calls us Negro.... We're not Negroes, and have never been until we were brought here and made into that. We were scientifically produced by the white man.[11]

The significance of X attacking the term "Negro" encourages his listeners to reconsider history, taking a deeper view of language and social conditions. Once the Negro realizes the enormous deficiency in being renamed, Malcolm then provides a new vision of and about Africa. The necessity of providing new information about Africa is based on the previous perspective of the continent consistent with the debilitation of the slave and the continuance of enslavement. White American statesmen since the 17th century discounted and discredited African culture and civilization. A sample of what Henry Louis Gates writes and quotes about the 18th century statesman David Hume centers on the enormity of the challenge to redefine the "so-called Negro": "Hume posited with all of the authority of philosophy the fundamental identity of [negro] complexion, character, and intellectual capacity":

> I am apt to suspect the negroes and in general all the other species of men (for there are four or five different kinds) to be naturally inferior to the whites. There never was a civilized nation of any complexion than white,

nor even any individual eminent either in action or speculation. No ingenious manufacturers amongst them, *no arts, no sciences*[12] [my emphasis].

Malcolm's history lessons about ancient civilizations such as Sumer, Meroe, Ghana, Mali, and, most importantly, Egypt refute the great philosopher. X says this about the Nile Valley:

> Now the black civilization that shook the white man up the most was the Egyptian civilization, and it was a black civilization. It was along the banks of the Nile which runs through the heart of Africa.... This tricky white man was able to take the Egyptian civilization write books about it, put pictures in those books, make movies for television and the theatre — so skillfully that he has even convinced other white people that the ancient Egyptians were white people themselves. They were African, they were as much African as you and I.[13]

The fundamental and colossal significance of linking Egypt (Kemet) to Africa carries an intellectual and cultural magnitude that dazzles even today. For example, the questions of how, why, and when the pyramids and the sphinx were built are still debated. Graham Hancock explains the difficulty the ancients underwent in order to square the base of the Great Pyramid. He concludes: "All that we can say for sure is that the base *is* square and that the monument *is* locked into the cardinal axes of our planet with great care and precision."[14] How could the ancients meticulously transfer, handle, and carve rock and stone weighing hundreds of tons? If the ancients were stargazers, as some Egyptologists claim, then how could Pythagoras, the touted father of mathematics, be the inventor of pi? John Anthony West argues that point:

> Arguments had long ranged over whether the proportions of the Great Pyramid were deliberate or purely fortuitous. The pyramid's height stands in a precise pi relationship to the perimeter of the base. Pi (3.1416...) is the transcendental that defines the ratio between the diameter of a circle and its circumference. At the same time, pi is related to another, more interesting, irrational, phi, the so-called Golden Section. It had been observed — and ignored by Egyptologists — that not only the Great Pyramid but the other pyramids as well made use of different phi relations in their construction.[15]

There is no debate among scholars, however, that the pyramids' construction occurred thousands of years prior to the Greek Pythagoras (sixth century BC). Pythagoras and others openly talk about their personal limitations in comparison to the Kemets:

> We Greeks are in reality children compared with the people with traditions ten times older. And as nothing of precious remembrance of the past would

long survive in our country, Egypt has recorded and kept eternally the wisdom of the old times. The walls of its temples are covered with inscriptions and the priests have always under their own eyes that divine heritage.... The generations continue to transmit to successive generations these sacred things unchanged: songs, dances, rhythms, rituals, music, paintings, all coming from time immemorial when gods governed the earth in the dawn of civilization.[16]

The enormity of the architecture in Kemet speaks to remote epochs when "gods governed the earth." Malcolm told the "lost/found black man" that he was the original man and a builder of civilizations. When Cheikh Anta Diop persuaded scholars to connect African history to the image of Kemet he promoted this same line of thought. Although Malcolm may not have read Diop because translations of his work never occurred during X's lifetime, they both advanced an African-centered perspective of history. W.E.B. Du Bois did as well, claiming the accomplishments of the ancients. Muhammad taught Malcolm about the "devil White man's" stripping of the Asiatic Black man from his position of power millennia ago. Diop, in his two-cradle theory, explains such abusive tendencies according to climate and its relevance to behavior:

> The history of humanity will remain confused as long as we fail to distinguish between the two cradles in which Nature fashioned the instincts, temperament, habits and ethical concepts of the [Blacks and Whites] before they met each other after a long separation dating back to prehistoric times.... The abundance of vital resources, its sedentary, agricultural character, the specific conditions of the [Nile] valley will engender in man, that is, in the Negro, a gentle, idealistic, peaceful nature endowed with a spirit of justice and gaiety.... By contrast, the ferocity of nature in Eurasian steppes, the barrenness of those regions, the overall circumstances of material conditions, were to create instincts necessary for survival in such an environment.... Man in those regions long remained a nomad.... He was cruel.... All the peoples of the area whether white or yellow, were instinctively to love conquest, because of a desire to escape from those hostile surroundings.[17]

In developing and discussing theories for racially distinctive behaviors, Diop, Muhammad, and X awakened the repressed psychological and the overt damage of American slavery and European colonization of Africa. X's searing language lifted a fog, or what W.E.B. Du Bois would call a veil, from the assimilating tendencies that the Negro at home and abroad adopted in order to survive. Malcolm's dichotomous racial language shifted the "Negro struggle" from desiring White privilege to building and creating institutions that would solely benefit his race. Following the institution building of Elijah Muhammad, once he separated from his spiritual father, X started his own organizations, the Muslim Mosque, Inc., and the Organization of Afro-American Unity, both in 1964.

Another side of Malcolm, Du Bois, and Madhubuti is a personal parallel. All were fatherless males. Malcolm had to remake himself by himself, borrowing clues from popular culture.[18] His older sister Ella Colllins became his surrogate mother, and later Elijah Muhammad became his spiritual guide and surrogate father. X's relationship with and reverence for Elijah Muhammad are well documented, so I will not revisit that kinship here. However, I want to emphasize how X, like many in the Black community, reassembled a family for himself once he lost his original kinfolk. This type of reassembling comes from the disaster of enslavement when families were deliberately torn apart and members instinctively refashioned new kinship elsewhere. Moreover, X refashioned himself from ideology, which also gave him a sense of masculinity.

W.E.B. Du Bois,' father Alfred disappeared from his life when he was two years old, and later the great sage explained his disappearance through blame of his fair skin and manners anathematic to his mother's family. The complicated human pain of a male losing his father shows up well into Du Bois's advanced age in an interview by a member of the Columbia Oral Project. The Pulitzer Prize winning biographer of Du Bois, David Levering Lewis, writes about this episode: "When a historian from Columbia University's Oral History Project delicately probed the subject the year before Du Bois left for Ghana, reproach gave way to raw indictment, exposing the festering wound inflicted by a father's absence upon a still-tortured son."[19] Du Bois was ninety-two years old. In *Dusk of Dawn, Autobiography*, and *Darkwater*, Du Bois does not speculate about the possibility that his father may have been married before or that he deserted his mother Mary Silvina.

Madhubuti, born in 1942, suffered abandonment by his father when his family moved from Little Rock, Arkansas, to Detroit when he was very young. James Lee deserted the family and Maxine Graves Lee deteriorated among the working poor, trying to raise a young boy and girl. She became increasingly dependent on drugs and alcohol. Working as a janitor, she hauled large cans of trash up and down stairs, and this anguished young Don L. Lee. However, despite living in unspeakable poverty, she encouraged her son to read, beginning with *Black Boy* by Richard Wright, and her son found himself and a future voice in literature. He located through reader-response a sense and idea of what it meant to be Black and male in America. Through Wright's narrative, which gives figurative essence to racism, his emotions assumed clarity and form. In his real world, however, his mother's lifestyle was causing constant disturbance, and at her death, she had a closed casket funeral because of extreme disfiguration. Madhubuti was sixteen years old.

Later when listening to Malcolm X, young Don L. Lee found a model of masculinity and revolutionary thought that stimulated him to build institutions. Madhubuti says, "listening to Malcolm X and deeply reflecting upon the books I was reading, I discovered the uniqueness and importance of culture. I now understood why Africa and African people were marginalized and diminished in the eyes of the world."[20] The examples of the race men that influenced the imagination of Madhubuti also encouraged him to step beyond language and into the realm of business ventures related specifically to the transforming Negro into the American-African or African American. Haki Madhubuti is the only Black Arts poet to found and build institutions that are still vital and prosperous today, and he and his wife Safisha are still building. Madhubuti's enterprises are Third World Press, 1967, The Institute of Positive Education, 1969, The New Concept School, 1972, The Betty Shabazz International Charter School, 1998, The Barbara Ann Sizemore Campus, 2005, and the DuSable Leadership Academy, 2005.

Summary

Great men influenced the maturation of Haki R. Madhubuti to not only write poetry but also to build institutions that solely relate to the positive transformation of Black people. Paul Robeson, W.E.B. Du Bois, Richard Wright, Malcolm X, and Cheikh Anta Diop put forward ideas that captured Madhubuti's imagination. Diop in particular developed a line of thought that is evident in Madhubuti's work and the direction of his life. Diop scientifically discovered the African-ness of the ancient pharaohs and he linguistically illustrated the similarity between African languages and the language of Kemet (Egypt). His findings startled the academic world during the 1940s and 1950s because he proved that Kemet was a part of Africa, not an appendage of Europe or the Middle East.

Diop urged all African scholars to connect their particular history to that of Kemet and to search for commonality within the cultures. Like Du Bois, Diop wanted scholars of African descent to locate continuity in history in order to isolate great successes that could be applied in contemporary times. Diop, like Malcolm X, desired a lived history, not an inactive or an inaccurate one.

In this notion of a living history, Madhubuti thought big about his contribution to the growth of African American advancement. For this reason, he built institutions from the 1960s that remain current and prosperous today. In the next chapter, we look closely at his institution building and how it relates to the oratory of Malcolm X.

SIX

Issues of Memory and Maleness: Malcolm and Madhubuti: Institution Builders and Educators

Malcolm X helped to shape the intellectualism and activism of the 1960s with his prolific interpretation of history, politics, and racism. He took this tripartite perspective and designed an American critique that exposed the textural and underlying reasons for the impoverished, imitative, and inferior positions of American Negroes. Most recognize X's influence on Civil Rights leaders and on the trajectory of the Civil Rights Movement (Asante 1993; Branch 1998: 3–20; Dyson 1995; Harding 1990: 44–46, 85–86, 222–223; Sale 1994). Hardly anyone, however, has studied his permanent effects on poets, literary critics, and contemporary culture. The examination of Haki Madhubuti's institution building and literature begins to fill that void because Madhubuti's imaginative and practical vision reflects the philosophy of Malcolm X.

This study does not concentrate on the dichotomy between Madhubuti and Malcolm X. Rather, it examines the complementary aspects of "twinness" between the two, concepts based upon principles of African philosophy that unite through harmony and balance. The philosopher Marimba Ani in her opus *Yurugu: An African-Centered Critique of European Cultural Thought and Behavior* (1994) scrupulously investigates the cultural contrasts among African, Indian, Oceanic and European peoples, identifying an African inspired return to a non-either/or interconnection. In Eurocentric thinking opposites — black/white, young/old, ugly/pretty — contrast in the negative. In Afrocentric thinking, opposites are often complementary: different but not in opposition to each other, with one privileged over the other. In African thought things are perceived as interrelated and of the same divine source, and this transcends the notion of the isolated self. Ani states that Eurocentric cultural approaches to understanding have objectified all that is not of European descent, and this objectification has devalued African people. To correct this situation, she argues for cultural alternatives that bring forward ancient thinking in order to accelerate empowerment for Africans throughout the Diaspora.

This approach to examining Malcolm X and Haki Madhubuti is unlike Harold Bloom's direction in *The Anxiety of Influence* (1973), where he envisions poetic influence hurting the creative process. He generally argues the Freudian Oedipal tendency to kill off the father in a literary sense to make creative corrections in the misreading of predecessor artists. His assumptions preconceive a patriarchal and Eurocentric body of writing and writers, and their probable anxiety because of the bulk of the past.

In contrast, Malcolm is a Muse to Madhubuti and other Black Arts writers, providing guidance, not anxiety. To study Malcolm from this perspective challenges the regularly repeated notion of him as a tragic hero. For over thirty years, Haki Madhubuti created literature and African-centered enterprises that manifest, vitalize, and restore Malcolm's memory.

This chapter then gives context to the unique and continuous ideology and culture transference that Malcolm through his lectures offered to millions of Negroes including Madhubuti, Larry Neal, and Leroi Jones/Amiri Baraka, architects of Black Arts.

Madhbuti and other Black Arts writers never desired separation from the male archetype and muse Malcolm X. On the contrary, in the oratory and image of Malcolm X, Madhubuti and other males found and fomented a new way of self and race presentation. Malcolm's masculinity and embrace of revolutionaries worldwide generated an intellectual stridency in male poets such as Madhubuti heretofore unknown.

Madhubuti reconstructed core components of Malcolm X's (his intellectual father's) philosophy, thought, and action. By engaging and rearranging Malcolm's dicta, Madhubuti reinvigorated the nationalism and internationalism of Malcolm, making it palpable for the current generation. Once he traced how Malcolm understood theory and phenomena, he decided that through art, institution building, and educational initiatives he would spread a malcolmian cluster of knowledge. Like Malcolm, Madhubuti imposed his will onto America.

A contemporary symbol of the 1960s, he is known today primarily as a poet and essayist, one who assisted in formalizing the Black Arts Movement, the artistic renaissance that fused literature and Black Power. In his twenty-eight books of poetry and essays, from 1966 to 2005, a steadfast purity, a reminder and expansion of Black Power and the 1960s neo-aesthetics remains. With age, his poetics have ripened, as they continue to reflect the focus, intent, and intensity of the 1960s.

Unlike other 1960s poets, Madhubuti decided to create institutions that would provide a foundation for his ideas and those of others functioning in the politics and rhetoric of Malcolm X. Therefore, along with his publications, he founded Third World Press in 1967, and in 1969 he started the Institute of Positive Education. The Institute of Positive Education was initially a Black independent early educational facility. Today, it is the governing board for the Betty Shabazz Charter School, a middle school, and for the New Concept pre-school. These educational facilities are independent of traditional, Western ideology. Instead, the curriculums are African-centered, housing the tenets of Malcolm's desire to reeducate Black people. Madhubuti, a teacher himself, is today a distinguished professor of English at Chicago State University.

However, his beginning was impoverished, painful, tragic, and insecure. Living in poverty in an existentialist environment, he found guidance in Malcolm, his muse, W.E.B. Du Bois, Richard Wright and others that gave him material for self and race reconstruction. Madhubuti made Black Power modern, aiming the abstraction to a living fount of activity through publishing and schools. An individual and collective thinker and practitioner, Madhubuti built enterprises that benefit more people than himself and his family. Forwarding the mythic essence of Malcolm, he promotes Black unification, African-centered reeducation, economic development, culture, history, and responsibility. He promotes Black Power, the mythic essence of Malcolm X.

Black Power and Nationalism: A Historical and Neo-Revolutionary Aesthetic

Black Power is a 1960s term, concept, attitude, and action that ushered in a new phase of political activism for the Negro people, who were quickly becoming a reconfigured "Black." On May 29, 1966, Adam Clayton Powell, then chairman of the Education and Labor Committee, declared in his baccalaureate speech at Howard University that "Civil Rights are man-made and Human Rights are God-made. To demand our God-given rights is to see *black power*— the power to build black institutions of splendid achievement."[1] A week later Stokely Carmichael/Kwame Tourè marched through Greenville, Mississippi, leading the marchers in the call and response chant

"We want black power, We want black power." Prior to the Black Power slogan, chant, and activism along with its fists pounding accompaniment, the traditional Civil Rights organizations such as the Congress for Racial Equality and the Southern Christian Leadership Council favored coalitions and integration with Whites. Black Power on the other hand carried forward 19th century ideology and nationalism that stimulated among others the writer and activist David Walker, the minister and abolitionist Henry Highland Garnet, and the fighter journalist Ida B. Wells. They felt that Blacks had to lead in order to gain respect and to respect themselves they had to lead. Sterling Stuckey in *Slave Culture* (1987) writes that Henry Highland Garnet saw nationalism as a means for achieving freedom in the United States and a means by which Africans might be liberated in a world prejudiced against them.[2] Garnet and David Walker both valued revolt and desired land redistribution. Ida B. Wells, the first American investigative reporter who reinterpreted why Black males were lynched, had a similar attitude. She said: "Although I had been warned repeatedly by my own people that something would happen if I did not cease harping on the lynching of three months before, I had expected that happening to come when I was at home. I had bought a pistol the first thing after Tom Moss was lynched, because I expected some cowardly retaliation from the lynchers. I felt that one had better die fighting against injustice than to die like a dog or a rat in a trap."[3]

Wells' revolutionary words rupture the stereotype of Victorian women, recalling the political activism of Harriet Tubman and the toughness of Maroon women who physically fought along with men to prevent enslavement. Ida B. Wells speaks in the revolutionary language (and action) of self-defense. Since slavery, Black men and women empowered a revolutionary ideology and action, and this spatial realm later penetrated the psychology of Malcolm X. Such consciousness had collectively always already existed.

In the 20th century the essentials of Black Nationalism pervaded the political philosophies of W.E.B. Du Bois, Marcus Garvey, Elijah Muhammad, and Paul Robeson. Du Bois called for "Negro islands" based on African communism.[4] This kind of African communism as defined by Chancellor Williams in *The Destruction of Black Civilizations* (1987) does not relate to Marx and Engels but to a system of democratic principles that Africans adhered to prior to the arrival of Whites.[5] Paul Robeson saw a unity in Black culture that cut across geographic boundaries whereby African people could seek out their common traits in order to expand and unify Black culture. Robeson also considered art an instrument of revolutionary change.[6] This line of reasoning culminated in the 1960s Black Power ideology, art and activism, and soon after it reformed again into Afrocentricity and African-centered thought.

The omnipotence of Black Power traveled internationally. In South Africa, for example, the activist and nationalist Stephen Biko coined this concept and attitude as "Black Consciousness." Art and activism as Paul Robeson noted were not separate issues, and in South Africa they overlap, intertwining into a dance that motions revolutionary fervor. In South Africa during the fight against apartheid, Blacks pounded fists in the Black Power salute and danced the *tsoi tsoi* (pronounced "toy-toy"). This dance blossoming from the energy of warriors accentuates dimensional rhythm, negotiating with and in time. Rhythm goes beyond the five senses, collecting epic (racial) memory, presenting it as now, containing all that ever was and what will be.[7] Dance master and scholar Kariamu Welsh-Asante summarizes critic and author Larry Neal's interpretation of rhythm: "Life and the experiences therein, that which comes into one's life to become experience, is interpreted symbolically, and seen again as the image or representation of Infinite Spirit manifests in one's presence and as one's presence."[8]

In America (and South Africa) the salute of slowly pounding raised fists and the Black Power chant exposes a multi-dimensional rhythm of resistance suggesting politics, art, and Ntu (the Life Force or vital energy). Kariamu Welsh-Asante charts this combination through *Umfundalai*, the "essential" in Kiswahili, writing that it operates in literature, dance, poetry, and the plastic arts. Allowing for individual and collective expression, *Umfundalai*, a school of thought, is both polyrhythmic and multi-layered, the "ethos of the African aesthetic."[9]

Black Power, the polyrhythmic, multi-layered complexity, manifests in dance, salute, and chant and erupts through symbols and group representation. According to Welsh-Asante one cannot evaluate, "appreciate and perpetuate the art form without a knowledge of symbols, history, geography, language and conceptual actions such as time, space and elements."[10]

Over time and space, the idea, image, and action of Black Power have both transformed and remained the same. During the 1960s when this term resurfaced in urban America, it revitalized the call and response participants at political rallies, either to fight segregation in the South or to stop police brutality, segregation, and inequality in the North. Chanting Black Power heightened the potency of rebellion, frightening White America in an old remembered way.

This White fear is similar to the reaction to 19th century Native Americans who chanted, sang, and danced the Ghost Dance. Dance for Native Americans and Africans meant and means more than athletic grace and personal expression. In the ethos of Africans and Native Americans, dance is a ritual mode of expression that can change what happens on earth. For example, the Native American Ghost Dance was performed as a final effort to retaliate against massacre, land theft, and removal to reservations. The native dancers danced to defy annihilation and assimilation. Carl Waldman explains this more fully:

> Many western Indians began practicing the Ghost Dance Religion. Its teachings offered hope to once free and proud peoples now living in poverty and depression on reservations in the midst of their conquerors. But Sioux medicine men — Kicking Bear and Short Bull of the Miniconjou band of Teton Lakota — gave the religion their own interpretation. They claimed that special Ghost Shirts could stop the white man's bullets. White officials became alarmed at the size of Indian gatherings and the renewed Indian militancy. As a result, they banned the Ghost Dance on Sioux reservations. But the Indians continued to hold the forbidden Ceremonies.[11]

Conjoining dance and religion, the forbidden ceremonies "renewed Indian militancy." The Black Power salute and the *tsoi tsoi* reflect and renew the ethos of fomentation. In the metaphysical world of Red and Black peoples, religion and dance link to political action engendering courage, new possibility, reality shift, and a metaphysical and physical merging. With the Ghost Dance, the South African *tsoi tsoi* and the Black Power chant overlapping the secular and the sacred, each ignited transformation. Each individually and collectively configured a symbol of resistance as a thing of beauty, a cultural and survivalist tactic, for as Welsh-Asante writes:

> Spirit, rhythm and creativity are the key criteria in discussing any aesthetic for African people. Spirit, rhythm and creativity derive from epic memory (Welsh-Asante, 1985) or sense of ancestorism (Thompson, 1975) or race memory (Larry Neal, 1972). African people can draw upon a collective aesthetic bank that houses images, symbols, and rhythms based upon history and subsequent mythology.[12]

In African thought, vibrations never end. This is why Africans practice ancestor veneration. With time being eternal, new experiences enter into the rhythm, shifting and maintaining balances and slopes. Collective consciousness culminates changes and combines the new while keeping the primal core.[13] This ontological synthesis emerged in the New World as nationalism once enslaved Africans were forbidden to speak their language and to worship in remembered ways. Yet, as scholars have pointed out, many Africans continued to clandestinely and overtly practice cultural traits now referred to as Africanisms (Conniff 1994; Herskovits 1941, 1990; Holloway 1990; Holloway & Vass 1997; Welsh-Asante 1994).

Thus, the Black Power fists' pounding and chanting that maintained relevancy for Africans in America might be much older than the 1960s. This fist symbol and its chant and dance accompaniment probably traveled the Atlantic Ocean in slave ships.

In New York City in 1996 at the discovery of a burial site of enslaved people, archeologists found a woman in her mid-thirties buried in 111 waist beads. In the video *Slavery's Buried Past* (1996), Dr. Cheryl La Roche of Howard University confirms the significance (and transference) of African culture in the Americas as something extremely important to African people.[14] In linguistics and language, Melville Herskovits in *The Myth of the Negro Past* (1941) was among the earliest pioneers to point out Africanisms in the English language. Cheikh Anta Diop in *The African Origin of Civilization* (1974) compared his Wolof tongue to the language of Pharaonic Egypt (or Kemet, the indigenous term). In *Slavery's Buried Past*, which included the New York burial, archeologists found another gravesite in James River, Virginia, where the enslaved were buried with tobacco pipes under the arms and beads around a child's neck. However, as it relates to Black Power, we find the symbol at the Hermitage, the house in Nashville, Tennessee, that President Andrew Jackson built.

Jackson, enslaving about one hundred and forty people, may have been unaware of the esoteric practices of those he held in bondage. Beneath the homes of Jackson's enslaved people, a century later, archeologists found charms or "hands" (the generic term) contoured like fists. They are startling artifacts, with vitality emanating from each one. The scientists found three different styles of encircled, clenched fists carved from pewter. Dr. Larry McKee, director of archeology for the Hermitage, said that he had no idea what the fist represented. However, he did know that it indicated the private world of the enslaved people and that it contained a kind of "power" to perhaps ward off evil or attract something to the wearer.

It is possible that the "hand," the clenched fist, represented a symbol of Black potency that African people utilized long before Whites entered or invaded the African continent. A clenched fist might relate to Ogun, a Ntr (god) of protection and war in the Yoruba tradition who is also a Black smith forging iron. Similarly, a clenched fist, in Kemetic (Egyptian) symbols "md-ntr" (pronounced "medu-neter") or sacred symbols (hieroglyphs) means to grasp, to seize, to capture, and to plunder. Mentu, a symbol of war and protection, one of the solar Ntru (gods), grasps a scepter in his right hand and grips an ankh in his left. The ankh is a religious symbol of life resembling a cross, with a circular shape on top. The scepter suggests authority. The md-ntr symbol of this hawk-headed man wearing a solar disk holding the scepter and the ankh highlights each fist, reflecting the meaning of "to grasp."[15] However, Mentu may not solely be a war symbol. This image also reflects the genius Imhotep, a healer and scientist whose methods set standards for ancient Kemet over two thousand years ago. Imhotep appears on "the wall of the chamber at Deir-el-Bahari ... carrying a scepter in one hand and an ankh in the other. The inscription reads, 'I have given you life combined with health and protection. I am the protector.'"[16]

When Stokely Carmichael/Kwame Touré clenched his fist and shouted "Black Power" in call and response, he reproduced a cultural and linguistic symbol in rhythm that exposed ancient African religion and thought, and his present, spatial continuum, his now. In his grasp, the fist, he rendered individual and collective synthesis, gathering a spiritual momentum for future political action. Carmichael/Touré's action called forward epic memory, one of the seven senses of Welsh-Asante's Nzuri model, a traditional response to the African ethos.[17] Spirituality, an aspect of epic memory, feeds on experience, calling upon the ancestors and divine metaphysical forces to allow the energy to flow into the artist or activist. Epic memory is embedded in the representation, Carmichael/Touré's fist.

When Malcolm X explained in oratory the significance of Black people studying indigenous Black history, he stimulated epic memory, which Haki Madhubuti houses in educational and publishing institutions and in his poetry from the 1960s to the present. Critics of Madhubuti condemn his African-centered Black Arts poetry because of his (and other writers') non-emphasis on class and White influence. For example, Tony Bolden (2004) writes the following about Madhubuti: "[H]is quest for a pure, black form undercuts the resistive thrust posed by the Black Arts Movement because it obscures the creolization of African American culture, which, in turn, challenges hegemonic concepts inscribed in such terms as 'American' and 'literature.'"[18] He also faults Madhubuti for not establishing a formal relationship to American White authors and poetry. And still later he decides that "Madhubuti's inability to understand racism as a component of an international class struggle leads him to the construction of a hierarchy not unlike that which he purports to raze."[19]

Quite troubling is Bolden's equalizing Madhubuti with racists. Madhubuti wrote against the centuries of Western aesthetics that mocked and made minimal Negro aesthetics and people. Marxist analysis is an important and singular way to interpret and investigate literary depth. However, critics overlooking the crucible of race when investigating Black authors commit a racial suicide that omits and dismisses the poison of racism and its effect on the psyche of American Blacks. Bolden overlooks the reality of and purpose for Black Arts poetry. Black Arts poetry was an art and act of war.

Black Arts poetry was aimed to defy White racist hegemony and to reverse self-defeating trends in the behavior of Negroes. Writing the art of war, the Black Arts poets and Madhubuti would never interconnect with "Anglo-Americans" and "creolization." Such inclusions lack logic when one fights an enemy. War is ugly. Metaphorically, it murders harmful ideas. Black Arts poets fought against integration. They wrote fighting words to eradicate White superiority. A Black and White "creolization" at that time would never yield what the poets desired, an African and African American aesthetic along with cultural, political, and economic (if possible) independence.

With Malcolm the muse of Black Arts poets, they sought to develop a neo-African identity. As in all Black Nationalism, the artists and practitioners were attempting to locate the particulars of Paul Robeson's and later Molefi Asante's paradigm. They were attempting to put together a theory and direction that assisted in the unification of African peoples in order to elevate said peoples towards self- and race-discovery, an importance dismissed since enslavement and colonization. To accomplish such ends, Black Arts poets including Madhubuti disassociated mentally and physically from the conquerors of Blacks. This disassociation occurred in a variety of venues: education, aesthetics, art, literature, and internationalism.

When Adam Clayton Powell explicated the difference between civil and human rights, he repeated a key Malcolm X declaration. Malcolm had publicly voiced the dichotomy between civil and human rights since 1964, confining "civil rights" to the United States, and his preference for "human rights" as those instituted in global struggles against oppression and tyranny. Always an internationalist, X discussed global issues even during his days studying under and representing Elijah Muhammad, head of the Nation of Islam. In oratory, X regularly demonstrated how "the so-called Negro" fits on the world stage of history, internationalizing the struggle of American Blacks. A century earlier, Frederick Douglass and Ida. B. Wells traveled abroad to gain support for the fight against legal human bondage in America. Malcolm X, in a 1964 interview, presents the "Negro" as a case study for international politics, saying:

> One of the organizations which we've now formed, the Organization of Afro-American Unity, has reached the conclusion, after a careful analysis of the problem, that approaching our problem just on the level of civil rights and keeping it within the jurisdiction of the United States will not bring a solution. It's not a Negro problem or an American problem any longer. It's a world problem, it's a human problem. And so we're striving to lift it from the level of civil rights to the level of human rights. And at that level it's international. We can bring it into the United Nations.[20]

Adam Clayton Powell learned from Malcolm X. Powell's definition of "black power" in his address cited earlier contained the X-factor distinction between civil and human rights. This borrowing and extending represents the mutual respect between Powell and X. Both men appeared at rallies together and regularly Powell invited X to speak at Abyssinian Baptist Church. Even in personal aesthetics they have much in common: both are tall, fair skinned, forthright, Black Nationalist ministers. Each carried the challenges and joys of Black people as emotional and intellectual centers of existence. Wanting to be replicated and understood, they strove to make conscious and accessible the process of speaking well, and Haki Madhubuti deliberately embraced this realm. With him fitting the above external descriptions, more than likely, the physical initially attracted him followed immediately by ideological wealth and progressive action. Powell, Malcolm, and Madhubuti recognized their inseparability from the realities of the Negro. In the words of W.E.B. Du Bois, they were race men.

However, for Madhubuti, Malcolm X was more than his muse, guide, and indirect teacher. In the words of Ossie Davis, who wrote X's eulogy, Malcolm X was Madhubuti's manhood. The image of Malcolm gave him and other males an archetype to challenge and in their thinking to destroy (and add to) the regular Negro male images in America, the brute, the coward, and the comic. Malcolm, as Madhubuti's muse, opened up his mind and his mouth.

The Muse

In the Greek tradition, Mnemosyne, the goddess of memory, is the mother of the Muses. Zeus is the father of the nine daughters who guide the arts and sciences, the Muses. A Muse is a guiding spirit, a source of inspiration, and a poet. The term comes from the Latin *Mūsa* and from the Greek Moûsa. Its derivative "men" has other important offshoots: mind, mental, mention, automatic, memento, comment, reminiscent, monitor, monster, monument, demonstrate, premonition, summon, mosaic, museum, music.[21]

Major male writers of the Black Arts Movement, Larry Neal, Amiri Baraka, and Haki Madhubuti, insist that Malcolm summons their exegeses. Such claims make Malcolm the music in the monster of "Black Arts," reminiscent of ancient memory that affected and affects Black music and poetry. Malcolm is a mosaic and a museum that Black intellectuals visit often for premonitions and commentary. Molefi Asante, the father of graduate studies in African, African American, and Africana disciplines, also makes this claim.

The people in ancient Kemet had a cycle of nine deities referred to as the Ennead. Sometimes this cycle represented the entire Kemetic pantheon and at other times the deities of particular locales. With the exception of (A)tum-Ra, the others were heterosexual pairs: Shu and Tefnut, their children (S)Geb and Nut, and their grandchildren Osiris (Asr) (Wasiri) and Isis (Ast) (Assata), Set and Nephthys. This pantheon encompasses at least ten thousand years before the Christian era.

Shu and Tefnut represent dry and moist air. Shu often assimilates to the sun god. He is air intervening at the moment of creation. Shu is also known as the god of light.[22] For Amiri Baraka, Haki Madhubuti, and Larry Neal, Malcolm the muse provided a guiding light in varying ways. Neal wrote poems to Malcolm and they demonstrate the complexity of X's psychological effect, his light, particularly for Black males. He awakened them. In "Morning Raga for Malcolm" we hear an awakening:

> O Allah receive him, a morning god
> bursting springily in ascendant
> colors of the sun — a crescent sword slices
> the shrill morning raga; ...
> the voice tears at blood
> streaked faces. Dispossessed eyes flash at
> the truth brilliantly black.[23]

Neal's "brilliantly black" suggests the "black" transformation of the 1960s spearheaded by Malcolm X and the Muslims. This transformational "Black" became ethical, revolutionary, African-centered, an entity multiple yet unified. The "dispossessed eyes" are synecdoche, recalling Ralph Ellison's projection of the "dispossessed" as a metonym in *Invisible Man* (1952). Ellison's "dispossessed" were the working class Blacks, portrayed as pawns for the communists in Harlem during the 1930s. X inverted the Western traditional use of "black" as evil, sinister, and ugly to a site of aesthetic beauty that encouraged an entirely new cultural mythos and behavior among those becoming African American. Elijah Muhammad's premonition (that became Malcolm's) that "black" was synonymous with "beautiful" happened exponentially because of Malcolm's oratory, his ability to speak accessibly and well. This new site of aesthetic beauty, "black," becomes a symbol in the transforming lexicon of vernacular in the 1960s. Because it is a social and biological construct, "black" measured through *umfundalai*, is an extensive, immeasurable core component of African-centered thought and behavior. For, this 1960s "black" upset and inverted the power of "white," providing the *ntu* for the poets to individually and collectively categorize themselves as other than Negro. In the above poem, Neal refers to Malcolm as "a morning god" because for him and thousands more Malcolm was the man/priest/god who resurrected the "necro," the corpse, the "negro." During the Harlem Renaissance, Langston Hughes penned the beauty of "black"; however, in the 1960s, Malcolm X compounded the black-is-beautiful aesthetic by regenerating it with political activism, African and African American culture, and nationalism.

"Morning Raga" is the second poem where Neal deifies Malcolm because of the profound transference of new ideas, thoughts, and insights that X instructed his people to adopt, halting negative assimilation ingrained since Reconstruction. Malcolm X caused Christians to become either Muslim, agnostic, or truth seekers. A monster to his enemies—Black and White—Malcolm offered an alternative to Christianity, calling it the enslavers' religion. Ripping through W.E.B. Du Bois's collective veil, X spoke to destroy the concept of double consciousness.

In addition to Neal perceiving X in a paranormal light, Amiri Baraka adapted and practiced Malcolm X's stridency. For example, he believed that he was imitating Malcolm when he insulted federal officials who funded his New York Black Arts project during the 1960s. He refused his funding sources access to his building. Baraka writes: "There was ... a positive overall effect of the Black Arts concept that still remains. We showed that we had heard and understood Malcolm and that we were trying to create an art that would be a weapon in the Black Liberation Movement."[24]

Creating a militaristic art that would reconfigure Blacks and repel Whites was the first stage of the poetic war with words against the dominant society. Prior to the 1960s, no Blacks signified on, or played the dozens with White people forthrightly. Instead, they recited seculars and toasts normally among themselves. X, however, spoke Elijah Muhammad's ideology and theology before the media, and his honesty and forthrightness caused Black male onlookers to adopt his new swagger in manner and discourse. This is the attitude that Amiri Baraka adopted, failing to realize immediately the independence of X's funding source. Malcolm X was not subservient to Whites because they did not employ him. Elijah Muhammad and the Nation of Islam allowed Malcolm X a freedom that few Black males ever achieve. Baraka on the other hand operated a program funded by the Whites he had insulted. Nevertheless, he stepped inside of a preconceived image located within Malcolm's daring monologues, and in general he manifested three important tributes to the recreation of the Negro: new thoughts, courage, and Black Power art. This new art was symbolically and literally a tight, clenched fist, pounding *ntu* (life force) vibrating with memory, an art reflecting an ancient memento.

John Henrik Clarke calls Malcolm's oratorical legacy a "philosophy of liberation,"[25] and it is this philosophy that Haki Madhubuti adopted in art and in institution building.

The X-Factor Influence on Madhubuti's Institutions

Malcolm's personal and metaphysical association with Africa differed from that of his spiritual teacher and guide, the Honorable Elijah Muhammad. Malcolm's musings on and projection of Africa also contrast with that of Alexander Crummell, the 19th century Episcopalian priest who lived and practiced ministry in Sierra Leone. Unlike Muhammad and Crummell, Malcolm like an imaginative architect projected Africa as a building block, a pyramid, and savior for Blacks. He projected Africa like David Walker in *The Appeal* (1829). Walker's small book encouraged Black people, enslaved and free, to resist oppression by taking up arms against enslavers. As well, Walker presented Africa and Egypt as one, identifying the unity within that relationship and how enslaved Blacks were a part of that ancient legacy. Linking human chattel to greatness, he intended to inspire. Similarly, Malcolm presented Africa to American Blacks.

In his final organization, the Organization of Afro-American Unity (OAAU), based on the Organization of African Unity, he illustrated his desire to transform American Blacks into a viable nation. Through the OAAU, Malcolm formulated a paradigm of self-reliance in order to stop Black people from depending solely on White leadership and economics. In the following, he makes that evident:

> [The OAAU is] responsible only to the Afro-American people and community and will function only with their support, both financially and numerically. We believe that our communities must be the sources of their own strength politically, economically, intellectually and culturally in the struggle for human rights and dignity.[26]

Haki Madhubuti was not an OAAU member, but he read about and listened to the oratory of X, and like many young people at that time, he digested X's philosophy. Unlike others, though, he rearranged his public and private life in order to institutionalize his version of X's legacy, memory, and philosophy of liberation. All of his poetry and essays speak to the subjects that pertain directly and unabashedly to African American people. For example, in *Don't Cry Scream* (1969), which sold half a million copies, he writes, "Blackpoetry moves to define & legitimize blackpeople's reality

that which is real to us" (15). For Madhubuti what is "real" is the relevancy of Black people demonstrating responsibility for and support of one another, and this message appears in his poetry, prose, and poetry recitations. By grounding his ideas in African-centered publishing and education enterprises, for over thirty years Madhubuti expanded his conception of "real" to impact current and future generations. This longevity is unique in Black and White America.

Madhubuti's enterprises accomplish what X explains as Black communities experiencing "their own strength politically, economically, intellectually, and culturally." Third World Press, the Institute of Positive Education, and the Gwendolyn Brooks Center for Black Literature and Creative Writing all exhibit a contemporary Black Power. As Adam Clayton Powell articulated during his "now" time, they are "institutions of splendid achievement." Powell spoke and predicted Madhubuti's future.

The following succinct review of Madhubuti's establishments demonstrates the X factor influence on the poet's practical vision.

Two years after the assassination of Malcolm X, Haki Madhubuti, then Don L. Lee, founded Third World Press (TWP) with the assistance of Carolyn Rodgers and Johari Amini on September 20, 1967. In his small basement apartment near 63rd and Ada Streets on the South Side of Chicago, Madhubuti started TWP with a used mimeograph machine and $400.00 from a poetry reading.[27] The founding of TWP inaugurated and grounded Black Power, 1960s activism and Madhubuti's Black Arts poetry and essays from *Think Black* (1966) to *Run Toward Fear* (2004) and *YellowBlack* (2005). As an artist and activist, Madhubuti refused to compromise his artistry; therefore, he never sought recognition and publication from White publishing houses. He had already mentally separated from White people in power, which Malcolm and the NOI had preached to the Negro. Before beginning TWP, Madhubuti, selling his poetry from coast to coast, on his own, had established a substantial following. In fact, mainstream presses approached him with offers that he refused once deciding to enact the 1960s code of conduct that demanded Black autonomy.[28]

In the early years, Third World Press solely published poetry, including Madhubuti's *Think Black* (1967) and *Black Pride* (1968), Johari Amini's *Black Essence* (1968), and Sterling Plumpp's *Portable Souls* (1968). In the 1970s and 1980s, the press varied its genres, publishing autobiography, fiction, nonfiction, children's literature, psychology, history, inspiration, politics, and culture. Black intellectuals Chancellor Williams, John Henrik Clarke, Amiri Baraka, Woody King, Hoyt W. Fuller, Ruby Dee, Mari Evans, Nathan Hare, and Frances Cress Welsing found a home at TWP. Today

Derrick Bell, Vivian Gordon, Lily Golden, Fred L. Hord, Kalamu ya Salaam, Useni E. Perkins, George Kent, Keorapetse Kegositsile, Geneva Smitherman, Asa G. Hilliard, and Acklyn Lynch join the list of authors. The press's bestsellers include *The Isis Papers: The Keys to the Colors*, by Frances Cress Welsing; *The Destruction of Black Civilization: Great Issues of a Race from 4500 BC to 2000 AD*, by Chancellor Williams; *Wise, Why's, Y's*, by Amiri Baraka; *Blacks*, by Gwendolyn Brooks; *Afrolantic Legacies*, by Derrick Bell; and *Black Men, Single Obsolete, Dangerous?*, by Haki R. Madhubuti. Each sold 50,000 or more copies.

In spite of his success as author and publisher, Madhubuti has never accepted royalty payments from his publications. Rather, he recycles his royalties back to the press, supporting his family (and the firm) with salaries from teaching positions beginning at Howard University in 1970 and currently at Chicago State.

Not surprisingly, the press's thirty-eight years have been unstable and sometimes tragic. For example, Black banks failed to support Madhubuti's efforts, placing him on the brink of failure at least five times. Yet, his determination, sacrifice, and effort never desisted and were noticed by a legend in American literature. Gwendolyn Brooks (1917–2002), poet laureate of Illinois and the first Black to receive a Pulitzer for poetry, generously switched to TWP from a mainstream publishing house, boosting the operation during the 1970s. Gwendolyn Brooks and Haki Madhubuti developed a nonbiological kinship. She became godmother to the motherless Don L. Lee, who lost his biological mother when he was sixteen years old.

Following the model of the defunct Broadside Press, founded by Dudley Randall in 1965, Third World Press today stands as a beacon of Black independence. According to Paul Coates, creator of Black Classic Press in Baltimore, TWP "is without precedent and one of the most significant things to emerge out of the Black Arts Movement. For him [Madhubuti] to provide an outlet for black thinkers and a center where those black writers could come together ... [is] as significant as Motown."[29]

Sixty percent of TWP's audience is African American. The texts sell nationally and internationally to bookstores, booksellers, chains, superstores, educational institutions, academic bookstores, and libraries.

Still located on Chicago's South Side, TWP, now a one million dollar facility, employs twelve people. Housed in a working-class neighborhood in a former Catholic school and church, it is more than an African-centered publishing institution. In its décor, it also promotes Afrocentricity. Inside, the hallways are lined with wooden bookshelves, and in large, welcoming rooms is African American art: paintings and hand carved sculptures and framed prints celebrate Paul Robeson, John Coltrane, W.E.B. Du Bois,

Gwendolyn Brooks, and Malcolm X. In fact, an enormous painting of Malcolm X sits in Madhubuti's expansive office. TWP is a tribute to and tributary from Malcolm X, who says in "The Ballot or the Bullet":

> Our people have to be made to see that any time you take your dollar out of your community and spend it in a community where you don't live, the community where you live will get poorer and poorer, and the community where you spend your money will get richer and richer.... If we own the stores, if we operate the businesses, if we try and establish some industry in our own community, then we're developing to the position where we are creating employment for our own kind.[30]

The conception and rigorous formation of Third World Press harnesses X's above vision about community control of businesses. This is why Madhubuti developed the fortitude to maintain his course despite heart wrenching obstacles designed for his failure. Malcolm's notion of "reeducation" affected him. This is why he sought the assistance of Black banks, that disappointed him, and on the other hand, this is why Gwendolyn Brooks offered her status and prestige to assist a small, Black, publishing house. Madhubuti had overwhelmed her with the fire of Malcolm, Black Power, and Black Arts. She learned from him that Black people must build and control businesses within their own geographic space. Third World Press's mission then and now is to bring before "the reading public, books that encourage creativity, inspire intellect, engender pride and spur engaged and informed critical debate over issues of race, culture, politics, and social health."[31]

Malcolm earlier defined nationalism and issues of race at a press conference on March 12, 1964, when he founded the Muslim Mosque Inc. (MMI), declaring his separation from the Nation of Islam. The MMI combined religious and political activism designed to rid the Black community of vices, such as drug addiction and drug selling. This organization would allow Malcolm X to enter the human rights struggle on his own terms. The MMI neutralized the religious controlling theme of the Nation of Islam by welcoming all Blacks, despite religious affiliation.[32]

George Breitman, editor of *Malcolm X Speaks* and other books containing X's oratory, summarizes X's MMI stage and thinking as transitional. He suggests that Malcolm's Black Nationalist phase does not represent all "the conclusions he reached before his death" (20). He refers primarily to the after-image of Malcolm: his return from Mecca and its multiple meanings, primarily his re-envisioning of Whites. Historian and scholar John Henrik Clarke interprets X's self-critique and self-revision that occurred after his trip to Mecca. Clarke writes:

When he returned home from his trip he was no longer opposed to progressive whites uniting with revolutionary blacks, as his enemies would suggest. But to Malcolm, and correctly so, the role of the white progressive was not in black organizations but in white organizations in white communities convincing and converting the unconverted to the black cause.... He was convinced that there could be no workers' solidarity until there was racial solidarity.[33]

Accordingly, John Henrik Clarke, a scholar and personal friend to Malcolm, observes that X's evolving argument and vision never left the center of African American consciousness. Welsh-Asante might say that it never left epic memory. It never left the creativity, rhythm and spirit of David Walker. It is in that appeal that he forged ahead as one of the greatest freedom fighters and orators for and of Black people. It is in that spatial realm and conception of racial analysis that Haki Madhubuti continues to dwell and build upon X's urge to control businesses within the Black community.

Malcolm X attempted to "wake up" Black people to a broader and more valid history that existed before slavery and subservience to global White supremacy. In many of his speeches, he interspersed African-centered history and politics, directly teaching his listeners the transforming power of gaining knowledge. His final lectures in Harlem prior to his murder were actually lessons in Black history, because Malcolm believed that

> When you deal with the past, you're dealing with history.... When you know the origin you know the cause. And if you don't know the cause, you don't know the reasons, you're just cut off, you're left standing in midair.... Now if we don't go into the past and find out how we got this way, we will think that we were always this way. And if you think that you were always in the condition that you're in right now, it's impossible for you to have too much confidence in yourself, you become worthless, almost nothing.[34]

To dissuade young Black people from lacking confidence, becoming "worthless, almost nothing," Haki and Safisha Madhubuti created the New Concept Development Center and its governing board, the Institute of Positive Education, in 1969. Begun in an abandoned storefront on Ellis Street, the New Concept Development Center and the Institute of Positive Education now sits in a separate wing of the current Third World Press location. Since the 1960s, New Concept and the Institute sponsored activities that fostered African-centered learning for youngsters and adults. Since 1972, the Institute serves as the legal entity for the operation of the New Concept School, and it leases space to the Betty Shabazz International Charter School founded by the Madhubutis in 1998.

New Concept is one of only three such schools in the United States dating back at least twenty years. Haki Madhubuti explains the philosophy of his educational facilities this way: "We're not talking about words on paper but creating a world in which children are being anchored properly. I see our mission as nothing less than providing the necessary foundation for a child to deal with the world from a secure and self-aware position."[35]

Safisha Madhubuti for sixteen years served as a teacher and principal at New Concept before leaving to finish her PhD at the University of Chicago. Today, she teaches at the University of Chicago in the School of Education at Northwestern under the name of Carol Lee. In an interview, she said: "Students who graduated from New Concept have grown to be lovers of Black people and contributors to the world. They are well mannered, not into gangs, not into drugs."[36]

New Concept once had enrollments of about one hundred fifty students whose parents were doctors, lawyers, plumbers, secretaries, and welfare recipients. Some parents volunteered in lieu of paying the $3000.00 annual tuition. Most of the parents, however, are public school teachers. Safisha Madhubuti provides insight into why so many public school teachers send their children to New Concept, saying, "The average dropout rate in the Chicago public schools is around 50 percent. There are high schools in Chicago where the dropout rate is 75 percent. I personally cannot name a single child who attended New Concept for even a year who did not go on to graduate high school. Not one."[37]

Mornings at New Concept start with the "unity circle," just before 9 a.m. The children and the staff gather around a large white circle painted on the gymnasium floor. The children recite a Black National pledge developed by the Council of Independent Black Institutions. In call and response the teacher begins "We are African people." The children respond with "We are African People. Struggling for national liberation. We are preparing leaders and workers to bring about a positive change for our people. We stress the development of our bodies, minds, souls, and consciousness. Our commitment is to self-determination, self-defense, and self respect for our race. We extend the right hand out for the fruition of Black power, for the triumph of Black nationhood. I pledge to my African nation to the building of a better people and a better world, my total devotion, my total resources, and my total power of my mortal life."

New Concept and the Betty Shabazz International Charter School aim to teach Black children a narrative and art populated by African and African American heroes, African rituals, fables, and values. The art on the walls expresses the aesthetics of African and African American people, as well as inspirational quotes from Black luminaries. On the landings between floors, the space is decorated with African prints, tables, and chairs, and educational passages printed large enough for display. A Zora Neale Hurston quote is on one landing, and on another, an African mathematical system. This use of space invites visitors and perhaps teachers to rest and relax with African and African American wisdom. The classroom windows are decorated with colorful *kente* prints, representative of African cultures. For, as Welsh-Asante writes, "African aesthetics can be expected to utilize and highlight *Kente, Adinkra, and Adire* rather than Scottish plaid and herring-bone designs.... Aesthetics can be descriptive in the context of history."[38]

At New Concept and Betty Shabazz, along with rows of lockers, children's projects such as a depiction of the solar system hang proudly along the walls. At recess, the children sometimes play a game called the Underground Railroad, where girls clamor to be Harriet Tubman. The principal, Dr. Elaine Mosley, says that the children learn Spanish and Swahili, and the teachers are referred to as Mama and Baba, mother and father in Swahili.[39] This allows the students a sense of non-biological family as it reinforces the instructors' commitment to familial values. This is also a representation of the African extended family. New Concept now has four teachers and the Betty Shabazz International School has nineteen teachers and eleven classes. Ann Ward, a teacher at Shabazz, says that the children learn art, music, music theory, science, reading, writing, math, social studies, and history.[40] When she was a student, Safisha Madhubuti might have thought this impossible had she listened to a guidance counselor.

Safisha Madhubuti was an honor student. Yet, a guidance counselor told her that Black children had limited ability, that graduate school and college level teaching were beyond their reach. This spurred Safisha's first impulse to start New Concept. When she met her husband at a poetry reading in 1968, she was teaching at a school known later as Kennedy-King College. She was twenty-three and he was twenty-six. Discovering that Black students needed assistance in learning prior to college, she later convinced her husband of the necessity to build an African-centered preschool.

The team began teaching Saturday classes where they instructed children from two to twelve. At the urging of parents by 1974, the school offered a full-time program from preschool to third grade. Expanding each decade, the school moved to its current location in 1991. Haki Madhubuti remains the main benefactor with profits from Third World Press supporting the Institute of Positive Education.

In a public speech at the Gwendolyn Brooks Center for Black Literature and Creative Writing, Madhubuti recalls many of his tribulations as he struggled to maintain all of his enterprises. He recounts sending Safisha and the children to her parents' home when he lacked capital to support his family, Third World Press, and the Institute of Positive Education. In private, he discusses his agony when his Black bookstores failed. Yet, he never wavered during the dog years of struggle and he proudly admits that he never missed a payroll in all the operating years of the Institute and the Press.

Getting along with diverse people is not a problem for graduates of the Institute of Positive Education because the students know and understand history and identity. They believe that not knowing an African-centered history is the impulse for anger. In the Institute's curriculum, Africa is the starting point, but not the closing one. Students also learn about the Chinese, Mayans, Native Americans, and Europeans. Safisha Madhubuti says, "[W]e teach about African values and what is useful today — critical thinking. We are realistic about how the world operates."[41] In this response, Safisha counters an important point that Malcolm X made when he said: "[B]y keeping us completely cut off from our past, it is easy for the man who has power over us to make us willing to stay at this level because we will feel that we were always at this level, a low level. That's why I say it is so important for you and me to spend time today learning something about the past so that we can better understand the present, analyze it, and then do something about it."[42]

The Institute of Positive Education provides the space for not only New Concept and the Betty Shabazz Schools, but also for programs with an African-centered purpose. It houses before- and after-school functions for students, and the Mary McLeod Bethune Teachers Training Center, headed by Safisha Madhubuti.

In 1990, Haki Madhubuti started another educational enterprise. With the assistance of the president of Chicago State University and the board of trustees, Haki Madhubuti started the Gwendolyn Brooks Center for Black Literature and Creative Writing at Chicago State University. Madhubuti labored to open this center in order to respond to the critical need to recognize and preserve the literary achievements of Gwendolyn Brooks, the first Black poet to receive the Pulitzer (in 1950 for *Annie Allen*). By starting the center while she lived, he honored his spiritual and cultural mother, and ensured her legacy.

The Gwendolyn Brooks Center for Black Literature and Creative Writing sponsors an annual literary, historical, and cultural conference that researches and disseminates information on noteworthy Black writers, especially Brooks. The Center's purpose is to strengthen the humanities and promote the study of Black writers locally, regionally, nationally, and internationally. Since 1991, it hosts a broad selection of programs to encourage community participation, foster literacy, and broaden access to the arts and culture. It hosts a Black history month film festival, a women's history month lecture series, a Gwendolyn Brooks readers' circle, a national poetry festival, poetry readings and workshops, and literary competitions for emerging writers, and it publishes *WARPLAND: A Journal of Black Literature and Ideas*.

These are three[43] of the institutions that Haki Madhubuti built, and they encompass creativity, spirit, and rhythm symbolic in a 1960s tight clenched fist — thus, emerging from an energy that vivifies his vision, purpose, and X-factor influence.

Summary

Malcolm X developed an American critique exposing the reasons for the inferior status of Negroes during the 1960s. Haki Madhubuti built institutions in publishing and education that house Malcolm X's philosophy of liberation. X is a representative of Black Power, replicated in the ethos, poetry, and essays of Haki Madhubuti. Black Power is also a creative and spiritual rhythm. It is a dance in South Africa, the *tsoi tsoi*, and in America and South Africa it is a chant with a fist-pounding accompaniment. To analyze this phenomenon, Welsh-Asante's school of thought, called *Umfundalai*, is most useful because it includes concepts of the African and African American experience. The Black Power chant and dance is symbolized in artifacts from enslaved people found in gravesites in 1996 in New York City and in Tennessee. This suggests that the Black Power emblem and behavior are much older than the 1960s, when Stokely Carmichael (Kwame Touré) popularized the symbol. The Black Power symbol might possibly have begun in ancient Africa.

X preached about the importance of studying Black history as he internationalized the "Negro" struggle with his preference for "human" rights instead of "civil" rights. With human rights, he placed the Negroes' struggle on the world stage. X's image of Africa and thinking are replicas of David Walker's 19th century nationalism. Madhubuti's enterprises, Third World Press, the Institute of Positive Education and the New Concept School, and the Gwendolyn Brooks Center for Black Literature and Creative writing, all exhibit an African-centered foundation and perspective. Gwendolyn Brooks saved Third World Press when Black banks failed Madhubuti. She is the first Black to receive a Pulitzer for poetry, and she became Madhubuti's godmother, a tradition in Black communities and culture. When listening to X and reading literature by Black males, he found self-definition and a route to manhood. Amiri Baraka and Larry Neal, other major writers of the 1960s Black Arts Movement, say similar things.

Third World Press stands as a beacon for other presses. Today it is located in a million-dollar facility and it employs twelve people. As X urged, Madhubuti's businesses remain in working class Black communities.

In part, because X preached that the Negro can become almost "worthless, almost nothing" when not knowing African history prior to American enslavement, Madhubuti and his wife Safisha started educational institutions. They started the Institute of Positive Education and the New Concept Development Center in 1969 and the Betty Shabazz International Charter School in 1998. New Concept is one of three such schools dating back more than twenty years. Safisha Madhubuti served as principle for 16 years, and she reports that none of the children dropped out of high school. All finished high school in a city, Chicago, Illinois, where the drop out rate among Blacks is as high as 75 percent. At New Concept and Betty Shabazz the children learn Swahili and Spanish and they learn about Africa as a starting point, not an ending one. They also study the Chinese, Mayan, and Native American cultures and histories, along with the dominant culture's discourse. As X said, learning about the past helps people analyze the present in order to make constructive changes.

The next chapter presents a comparative analysis of Malcolm X's rhetoric with a closer examination of the Institute of Positive Education and the personal and public relationship of Haki and Safisha Madhubuti.

SEVEN

Malcolm and Haki and Safisha Madhubuti on African-Centered Education and Africa in the Imagination

Establishing independent Black schools demonstrates how Haki and Safisha Madhubuti precisely grounded Malcolm X's major idea about educating Black children in Black schools. Such institutions are not solely based on race, but are those that incorporate an African-centered curriculum. This marks the difference between developing a school segregated for Blacks and one that rejoins American Blacks to the culture, history, science, and spirituality of Africa. The New Concept and the Betty Shabazz International Charter Schools under the hegemony of the Institute of Positive Education have successfully put together a global and national curriculum that amplifies the relationship that students have to Africa. This chapter highlights Madhubuti's educational initiatives as well as the influence of his wife and partner Safisha in beginning and maintaining these endeavors. Together this team manifests a complementary gender difference, not gender opposition. She is an extension of his "twin-ness" to Malcolm X. Twin-ness is a traditional African concept that relates to appositional complementarity, explored in earlier chapters. For, as philosopher and anthropologist Marimba Ani writes in her tome *Yurugu* (1994), "In the African and Eastern conceptions, harmony is achieved through the balance of complementary forces, and it is indeed impossible to have a functioning whole *without* harmonious interaction and the existence of balancing pairs."[1] In viewing the Diaspora and its relationship to the continent of Africa, the Madhubutis are a balanced pair, having similar visions, rooted in the ideology of Malcolm X.

When Haki and Safisha Madhubuti founded the New Concept Development Center and the Institute of Positive Education in 1969, each agreed that the children should learn Swahili, fostering globalization skills along with a relationship to Africa. Deciding that language must be a significant part of the curriculum, they manifested Malcolm X's advice to his listeners when he said:

> We must revamp our entire thinking and redirect our learning trends so that we can put forth a confident identity and wipe out the false image built up by an oppressive society. We can build a foundation for liberating our minds by studying the different philosophies and psychologies of others. Provisions are being made for the study of languages of Eastern origin such as Swahili, Hausa, and Arabic. Such studies will give us, as Afro-Americans, a direct access to ideas and history of our ancestors, as well as histories of mankind at large.[2]

Urging the Negro to go beyond American boundaries, Malcolm X privileges African language instruction. Also, reconfiguring the English language, he substitutes "Afro-American" for Negro, formulating a racial classification that connects to Africa. Malcolm X does not perceive the African as the savage other. Rather, he embraces the concept of the other in opposition to Western thought, where the unfamiliar and the different, the "other," is inferior and repulsive. Malcolm interjects no distance or difference between himself, as a representative of Black America, and the African, desiring entry into the multiple systems of thought and ethnic splits on the continent. Involved in making provisions for instruction in several language variations, X speaks into power a school and new school of thought. Returning the Negro to Africa (by way of language), Malcolm qualifies the importance of history. Similarly, Molefi Asante (1993) writes: "The past is alive only to the degree that we capture it in our own depths. History allows us access to the living models of Afrocentricity. There was a time when Harriet Tubman walked the earth. Ausar and Auset did exist. By studying the past [we] can gain some access to their lives, to their histories, to their power."[3]

With Malcolm turning his incarceration into a university education, years later, he naturally included a school within his final organization, the Organization of Afro-American Unity (OAAU). Sharpening himself into a scholar and activist, he loved learning and not just for the sake of process; emerging out of a Black Nationalist tradition, he studied to discover new and better choices for Black people.

X's close friend James Campbell assisted in conceiving and coordinating the OAAU's liberation schools. Although modeled after the Southern "freedom schools," they offered more academic subjects.[4] During the 1960s, the freedom schools sprung from the Freedom Movement when northern Black and White volunteers went to Southern states to register Blacks to vote. The volunteers recognized that the disenfranchised people required knowledge of civil liberties and Black history, so they started educational facilities for the first-time voters. The courses were ad hoc sessions with pupils from eight to eighty.[5] The teaching foundation was based on history.

Like a professor, when Malcolm spoke, he often lectured on history. We see this most clearly in *Malcolm X on Afro-American History* where he begins a systematic study of African civilizations. He articulates Pan-African nationalism by way of outlining the historical significance and connection of African civilizations from the North to the South. He was well aware of the importance of teaching Black adults and children because the Nation of Islam had started schools across the nation, named after "the Messenger's" wife, Clara Muhammad.

The OAAU schools, however, had a more international curriculum that did not abandon domestic issues. They had age consistent courses that served the youth, older people, and married couples. Parents were even taught how to shop and how to care for children.[6] William Sales tells more: "The curriculum of the Liberation School provided weekly school sessions in African and African American history, political education, and consumer information and skills. The Saturday morning sessions focused on African and African American history. First the children and young teenagers (the junior high school ages predominated) came while their parents shopped from 10:00–11:30 a.m. From 11:30 a.m. to 1:00 p.m., the adults held class."[7] Diverse speakers lectured in the OAAU's educational units: members of the Universal Negro Improvement Association, the Communist Party, and others with topics of African-centered interest.

To ground an African-centered perspective for youngsters, Haki and Safisha Madhubuti implemented African language instruction throughout New Concept and the Betty Shabazz International Charter schools. Following Malcolm, such inclusion enables the students (and teachers) to have "access to ideas and history of [African ancestry]." Swahili is incorporated into the everyday communication among the teachers, students, and administrators. Swahili, a Bantu language, is one of the most widely spoken African languages. It is the official language of Tanzania and Kenya and is spoken throughout most of East Africa and parts of Central Africa. Using Kiswahili, as it is also called, at New Concept and Betty Shabazz, teachers are referred to as *Mwalimu* and the students, *Mwanafunzi*. Teachers, male and female, are additionally called Mama and Baba. The *Nguzo Saba*, created by Maulana Karenga, further augments the American African students (teachers and administrators) with governing codes from the continent. The curriculum's matrix is the *Nguzo Saba*, a Black value system, and the foundation for *Kawaida* (which means tradition or reason). Today, many recognize and honor this teaching matrix as Kwanzaa, a celebration of acts of faith for seven days following Christmas. The seven principles are as follows: *umoja* (unity), *kugichagulia* (self-determination), *ujima* (cooperative work and responsibility), *ujamaa* (cooperative economics), *nia* (purpose), *kuumba* (creativity), and *imani* (faith). Practitioners of Kwanzaa during the holiday period pledge to abide by the principles throughout the year. Those attending or employed by New Concept or Betty Shabazz not only engage the concepts during the holiday season but also have daily opportunities to apply each one.

Haki Madhubuti refers to the formation of New Concept as one of his most significant accomplishments. Building African-centered educational facilities, according to Madhubuti, enables children to negotiate the world from a position of self-awareness.[8]

In this vision and practice, he challenges and resists the traditional American school curriculum that fails to adequately address the history of African and Native American people. Simply busing children to so-called "better" schools, meaning White schools, has not solved the educational disparity between Black and White youngsters. The social scientist and psychologist Amos Wilson critiques this disparity in *The Developmental Psychology of the Black Child* (1980), concluding that:

> Schools, whether primary, secondary, collegiate, vocational, etc., are cultural products and are established to maintain and advance a cultural way of life. Schools exist for the culture not the other way around.... With these facts in mind, it should not be surprising to find that black students' academic performance "lags behind" that of whites in a school system designed for the purpose of maintaining white dominance, for the advancement of white culture and in school system[s] based almost purely on white cultural needs, values, and orientations.[9]

New Concept and Betty Shabazz reverse this defeating orientation that secures White supremacy. In *From Plan to Planet* (1979), Haki Madhubuti poses a related educational dilemma for instructors to consider when designing an atmosphere of African-centered scholastics for the next generation. He writes:

> In the 1970's the question that is elementary to our predicament is, can we create or re-create an Afrikan (or Black) mind in a predominantly European-American setting? This is critical. One cannot expect change

unless one creates a climate for change. One cannot expect a sincere revolutionary movement of thirty-five million Afrikans outside of Afrika unless we create an Afrikan mind that dictates such movement. No European can create an Afrikan mind. Only an Afrikan can do that. Yet, Afrikans cannot be created out of a vacuum. We need structure.[10]

This imaginative structure suggests international nationalism urging racial responsibility. Calling forth the creation of neo-African teachers, he shows the importance of institution building, and planning for a distinctly different generation. Also in the above paragraph, Madhubuti assumes leadership in deciding to rearrange language beneficial to African people, indicative in his spelling of the term "African." Like Malcolm, eliminating the appellation Negro, preferring Afro-American, Madhubuti removes the "c" in Africa, and replaces it with a "k" deliberately. He does this for the following reasons:

1. Most vernacular or traditional languages on the continent spell Afrika with a K; therefore the use of K is germa[ne] to us. 2. Europeans particularly the Portug[u]ese and British, polluted our languages by substituting C whenever they saw K or heard the K sound — as in Kongo and Congo, Akkra and Accra, Konakri and Conakry — and by substituting Q wherever they saw KW.... We are not certain of the origin of the name Afrika, but we are sure the name spelled with the C came into use when Afrikans were dispersed over the world. Therefore the K symbolizes our coming back together again.[11]

Madhubuti wrote about this coming back together again three decades ago. Yet, today some African scholars still wrestle with whether or not to write Africa with a "c" or a "k." Maurice Tadadjeu, professor of African language and linguistics at Yaoundé University in Cameroon, is an example of that ambivalence. Yet, he celebrates graphic designer Saki Mafunkikwa for writing *Afrikan Alphabets: The Story of Writing in Afrika* (2004) and the author's obvious use of the letter "k." Tadadjeu comments:

What is the point in writing the name Africa in English with a k? What is the difference between Africa and Afrika? Obviously one difference is the visual appearance of the two spellings of the same name. The two sound identical but look different.
  It was not until I met the author of this book, Saki Mafundikwa, that such a difference became rather embarrassing to me. In fact, I cannot recall any African language that spells Africa with a c. Africa is spelt Afrika in Afrikan languages.[12]

Hence, Madhubuti's reclamation of the indigenous spelling of Afrika was not solely an awakening for the domesticated Negro. His "coming back together again" signals the dispersal and enslavement of African people in America, colonialism on the continent and the psychological harm of each. Notice the professor's previous unawareness of the c-k variation until one of his own wrote a text imposing an African-centered perspective on language. Professor Tadadjeu must have worn a Du Boisian veil. His inability to see clearly reflects a truism about the effects of colonialism and slavery. Although many are quick to claim that slavery has no effect on contemporary Blacks, Tadadjeu's uncertainty and embarrassment suggest otherwise. The social scientist Dr. Joy Leary would call his behavior a product of "post-traumatic slave syndrome."[13] In her findings, she details the relationship between violence and slavery, self-negating behaviors and slavery, victimization, violence and slavery. From her research, conducted primarily on 200 Black young males, 100 incarcerated, the other hundred participants in rites of passage programs, she concludes the following. Black males feel discomfort in their own skin. Black males experience disrespect from the dominant society and it is negatively amplified and engaged within the Black community. The connecting web between both groups of men, incarcerated and free, is that each group responded the same way to questions. The college graduate and the inmate thought alike.

Leary lectures that "America's pathology is her denial of race. What is the symptomology of the denial? [Whites] would rather erase [Blacks] than acknowledge [they] are there. Blacks cause cognitive dissonance." And all human beings work to reduce cognitive dissonance. Some would argue that this accounts for the large amount of incarcerated men of color and the creation of ghettoes that have built in systemic routes to incarceration. Haki and Safisha Madhubuti built schools to counter this downward trend.

When Haki and Safisha began a Black school with an African-centered curriculum, they created an imagined Africa in the geography of America to reacquaint children, teachers, and administrators with the ontology of self and race determination. This race-first concept[14] was based on life, existence, culture, spirituality, and history prior to the destabilization of Africa. Free to select the continent's useful concepts and practices, they remembered the American African, a Negro, to a geographic base that does not begin with a people in bondage. Ironically, continental Africans were watching and mentally investigating this activism of the 1960s, and this line of thought shifted how the continentals imagined one another. For those on the continent and the renamed Negroes in America, Madhubuti's concept of "coming back together again" boomeranged.

In *In Search of Africa* (1998), Manthia Diawara poignantly describes and analyzes this boomerang, the triple effect of the transatlantic presentation of culture. He explores this multiplicity through the genius of James

Brown, who grunts, growls, and hollers in syncopation with his singing and dancing. Brown's nonverbal nuances are African and today African artists now study Brown in order to mimic and to create new combinations in music. We then have an African, fused African American, and back-to-African sound and performance style. We have fusion with variation that suggests the modern and postmodern methods that continental, Diaspora, and exiled Africans now re-envision Africa.

When Haki Madhubuti was turning out and performing Black Arts poetry, building Third World Press and independent Black schools, Manthia Diawara and his African crew were watching and imitating the neo–Black Americans. Diawara writes:

> Seydou Ly (Sly) and I, along with a few others in the group, thought that our Afros had power enough to set us apart from our peers in Bamako and to transform us into black Americans, whom we admired so much. The imagination of the youth in Africa at the time was captured by the defiant images of George Jackson, Angela Davis, Muhammad Ali, Eldridge Cleaver, Malcolm X, and James Brown. We used to spend hours washing our hair with special shampoos and combing it. We dressed to resemble our black American heroes. We walked tall in packs and pretended we couldn't speak French. We called one another by our American nicknames, and slowly we became aware of race in our daily relations with French people. We began to see racism where others before us would have seen colonialism and class exploitation.[15]

Again, the power of the veil: the African Black Power proponents did not or refused to see racism until their American counterparts took action against its domesticated form. Ironically, as the Black Americans claimed Africa for culture, history, and essence, the continentals not only imagined Black Americans for courage, but also culture, imitating the American Africans in dress, language, and style. The continentals and the Diaspora Africans became family again, as Walter Rodney might assert. In his seminal work *How Europe Underdeveloped Africa* (1982), Rodney distinguishes the African core of cultures or civilizations as expressing dance, song, religion, and family as common cultural aspects throughout the continent.[16]

At the New Concept School, where the ages were once from two to six, and seven to twelve, the courses interspersed and combined with science and art.* For instance, after completing a human anatomy lesson, the *mwanafunzi* danced. This motion gave the abstract book knowledge a phys-

---

*With the founding of the Betty Shabazz International Charter School in 1998, New Concept is now a preschool, teaching children from two to six years old. Betty Shabazz International Charter School is a middle school, with ages from six to twelve.

ical and personal dimension in addition to an African textured meaning. For example, to dance, in African systems of thought, opens communication with God. Dance master and scholar Welsh-Asante explains this in *The African Aesthetic* (1994):

> The process of perception in an African centered worldview combines the sacred and the profane, mind and body, the natural and the supernatural as organic dynamic entities, able to manifest themselves in all sorts of combinations and disciplines.[17]

At New Concept, when the children danced they reinforced the anatomy lesson in a rhythm more complicated than simply having fun. Dance binds the children to cultural performance both familiar and African. As a cultural facet, it shares commonality with all African ethnic variations (throughout the Diaspora) reaching back into epic memory. By dancing, the children not only learn about African culture, they reproduce it.

Africa on Madhubuti's Mind

Madhubuti says that Malcolm X's foresight regarding the need to internationalize the Black condition in the United States helped him make later choices to become directly involved in the African liberation struggle.[18]

As such, since 1969, Madhubuti has been writing about and traveling to Africa, gaining the attention and respect of African heads of state. For instance, he participated in the First Pan African Festival in Algiers, and in later years, African governments invited him to organize and join political and cultural forums, such as Pan African Congress sessions. Like Randall Robinson, former head of TransAfrica Forum, which helped defeat South African apartheid, Madhubuti argues and works for African autonomy. In 2004 the Senegalese president Abdoulaye Wade requested his presence and input in Senegal's political and cultural renaissance.[19]

Early in Malcolm's career in 1959 he traveled to Africa with his beloved "Messenger," Elijah Muhammad. Years later, after leaving the Nation of Islam, Malcolm returned to Africa with a document that charged the United States with abuses against the Negro people. Encouraging the leaders of African nations to take his grievances before the world court, Malcolm was the first invited African American to attend a summit of thirty-four state leaders. Malcolm presented his historic memorandum at this Cairo summit in July 1964.[20]

Historian and scholar John Henrik Clarke (1991) says Malcolm's reception in Africa was an enormous accomplishment, commenting that "Malcolm X had succeeded where other black men had tried and failed for over a hundred years. From the middle of the nineteenth century, and afterward, every genuine black nationalist has dreamed of a union with Africa and other people of African descent scattered throughout the world."[21]

Malcolm's African study and travel stimulated his elucidation of neonationalism and Afrocentric thought. He sought similarity and victorious consciousness among Africans, two hallmarks of Afrocentric theory. When attorney Milton Henry interviewed him after the Cairo summit, Malcolm's search for African commonality was obvious. He said:

> First, I want to point out that we are sitting here along the banks of the Nile, and the last time I spoke to you we were in Harlem. Here along the banks of the Nile it's not much different from Harlem — same people, same feeling, same pulse.[22]

The juxtaposing of Harlem and North Africa is another tenet of Afrocentricity, a contemporary and controversial paradigm because of its challenge to White studies as universal. Yet Malcolm before his assassination spoke and lived by this system of knowledge, years before Molefi Asante coined and charged the term. Demonstrating the common "pulse" among all African people, Malcolm's observations recall Paul Robeson's earlier commentary on culture and similarities among African and Diaspora ethnic splits. Malcolm X is talking about the study of and African connection to Nile Valley civilizations, the earliest and most advanced cultures of all peoples. He continues with his observations:

> I pointed out ... that as independent heads of states we looked upon them as the shepherds not only of the African people on the continent, but all people of African descent abroad; and that a good shepherd is more concerned with the sheep that have gone astray and fallen into the hands of the imperialist wolf than the sheep that are still at home. Afro-Americans in the United States were still Africans[.] [W]e felt that the African heads of state were as much responsible for us as they were responsible for the people ... on the continent.[23]

Malcolm had already politicized at home the original connection between Negroes in America and Africans on the continent. In the above, we see his reminding the Africans of their responsibility to those in America. Malcolm possessed the boomerang effect. This is a unique revolutionary strategy that does not display any romanticism about Africans. This goes beyond wearing African clothing and speaking African languages. It importantly illustrates that X had more on his mind than a religious conversion when traveling to Africa. It displays how shrewdly his rhetoric carried multiple meaning. X urges Africans to remember that American Negroes are Africans, not just Americans. Malcolm collapsed the distance between continental Africans and those in the Diaspora, turning distance into dividend. He influenced Madhubuti to write in *From Plan to Planet*, first published in 1973, that "Our ties to Afrika are cultural, political, economic, and emotional."[24]

Early in his career, one discerns Madhubuti's critical assessment of Africa as well when he disagrees with President Julius Nyerere of Tanzania and Sékou Touré, head of Guinea, at the Sixth Pan-African Congress, in 1974. Sounding like Marcus Garvey's sloganeering of "Africa for the Africans," Madhubuti faults the presidents for allowing non-Africans to join the Pan-African Congress. He emphatically writes: "It is clear to me that at one level Pan-Afrikanism has become a trap for Black people when it includes white people and Asians. *Where is it in the world where Black men and women can sit down as a world people and talk about our problems and our solutions and not have white people there?* White people have the North Atlantic Treaty Organization (NATO): no Blacks allowed; Europeans and Asians have the Southwest Asian Treaty Organization (SEATO): no Blacks allowed; Arabs have the League of Arab States, the Arab Financial Organization and the Arab Common Market: no Blacks allowed. And *all* are accepted in the international arena. But anytime we Blacks try to move among ourselves, for ourselves, by ourselves, the world can't take it and we are accused of racism, of being metaphysical and not scientific"[25] (emphasis in original).

Conjoining metaphysics and science at New Concept School, Haki and Safisha Madhubuti developed an educational system that emphasized African and African American art, culture, and geography. They sought to "revamp thinking" to "redirect learning trends," as X had earlier stated. In the beginning years, the children memorized traditional names of African nations from books and magazines in order to foster a Pan-African consciousness. The children then and now are taught to think internationally and to value African and African American knowledge, philosophy, aesthetics and culture in addition to traditional dominant cultural studies.

The drum is a component of the African culture studies and community drummers instruct the children. Drumming, an original African (and Native American) art and religious form, specific to males, normally involves noncompetitive performances. These events, like secular singing competitions among Black American rhythm and blues artists, encourage participants to push individual talent to its pinnacle.

I have witnessed rock and roll, rhythm and blues concerts during the 1960s where such vibrant challenges took place. These cultural exhibitions, called "The Battle of the Groups," took place at the Uptown Theater in Philadelphia, sponsored by WDAS and Georgie Woods "the man with the goods" and were sometimes emceed by Jimmy Bishop, a disc jockey who danced onstage. The Uptown Theater was known for its stellar performances that showcased the Motown sound: Smokey Robinson and the Miracles, the Supremes, Gladys Knight and the Pips, the Marvelettes, the Coasters, the Drifters, the Four Tops, the Tempting Temptations. The "Battle of the Groups" occurred after all the featured acts had finished. With a drum roll in the background, the master of ceremonies called the opposing groups back onstage: the Four Tops challenged the Temptations to a duel in song. The energy and music merged like magic. Eddie Kendricks and David Ruffin of the Temptations and Levi Stubbs of the Four Tops hit incredible lyrical levels that, along with audience participation, blew the roof off the Uptown theatre. It was impossible to select a clear winner. Like the Jackie Wilson song, each performer (and group) lifted lyric and dance "higher and higher," each showcasing his particular "philosophical and spiritual aspect of being an artist."[26] Drumming competitions excel the talent of children.

From performance and culture to history projects, the *mwalimu* at New Concept design science and educational projects where the older *mwanafunzi* help younger students. This feature and recurrence resembles the age-set groups that Chancellor Williams discusses in *The Destruction of Black Civilizations* (1987). Prior to first contact when Africans greeted Europeans, their social system involved age-set groups with in-group obligations to one another and to the society at large. Williams writes, "The age-grade or age-set (also called 'class') was the specific organizational structure through which the society functioned. Classification was determined by the period to which one was born in the same year, or within a general but well-defined period before or after a given year.... There was seniority within each grade according to age and intelligence."[27]

At New Concept, the interaction between the age-set groups fosters and introduces the process of "collective work and responsibility" to the *mwanafunzi* as it weakens the desire for negative competition between the youth. Parental involvement is welcomed and obligated at New Concept. Madhubuti writes:

> If our children are to be responsible to us, we, in their youth have to be responsible in educating them. Nobody can instill black values except Black people. Our ability to conceptualize and act for our future depends upon who's been feeding us our concepts.... We need doers rather than sayers. To continue to send our children to strangers for the cultivation of their minds will make them strangers to their own people.[28]

Safisha Madhubuti

Safisha Madhubuti has spent her life developing theory and programs that would offset Black children behaving as "strangers to their own people." Before leaving to finish her PhD at the University of Chicago, she was teacher and principal at New Concept for sixteen years. Safisha, a former high school teacher, had heard White educators belittle the ability of Black youngsters. This helped her decide to devote her life to designing schools directly for Black students. Today, similar to her husband, she too articulates New Concept as a proud victory. About a New Concept reunion, she recalls: "I remember looking around the room with great pride.... These were young people who were centered. They are black and love being black. They feel a need in their lives to contribute to the greater world, to make a contribution as African Americans to their world. They are well mannered. They're not into gangs and not into drugs. They're wholesome young people who have big views. They think big, which is what we wanted them to do."[29]

Gayle Tate in *Unknown Tongues* (2003) historically examines the victorious consciousness — wanting students to think big — and practice of Black women like Safisha Madhubuti. Tate, a political scientist, provocatively emphasizes the invisible boundaries of resistance that enslaved and later free Black women brought to American culture and to the work force. Arguing that Black women's resistance emerges from African spirituality, Tate says this force then commingled with New World religions. In that commingling cultural aspects emerged relevant to the rigors of the new geography. Women discovered resistance through literacy, for themselves, and in instructing young people and others to read and to write in order to form resistance cells. Coming from a tradition of collective politics, which springs from epic and collective memory, women contoured an Afrocentric worldview to cope with and defy racial oppression.[30] Tate points out that

> As slave women created the infrastructure of resistance into the fabric of the slave community, they were transforming their labor activities to challenge the slave hierarchy. The significance of black women's labor will was the symbolic and substantive representation of the cultural retentiveness of an African heritage and the resolve of slave women to transcend the powers of enslavement. Just as enslavement and the Southern economy shaped the political and social role of female slaves, industrialization and urbanization in the "freedom cities" of Boston, New York City, and Philadelphia would transform antebellum free black women's social and political activism. Amid the industrializing process and their marginalization in the marketplace, black women would contour an agenda of urban resistance [59].

When Safisha Madhubuti, then Carol Hall, convinced Don L. Lee (Haki Madhubuti) of the potency of early education for Black children, she was forwarding her "agenda of urban resistance." With the formation of New Concept, she directly created an infrastructure that challenged White supremacy. She knew, as Komozi Woodard writes in *Nation Within a Nation* (1990), that African American children (and people) were not assimilated into American society. They were "urbanized and modernized in a very separate manner that laid the foundations for a black national political community."[31]

Safisha Madhubuti's consciousness developed out of a nationalism that expanded her role from lover and helpmate of Haki Madhubuti to partner of Haki Madhubuti. Their relationship joined for larger purposes than individual self or couple gratification. They made a union in order to transcend the omnipresence of unequal rights in America. Contributing her labor will to reduce the effect of racism and to construct institutions for Black empowerment, Safisha Madhubuti confronts and challenges capitalistic and racist hegemony. As the principal of New Concept for sixteen years, she impacted her vision into the curriculum matrix. Her personal transformation revealed itself when she returned to college in order to strengthen her credentials and pick up where she left off once meeting Haki.

Haki has publicly discussed their long, successful partnership. When they met in the summer of 1968, their courtship included operating Third World Press — his publishing house — and founding the Institute of Positive Education. Haki, along with Carolyn Rodgers and Jewel Latimore (Johari Amini) started Third World Press in 1967. Safisha entered Haki's life when he was grounding his X-factor idea of controlling his art and the art of others that addressed Black Power and 1960s nationalism. They have struggled together and with the larger society for over thirty years, marrying in 1974 after she sent him a letter forcing a decision about their intimate involvement. Safisha says, "I had invested five years of my life with this man."[32] The scholar Clenora Hudson-Weems (1993) in general elucidates Safisha's personal and political investment, noting that

> The Africana womanist is also *in concert with males* in the broader struggle for humanity and the liberation of all Africana people. The ideas of the intertwined destiny of Africana men, women, and children [are] directly related to the notion of the dependency upon the male sector in the participation of the Africana womanist's struggle for herself and her family. Unlike the mainstream feminist, whose struggle is characteristically independent of and oftentimes adverse to male participation, the Africana womanist invites her male counterpart into her struggle for liberation and parity in society, as this struggle has been traditionally the glue that has

held them together and enabled them to survive in a particularly hostile and racist society.³³

Haki found Safisha special when they first met because as he recalls, she had "something serious to say." Her conversation was about "liberation," "struggle," and an X-factor education. With apparent twin-ness, she complemented him.

Similarly, when Malcolm X decided to court Betty, he too made this decision because Betty X had much that was serious to say. Malcolm deliberately selected an educated woman to marry, and he remarks about this interest in Betty X in the *Autobiography*, saying: "I was halfway impressed by her intelligence and also her education. In those days she was one of the few whom we had attracted who had attended college."³⁴ Betty X had been an education major at the Tuskegee Institute in Alabama. In New York, studying nursing, Betty X lectured to Muslim girls and women on hygiene and medical information.

When Safisha Madhubuti returned to the university to complete her education, she too majored in education. Currently teaching at Northwestern University, she remains chair of the board of the Institute of Positive Education and New Concept School. Betty X, Safisha, Malcolm, and Madhubuti are all teachers.

Benjamin Karim provides evidence of Malcolm's commitment to teaching. Once, at a New York museum, Malcolm led Muslim children in a discussion about Eskimo culture and sea animals. He explained how Eskimos carved clubs, knives, fish hooks and combs from the walrus.³⁵ Encouraging the children to question him, he gained the "attention of not only the kids from the temple but other kids, too, black and white, and some of them would be perched up on their parents' shoulders so they could see."³⁶

Malcolm exhibited what Haki Madhubuti would later demand of his teachers, the preparedness and attitude to be ready always to teach. Among the first modern scholars to instruct the Negro about his and her relationship to Nile Valley civilizations, Malcolm intended to "liberate [Black] minds."

Haki Madhubuti wrote a faculty handbook, so to speak, outlined in *From Plan to Planet*, where he encourages investigative self-analysis, a teaching pedagogy, and an ethos to discipline and create exceptional teachers. This is Madhubuti's pedagogical philosophy.

1. Be the example of what you teach. Your personal contradictions can wipe out years of hard work. You must be direction for the young, be what you teach....

2. Always impart knowledge with an eye on reality. Pull your examples from the real world that we're involved in daily. High sounding philosophy belongs in philosophy classes that divorce themselves from life. Knowledge without understanding and practical application is like owning the land without being able to cultivate it.
3. Never tire of teaching. An instructor who believes in what he's teaching can teach anywhere and at any time and is always prepared to teach; his lifestyle should be a lesson. Concentrate on the four ingredients for an Afrikan reality: to work, to study, to create, and to build.[37]

These are applied ethics in the Betty Shabazz International Charter School. With affirmations and pledges, the principal and director, Dr. Elaine C. Mosley, starts and ends her school day. In the morning all the students begin with the pledge created by the Council of Independent Black Institutions. (The full script is in chapter six.) The children stand in a circle and recite the following pledge, partially excerpted here: "Our commitment is to self-determination, self-defense, and self respect for our race. We extend the right hand out for the fruition of Black power, for the triumph of Black nationhood. I pledge to my African nation, to the building of a better people and a better world."

As she speaks, the regal and affirming Dr. Mosley exudes a visionary's commitment to improve the lives of children. When asked about the most important aspects of instruction at Betty Shabazz, she responded:

History and culture are important aspects in the learning process and that along with making sure [the students] have the basics, math, reading, science, I strive to create a welcoming environment for the children. I want them to know that they can be all that they choose and that they have the school, the teachers, and myself here to help them.[38]

The Madhubutis' schools are, in an African sense, more than educational enterprises. They have a family-type infrastructure. Safisha Madhubuti says that "by appreciating their culture and history, the students realize that true education goes beyond learning the basics."[39] At New Concept and Betty Shabazz the children, the *mwanafunzi*, learn to feel comfortable in their skin, and the teachers and administrators activate this process by fostering kinship through language.

Like the structure of the school, Haki and Safisha Madhubuti publicly and personally have extended family. Haki has two children from previous relationships: Don, 34, and Mari, 30. Safisha and Haki have three children together: Laini, 28, Bomani, 26, and Akili, 24. And along with Safisha's mother, Inez Hall, residing with the Madhubutis, Safisha and Haki talk about the people at New Concept, Betty Shabazz, and Third World Press as family. This does not count their worldwide affiliations or kinship ties.

This expansive dominion of "family" probably increases the confidence of *mwanafunzi*, stimulating high performance, and correcting family deficiencies at home. Solomon Dumas, an eighth grade student at Shabazz, calls the school "a blessing." "Brandon West, who is in his first year at Shabazz, appreciates the school's enforced discipline."[40] He watched fist-fights at his former school where teachers rarely intervened. Given a personal tour of Betty Shabazz by Ann Ward, a Julliard graduate and music director, I asked about this notion of nonbiological family. Ward responded:

> I have students who I am very involved with because they need the extra attention and I have no problem giving it to them. Most of the teachers here feel that way. We took these jobs because we wanted to make real differences in the lives of our children.[41]

Ann Ward's use of "our" seals the familial connection. It signals the family without blood ties. Although the Institute of Positive Education and New Concept School started in an abandoned Chicago storefront, it has garnered attention from the state of Illinois. Although some opponents of charter schools argue their monetary subtraction from public facilities and a so-called glorification of race over practical knowledge instruction, the Madhubutis' African-centered facilities are among the top ten in Chicago.

This success has come at great personal and financial cost, but because the Madhubutis are committed to Black empowerment they endured. In their determination to accept responsibility for creating generations of young people who combine intelligence and African-centeredness, the Madhubutis have succeeded against the odds. In fact, the Chicago Board of Education recently acknowledged their achievements by presenting a request. They asked the husband and wife team to start a high school, the first of its kind in America.[42] Called the Barbara Ann Sizemore Campus, this high school honors a prolific educator.

Summary

With the inspiration from Safisha Madhubuti, Haki and Safisha built the Institute of Positive Education and New Concept School in 1969, two years after Haki Madhubuti established Third World Press (with Carolyn

Rodgers and Johari Amini). In part, the idea of the school and the publishing house manifests from Malcolm X's rhetoric. Additionally, Malcolm X had articulated the importance of creating institutions where African languages were prominent. The staff, students, and administrators at New Concept and Betty Shabazz speak Swahili, incorporated specifically in titles. Like Malcolm, the Madhubutis believe that African-centered learning puts confidence in Black students.

Haki and Safisha Madhubuti have maintained independent Black schools for over thirty years with Afrocentric curriculums that foster high achievement, internationalism, and race responsibility. The founders studied the purposeful concepts of African culture and applied a unique pedagogical style African-influenced in learning basic academic subjects.

Imposing her will onto the teaching matrixes of New Concept and Betty Shabazz, Safisha Madhubuti advances an agenda and site of resistance using education. Based on the *Nguzo Saba*, an African value system, the schools curriculums engage codes from the continent. Safisha continues a tradition started by Black foremothers during enslavement and nominal freedom. She utilizes literacy from an African-centered perspective to empower *mwanafunzi* (students) and in this configuration and action she directly challenges White supremacy and capitalistic America.

Malcolm X spoke earlier about learning from an African-centered conception and during the 1960s, Africans on the continent defined American Africans, like Malcolm X, as heroes. In culture, specifically music, the continental Africans imitated American Blacks, which began a cultural exchange and fusion that continues today. Ironically, American Blacks redefine themselves using African cultural codes and Africans on the continent refashion themselves based on Black American behavior.

Teachers and administrators at the Betty Shabazz International Charter School project and incorporate an extended family attitude, perspective, and situation as they instruct the students. They go beyond teaching the basics. They provide extra support and care because of the devastation Black students and families have endured in this country.

For Haki and Safisha Madhubuti, their long, hard sacrifices to maintain Afrocentric educational facilities have been rewarded. In 2004, the Chicago Board of Education requested that they build a high school. The Barbara Ann Sizemore Campus sets a precedent in America.

In Chapter Eight, we leave education to examine the influence of X on Haki Madhubuti and Huey Newton, cofounder of the Black Panther Party.

EIGHT

Malcolm X and Madhubuti: A Physical and Personal Merging

New Concept and Betty Shabazz students experience a lifestyle transformation because of the globalization and the unified African cultural codes grafted into the curriculum and in the teachers' pedagogy. Yet, a lifestyle transformation includes more than examining knowledge. For the Muslims and for Madhubuti, it incorporates shifts in eating habits, diet, and philosophy. For instance, along with independent building, following Elijah Muhammad, Malcolm X inspired Haki Madhubuti to live and to preach the significance of quality health. The main health adjustment involved eliminating pork from the diet. The consumption and image of the "pig" had multiple streams of thought that effected not only Madhubuti but also the 1960s leaders of the Black Panther Party, Huey Newton and Bobby Seale.

On another subject that involves the image of X himself, we will also review a contemporary malcolmian attitude in Allen Iverson, star guard of the 76s' basketball team. However, since Malcolm X received much of his perspectives, attitudes, and philosophy from Elijah Muhammad, we will begin briefly with him to understand the background and the backdrop for the Nation of Islam.

Born October 7, 1897, to sharecroppers Wali and Marie Poole, Elijah grew up in poverty along with twelve brothers and sisters in Bold Springs, near Sandersville, Georgia. Witnessing a brutal lynching when he returned home from school, young Elijah was indelibly and negatively affected early in life by White tyranny. The lynched man had been a member of his father's church. In his adult life, Elijah Muhammad searched for answers to horrific White behavior and for Black independence from White America.

After marrying Clara Evans in 1917, he became a Pullman porter until racism, an attack by a White man, caused him (and his family) to leave for Detroit where he met a Northern version of "racism, discrimination, hunger, and despair."[1] Continuing his search to understand White supremacy and to develop Black autonomy, Elijah Muhammad joined Marcus Garvey's Universal Negro Improvement Association. Garvey's Black Nationalist organization developed businesses, an army, and an ideology of self and race empowerment. Garvey had a plan and a mission to send Blacks to Africa to rebuild the motherland. However, hounded and harassed by federal officials, the police, and integration-minded Blacks, Garvey was exiled from America in 1929. In 1930, Elijah joined a religious group in the Paradise Valley section of Detroit where he met Wallace Fard Muhammad, "a mystic who taught a radical religion named Islam. Muhammad's religion taught that blacks are mutually good and that whites are devils."[2] In *Inside the Nation of Islam* (2001), Vibert White explains the monumental importance of Wallace Fard Muhammad's impression on Black people. He writes that

> Fard, as he was often called, not only cleaned people's homes in exchange for a captive audience but he occasionally paid people twenty-five cents to come to Nation of Islam Sunday meetings to hear his lectures. According to many of the first followers, this was the only way to get blacks to hear Fard's fiery and antiwhite rhetoric. To an oppressed people hearing someone call them great, wonderful, and gods, while referring to white store owners, landlords, and racist police as swine, devils, and the great Satan, allowed them to redeem a little of the self-worth that white America had taken from them.[3]

Scholars have documented Fard's criminal activities and deceptions.[4] Likewise they point to what some call the "bizarre" religious narrative, the foundation of the Nation of Islam's theology, the grafting of Whites from Blacks.

Yet, this theology assisted in motivating the believers to attempt self-reliance as opposed to sole dependency on White America. Similarly, Elijah Muhammad is often dismissed as a religious faker, adulterer, dictator, and racist. He has been compared to Hitler and Mussolini[5] and presented as a hypocritical criminal for taking money from White supremacist organizations. Yet, whatever his contradictions, Elijah Muhammad created from meager sources an empire on which Blacks and Malcolm X in particular could fly. The Nation of Islam, once Fard Muhammad "disappeared" and

Elijah Muhammad headed the organization, became the most powerful and independent economic enterprise for American Blacks. It practiced a separatist ideology that forced the members to think and to behave in terms that related to one another, not to a government or a society where they faced daily humiliating injustices. This is a continuation of 19th century nationalism. Elijah Muhammad entered energy already in America and he augmented it with a new God, a new code of conduct, based on belief in self and race.

Recruiting from the lowest echelons of America, the Nation of Islam taught theology from an African American–centered perspective, reforming criminals such as Malcolm himself and guiding aimless men and women toward purpose and meaning. In the NOI temples, the ministers gave public lectures three days a week. At the temples, on the days in between, the faithful studied history, the Bible, and the Koran. Benjamin Karim tells more:

> Friday night at the temple was called General Civilization Night....
> Malcolm would always start off the meeting with a big question from one of our Muslim lessons. "What is civilization?" he might ask, or "What is the duty of a civilized man?" He might end up however talking about breastfeeding or eating bean pie. Diet, language, table manners, liturgy, scriptures, polished shoes, they are all parts of the same elephant.... For generations, he pointed out our people have been divorced from their native culture, so the history of African Americans in the United States has become a history of losses.[6]

When Elijah Muhammad, head of the Nation of Islam, put men to work, he enacted a specific kind of masculinity and purpose for male members, which Minister Louis Farrakhan, head of the Nation of Islam today, continues. For example, on major streets across the country, Muslim males in suit and tie still sell the NOI's famous bean pies along with carrot cakes, spring water, and the Muslim newspaper renamed *The Final Call*. Others own restaurants and stores specializing in non-pork dishes. In contrast to Farrakhan's Nation of Islam, Wallace Deen Muhammad, Elijah's son, leads an orthodox group of followers of the Islamic religion, and all racial groups are allowed to join. This is a considerable break from the perspective of Elijah Muhammad, whose original organization restricted membership to Blacks only.

When Elijah Muhammad branched from his God, Master Fard Muhammad, he sought to transform Negroes into a Black, self-serving nation. Legal segregation was prominent during this epoch. With the idea of racial transformation an important component of reshaping the habits and behaviors of the then Negro people, the religious dietary restrictions and moral, religious, and cultural code challenged the assimilation tendencies of Negroes.

The cultural code of the NOI encouraged a new social system for adherents to follow and maintain. This system reached into almost all aspects of the members' lives. For example, men did not randomly date sisters of the faith. The dating process had an inherent formality. Leaders in the organization arranged chaperoned heterosexual outings. This kind of arrangement implicitly addressed the preference for sexual abstaining before marriage, as it protected the Black Muslim woman from abuse. Elijah Muhammad sought to recreate a Black familial culture through a unique version of Islam that without the cultural focus resembled Victorian values.

Malcolm X carried this gender specific masculinity of the NOI. In his appearance and attitude he also revealed a dynamism which attracted other males in search of authenticity that could provide direction and leadership. When Malcolm spoke before audiences, his listeners absorbed more than his message. Taking in his appearance, they also imitated his sense of style.

Malcolm's style, reflecting the Muslim moral code and diet, impressed Haki Madhubuti as well as Huey P. Newton and Bobby Seale, founders of the Black Panther Party for Self Defense. Each male imitated Malcolm differently, taking sections of this new American hero to boost and to guide their African-centered enterprises. In *Claiming Earth* (1995), Madhubuti admires X because of his intelligence and self-discipline (77).

Personal Madhubuti and Malcolm

Malcolm X's self-discipline, like all Muslims, included the elimination of pork from his diet and this exclusion was sometimes mentioned in his speeches. In Elijah Muhammad's book *How to Eat to Live* (1967), he exhorts his followers to eat one meal a day or one every other day between four and six p.m. for long life. He did not promote vegetarianism, but strictly prohibited the eating of pork. Writing about fasting as a way to rid the body of poisons, he explains Black people's contemporary eating habits as unhealthy because they began in slavery.

Muhammad knew that slaveholders for the most part determined what the enslaved consumed, causing those in bondage to base their diet on whatever was available. On many plantations, meat was a premium, often denied to the enslaved. The enslaved Africans, however, inverted the world of slavery into a more manageable realm of existence. This included not only resistance (masquerading for White approval) but also finding ingenious ways to widen their diet. For example, Black people turned chitterlings (pig intestines) into a delicacy, because pig guts were unwanted by Whites. With chitterlings as a main source of meat for many, they celebrated what the Whites discarded and this celebration continued from slavery into this contemporary period. In my family, for instance, during the 1950s and 1960s, when my Uncle Charlie returned from serving his country, my aunt Helen always prepared a festive meal of fried chicken, potato salad, collard greens, lemon meringue pie, pig feet, and chitterlings. During slavery, in Black folklore, tales abound about the enslaved stealing pigs. Therefore, the pig has a very special and complex meaning to Black people.

Yet, on being a Muslim, one had to give up pork, collard greens, black-eyed peas, corn bread and other African American dietary delights. Muslims also abstained from alcohol, tobacco, and drugs. These restraints were amplified in Malcolm's oratory and this new behavior impacted many of his serious listeners such as Madhubuti. In *YellowBlack* (2005), Madhubuti says that Malcolm's "ascetic lifestyle appealed to [him]."[7] Malcolm's diet as well as his fresh religious and secular ideology related not only to deconstructing racism but also to deconstructing American dietary habits.

Noted historian John Henrik Clarke, in the documentary *Make it Plain* (1994), discusses Malcolm's gentle chiding of him for eating pork. Clarke says about Malcolm:

> He had a beautiful sense of humor, especially when he was kidding me about pork. And whacking me on the back saying that, "You're a decent human being, smart historian. I'm going to give you 99 as a human being and if you stop eating pork. I'm going to give you 100."

Malcolm's disdain for pork paradoxically affected the Panther founders Newton and Seale. In Oakland, California, in 1966, Newton, along with Bobby Seale, legally armed himself to patrol the police, a tactic to stop police brutality. Within this strategy, new language emerged with Newton renaming the police "pigs" and "swine," lingo for pork. Newton may not have realized that during the 1930s Fard Muhammad called the police "swine." Thus, Newton brought forward a resurgence of an original Muslim reference. The Panthers' boldness and popularity, arming legally in order to police the police, caused their admirers and others to replicate his coinage for cops. He initially called the police "dogs," gods spelled backwards, but it never captured the imaginations of the people. "Pig" had an impressive effect in the 1960s and today it is not only in the vocabulary of American vernacular, but also in the dictionary as a negative synonym for the law.

A law student himself, Newton deliberately disqualified obscenities when renaming the police. In his autobiography *Revolutionary Suicide*

(1973), Newton says that he, Bobby Seale and Eldridge Cleaver stumbled onto the term from a postcard of a slobbering pig under the caption "Support Your Local Police." Newton writes: "Thus, even though we came to the term 'pig' accidentally, the choice itself was calculated. 'Pig' was perfect for several reasons. First of all, words like 'swine,' 'hog,' 'sow,' and 'pig' have always had unpleasant connotations. The reason for this probably has theological roots, since the pig is considered an unclean animal in Semitic religions."[8]

Newton never mentions Elijah Muhammad's depictions of the pig in the newspaper *Muhammad Speaks*. Nor does he mention the close resemblance of the Panthers newspaper, *The Black Panther*, started by Bobby Seale, to the Muslims newspaper format detailing the group's philosophy. *Muhammad Speaks*, started by Malcolm X to provide an overview of the Muslim's philosophy and ideology, had a section entitled "What the Muslims Want" and "What the Muslims Believe." Years later, *The Black Panther* had a very similar format for the ten-point platform and program of the Black Panther Party under the caption "What We Want/What We Believe." Newton and Bobby Seale both write how they read about Malcolm X in the Muslim paper and that Malcolm X's spirit guided the founding of the Panthers. Therefore, from folklore, history, culture, and diet, Newton probably had 'pig' on his mind for reasons other than seeing one on a postcard.

In *Revolutionary Suicide* (1973), Newton sets the parameters for Panther ideology using existentialist and European conceptions. His intellectualism, steeped in the master narratives of White supremacy, probably overshadowed sources closest to his own culture.[9]

Newton was close to the youth culture in California where drug usage often proliferated. Yet, because of the power and ascetic lifestyle of X, Newton and Seale removed themselves from such influence in contrast to another Panther leader, Eldridge Cleaver. The following excerpt illustrates their malcolmian behavior. Newton writes:

> Because Bobby and I had started out as Black nationalists and were influenced by the Muslims and Malcolm X, we steered clear of the drug scene. Unlike Eldridge, neither of us identified with Haight-Ashbury or Telegraph Avenue, and especially not with drugs.[10]

Haight-Ashbury was a popular drug culture site during the 1960s where mostly young radical (hippie) Whites lived, worked, and played; however, this fantasy area that impressed Cleaver did not affect the Panther founders, largely because of Malcolm X. The Muslims under Muhammad and Farrakhan are known for their successful methods in reforming drug addicts.

Haki Madhubuti has never experimented with drugs, alcohol, or cigarettes. Abstaining from all meats, poultry, and fish, Madhubuti today is more exclusive in diet than X and the Muslims. As a vegan vegetarian, he discusses health-centered issues during his poetry readings, a mix of oratory and poetry recitation. In fact, in *From Plan to Planet*, Madhubuti writes that one should "eat to live not live to eat,"[11] which is verbal play on Elijah Muhammad's book title *How to Eat to Live*.

Historically, innovators and resistors have selected a natural diet. Harriet Tubman, familiar with farming, picked appropriate roots and herbs for healing and eating.[12] Before Harriet Tubman, "Toussaint L'Ouverture lived on berries and nuts and often counseled his men on the proper foods."[13] Clearly, Malcolm's proselytes not only imitated his rhetoric and key ideas. Some like Madhubuti made food consumption an important route towards liberation and longevity. This is how Madhubuti explains his dietary choices in *Enemies: The Clash of Races* (1978):

> If one is serious about struggle in the U.S. the crucial question becomes how does one maintain a healthy balance between mind, body and the outside world? It is a contradiction of the highest level to speak of an educated person purely from the perspective of having a superior mental capacity in a certain area. That is to say that a person may be the greatest living authority on nuclear physics while at the same time each and every day maybe unknowingly killing himself or herself through the intake of bad food, lack of proper exercise, lack of proper sleep, inadequate sitting and walking postures while maintaining many other poor habits such as smoking, high alcohol intake, etc.[14]

Haki Madhubuti projects word power for the health of his listeners, incorporating this subject with his facts about racism and resistance. When interviewing writers who attended Madhubuti's annual Gwendolyn Brooks Black Literature and Creative Writing Conference, one of the running jokes concerned his proclivity for vegetarianism. His writing comrades laughed heartily at his refusal to eat "anything with a face or legs." They boasted that they eat the "face, legs, neck, everything." Jocularity notwithstanding, they respected Madhubuti's discipline to gain good health. Vegetarian meals are served at all of his functions.

Revolutionary Attire: Malcolm, Madhubuti, and Huey Newton

In addition to the contrasting variations with "the pig" and diet, Madhubuti and Huey P. Newton also responded to X's style of dress and demeanor. Huey P. Newton, the college student and co-founder of the Black Panther Party, writes in his autobiography *Revolutionary Suicide* (1973) about the attraction of Malcolm's style:

I first heard Malcolm X speak at McClymonds High School in Oakland, when he attended a conference sponsored by the Afro-American Association on "The Mind of the Ghetto." Muhammad Ali (then Cassius Clay) was with Malcolm, and he told about his conversion to Islam. He was not yet the heavy weight champion. Malcolm X impressed me with his logic and with his disciplined and dedicated mind. Here was a man who combined the world of the streets and the world of the scholar, a man so widely read he could give better lectures and cite more evidence than many college professors. *He was also practical. Dressed in the loose-fitting style of a strong prison man, he knew what the street brothers were like, and he knew what had to be done to reach them*[15] [my emphasis].

The aesthetics and dance scholar Welsh-Asante might say that X recognized himself as art and as art he initiated the visual significance of symbols relative to his audience. Thus, Huey P. Newton's gaze borrowed the stylized image of Malcolm and it attracted him. It is something remembered, yet Muslim and distinctive. A strong prison man is a formidable man. Huey was a prison man.

A prison man is a legend in folklore, the brother on the chain gang, the outlaw, caught briefly. A prison man is Stagolee, who keeps on returning. He is Slim Greer of Sterling Brown's imaginative pen. A strong prison man is an unbroken man, steel-fisted enough to smash through all the mires of White supremacy, and still look pretty. As Malcolm X stands before Huey P. Newton at McClymonds High School, he is the ideal and work of art of the "street brothers," allowing the lumpen proletariat, a borrowed Panther term for urban men, to see him at his best, controlling, intelligent, independent, Afrocentric, and futuristic. Newton's multiple attraction to Malcolm contains more than receiving information or ideology. His attraction includes a matter of aesthetics.

African American aesthetics and Malcolm's reflection of masculine appeal gave Newton a sense of re-affirmation and recognition, affirming his sanity in the world of the Negro becoming Black. Malcolm was an example of the best of his people. Welsh-Asante (1994) confirms that "Africans have a highly developed spatial, kinesthetic and design sensibility. The idea of just creating for the pleasure of an individual is considered to be an aberration outside of society.

Works of art must be created based on tradition, heritage and reasoning."[16] Malcolm, intuiting himself as art, chose his attire for audience appreciation and acceptance. He well knew that he was extending and creating a tradition that would inform Black masculinity. Malcolm located himself into (and reshifted) the acquired sartorial tastes of Black men, and his skillful manipulation of language, mythology, history, and iconography caused Newton to emulate and imitate him.

The attire of 1960s activists projected a political defiance of American conformity, and a unification of African aesthetics. Malcolm allowed his hair to grow long, a small afro; he grew a goatee and he wore dashikis. Newton and Bobby Seale wore afros, black leather jackets, blue shirts and black berets. Madhubuti in 1969, the "Black writer-in-residence" at Cornell University, wore H. Rap Brown's trademark sunglasses, afro hairstyle, goatee, and dashiki. H. Rap Brown is the college student who left Southern University in Baton Rouge, Louisiana, to devote his entire life to the Civil Rights Movement. A prominent speaker who rose to chair the Student Non-Violent Coordinating Committee after the resignation of Stokely Carmichael, Brown advocated, like Malcolm, Black self-defense as he condemned racism.

Consistently harassed and hounded by the police and FBI, Brown became a 1960s symbol of Black pride and resistance. Thinking his public discourse incendiary, authorities in Maryland, Ohio and Virginia indicted him in 1967. With the police and FBI constantly following him, while under indictment, Brown was arrested for carrying a legal weapon across state lines.[17] H. Rap wore dark sunglasses and sported an afro, and his image in popular culture is captured in a poster where he holds a lighted match with the caption, "burn baby burn."[18]

Madhubuti's image at Cornell University closely favors Rap Brown's. His picture in *Ebony* magazine is the epitome of the angry student or teacher intellectual of the period. Introduced at the International Poetry Forum in Pittsburgh by Gwendolyn Brooks, the following exchange signals the contrasting elements between the two. Once Brooks, then Madhubuti had performed an author writes: "Miss Brooks was approached by an ingratiating black matron who sought to assure her that her works had been well received. Then, pointing to the wiry, bearded figure walking a few steps ahead, she whispered: 'But *he* frightens me.' Brevity as a value has roots in Miss Brooks. 'He should,' she responded dispassionately, keeping her pace."[19]

Yet there is a profound distinction between Madhubuti, H. Rap, and Newton although each stirred fiery images during the 1960s and 1970s. An area of difference is in ideology and directed action. For example, Madhubuti disagrees with a major point and position articulated by Huey P. Newton in the 1970s. In *From Plan to Planet* (1973), Madhubuti emphasizes the need for Blacks to "live for the people." The phrase "to live for the people" is a replay and twist on Huey Newton's book title and Panther mantra *To Die for the People* (1972). This is a saying also echoed by Fred Hampton, the slain Panther leader in Chicago where Madhubuti lives. The poet puts it this way: "We must never say 'to die for the people.' We should always be about living for the people. A people are not renewed or redeemed through the sacrifice of martyrs; in many cases martyrs are, in the final analysis, very selfish men who have failed to build a movement (institution) void of their egos, have failed to build a movement around a solid ideological base that relates and fulfills the needs of the people."[20]

According to Ethel Paris, a former member, Panthers did not necessarily seek death or wish to die. They accepted the possibility of death because of the war against individual members and the collective organization. The counter-intelligence program infiltrated the Panthers nationwide, and assassinations were set up such as the murders of Fred Hampton and Mark Clark. Ethel Paris explains how members thought about death or "dying for the people": "Yeah, we talked about death a lot because we had to be strong enough to accept it, because we believed that to get our freedom, we had to be unafraid to die."[21] Also, Malcolm X stepped into martyrdom; so did King. Once guiding principles and race love of both men enlarged extraordinary dimensions, accepting death was inevitable with threats a part of their daily lives.

Yet, Madhubuti's "living for the people" exerts a kind of attitude, discipline, and direction that ensures the unification and life of a belief system beyond epochs, incarcerations, and assassinations. Institutions do build a fulfillment of "the needs of the people," ensuring the "life" of an ideology. When institutions or movements diminish, often the glorious ideas of the progenitors disappear.

The original BPP has disappeared, and Madhubuti's institutions have not. Yet, there is a political absence in contemporary hip hop culture that weakens the imagistic stridency of the 1960s. However, there is a basketball star who bridges some of the aesthetics of the 1960s.

Allen Iverson, the star guard of the Philadelphia 76rs, ignites a visual Black Power tension today. He is possibly the first NBA ball player to publicly wear cornrows on and off the court.[22] Cornrows are an African hairstyle that followed the afro in the 1960s. He is also a star guard who wrongly received a maximum prison sentence at seventeen years old, when in high school.[23] Iverson, a high school football and basketball star in Virginia, was the only person incarcerated when a brawl occurred in a bowling alley between White and Black youths. His high school celebrity, inner city attitude, and poverty negatively impressed those in authority. Youth, Black masculinity, extraordinary ability, ghetto identification and representation, bravado, corporate endorsements, and upcoming wealth isolated Iverson for jealousy and for neutering. Because of his mother Ann Iverson and the lawyers' relentless work, Governor Douglas Wilder overturned the original five-year sentence. That was 1993. Allen Iverson was eighteen years old.

Allen Iverson carries the appearance of an urban African warrior, and he lives cultural tendencies of "brothers in the hood." For example, despite his millions, he maintains his same circle of Black male friends who grew up with him in "the hood." They took care of his family, his mother and sisters when he was incarcerated. He says he would never leave them now; his friends are extended family.

Allen Iverson dresses not in tie and suit but in urban, loose-fitting, hip-hop chic, refusing to project any image untrue to himself and his roots, he says. For these reasons Iverson alarms the corporate sponsored media, in this current age of race neutralization. Because of his cornrows, Cleveland fans booed him in 1997. Additionally, "Athletes' agents, still wedded to the crossover model of marketing, wouldn't countenance cornrows, which were seen as too in-your-face, too black."[24]

The media and corporate sponsors, with no understanding of and little respect for African or African American culture, have made Allen Iverson's wearing of cornrows synonymous with thug, "gangsta" culture. The media have taken cornrows out of Africa, away from 1960s Black Power, from Black imposition onto American aesthetics, and replayed the hairstyle as anti-social. Sports writer Rick Reilly, friendly to Iverson, reveals the corporate neo-American anti-aesthetic this way: "[When you see Iverson,] now you see the cornrows and the tattoos and the pierce-holes dripping gold, and they bug you, right? You think *thug* and *rapper* and *criminal*."[25] Subscribers to *Sports Illustrated*, disturbed when Iverson appeared on the cover, followed with such lines as "Don't you have enough ... corn-rowed freaks on the inside [of the magazine]," and "The cover with Allen Iverson made me sick to my stomach."[26]

Another friendly writer to Iverson types him this way in contrast to the more acceptable Vince Carter at that time of the Toronto Raptors. "[T]here is Iverson, all tattoos and piercings and braids and attitude, the anti-hero that the NBA fears...."[27] Celizic knows not the difference between braids and cornrows. He uses one for the other and these writers are not alone. Larry Brown, Iverson's former coach, misspeaks about cornrows in the media and on Allen Iverson's compact disc (2001). To paraphrase the coach, he says, when discussing a positive change in Iverson's behavior that, now, when people see Allen they look away from the cornrows. They accept him as a person.

Larry Brown obviously views cornrows as a negation and a reflection of non-personhood. This is the arrogance and Eurocentric racism that suggests only White critics, historians, philosophers or explorers can decide who "people" are, and those who get this classification must act, think, dress and look like Europeans or Anglo-Americans. This is a throwback to when Blacks were wooly headed, big lipped savages. It is also a reminder of how Whites consistently disregard, lack the knowledge of, and devalue Black or African aesthetics.

Brown and the other writers are not overt racists. However, their insensitivity to Black culture and American history recalls a naïve brand of White supremacy. Their comments about Black hair insult not only Allen Iverson but also all Black people. This language and thinking recalls the reasons that the 1960s developed a "Black is beautiful" aesthetic. The Black Arts and Black Power movements occurred in order for African Americans (who were Negroes then) to stop modeling Whites in appearance and in behavior. The Black Power hairstyles, the afro, braids, cornrows, locs, and other African-inspired coiffures permitted American-Africans to locate value and aesthetic pleasure in their own unique beauty.

In this current age of euphemisms for race such as "minority" and "multicultural," Allen Iverson's appearance and confidence mark him as threatening, because they mark him "Black."

Back in the 1960s, Madhubuti frightened his poetry public especially in contrast to Gwendolyn Brooks, also undergoing a transformation because of the times and her relationship to Madhubuti. Brooks and Madhubuti exchanged reciprocal energy as she mentored him, and in their intimacy, Malcolm X loomed large, because Madhubuti's controlling images derive from X's rhetoric. I recall how a White colleague in English mentioned his preference for Brooks' poetry prior to the 1960s. Before the Black Power Movement, Brooks wrote comfortable poetry, non-disturbing to Whites. Before exposure to Malcolm and Madhubuti, her poetry safely and beautifully regaled Black (Negro) life, not Black change. She represented well the values of her era, the 1950s: integration and conformity. Before her decision to craft poetry infused with Black nationalistic tendencies, she wrote memorable Negro portraitures. After her involvement with Madhubuti and the Black Arts poets, her aesthetics focused on a neo-African identity and what Madhubuti called "what is real to us." The dislike that my colleague expressed spells the absence of Eurocentric ideology in content and poetics. For Brooks to manipulate English in patterns that represented, like hair, Black cultural interests, bothered him.

When African Americans cause dissonance among Whites, they are isolated, written against, killed, or neutralized in some manner. This is a reaction to a psychological fear and guilt rooted in enslavement of the African. Probably, this is the psychological fear that Whites have of Allen Iverson today and his crew of non-smiling, young Black men. However, history proves that serious, outlaw-like young Black males have not initiated a war with Whites. Rather, non-smiling Black males are practicing a cultural stream of manhood developed to offset the hostile environs of urban America.

Summary

Based on oratory, style, demeanor, and diet, Malcolm X influenced a personal life style change for Madhubuti, Bobby Seale and Huey Newton. In diet, Malcolm's Islamic restraint from pork inspired Madhubuti to change his eating habits even more. He is a vegan vegetarian, and sometimes when he recites poetry, he expresses the benefits of eliminating meat from one's diet. Newton on the other hand used meat, particularly pork, in another way. He projected the symbol and image of "the pig" to represent abusive police behavior, and this usage found a place in the American vernacular.

Much of Malcolm's philosophy and ideology are not his alone; they come from his spiritual teacher, Elijah Muhammad, referred to by his followers as "The Honorable Elijah Muhammad." Since Newton and Madhubuti were disciples of Malcolm X, they continued (of course with variations) the 19th century Black Nationalist tradition that Elijah Muhammad had embraced during the 1930s.

Madhubuti warned Blacks to "live for the people," which is the inverse of Newton and the Panthers' slogan, to "die for the people." According to Madhubuti, living for the people is the hardest achievement for serious activists. Because of assassinations, old ideologies strut in the public domain as new and empowering ones disappear.

For example, Malcolm wore his hair naturally and sometimes wore dashikis, an act of redefining and incorporating global Black behavior. The Panthers and the 1960s poets donned the afro, which began a string of new hairstyles such as cornrows based on Black hair texture and culture. Yet today, White writers and speakers insult cornrows, an African inspired hairstyle worn by Allen Iverson (and others), star guard of the Philadelphia 76rs basketball team. Mainstream journalists have associated cornrows with "thug" or "criminal behavior." White sports writers and others often reject Allen Iverson because his appearance is "too black" and he fails to leave the ghetto element (his friends and nonbiological family) in the 'hood. Once again, Whites expect Blacks to behave in ways and to appear in images that they deem appropriate. Such ideas have gained validity again because of the omission of the 1960s transformation in Black culture and the contemporary neutralization of race and racial issues.

In Chapter Nine, we review the concept of extended family and shifting familial roles through a comparison of Madhubuti's relationship with Gwendolyn Brooks, and Malcolm X's to Ella Collins.

NINE

Communion: X, a Magnet for Madhubuti and Brooks

The relationship between Haki Madhubuti and Gwendolyn Brooks is a contemporary reminder of the behavior of dispersed enslaved people during the epoch of American slavery. Madhubuti and Brooks did not deliberately go in search of one another, but once they found each other, they never parted. The motherless Don L. Lee found a substitute mother in Gwendolyn Brooks and she another son in the young Don L. Lee.

When Gwendolyn Brooks met Don L. in 1967, he was carrying the stridency and swagger of X and the war poetry of the Age of Malcolm. In this chapter, we will examine the significance of Brooks in Madhubuti's life and literature as well as X and his relationship with his big sister Ella Collins. By viewing surrogate parenting, we can discern a generosity specific to Black women, and we can examine its effect on young Black men. We begin with young Don Luther before he was a poet and before he met his non-biological mother, Gwendolyn Brooks.

After interviewing the poet's family members to get a sense of young Don Lee's early life, I found the depth of his poverty astounding. Like Richard Wright in his literary masterpieces, *Black Boy* and *Native Son*, Don L. Lee had suffered literal hunger. One relative specifically discussed Don Lee's regular arrival at his home requesting food for himself and for his family. In *YellowBlack* (2005), the poet for the first time provides through essays and poetry an honest glimpse into his first twenty-one years. His early life penetrates as deeply as the childhood of Malcolm X in the *Autobiography*.

From childhood deprivation, Don Luther created himself out of Black music and the literature and language of W.E.B. Du Bois, Paul Robeson, Richard Wright, and Malcolm X. It is clear that gender specific, intellectually expanding race conscious role models matter, because if Lee had not found masculine literary figures, we might not have sampled his genius today.

As a fair-skinned Black, he suffered a particular sarcasm from his own people. Yet he resulted in becoming a race man because of his literary role models. He says it best: "Light skinned or fair skinned or fair skinned Black folks were /considered the benefactors, materially and / culturally, because they are the closest to / the hue of white people. If being one half, one / third, or one forth white was a benefit, I am / here to dispel that myth. My life has been that / of an outsider...."[1]

Malcolm X also speaks about the complications of color in the *Autobiography* when he differentiates between his parents' behavior towards him. X says that his Black Nationalist father, Reverend Earl Little, allotted him special treatment because of his light shade. The exact opposite occurred with his fair-skinned mother, also a Nationalist, a member of the Universal Negro Improvement Association, who whipped him for childhood infractions. X believes that Louise Little's severity arose because of his complexion, his shade a reminder of her origins, the result of rape by a White male in Grenada. Such color complications occur within the Negro-becoming-Black race due to the gradated hierarchy that developed during the enslavement of Africans in America.

Don L. Lee's family moved from Detroit to Chicago after he was born in Little Rock, Arkansas, February 23, 1942. His mother was fourteen years old, and four years later his father left the family that now included his little sister Jacklyn. Young Don L. became the man of the house and a man much too soon in a culture of "Black inferiority and white answers" (xv). *YellowBlack* is mostly about his mother, who died when young Don was sixteen years old. About his mother Maxine Graves Lee, he says that he didn't know "that her life would be short and / full of vacancies and violence" (5). About his father in the poem "Jimmy Lee: One," the poet writes: "My father was a fast question" (7), and from the poem "Jacklyn Ann," he continues about his father's absence:

> ...
> My father disappeared..., stating
> that my sister was not his child
> this was like a razor cut in the body of my mother

> a seventeen-year-old girl who had only
> known one man. My mother, a woman with
> little education, extraordinary good looks, a
> great body, southern smile, light skin with long
> straight Black hair, the beauty that could turn
> the heads of blind men. She was left with two
> children under the age of four, the stars didn't
> shine that night and it was the first, but not the
> last time there was real fear in my mother's eyes.
> It was also the last time she cried over a man [18–19].

Malcolm X's family life involved the tears of his mother flowing when Earl Little was killed. Although Malcolm experienced the support of a father in the house, one who headed the household, this normalcy was disrupted after Earl Little's death. To the point of insanity, Louise Little struggled to raise and economically support her children. When insufferable hardships caused a mental breakdown, the state of Michigan separated her children into foster care facilities.

After the family split up, Malcolm X drifted into crime and then jail at the age of 21. In prison, he made the transformation from hardened hustler to astute student of the teachings of the Honorable Elijah Muhammad and of history and politics. Madhubuti after his mother's death continued Dunbar Vocational High School, holding a series of jobs from paper routes to cleaning a bar during predawn hours. Madhubuti's unmarried sister, a year and a half younger than he, had three children before the age of twenty-one.

In 1960, he enlisted in the military for three years. During this period, Malcolm, released from prison in 1952, was traveling the country preaching the teachings of the Nation of Islam and becoming a political power broker in the Civil Rights Movement. In the military, Madhubuti read close to a book a day. His mother had stimulated his interest in literature when at thirteen she had him go to the library and check out Richard Wright's *Black Boy*. Madhubuti writes about this incident as a pivotal moment: "I refused to go [to the library] because I didn't want to go anywhere asking for anything Black. The self-hatred that occupied my mind, body, and soul simply prohibited me from going to a white library in 1955 to request from a white librarian a book by a Black author, especially with 'Black' in the title."[2]

Once he obeyed his mother, sat down at the library, and read some of the book, he had a life altering epiphany. He writes: "For the first time in my life, I was reading words developed into ideas that were not insulting to my own personhood. Richard Wright's experiences were mine even though we were separated by geography.... I checked *Black Boy* out, hurried home, went into the room I shared with my sister, and read for the rest of the night. Upon completing *Black Boy* the next morning, I was somehow a different type of questioner in school and at home.... I became more concerned about the shape of things around me."³

Madhubuti's mother planted and left an extraordinary love for literature in her only son. Yet, their relationship was often agonizing for more than her personal problems with drugs, alcohol, and prostitution.

As a child, Madhubuti hated his inability to assist his mother in her janitor's job. He anguished watching her carry heavy trashcans up and down apartment steps. Advice she gave to her only son before she died became the book title of his first best seller. She told him, "don't cry, scream." He writes in the dedication, "first to all blackmothers & especially mine (maxine) who will never read this book but said to me in my early years:

> nigger, if u is going ta open
> yr/mouth **Don't Cry, Scream**.

Which also means: **Don't Beg, Take**" (emphasis in original).

Madhubuti received his associate's degree from Chicago City College in 1966, and he attended Roosevelt University in Chicago, 1966 to 1967. During the 1960s, he was an apprentice curator for Chicago's Du Sable Museum of African History, directed by Margaret G. Burroughs. Simultaneously, he worked as a stock clerk, a post office clerk, and a junior executive for Spiegel's. In 1967, he devoted his time fully to publishing, writing, and teaching others. His heart and intellect became the world of Black people. In 1984, he earned a master's in fine arts from the University of Iowa.

Malcolm X was born in Omaha, Nebraska, on May 19, 1925, to Black Nationalist parents under the leadership of Marcus Garvey, head of the Universal Negro Improvement Association. Malcolm's family was destroyed when racists murdered his father[4] and his financially strapped mother succumbed to the inability to care for her four children, Wilfred, Hilda, Philbert, and Malcolm. Malcolm's mother was placed in a mental institution. Don L.'s mother performed odd jobs and prostitution, turned to alcohol and drugs, and died when her only son was sixteen years old. Madhubuti writes, "[M]y family's condition of poverty drove my mother into a culture that dictated both her destruction and great misery for my sister and me. By the time I was thirteen, my mother was a confirmed alcoholic and was fast losing her health. When I turned fifteen, she had moved to hard drugs and was not functional most of the time."⁵ Maxine Graves

Lee, Black in a racist America, was refused help in a nearby hospital. She died from hemorrhaging of the brain before family members could get her to the Detroit City hospital.[6] So sexually and physically disfigured at her death, Maxine Graves Lee had a closed casket funeral. This agony was so isolated and private in Haki Madhubuti that it took him forty-two years to write about his mother. In his latest memoir, one poem about his mother goes:

> ...
> She was music unemployed
> She wanted to be a dancer
> She wanted to be warm weather year round
> She wanted to know the origin of walnuts and wealth,
> She wanted to play the harmonica and sing like Billy Holiday,
> She believed in God, kind Negroes, reciprocity and southern food
> Her clothes got in the way of
> Men taking them off.[7]

The depth and layered nature of Madhubuti's poverty is reflected in another poignant, childhood memory.

> One Christmas stands out in my memory. I was about thirteen and we lived in a wood frame house next to the railroad tracks on the east side of Detroit. The house was built with cracks throughout its foundation. It literally whistled in the winter and summer wind, and we tried to fill the holes with cloth, mainly old towels and when possible tacked the holes with cardboard. In fact, cardboard fixed everything, especially the holes in my shoes. The only advantage living next to the railroad tracks was that often the freight trains that carried coal to the city's industries would park overnight outside our house, and I would steal coal from the open cars for our pot-belly wood and coal burning stove that set in the middle of our five room house. I would also walk the tracks, miles in each direction collecting coal that fell off the train as well as wood and other items that could be burned to warm our small house. It never was enough. We were always too cold in the winters or too hot in the summers. My nose never stopped running no matter the weather.[8]

Because he wore Salvation Army clothes, young Madhubuti was laughed out of Sunday school. After his mother's death and his remarkable self-education, although accepted in Detroit's best high school, then Cass Tech, he could not afford the books and supplies. After a stint in the army and back to Chicago, Madhubuti worked on the docks where non-English speaking Whites got better jobs than Blacks. Differently, Malcolm X refused to go into military service, feigning insanity when he was called to duty. This was during his hustler phase, pre-incarceration. Yet, the military provided

Don L. with food regularly, racism, and his Black self education. He read as much as possible, mostly nonfiction and poetry. After the military, he attended Wilson Junior College and found employment at Du Sable Museum where the director Margaret Burroughs encouraged his writing talent. This is when he met Gwendolyn Brooks.[9]

> Madhubuti first met Brooks when she was conducting writing workshops for south side Chicago gang members. Madhubuti's voice fills with admiration as he recalls how this diminutive woman asked the gang members to check their weapons at the door. Brooks helped him get his first teaching job, he says, and they have been "glued like mother and son" ever since.[10]

It is not uncommon for motherless children to find women (and sometimes men) who informally adopt them. Although James and Maxine Graves Lee gave birth to Madhubuti, Gwendolyn Brooks became his new mother. In literary history, she links him between poetry of the modern era and the eclectic, race-centered war poetry of the Age of Malcolm X. Widely influenced by Malcolm X, probably largely due to Madhubuti, Brooks wrote poetry to X in *In the Mecca* (1968). Her relationship to Madhubuti expanded into a close bond. Consider the following example. Once, she phoned him saying that someone was breaking into her house. His response: he drove the wrong way up a one-way street to arrive faster. On arrival, the police, more concerned about his driving in the wrong direction, questioned him until he shouted, "This is my mother. Somebody's trying to break into her home."[11]

In 1967, when Madhubuti and his circle of writers met Brooks, no one imagined the lasting impact. The artist Oscar Brown Jr. (1927–2005) had arranged the workshop for the gang members, and the new 1960s poets attended and later talked to the poetry legend about art. Brooks, at fifty, decided to give the young writers private lessons in her home. Madhubuti was twenty-five years old. Her approachability and kindness impressed not only Madhubuti but also all of the writers. They were in awe of the first Black American male or female to receive the Pulitzer for poetry. The writing workshops continued for years, and something remarkable happened in 1969: when the young poets gathered for their writing lessons, Brooks entered the room with a new hairstyle: the afro. "'Everybody howled Madhubuti said. It was symbolic of a refocusing of her poetry of her decision to write, consciously and directly to blacks rather than having a general readership in mind. She said that, by meeting us, it had blackened her language, and I imagine it blackened her soul.'"[12]

However, this appreciation and imitation of 1960s aesthetics did not mean that the poetry giant agreed with Black Arts poetics. In the poetry of war, Brooks disagreed with the presentation of Whites. In her work, she illustrated Black humanity in portraitures. The new poets, however, wrote resistance poetry to attack assimilation and racism, and to design a neo-African collective perspective. This war poetry represented a response and an attack on current and historical violations of Negroes' human rights. This is the only kind of poetry Madhubuti composed.

Madhubuti, who personally visited Brooks three or four times weekly, had another problem. She disagreed vigorously with his diction. Mainly, they clashed over the appropriateness of using profanity in poetry. Because of this issue, Madhubuti stormed out of her house on more than one occasion. In fact, Brooks scolded him, calling profanity an easy reach. Madhubuti recalls, "She was always trying to push for the best.... She taught me kindness, and I was rough.... I was angry; I was ready to fight. And she taught me how to negotiate the world more effectively."[13] On one occasion after not speaking with Brooks for a period of time, Madhubuti looked closely at his work. He reconciled himself with his Black Power poetry that attacked without retreat. He then reminisced on the beauty of Brooks' poetry and on her absence before meeting her. His melancholy and compelling admiration urged his return, and they both agreed to seek verbal harmony. Brooks reached out and taught Madhubuti with care and concern, showing him how to fight and how to love, helping him to become one of America's important poets.

In bars around the South Side during the 1960s, they often read poetry together. He remembers her saying when they walked into taverns that they were "gonna lay" some poetry on the people.

This unusual couple — unlike the normal duo one sees in cinema, television, narratives, and the news — worked together to emphasize the significance of poetry to grassroots people. How often does one glimpse a contrasting twosome — opposite genders and ages — coming together for the validation of Black people, Black language, and life? The tall lightly colored man and the shorter deeply hued woman were a pair, representing a tradition in the Black community that some say has dwindled. This duo brought poetry to the disadvantaged, not normally an audience who purchases poetry books.

Gwendolyn Brooks also wrote poems for children and enjoyed reading to youngsters. Using her own funds, she established the Young Poets Award, for thirty years, and sponsored public readings to reward new writers. Brooks, like Madhubuti, recognized a missing piece in Black culture that she sought to rectify, using her own resources. This heightened sense of giving they commonly shared, and the son seeking to honor her while she lived, created at Chicago State, the Gwendolyn Brooks Center for

Creative Writing. Now in her physical absence, the Center continues her legacy. Together, Brooks and Madhubuti invigorated collective, epic memory and the spatial realm once actualized by the ones enslaved. What I mean is this: The institution of slavery tore families asunder and often those enslaved located new kinship on different plantations, in different geographies. Madhubuti very naturally missed his mother, therefore suffering maternal absence. Gwendolyn Brooks probably intuited this lack and opened her life to receive him (and his family) as Black foremothers have always done.

Similarly, when young Malcolm lost his family to racism: after the killing of his father, and the disorientation of his mother, Ella Collins took his mother's place. Collins, his sister by Reverend Earl Little's first wife, had not specifically known Malcolm until the dissolution of his family. When he arrived in Boston from Lansing, Ella, like Brooks with Madhubuti, encouraged him to learn his environment in a casual pace. When Malcolm first went to Boston to live with her, in the autobiography, he says that she did not insist that he immediately find a job. She allowed him time to explore a new city. However, in *Seventh Child* (1998), Rodnell Collins, Ella's son and X's nephew, states that on his second day in Boston, his mother took Malcolm to an uncle's parking lot business and got him hired.[14] This first job being a part-timer may account for the discrepancy between the narratives. Ella Collins later secured X's first full time job at an ice-cream parlor. In the autobiography, X says this about his sister's generosity:

> About my second day there in Roxbury, Ella told me that she didn't want me to start hunting for a job right away like most newcomer Negroes did. She said that she had told all those she'd brought North to take their time, to walk around, to travel the buses and the subway, and get the feel of Boston, before they tied themselves down working somewhere.[15]

Malcolm had just graduated the eighth grade — he was between fourteen and fifteen years old. Indeed, Ella Collins was a sister and mother figure to him. In "get[ting] the feel of Boston," X discerned intraracial class distinctions and culture. From this discernment, he recognized his comfort level among the ghetto poor, those with hip culture. Among Shorty and other friends from the hood, X brought his first zoot suit and got his first conk.

Ella helped Malcolm to settle into a new life after a former White teacher discouraged him from making law a career. Providing him with a sense of importance and love from the very beginning, she arranged a welcoming dinner when he arrived in Boston from Lansing. She got him the soda fountain job at the Townsend Drug store, where he hated to be called a "soda jerk." And later Ella behaved like a proud mother when Malcolm brought home the refined Laura to take to a big band dance. During his time with Ella Collins, she remained his guiding force whether or not he followed her suggestions.

The emotion of the above mother and son relationship is reflected in the poem Brooks wrote on the birth of the Madhubutis' daughter Laini Nzinga, titled "A Welcome Song for Laini Nzinga (Born November 24, 1975)." It reads:

> Hello Little Sister.
> Coming through the rim of the world.
> We are here! To meet you and to mold and
>   To maintain you.
> With excited eyes we see you.
> With welcoming ears we hear the
> clean sound of new language.
> The language of Laini Nzinga.
> We love and we receive you as our own.[16]

The Madhubutis and the Brooks-Blakelys attached into extended family. Safisha, Haki, the poet's daughter Nora, and a family friend were at Gwendolyn Brooks' bedside when her physical body left for the other side. Although unable to communicate with her, they read aloud her poetry and other enjoyable literature until she expired. Third World Press has published Brooks' final book of poetry, *In Montgomery* (2003). On meeting Haki Madhubuti, Gwendolyn Brooks received another son and he another mother.

He captures their intimacy in the following poetic statement printed in the funeral program. Over two thousand people attended the service, Monday, December 11, 2000, at Rockefeller Chapel, University of Chicago campus. The son writes:

> I've grown up in your magic, shadows and words, I've seen you manage pens, paper, poor eyesight and gift-giving. I've measured the recent dip in your walk, noting the way the wind leans you into its current and I worry. What if I'm not there to catch your arm to gently steer you away from a fall, missed step or away from harm's way but you've always been your own clock and as the seasons disappear and rise you know exactly what time it is, beating the beat in storms not of your making. See you on the bright side.
>
> Haki R. Madhubuti
Your Cultural Son

This poetic statement has been beautifully revised into a poem entitled "Eighty-three Is a Wise Number" with an additional stanza that brings "peach and hurricane water" in *Run Toward Fear* (2004). Madhubuti and Brooks shared what Marimba Ani calls ethos and worldview. Both include shared historical experiences, along with a common and emotional culture.[17] To particularize this relationship, to explore the African inspired nature of this relationship and its outcome, the Gwendolyn Brooks Center and poetic texts, Welsh-Asante's *Nzuri* model is useful. The *meaning* of Brooks and Madhubuti's coming together coalesced to highlight the "significance [of literature and love] in relationship to individual and community." Neither artist wrote in a vacuum. Each produced art to effect people turned into inferior subjects in Western civilization. The *ethos* of their literature, artistic presentation, and relationship exuded "spirit, emotion, and energy," again combined historical roots. The quality of their relationship and literary expression enhanced the two and everyone who viewed this joining, that extends in energy and spirituality beyond America and beyond culture. For example, in African spirituality in the pantheon of deities, they have children and some adopt other children.[18] Thus, even in the metaphysical world of the African, the concept of extended family assumes an integrated dimension. Brooks assisted in his becoming a better wordsmith, and their poetry functioned as a magnet to Black listeners for reconfiguration in language, specific to their own culture and world view.

The mission of the Black Arts poets was more than a collective writing group. They intended to produce a neo-African worldview as they developed neo-African culture. A Black aesthetic was to defeat White supremacy, and this aesthetic and dynamism influenced Brooks. She left a prestigious publishing house in order to allow Broadside Press and later Third World Press to publish her poetry. Welsh-Asante says that the undercurrent of the seven senses of *Nzuri* spring from three sources, spirit, rhythm, and creativity. Linked to the soul, spirit cannot die, and it is a link to the "inner world of ideas, thoughts, and emotions." It is through ideas, thoughts, and emotions that Madhubuti was joined to his new mother. Together they established a heightened significance to not only Black writing, but also institution building. Many people during the 1960s talked about the importance of institution building yet Madhubuti, with the assistance of Brooks, and his wife, extended themselves beyond the talk.

Summary

X and Madhubuti emerge from the working class, urban lifestyle. Both are self-educated men who used this learning to elevate the status of the then Negro people. They have much more in common. Both lost their parents and each went in search of new family, whether consciously or not. Each recreated his masculine self from the words of male writers; X, more so from the teachings of Elijah Muhammad, Madhubuti from Du Bois, Robeson, Wright and X. Both males were assisted and directed positively by extraordinary Black women. Madhubuti found Gwendolyn Brooks, like X idolized his big sister Ella Collins. Mentoring their young male charges, these women continue a long established pattern in African American culture that has roots in enslavement, when those either sold or previously in bondage found new family. This kind of informal adoption is present in African spirituality where the Divine principles have children and adopt other children.

Because of his disturbing childhood, it took Madhubuti over forty years to write about his private life, particularly his mother, Maxine Graves Lee. In opening up his world during his first twenty-one years, we now experience a male's search for comprehension in an existentialist venue of racism and poverty. Knowing his earlier circumstances makes his achievements even more remarkable.

TEN

The X-Factor Influence: A Theoretical Frame for Resistance Poetry

In the previous chapter, we examined two important mother figures who assisted in the intellectual and personal growth and development of X and Madhubuti. In this chapter, we examine discourse as opposed to human relationships. We visit the rhetorical strategies that Malcolm X engaged — to transform the Negro — that enormously influenced, inspired, and shaped how Madhubuti designed his art of the 1960s. 1960s art springs from patterns in poetics originating in the expressions of Langston Hughes and Marcus Garvey.

Langston Hughes, Marcus Garvey, Malcolm X, and Haki Madhubuti choreographed in art the process of re(re)naming. That is to urge the Negro people to name change, after three centuries of wearing a bastardized, demeaning appellation that to paraphrase Madhubuti emerged from "the basement of other people's mind." In oratory, Malcolm, forwarding instructions from Elijah Muhammad, his "Messenger," directly persuaded the Negroes, a conquered people, to name change, to become African Americans. Once the Negroes collectively name changed, they overturned more than three hundred years of negating (re)naming. Hence, the re(re)naming of the Negro to African American is an important feat in the history, psychology, and aesthetics of a once enslaved people. It is an act of independence that Malcolm X powerfully encouraged: at the level of a zealot, X is the first public intellectual to demand this linguistic and racial disappearance. In urgency, his oratory often carries this subject, which reached its goal twenty-four years after his assassination. The Negroes officially adopted his term, African American.[1]

In this chapter, to determine exactly how Malcolm X accomplished desirable race-specific results, we deconstruct excerpts of his speeches.

In X's speeches, the re(re)naming issue separates him from other 1960s leaders who never argued for a racially distinct or African connected terminology relative to the Negro. Most 1960s leaders protested against domestic injustices, which were ontologically demeaning, and this fight caused incarcerations, beatings, lost employment, and death. However, Malcolm in oratory fought those same battles as well as forwarding domestic and international concerns for the "so-called" Negro *and* the continental African. Yet, in his multi-purposeful argument, he consistently articulated the problematic nature of the word "negro," which Richard Moore had urgently discussed before him, and he devised a linguistic campaign to accelerate the re(re)naming process. Examining this critical phenomenon in African American literature and history resumes the complementary method of investigating Black achievement. Because of the damaging effect of chattel slavery and the historical omission of the study of African civilizations from an African-centered perspective, it is vital to re-frame African Diaspora history and culture. Evaluating the life of Malcolm X according to principles of African-centered thought architects a new paradigm and worldview, as it additionally surfaces a line of thought and a matter of existence too often dismissed or omitted in discourse. Malcolm X is an antecedent of the Negro's journey from guinea, or negro, to African American because of his persuasive and prescient oratory. This is one among many major accomplishments that Malcolm bequeathed to his people. Yet, scholars too often concentrate on what they call Malcolm's articulation of "rage" as his gift to the American Africans. Cornel West in *Race Matters* (1994) explains a "psychic conversion" of Malcolm that emerges from a "rage" that had few places to find legitimate "spaces." In other words, a "falter[ing]" of Malcolm sets the tone and the stage of his legacy. Malcolm in my view is much larger than that. His internationalist and Pan-Africanist perspective generated a school of thought that he made new for the multitudes influenced by his persistent message.

Malcolm's Oratorical Approach

Malcolm never taught a class in a university. In fact, he failed to finish middle school and he certainly never returned to traditional educational institutions to acquire the appropriate degrees that equal a doctorate of philosophy. Yet, as Huey P. Newton notes in his autobiography, *Revolutionary Suicide* (1973), Malcolm was more learned and astute than many with a degree, and Newton himself was a university student when he made that claim. Malcolm's pedagogy spins a new historicist approach where he teaches his listeners to revisit the construction and the operation of America. He deconstructs traditional history, isolating for examination the hierarchy that favored Whites over Blacks. In his oratory he inverts the patriotism of traditional history and speaks completely from the perspective of the "so-called Negro" who has the potential and the obligation to become someone else. Along with addressing intellectuals, Malcolm's attraction involved his speaking the language of the urban male and female, the working class populations and the youth. Speaking from their perspective in the style of urban culture, he offered a new identity and direction to a people that considered themselves the sons and daughters of the enslaved, used and abused for centuries. Taking the Negro back to an Africa with civilizations instead of savagery expanded the group's perspective and it complicated thought about American roots.

Additionally, when X concentrates on the topic of enslavement, he inverts the democratic initiative promoted in the founding of America. The inverted notion of patriotism shows exactly how one group of people experienced privilege while others experienced servitude. Offering the historical hypocrisies and flaws inherent in an educational system that upholds this master narrative, Malcolm's lectures encouraged many to self-educate, start study groups, and organize literary circles. He lectured to his listeners about origins, societal segregation, and the disparaging, inaccurate media representations, putting his listeners on notice to examine their environment in total. Public talks about racism were not the American norm. Similarly, discussing the psychological harm and hurt of racism were publicly uncustomary in America.

Armed with a Nation of Islam inspired re-education, Malcolm preached to males to take responsibility for themselves, the family, and the Black nation. Such responsibilities refigure the composition of manhood in America. Black manhood, particularly young Black manhood in urban enclaves, lauded the hustler persona, with a stable of women. This image still reverberates in hip-hop videos and films. Malcolm X spoke to that energy, reinvigorating it into another possibility, and because he himself was a product of poverty, he had the similar seductive language, a convincing spirit, creativity, and rhythm to persuade his listeners to listen.

As a fighter intellectual, Malcolm pounded with words, which probably relates to his always present desire to be a lawyer. He represented the repressed desires of an entire people. All of his experiences culminated into his becoming an organ for the Nation of Islam, his platform for growth that took him out of America physically and mentally. The NOI assisted his fashioning a population into a nation with an internationalist point of view. Like Cheikh Anta Diop, Malcolm connects the history of the Diaspora African back to the continent, beginning a new school of thought: Afrocentricity, and Malcolm spoke like a free African man.

However, Patricia Hill Collins states that Malcolm failed to incorporate social class theory into his rhetoric; therefore, he omitted divisions among Whites. She says: "Malcolm X alludes to the differences between working-class and middle-class Blacks. No such distinction is made for whites. They remain part of an undifferentiated mass lumped together under the label 'the white man.'"[2]

Collins is partly correct. Malcolm, a self-taught intellectual, was first and foremost engaged with the empowerment of the becoming Blacks. He did not, as most scholars are taught, uphold the ideology of Europe and White America. As the chief representative of the NOI, he stepped into a Garvey-type independence that dissolved any vestiges of Du Bois's double-consciousness. Malcolm, before the Black Arts poets and Haki Madhubuti, was at war with America. He lived in a time considerably different from the current day, when scholars can amass information on stratifications among groups and multicultural perspectives. When Malcolm lived America had open apartheid. Plus, his invitations from the socialist labor forums suggest that his White constituents understood why he spoke about Blacks and Whites as wholes, not parts. Malcolm understood the textured meaning of manifest destiny that enabled *all* Whites to partake of supremacy and privilege. Malcolm spoke, fought, and organized for a people openly segregated against and vulgarly denied human rights. With the financial support of the NOI, he did not have to muzzle his mandates for Negro humanity and dignity. Even more importantly, he could re-envision himself through the eyes of a new ideology and religion where he and his people occupied the center of existence. In the pervasive master narrative, where a White or European perspective is the center, the emphasis implies a universality that does not exist. In Malcolm's budding Afrocentric rhetorical discourse, he made no pretense to universality. He addressed issues from the point of view of African Diaspora people who sought to define kindred and commonality among all the variations within the Diaspora. To be African is to be human. That is, any racial group can locate an interconnection within the rhetoric of Malcolm. Just like anyone can sympathize with and understand perspectives of Asians, English, Scottish, Alaskan and other peoples.

Malcolm was able to speak from his own perspective because the NOI support provided a gateway to independence that permitted his confident and aggressive voice to sing the song of the oppressed. Rupturing the stereotype of the 1950s male, Malcolm X was a nonconformist to decorum, religion, and passive methods of protest. Malcolm refused to be among those kicked, punched, cursed, and spat upon while peacefully marching for rights that no man or woman has the authority to give. Malcolm instead brought the rhetoric and attitude of the disadvantaged urban class to television cameras. He gave verity and credence to urban crime and the 'hood. Like contemporary hip-hop artists, he found source material and worth in urban so-called underclass life. He was not ashamed of his unlawful behavior, explaining that impoverished areas and poverty serve the interests of the constructors of the ghettoes. In his nonconformity, his creativity flourished.

Spirit, rhythm, and creativity are units of *ntu* (life force, vital energy), composed in the cosmological energy present in all things. This energy unites and flows through everything in existence. Malcolm's labor of language had more than one effect and purpose. It was for him and for humanity, enabling listeners to inwardly (and outwardly) experience new directions and dimensions. With Malcolm's ministerial creativity, he responded to metaphysical as well as physical means. His creativity is what Silvano Arieti would call "the perennial (and almost always unverbalized) premise of creativity to show that the tangible, visible, and audible universe is infinitesimal in comparison to the one that awaits discovery through exploration of the external world and of the human psyche."[3] Malcolm's oratory penetrated the "internal world" of the psychology of the Negro, setting the stage for discovery and enlightenment, his *ntu* relating to predecessors in literature and life.

The Tradition of the Badman

In literature and in life, X represents thought and action existing since enslavement, in the badman tradition that disrupted enslavement and later segregation, discrimination, and the law. In fiction, Frederick Douglass begins this tradition in literature when he pens his first and only novel, *The Heroic Slave* (1853) and Martin Delany makes variations on this theme in *Blake or the Huts of America* (1861–2). Douglass's resistor was an actual person, Madison Washington. Delany's character Blake was imaginary with the possibility of a human counterpart. Douglass's *Heroic Slave* is not only the first Black novella in America. It is also the first literature of resistance in America. Yet, not surprisingly, it is absent in the first encyclopedias on

African American culture, literature, history and experience. These encyclopedias are the results of a wish, desire, and project of the great sage W.E.B. Du Bois. Cornel West, David Lionel Smith, and Jack Salzman edited the *Encyclopedia of African American Culture and History* (1996) and Henry Louis Gates and Kwame Anthony Appiah edited *Africana: The Encyclopedia of the African and African American Experience* (1999). Each hefty tome omits the first literary resistance in history written by an important and familiar abolitionist.

These are not insignificant omissions. These absences hide a human aspect of resistance, limiting the range of responses that Black people engaged to overturn enslavement. Additionally, such omissions restrict how Douglass (and other men and women) thought about masculinity, humanity, and heroics. Madison Washington is a hero to Douglass, not necessarily one to Whites. This important point of opposition illustrates the inverted way in which Black people view the world based on their experiences. Washington commandeered a slave ship, fought and killed Whites and escaped into the West Indies. The Blacks (and well meaning Whites) would cheer such an escape. Enslavers and those with the enslavers' mentality would not. This absence is a disconnecting and dislocating one from the *ntu* of resistance. The spirit and creativity of resistance when disappeared has no spaces on which to link, flow, and transform. Such omissions bury the love of humanity and freedom in the enslaved, suggesting a nonexistence. Yet, Madison Washington, after escaping bondage once, faced re-enslavement in order to gain his wife's freedom. His story is magnificent.[4]

Washington's absence and others similar in Black encyclopedias is a reaction to the master narrative. It attempts to erase the full anger and revolutionary potency that men and women considered as options. This disappearance appeals to the fears of Whites. If the general public never views a courageous revolutionary image, then perhaps it does not exist. Plus, in this vacuum, when revolutionaries do emerge, the media then images fervent people as anomalies. Such erasures try to ensure that the general public only discerns a specific kind of activism.

In reality, the badman character lives in all areas where Blacks reside. He is the unnamed enslaved man (or woman) who resists his master and later the one who refuses to abide by laws that restrain the reaching of full potential. He is the boxer Jack Johnson, the orator and organizer Marcus Garvey, the courageous Ida B. Wells. Also, some are unnamed, working at low volume, keeping the people thinking and motivated.

Malcolm X did not write books, but, like David Walker (1785–1830), he delivered emancipating discourse. David Walker was born in Wilmington, North Carolina, on September 28, 1785, to a slave father (who died before David's birth) and a free mother; therefore, he was a free Black because the status of the mother determined the condition of the child. Walker as a young man traveled throughout the South observing the inequities and the horrors of slavery. Influenced by the Methodism of Reverend Richard Allen, he left for Philadelphia for a while and then settled in Boston where he became a leader of a small group of free Blacks. He married, opened a successful new and used clothing store, learned literacy, and became a prominent member of the Massachusetts General Colored Association. This organization was to abolish slavery and better local conditions for Blacks. Walker backed the first Black newspaper in America, *Freedom's Journal*, in 1827. Walker's *Appeal* (1829) and his activism probably caused his death. In the South he had been wanted dead or alive for up to $10,000. On June 28, 1830, he was found dead in the street close to his clothing shop, perhaps poisoned.[5]

He like Malcolm X had his own individual way of illustrating creativity in order to eradicate bondage. In Walker's epoch the bondage was both physical and mental. In X's age the restraints were societal and mental. Living during the era of enslavement, Walker could not make incendiary public speeches, but Malcolm could. Walker spoke to small groups of free Blacks in Boston while Malcolm traveled the nation and the world. Malcolm, alive during the modern era, stood on "The Messenger's" shoulders and spoke some of Walker's previous ideology. Both men with similar literary and oratorical purposes urged revolt against slavery and separation from White America. They are joined in *ntu* in commonality. Walker's *Appeal* was the most notorious publication in America. Walker footnotes:

> I would not be afraid to stake down upon the board Five Cents against Ten, that there are in the single State of Virginia, five or six hundred thousand Coloured persons. Four hundred and fifty thousand of whom (let them be well equipt for war) I would put against every white person on the whole continent of America. (Why? why because I know that the Blacks, once they get involved in a war, had rather die than to live, they either kill or be killed.)[6]

Malcolm similarly argues in *Malcolm X: The Last Speeches* that

> It's not wrong to expect equality. If Patrick Henry and all of the Founding Fathers of this country were willing to lay down their lives to get what you are enjoying today, then it's time for you to realize, that a large ever-increasing number of Black people in this country are willing to die for what we know is due us by birth.[7]

According to Welsh-Asante's Nzuri model, the *ntu* in spirit, rhythm, and creativity cannot die. Hence, David Walker and Malcolm X are bound in "the inner world of ideas, thought, and emotions,"[8] where they both value group identity over the individual. When Cornel West talks about Malcolm's rage he is also implicitly referring to the rage of David Walker. Walker's tone projects his anger. Readers (hear) and view it in the text where he prominently places a series of exclamation marks when punctuating important and frustrating observations. For example, when Walker explains his disfavor of interracial marriage, he writes "that the black man, or man of colour, who will leave his own colour ... and marry a white woman, to be a double slave to her just because she is *white* ought to be treated by her as he surely will be, ... as a NIGGER!!!!"[9]

In this *ntu* of fomentation appearing in literature, oratory, and life, David Walker also casts aspersions against Whites. Elijah Muhammad and then Malcolm X stepped into this ideological and linguistic style, and X proliferated it throughout the nation and the world during the 1960s. This unique oration is the narrative outcome of seculars from enslavement. During that time, the enslaved could not forthrightly express themselves, but the displeasure is obvious in various poems. Consider "Raise a Ruckus Tonight": "My ol missus promise me / when she die she set me free. / Lived so long her haid got ball / Give up the notion of dyin atall."[10] This secular, in wit, humor and signification (mocking and indirection), expresses displeasure with White enslavers. Walker, a nominally free man, attacks Whites similarly, directly and historically:

> We view them next in Rome, where the spirit of tyranny and deceit raged still higher. We view them in Gaul, Spain, and in Britain.—In fine, we view them all over Europe, together with what were scattered about in Asia and Africa ... and we see them acting more like *devils* than accountable men[11] [my emphasis].

Walker attacks the "spirit" of the Whites, describing it as "tyranny and deceit." In the *nzuri* model, beauty and good are interchangeable, regarding perceptions and values as complementary. Spirit as a manifestation of *ntu* has a contrasting and similar ethos when applied to the behavior of Whites. The similarity occurs in the unchanging nature of spirit through time and geography. However, its difference is in the source of spirit as a unit of *ntu*. In *nzuri*, spirit bonds to soul, the necessary impulse for creativity. It is the inner realm of the individual and collective bridging the metaphysical world, the harmonic divine, and secular to the realm of ideas. The spirit of enslavers stands in opposition, outside of this *ntu*.

Walker projects the term "devil" as a synonym for White behavior, contrasting goodness in the religious and secular worlds. Walker, like Malcolm X a century later, groups Whites collectively because whether or not an enslaver, every White American had the opportunity to purchase people of African descent.[12] In the Age of Malcolm, his listeners attributed the creative use of "devil" to him and to Elijah Muhammad. Walker's *Appeal* (1829) demonstrates that this descriptor and characterization of Whites had long been a functional belief within the lexicon of the enslaved and the free. During slavery, the enslaved created, for example, "De Ole Nigger Driver" with the subsequent stanza: "Nigger driver second devil / O, gwine away! / Best ting for do he driver / O, gwine away! / Knock he down and spoil he labor / O, gwine away!"[13]

The "Nigger Driver" was the overseer in charge of the enslaved who performed brute labor from sun up to sun down. The above one is cruel, called the "second devil"; the implication is the master and his mistress are the prime devils on earth. Hence, the term devil and its *ntu* applied to Blacks and to Whites. It maximizes behavior more than biology. Also like Walker and his understanding of Black resistance, these enslaved laborers recognized physically fighting as an option: "Knock he down and spoil he labor." Therefore when Malcolm characterized Whites as avatars of evil, he was recalling the narrative ideology of David Walker and those in bondage. Malcolm X in a public speech in New York City in Harlem called Whites "devils," "old pale things," "exploiters," "robbers" and other defaming descriptors. Both Walker and X employ "devil" in the Christian, historical version, dissimilar from the rendition found in Negro or Black folklore.

In folklore, the enslaved Africans visited "the devil" with High John the Conqueror, and not only did they have a bar-be-cue in hell, they also held an election between John and the devil and John won.[14] This inversion well served the people. Those in servitude for life manifested a champion that they resembled and one who could outwit the metaphysical forces that assisted in perpetuating slavery. High John, as Zora Neale Hurston tells us, was a whisper in some places and a song in others. Only the enslaved could hear or see him when he decided to take on flesh and roam the plantations unbeknownst to the master class. High John assisted in managing, enduring, and defeating a legal system that dismissed the Negro's humanity and classified murder, brute labor, and disenfranchisement as normal.

A masculine conception of a metaphysical hero, High John demonstrates a probable African-inspired revelation of the trickster in religion. Papa Legba, or Lebas as he is known in Haiti, is a god who causes confusion, and the people respect him. Sterling Stuckey writes about this figure as a cross between Jesus Christ and Elegba, which will be discussed in chapter eleven. This *ntu* is a tradition international in conception. Walker and X reflect this *ntu* in the badman tradition, which complicates and inverts the ideology and ethos of enslavers and oppressors, causing that system of thought to turn for the advantage of the Black. The enslaved people's imagining a champion on earth who could defeat their idea of the "devil" illustrates a new American spirit and creativity that is included in the theory of David Walker. David Walker was a free Black and a champion for Blacks enslaved and free. He offered his wings and his words to elevate the enslaved and the free into an unfamiliar independence. His wings are synecdoche of the black crow that carried High John and the enslaved into hell (and heaven as well), as the folk tale goes.

High John was a narrative among enslaved people. David Walker and Malcolm X, however, lived the lives of scholars reading mostly history. In that pursuit, they both acknowledge that in Western thought Africa lacks civilization. Malcolm attempts to eradicate this rusty myth just as Walker before him connects American Blacks to the Egypt of the Pharaohs. In Malcolm's lectures on African history, he journeys from north Africa to south illustrating a continuity of "highly developed" civilizations inherent to the "so-called Negroes'" history. When Malcolm visited Egypt, he called Egyptians and Harlem residents the same. Claiming Egypt and the pyramid builders as his own, Malcolm insisted that ancient Blacks initiated the arts and sciences. Establishing this link, X in his oratory resituates the "Negro" to accept a radical shift in thought and naming.

Before Malcolm, Walker identifies a connection between Nile Valley civilization and Africans on the continent and throughout the Diaspora. Referring to the Egyptians as African, he compares the complexions of his present day Negroes to those of the ancients.[15] Such a comparison links the enslaved and the free in America with a classical civilization that started the arts and sciences. It allows those subservient in America to penetrate the idea of being whole human beings and members of a great historical civilization. This knowledge awakes a dormant energy *ntu* that affects the abstract on earth and in other spheres in African thought. With creativity as the metatext for creation, this is the fire that sparks the boomerang effect.

This critical adoption of antiquity is similar to the thinking of White scholars during the 19th century when David Walker walked the earth. During the height of American slavery, the Whites decided to realign the Greeks with European and Anglo-American history in order to establish classical roots. Contemporary Afrocentric scholars attempt the very same but with different motives. The enslavers were building a historical supremacy to continue to deny the opportunity of empowerment for Negroes. The neo-African scholars who align Diaspora history with that of the continent are reconstructing because of the immeasurable loss of culture and history. This historical loss happened because of, as Walter Rodney insists, the underdevelopment — slavery and colonialism — of Africa.

Malcolm fought against injustices with organizing and oratory. Killing off the word "negro" was a protracted battle that he never yielded. Developing a masterful strategy that encouraged discarding the term, he became a metaphor for the process itself. Knowing that identity, naming, and ontology intersect and interlock, he constructed a methodological and linguistic death for the term "negro." The highlights of his verbal strategic discourse are (1) He placed "so-called" before "Negro" creating doubt in linguistic nearness. (2) He positioned "Negro" between degrading synonyms. (3) He substituted degrading synonyms for "Negro." (4) He systemically explained the historical formation of the negro. (5) He surrounded "Negro" in sarcasm and signification. (5) He differentiated between "Negro" and other preferable racial indicators. Following is an example of how Malcolm discredited the term using negating synonyms. He says:

> We ... believe that the presence today in America of The Honorable Elijah Muhammad, his teachings among the 20 million *so-called Negroes*, and his naked warning to America concerning her treatment of these 20 million *exslaves* is all the fulfillment of divine prophecy[16] [my emphasis].

"So-called" prefixes "Negro" with doubt and the expectation of something else, a mystery unknown, and "exslaves," a synonym for "Negroes," associates many degrading meanings. A reminder of American bondage, it recalls shame, sorrow, anger, humiliation, hurt, defeat, cowardice, and rage. In this psychological fusion, Malcolm enters the divinity aspect, which in African thought overlaps into secular events and occurrences. Even today, for example, notice how African American rap artists, singers, and actors when receiving a public award normally thank God, first. In Africa an allegiance to God ($N\underline{t}r$) and God Forces ($N\underline{t}rw$) is commonplace. Among the Yoruba, people consult the Odu for direction in matters of existence because divinity exists in all things. All things have *ntu*. In this combining of the physical and metaphysical Malcolm establishes the groundwork for re(re)naming, and he prophesizes.

Benjamin 2X (Goodman), a student and close associate of Malcolm X, further explains this language performance. Benjamin 2X is the master of ceremonies who introduced Malcolm at the Audubon Ballroom minutes before the assassination. He explains how Malcolm X taught that "negro" was a derivative from the prefix "necro," which means "death," "corpse," and "dead tissue."[17] Such denotations reflect in the image of Africa in the poetry of Claude McKay and Countee Cullen, with McKay a "ghost" in the poem "Outcast" because of lacking clear understanding of and identification with Africa. And Cullen, influenced by the term "negro," sought death over life in "Shroud of Color." In the imaginations of both poets, living beneath "negro," they reflect Malcolm's funerary associations.

Elijah Muhammad instructed X on "the Negro" because he believed the (re)naming enforced and capitalized on the parent-child relationship between the White and Negro. Parents name children, and in African thought, names must mean something culturally and spiritually important or at least have human relevancy to the actual world. For Muhammad, who spent his life studying the hatred of Whites for Blacks, realized that his people wearing a name that meant "death" signaled the automation of the Negro. Therefore in re(re)naming, he expected the Negro to become human and to mature.

X's connotations for "death" and "corpse" are different from the early writings of the ancient Africans on death. Death among the ancients was a ritualized judgement and a transformation that implies a similarity between heaven and earth. This is why the imperial treasures were buried with the royalty, and sometimes the servers of the rulers were buried alive as well. According to this culture and thinking, activity continues after one expires. Throughout African cultures, the deceased are involved in assisting in earthly matters. The Yoruba God, Egungun, incarnated the spirit of the past. He whirled in ceremonies, and he entertained, judged, and provided wisdom.[18] However, for Muhammad dealing with Negroes, "death" meant something else, lacking knowledge of a relationship to the great continent of Africa. Muhammad taught Malcolm that like Jesus resurrecting Lazarus, re(re)naming would stimulate the Negro to life and activity. Yet, Malcolm adopted more of the African cultural transformation than Muhammad had suggested.

Excerpts from Benjamin 2X's compilation of Malcolm's speeches show *how* Malcolm set up his oratory to destroy what Richard Moore called "the evil name," "Negro." X preached:

> The Honorable Elijah Muhammad teaches that the "so-called Negro" is the one that the Bible is talking about....[19]
>
> Once the American "so-called Negroes" have been awakened to a knowledge of themselves and of their own God and of the white man, then they're on their own....[20]
>
> You may ask what does the religion of Islam have to do with the American "so-called Negro's" changing attitude toward himself, toward the white man, toward segregation, toward integration, and toward separation....[21]
>
> The Honorable Elijah Muhammad teaches us that no people on earth fit

the Bible's symbolic picture about the Lost Sheep more so than America's twenty million "so-called Negroes."[22]

The "lost sheep" substitutes for "Negro," couched in nebulousness because of "so-called." In contrast this is not identical to the previous excerpt and the association with enslavement. The prior one visits the inner and outer world of the Negro. This one centers the so-named group in religion. In total, Malcolm combines the social, secular, and spiritual, intersecting race, religion, and nationalism. Preparing his audience for new ideology, he negatively critiques Christianity; however, he makes the so-named the stars of the Bible, a position they have secretly enjoyed since slavery. Blacks identified with the Jews in the Bible. Religion and racism figure together in the above excerpts. By way of critiquing Christianity and racism, X prompts his audiences to rethink the past and present role of God in secular life, similar to what Langston Hughes accomplishes in his controversial poem "Good Bye Christ."

Benjamin 2X says that Malcolm's speeches were normally two hours long. To conduct a quantitative analysis to determine how often he mentioned racial indexes, I next isolate three speeches and a speech-interview. This will illustrate how often his oratory emphasized this subject, in preparation for future success. The speeches are "Black Man's History" (1962); "The Old Negro and the New Negro" (1963); "God's Judgement of White America: The Chickens Are Coming Home to Roost" (1963); and a speech-interview conducted by A.B. Spellman on March 19, 1964. The first three are found in 2X's text; the Spellman interview is in *Malcolm X: By Any Means Necessary*.[23] Below are the results.

Beginning with "Black Man's History," Malcolm says "so-called Negroes" fourteen times. In "The Old Negro and the New Negro," he states the phrase fourteen times again, with a questioner mentioning it once, showing the Negro's acceptance and willingness to change. In the speech-interview with A.B. Spellman, Malcolm asserts "so-called Negroes" ten times. In all, the median number is 12.6. Whenever Malcolm speaks, he repetitiously defames the term "Negro," readying the audience to abandon its usage. In his fourth speech, "God's Judgement of White America: The Chickens Are Coming Home to Roost," he omits "so-called Negroes." Instead he substitutes "so-called Negroes" with "lost sheep," "lost tribe," "lost people of God," and he couples "Negro" with "exslaves" seven times. His powerful metaphor, "Politically the American Negro is nothing but a football, and the white liberals control this mentally dead ball through tricks of tokenism: false promises of integration and civil rights,"[24] accentuates the root *necro*, "death."

Before Malcolm reached national and international prominence, he lectured at Temple #7, located at Lenox Avenue and 116th Street in Harlem, three times a week. According to 2X, he lectured twice during the week and once on Sunday from the 1950s to the early 1960s. With this schedule, re(re)naming spread quickly across Harlem and, when he traveled, across the country. In 1957, Malcolm's popularity soared when he challenged the Harlem police to release Hinton Johnson, a Muslim, the police had unmercifully beat.[25] With 500 Muslims surrounding police headquarters to support Malcolm and Hinton, the media made the minister into a national figure. In 1961, the author C. Eric Lincoln claimed that the entire membership of the Nation of Islam was approximately 100,000.[26] Malcolm, himself, in 1965, said to his cousin and fellow Muslim Hakim Jamal that "there are over a hundred and twenty-five thousand brothers right here in Los Angeles who I, myself, converted to the Nation of Islam."[27] In *Seventh Child* (1999), Rodnell Collins writes that Malcolm and the Little family were the greatest fishers of men and women who joined the NOI.[28] Malcolm's personal effect on the upsurge in Muslim membership suggests that his oratorical themes reached a great many people. From 1957 to 1964, Malcolm and other Muslims carried the "so-called Negro" narrative all over the country; therefore, the idea of re(re)naming assumed an awesome momentum. Malcolm says that

> This integrationist Negro is the one who ... is ashamed to be black—... So he calls himself a Negro — an American Negro —... whenever he sees himself on the American stage he sees himself as a minority in the company of a white majority. So he is the underdog.... And for everything that type of Negro seeks for himself he takes a begging attitude, a condescending attitude.[29]

In the above, to accentuate his analysis, Malcolm blends demeaning terminology with the "N" word: "minority," "underdog," beggar. Moving into the "N" word's interior, he explains a collective reflection of defeat, death. This disturbing mental picture describes the ailments of the Negro and like a psychiatrist, it forces the so-named to strip away the silence and the omission to visit a troubling truth about him- or herself.

Also about the so-named, Malcolm promotes "Black," like Hughes and Garvey, but he adds elements of ethics, nationalism, and revolution to the term. As he prepares for this promotion, to bind his listeners, he continues to cast doubt on the term "Negro," by sweetening, separating from, and then transforming it. He says:

> Yes, I think there is a new so-called Negro. *We don't recognize the term "Negro"* but I really believe that there's a new so-called Negro here in America. He not only is impatient. Not only is he dissatisfied, not only is he disillusioned, but he's getting very angry[30] [my emphasis].

Here, Malcolm describes the phases that the "so-called Negro" underwent when listening to his messianic message on racial (re)naming: dissatisfaction, disillusionment, and anger. Malcolm merges the Negro into the Black concept that excites agency and anger. Threatening his White audience with non-smiling Black men, he conjures up a mental portrait of the males who surround the 76rs star guard, Allen Iverson, and the ones in rap videos. Conjuring the "badman" in Black culture and literature, Malcolm's *ntu* circulates the nonverbal fighting of Frederick Douglass with the "nigger breaker" Covey in Douglass's narrative, and in his literary imagination, the fierceness of Madison Washington along with the shrewdness of Martin Delany, the creator of Henry Blake (1861). Following, in another context, Malcolm sympathizes with the so-named Negro as he encourages re(re)naming, serving up a different version of the "exslave."

> [T]he poor so-called Negro doesn't have his own *name*, doesn't have his own language, doesn't have his own culture, doesn't have his own history. He doesn't have his own country. He doesn't even have his own *mind*[31] [my emphasis].

This image is the collective Negro, nebulous, "out of time," "bending to alien gods," in Claude Mckay's "Outcast." Dislocated, functioning without African-centered history and culture, this is also the haunted, empty Negro agonizing for an imaginary Africa in Cullen's tormented verse. This no-thing Negro: no *name, language, history,* or *land* has no thing and everything — an absence of the African self. And this lack erases any "real" substantive sensibility. Yet, in contrast, this nothing Negro has an absence, not completely void. This absence contains the torment of bondage along with associations of currency, commodity, and bestiality. Like Garvey's lament, "Win the Fray," this image of Africa awaits the day when the Negro will make himself a man (and woman). The Garvey poem and X's lament are to hasten the spirit, rhythm, and creativity intended to bond audience and artist. In the following question and answer segment a gentleman inquires about self-identification on an application, and Malcolm replies:

> [N]ever put down Negro. The worst thing that you can call yourself is a Negro. If you don't think so just call yourself that and immediately you will find all the doors closed. But at the same time the blackest man from Africa comes here and he rejects the term Negro. He will tell you he is an African and every door is open.... Which shows you that there is a difference between being Negro and being black.[32]

Showing a linguistic deference for "African" and "black," he elevates both, privileging each over "Negro," disqualifying the validity of the latter. Favoring "black," he makes it a synonym for "African." Similarly his activist foremother Francis Harper distinguishes between a continental African and an American Negro. X's African is Harper's "Guinea man." Critiquing White behavior that separates the Negro and the African, he implicitly highlights the absurdity of racism. Lastly, in his reconfiguration of Black, he fortifies it with revolution: a concept that Malcolm asserted if the ballot failed to bring gratifying results.

> There's been revolution, a *black* revolution going on in Africa. In Kenya, the Mau Mau were revolutionary; they were the ones who brought the word "uhuru" to the fore. The Mau Mau, they were revolutionary, they believed in scorched earth, they knocked everything aside that got in their way, and their revolution was based on land.... The only kind of revolution that is non-violent is the *Negro* revolution[33] [my emphasis].

Malcolm makes a serious distinction between "black" and "Negro" revolutions. The nonviolent revolution is a fantasy to him while the Black or African one reflects the ugliness or beauty of the term. In his perspective, nonviolence and the term "Negro" are equally useless. Positioning his people on par with other nations, specifically Africa, he demands that his people behave as other nations. He implicitly questions, on what is the "Negro" revolution based? His answer, on the assimilating Negro who upholds White supremacy. When X compares the Kenyan revolution to the nonviolent American one, he trivializes nonviolence and signifies on Martin Luther King, and his "turn-the-other-cheek."[34]

In Malcolm's redefining racial terminology, he inverts traditional and racist symbolism. Like the poet Langston Hughes, he also inverts derivatives, like the word "dark," saying:

> Today *dark* mankind is waking up and is undertaking a new type of thinking, and it is this new type of thinking that is creating new approaches and new reactions that make it almost impossible to figure out what the *black* man is going to do next[35] [my emphasis].

This is Langston Hughes's "Dear Dark" in "Black Seed," and this Black man is the worker who told the master to leave him alone. This once again is the action-oriented neo–Black man who is an agent of change and transformation. Malcolm also with subtlety signifies on his White audience. A common White fear is not knowing "what the black man is going to do next." Laws were designed to restrict Black male (and female) behavior.[36]

Even in supposed openings for Negro expression Malcolm found flaws. Consider Negro History Week. He argued that this time period sought singly the advancements that American Africans made in the United States, therefore allowing White overseers or tutors or slave masters to receive all of the credit. However, Malcolm thought that the following was the worst "trick of all," a trip back to naming:

> ...when he names us Negro and calls us Negro.... We're not Negroes, and have never been until we were brought here and made into that. We were scientifically produced by the white man.[37]

Matthew Frye Jacobson in *Whiteness of a Different Color* (1998) explains the historical moment when scientific classifications served the social order of the power structure. He writes that "the new sciences that arose to theorize the relationship among the world's peoples — ethnology, anthropology, craniometry, anthropometry, and phrenology among them — owed a great deal to precisely those social questions generated by Euro-American expansionism and the intensifying slavery debate."[38] Thomas Jefferson exhorted "explorers" to go among other peoples to get knowledge in order to "control," "civilize," and "instruct" them. David Spurr says it best when he states, "[K]nowledge of racial difference is made a condition for political power."[39] Racial science was "racializing sciences."

The famous 19th century scientist Louis Agassiz, who believed in the polygeny school of anthropological thought, on first seeing the "negro" described all as hideous animals.[40] Indeed, when he studied the races he capitalizes the "I" for Indian and the "M" for Mongolian but he lowercases the "n" in "negro." The scientist Stephen Jay Gould scrupulously argues that science is a social phenomenon. The history of scientific views on race serves as a mirror of shifts in society.[41] In other words, racist scientific perspectives fed the social powers without any notion of objectivity. The questionable search for truth and objectivity is based on racial assumptions, summed up in the following quip: A 19th century Englishman touring America said that if every Irishman killed a Negro and got hung that would solve the race problem.[42]

Who Is the Race Problem

The crux of Malcolm's ideology was to evaporate Black adoration for Whites. This accounts for his comparison of Whites to scientists with Dr. Frankenstein implications. When one group, collectively called a "man," "makes" and renames another group, then, in fact, the man-makers are gods. Also, when Negroes only understand themselves in the American context, the birth of the word "negro," they are likely to, as Wheatley did, envision Africa as a "land of errors."

Malcolm intuits that if the Negro relates him and herself to Africa, the vision of "self" complicates; therefore, his romantic interpretation of Africa allows the composition of a powerful African space, a home, human identity, and culture for the Negro. Thus, Malcolm deliberately learned about African culture and politics, searching for commonality among Diaspora Africans, anticipating the current trend of globalization forty years ago.

In order to educate others, Malcolm taught himself many disciplines.[43] His study of science enabled him to preach and lecture on the divisions that emerged during enslavement. With science and culture operating in the interests of those in power, he offered a rational truth that provides evidence of the intertwining results of the Negro's bondage. Expansionism, greed, racism, science and society, in particular the media, assisted in the Negro's creation and proliferation and in the African's shift into savagery.

> Having complete control over Africa, the colonial powers of Europe projected the image of Africa negatively ... jungle savages, cannibals, nothing civilized.... you and I began to hate it. We didn't want anybody telling us anything about Africa, much less calling us Africans. In hating Africa and in hating the Africans, we ended up hating ourselves, without even realizing it. Because you can't hate the roots of a tree, and not hate the tree.[44]

Self-hatred is a cultural and educational construct. Images in books, newspapers, and cinema have historically harmed the Negro. From *Birth of a Nation* (1918), the first film Hollywood, produced to *Training Day* (2002) and *Monster's Ball* (2002), Hollywood depicts the Negro and now the handsome African American as a rapist, killer, and brute. And the highest awards are given for such depictions. To juxtapose and contrast the dark beast, they make heroic White male characters. Yet, Whites have not had to navigate between and around state sponsored apartheid. Elijah Muhammad separated from this navigation, and taught X the language and concepts to fight poisonous images and racism, teaching that

> This name "beast" when given to a person, refers to that person's characteristics, not to an actual beast. Study the history of how America treats the freedom, justice and equality which is supposed to be given to all citizens of America (of course, the Negroes are not citizens of America). A citizen cannot and will not allow his people and government to treat him in such a way as America treats her so-called Negroes. To call a person a "beast" is simply to say, according to the English language: nouns — violent person, berserk or berserker, demon, fiend, shaitan or sheitan or Satan, or dragon, evil spirit, Satan as, devil.... The so-called American Negroes have and still suffer under such brutish treatment from the American Christian white race, who call themselves followers of Jesus and his God.... They (white race) are the people described as "beast" in the Revelation of the Bible.[45]

When Malcolm following Muhammad objectifies White people, he moves into biblical language and imagery, building a concept that the "so-called Negro" would find horrifying and satisfying. Malcolm said: "When you call him devil you're calling him by his name, and he's got another name — Satan; another name — serpent; another name — snake; another name — beast. All these names are in the Bible for the white man."[46] This assault on "White" encourages separation from American (White) aesthetics, politics, values, religion, and philosophy. In renaming the White, Muhammad and X awakened the Negro, the major purpose and function of Muhammad's ideology.

In the following excerpt, Malcolm demonstrates his masterful rhetorical style, which awed, entertained, and educated listeners, Egungun. At Abyssinian Baptist Church, Malcolm was with Adam Clayton Powell, who questioned him about the contradiction of practicing Islam and barring White membership. Powell asked Malcolm if he hates the White man, and X replied:

> We don't even think about him. How can anybody ask us do we hate the man who kidnapped us 400 years ago, brought us here and stripped us of our history, stripped us of our culture, stripped us of our language, stripped us of everything that you could use today to prove that you were ever part of the human family, brought you down to the level of an animal, sold you from plantation to plantation like a sack of wheat, sold you like a sack of potatoes, sold you like a horse and a cow, and then hung you up from one end of the country to the other, and then you ask me do I hate him?[47]

X never answers if he hates the White man. Instead he signifies in verbal Black fluency that Geneva Smitherman describes and explains in *Talking and Testifying* (1977). "Indirection," "circumlocution" and the "logically unexpected" are among many characteristics of signifying.[48] Malcolm's wit and humor implicit in his remarkable response circle his understated answer. Instead of his normal forthrightness in oratory, X provides a scathing indictment against White America listing historical atrocities that invert the image of White from lofty to beastly.

The fact that this inversion is based on history shocks the listener into the omission of the Negro's specific circumstances, either neutralized or erased in educational institutions and the media. It also reminds everyone of the uneven disparity between the races. X was labeled a "hater" and "violent" because of such unflattering reminders and this labeling assisted in his assassination. Publicly commenting against Elijah Muhammad and being barred from speaking in Paris also suggest an international opening to a dangerous course.

In another direction, Malcolm spoke, for the most part, in formal

English, yet his words never left the vernacular, the soul of the streets. For example, repeated throughout his speeches is a colloquial expression of his generation. After Malcolm makes specific observations, he concludes with, "pick up on that." This expression from a Black lexicon is equivalent to contemporary closures such as "check it out," "are you hip to this," "are you down with that," or "see what I'm sayin.'"

Malcolm's verbal fluency and intelligence "picked up on" the new racial name most appropriate for the once negro people. He started substituting Negro with this new term around 1964, along with inserting "Afro-American" and his redefined "black." This X generated race name was the final solution to the Negro name change, solving the dilemma of juggling "negro," "Negro," "coloured," "Negrosaxons," and "Afro-Americans." His consistent search for an appropriate racial appellation culminated in a remark he made while wailing "The Ballot or the Bullet." This extemporaneous remark pushed out from metaphysical power, *nommo*, when Malcolm preached on April 3rd, 1964:

> Right now, in this country, [we are] 22 million *African Americans*—that's what we are ... [African-Americans].

The Founding of a People

Calling a new race of people into being normally involves warrior leaders. All ethnic groups have epic narratives about the founding of the nation. Malcolm X founded the African Americans. Malcolm X during the Age of Malcolm consumed himself with the idea, practice, and linguistics of racial reformation and empowerment. He started with an extraordinary teacher who had studied racism along with self-negating habits of the "so-called Negro." Malcolm took the teachings of Elijah Muhammad, made them modern and complicated those instructions with his own sense of politics and the international. In consuming the burden of love of Muhammad, X sectioned out new routes of awareness and new remedies for the obstacles that the re(re)named encountered. From the moment he fastened onto the ideology of Muhammad in the 1950s to his final day at the Audubon Ballroom, Malcolm thought singly about the transformation of his people. In such concentrated attention, over many years, he provided ideas that manifested after his martyrdom. People clung to the familiar racial appellations for years following X's death. However, the spitting out of "African American" never disappeared, entering the culture and media formally in 1988. The linguistics lingered in spirit, rhythm, and creativity among African Americans from the Age of Malcolm to that date. With these ontological sources of *nzuri* vibrating with *ntu*, in 1988, Jesse Jackson assumed the linguistics of leadership and presented the racial replacement at a news conference where the skeptics were aplenty.

Haki Madhubuti after X's physical death kept malcolmian issues prevalent in poetry, transforming the image of Africa and urging the Negro to re(re)name. With the replication in written art and the repetition in spoken word, Madhubuti forced the re(re)naming issue to linger in society. Because of him and others, Malcolm's prediction that "what I've already set in motion will never be stopped," and "The results of what I am doing will materialize in the future,"[49] came true. Malcolm X and later Haki Madhubuti and the Black Aesthetic poets taught the once "negro" people to adopt the brand new name that X uttered in 1964. Haki Madhubuti, filling the twenty-four year window and physical absence of the flesh but not the *nommo* with the wisdom of Malcolm, invigorated malcolmian creativity. In the final chapter, Haki Madhubuti brings malcolmian motifs alive in his poetic *nommo*.

ELEVEN

The X-Factor Influence on the Transformed Image of Africa in the Poetry of Haki Madhubuti: Issues of Re(re)naming and Inversion

In the previous chapter we examined the rhetorical strategies of Malcolm X and the linguistic creation of a new people, the African American. After X publicly uttered the term, its adoption was not immediate. After the assassination, Haki Madhubuti and other Black Arts poets took on the malcolmian mandate to re(re)name, to drop "Negro" and accept his term, "African American." Madhubuti produced art, activism, and institution building that not only reflected Malcolm's charge to name change, but also X's philosophy. In this chapter, we will review Madhubuti's poetry that specifically carries malcolmian motifs, evident in the poet's first book, *Think Black* (1966), and most recently in *YellowBlack* (2005). His latest book of poetry and essays, *YellowBlack*, dedicated to his mother, traces his first twenty-one years, which includes his introduction to the rhetoric and personality of Malcolm X.

Madhubuti admits that the ideology and personality of Malcolm X influenced his thought, behavior, and creativity.[1] Just as Malcolm preached to Muslims to be "black and brave" and to study word origins, this message reached and stimulated Madhubuti, who assisted in shaping the Black Aesthetics Movement. The 1960s Black Aesthetics or Black Arts Movement sought to identify and promote ideas for racial reconfiguration for those becoming African American.[2] This necessary step challenged all previous versification by Negroes, often imitative of White ideology and aesthetics examined in earlier chapters. The purpose of the 1960s Black Arts then was to overturn such imitation in art and to produce a body of poetry that captured a neo–African worldview. As such, this body of poetry contains a resistance paradigm that emerges from the rhetoric, rhythm, and spirit of Malcolm X.

C. Tsehloane Keto (1991) defines African-centered as beginning in Africa, the "historical core from which to build the narrative and the analysis of the experiences of people in Africa and peoples of African descent throughout the world."[3] The historian Keto further broadens his theoretical paradigm to include African "centers" which are of "local focus." This local centrality is anywhere and everywhere throughout the Diaspora in such places as Jamaica, Brazil, and the United States. In the United States, Haki Madhubuti designed poetry that persuaded the "local" metaphysical "focus" of Negroes or Blacks to remake themselves into an identifiably neo-African nation. He designed poetry as a means to steer and assist his people to recognize and reform harmful American habits that discredited Africa as point of origin and the American African as a human being. Following the plight of the "so-called negro" established by Malcolm and the Muslims, his expressions also sought to destroy the term "negro," a synonym for slave and slavery. To "loosen the language" of Madhubuti's poetry, sections of my interpretive frame come from the muse and deity Ogun, the god of war and of the artisan in the Yoruba tradition. My attempt to appropriate this muse satisfies precisely the intention behind the expressive output of Black Arts poets: they molded language into weapon. The critic of African discourse, according to Henry Louis Gates, should look to Esu Elegbara, a double-faced, double-mouthed deity, to clear the way for the understanding that comes between truth and meaning. My intent is to perform an Esu-'tufunaalo* on selected poetry of Madhubuti to illustrate his exact interplay between lyricism and X's oratory. This principal method is also relative because Esu during enslavement in Brazil became the liberator of the slaves and therefore the enemy of the master-class.[4]

In early works, Madhubuti urges liberation and transformation through re(re)naming: persuading Negroes to adopt racial indicators that spring from African continuity. This chapter documents his contribution to the actual re(re)naming of Negro people, which took place formally in 1988.

This coinage is in The Signifying Monkey *by Henry Louis Gates (p. 9). He received it from Wole Soyinka.*

This monumental event would not have occurred had it not been for Malcolm X, the Black Arts and Black Power Movements.

The Black Arts or Aesthetic Movement (BAM) gave 1960s artists a new way of viewing and producing art, causing a number of prismatic projections for poetry. They include poetry that challenged racism; poetry that transformed subservient thinking; and poetry that urged nation building. In sum, this movement encouraged writers to individually produce but for the Black collective, an assumption and reflection of *nzuri* and the ontological presence of spirit, rhythm, and creativity in African-centered thought and aesthetics. Black Arts poetry reflects "resistance," precedent setting in the public arts, where the word was the weapon. In this artistic movement, themes derive from ailments associated with the Negro and the purpose of writing is to resolve those problems. The *ntu* (energy) of this art was collectively to make things happen and to call things into being. The verses enlivened callers and respondents displaying the *ntu* between them and the collapse of audience and artist separation. Dance historian and scholar Kariamu Welsh-Asante designed the *nzuri* model, which enables an evaluation of the arts from an African-centered filter. *Nzuri* has seven aspects. The first one is *meaning*: the "significance of expression in relationship to individual and community. The second is *ethos*: the "quality of expression that exudes spirit, emotion and energy." The third is *motif*: the "incorporation and use of symbols in artistic product that reflect a specific culture and heritage." *Mode* is the fourth: the "manner in which artistic product is expressed." The fifth is *function*: the "operative relationship of artistic product to individual and community." The sixth is *Method or technique*: the "practical, physical and material means of realizing artistic product." *Form* is the final sense: the "status of artistic product in terms of structure, shape and composition."[5]

When Amiri Baraka composed "Black Art," where he sings that poems should "kill" and "wrestle cops into alleys,"[6] his language *form* is a warrior poem written in a portable *technique* to easily share with many people. The operative *function* of such a poem is to make the audience aware of the champion genre that will defend their rights. The *mode* and *motif* display a serious, angry, and ready-to-fight voice only for Black people, the historical victims of police brutality. Baraka's *ethos* and *meaning* exude with the emotive and spiritual elements that derive from past and present resistors to European oppression on the continent and in the Americas. The *meaning* of "Black Art" to the author and the audience is to halt the police brutality that has always been prevalent in Black America. Amiri Baraka in "Black Art" personifies the language of war, confronting the White privilege of murdering Black people with impunity (Fedo, 1979;

Ginzburg, 1997; Miller, 1999; Nelson, 2000; Patterson, 1971; Zangrando, 1980).

This motif of war was a new disposition coloring art, transforming the world of the Black (and the White). It was an art not to remain in books for a specialized audience, but an oral art, ripe for performing. Baraka's tone and diction veer dramatically from previous Negro writing, because "Black Art" was to make things happen.

The Art of the Warrior

In "Black Art," Baraka signifies the uselessness of poetry unless it has "teeth," an association to talking that demonstrates a rough speakerly quality that Henry Louis Gates defined in *The Signifying Monkey* (1988) as the "speakerly text." Gates explains this concept as one that signifies with a play of "voices" at work in "free indirect discourse," that speaks across texts. This notion of textual speaking explains how and why the Black Arts poets created spoken and written literature to influence and inform readers and listeners to activate and to take action. Activating the power of *nommo* the word, logos in African discourse, this poetry generated malcolmian ideology. The Black Arts had a deliberate conversational quality in order to generally appeal to the Black community, specifically young Black men. Instead of ambiguity and subtlety, this art penetrates the warrior mentality in young Blacks disenchanted with American living.

Resembling Marcus Garvey's lyrics, the Black Arts Movement inspired the poetry printed in *The Black Panther*, the newspaper of the Black Panther Party. Black Panthers considered themselves the vanguard army for Black people, and the Black Arts poets identified with the image, idea, and practice of self-defense. Thus, Black Arts poetry reflects the Revolutionary Action Movement, US, the Republic of New Africa, and other Black Power affiliates. This is the realm in which Haki Madhubuti started his writing career. As an author of war poetry that exposes victory and defeat, he writes "One Sided Shoot-out (for brothers fred hampton & mark clark, murdered 12-4-69 by chicago police at 4:30 am while they slept."

>...
>were the street lights out?
>Did they darken their faces in combat?
>Did they remove their shoes to creep softer?
>Could u not see the whi-te of their eyes,
>The whi-te of their deathfaces?
>Didn't yr/look-out man see them coming, coming,
>Coming?

> Or did they turn into ghostdust and join the
> Night's fog?
> ...
> it was murder.[7]

Madhubuti selects a real time incident that affects Black people and makes a decision that closes the poem: "it was murder." Like his literary foremother, Frances Harper, Madhubuti narrates current events, giving the date and the time of the assassinations. His *meaning* is a resistance to genocide, a latent quality intuitive in Blacks, and his *ethos* exposes the energy of past similar atrocities that exudes, paradoxically, a creeping softness. His *motif* speaks specifically to Black people because of the subject matter: police brutality and its horrific results, and the whole poem *functions* in one aspect like a newspaper. Madhubuti's *method* and *technique* deviates from other Black Arts poets because his "physical and material means of realizing [the] artistic product" (the poem) are all his own. Madhubuti started his own publishing company, Third World Press, in order to publish his versification and that of others, offering a malcolmian vision in verse. The "status of [the] artistic composition," the *form*, is like Baraka's "Black Art," a defender poem. With the title reading like a newspaper caption, and the body like the sketch of a short story, the *mode* asserts and predicts the outcome from an independent African-centered, not an assimilating, perspective.

Madhubuti's tone does not reflect sorrow about a battle lost. Instead, it reports and holds up a mirror to racism and state sponsored murder. The *function* here alerts the listeners and readers to inappropriate police action, and it presciently predicts an outcome. Years later through legal procedures the families of the murdered Panther leaders Fred Hampton and Mark Clark were awarded recompense for the police misconduct; therefore, as Madhubuti exactly alerted: "it was murder."

Yet, Madhubuti does not romanticize the assassinations by painting the Panthers as totally noble heroic victims. Notice that he raises doubt about Panther security, "didn't yr look-out man see them coming, coming, coming." Presciently, again, years later, Madhubuti's inquiries prove correct. On the 1990 television series *Eyes on the Prize*, a former Panther security person admits to aiding in the police assassinations of both Panther leaders.

In "One Sided Shoot-out" Madhubuti records an important event that yields historical memory: "[I]t functions as a commitment to a historical project that places the African person back on *center* and as such it becomes an escape to sanity"[8] (my emphasis). More Blacks than Whites witness and are victims of police treachery and brutality.[9] Blacks have the historical memory of the "paterrollers," the Whites who patrolled the roads for escaping slaves. The legacy of slavery has not disappeared in the imagination, the mind, and the psychology of Black people. For example, when my students give oral presentations in class on subjects that relate to enslavement, they use pronouns that link the contemporary to the past. For instance, when discussing an issue about the enslaved, they will say "we" as if they too are a part of that experience. It is not surprising then that the police are a contemporary version of the paterrollers, a name coined by those in bondage, and tragically the brutality from the past has not ceased. The whipping of Rodney King is ingrained in American lore along with the torture of Abner Louima and the murder of Amadou Diallo, shot 41 times.[10]

Therefore, when Haki Madhubuti documents this abuse in poetry — the assassination of two Panther men — he provides "an escape into sanity." He makes central an important and horrible event in Black culture, life, and history. As a defender poem, in his poetic challenge to White supremacy, he equalizes the Black and the White. Like X, for example, he employs signification in "One sided" with the image "white," reducing its power. His *motif* of devaluation appears two ways: in the spelling and in the pronunciation. In the spelling, he separates "whi" from "te," for the pronunciation whi-tee, and in the symbol inversion, the whi-te turns into a spectral presence. He inverts the pre-1960s artists, Countee Cullen and Claude McKay's image of the omnipotent and omnipresent White. The White in Madhubuti's conception ironically is similar to the unsubstantiated Negro of Cullen and McKay; with a ghastly, ghostly inner life because he lacked what X stated: history, land, language, and religion. Thus, Madhubuti shifts previous insulting images away from the Negro and onto the Negro's creator, the whi-te. He equally plays the game of White supremacy, like two opponents at chess. The *meaning* expressing the relationship between the community and the individual shows the listeners how to fight an oppressor in language by inverting symbols and signifying. As a defender of Blacks, in public threatening discourse, he projects Black power language like the advocate Kwame Touré (Stokely Carmichael).

On another track, in the repetition of "coming," one can pose male ejaculation parallel to the killing act and the act of killing. In the possible weakening of the police as they approached the sleeping Panthers, the undulation of fear and murderous intent in the patrollers vibrated from weak to strong again and again because of silent deception, dormant Panthers, and superior weaponry. The approaching police align with "ghostdust" and "night fog," pictures of milky or filmy substances without particular *form*, leaving life, shadowing the planetary surface or beckoning and welcoming death, evident in "deathfaces." The manner of the *mode* in this section expresses an image of danger and deception for the Black victims.

Another example of the symbol inversion *motif* occurs before this section, where a brief notion of minstrelsy sneaks into the poem: The combatants may have "darkened" their skin. As Susan Gubar asserts in *RaceChanges* (1997), White people in black make-up express a complicated need to darken the skin while reviling, segregating, and disenfranchising Black people. This darkening process was once popular and profitable art in American culture, as American as apple pie and Shirley Temple. Of course, in the above, the police darken to blend in and become the night; however, the complexity and profundity are in the hands that may have darkened to kill the dark.

In presentation, Madhubuti deconstructs this behavior, indirectly exposing racist White brutality towards Blacks, especially those who find independent solutions for overturning injustices. Therefore, his revolutionary art illustrates both the racism paradox and the political and revolutionary fervor that molded American society during the 1960s. It records and projects what Molefi Asante calls a "rhetoric of resistance" which describes precisely the oratory of Malcolm X (Neal, 1968; Harris, 1985: Randall and Burroughs, 1973).

Madhubuti, maintaining recurring motifs from the rhetoric of Malcolm X, (1) started history in Africa, not in America; (2) preached to transform black from negative to positive; (3) ordered the negative qualities of white; (4) urged Blacks to nation-build, and factored ethics into culture; (5) urged destroying or devaluing the term "negro"; (6) employed race-centered deictics; (7) signified; (8) used history for analysis; (9) insisted that Negro culture turn into Black and African culture; and (10) created revolutionary rhetoric.

In a transformed image of Africa (all references for African people) Madhubuti shifts his versification sharply from Euro- to Afrocentricity. This independence for a Black man caused Madhubuti to gain detractors. He and other BAM writers faced critics who dismissed their lyrics as other than art (Crouch, 1989; Kessler, 1973). Likewise, Gates (1987) mocks early, independent aspects of literary interpretation of the Black Arts before he assumes elements of Afrocentricity in his own paradigm. Below, he ridicules Stephen Henderson's original attempt in *Understanding the New Black Poetry* (1973) to explain the art of the 1960s. In Gates' critique, his unawareness of war or resistance language and the redefinition of a people, two fundamentals of the new Black Aesthetic, surface. He criticizes Henderson's analytical tool, "saturation," this way:

> His final category, **saturation** is the ultimate tautology: poetry is "Black" when it communicates "Blackness." The more a text is saturated, the blacker the text. One imagines a dashiki-clad Dionysus weighing the saturated,

mascon lines of Countee Cullen against those of Langston Hughes, as Paul Laurence Dunbar and Jean Toomer are silhouetted by the flames of our own black Hades.[11]

In his homage to the Greeks, Gates' misunderstanding or misreading of the Black aesthetic is immediately obvious. Dionysus is straight out of a Grecian heritage; therefore, he is ill equipped to contain and investigate African writing. Using European references to decipher Black art is the very straitjacket that Malcolm taught the "so-called Negro" to tear apart. Yet, Gates has redirected a transformed image of Black back to a Eurocentric symbol and meaning, which the 1960s artists previously defied. His language overall suggests an obscurity of "location," because he isolates an African local focus but begins it in Western iconography. For my purposes, Gates would have been more in line with African-centeredness if he had found the god from which Dionysus derives. The physicist Cheikh Anta Diop tells us that the term "Dionysus" is the renaming of another Greek word, Osiris.[12] Historian Tony Browder adds that "Osiris" stands for the original Kemetic (Egyptian) word *Ausar*,[13] actually *Asr*. The added vowels help contemporary readers pronounce the possible name. The differences from Dionysus to Osiris to Ausar demonstrate the flux of naming and *meaning* and the consequences of war and conquest. Egypt has had consistent invasions beginning with the Hyksos, 1786–1570 b.c., and then the following: the Assyrians, 712–663 b.c.; the Persians, 525–404 b.c.; the Macedonians (Alexander) 405–332 b.c.; the Romans, 58 b.c.-180 A.D.; the Turks (Ottoman), 1517–1914; and Britain and France, 1953. When conquerors conquer, they normally rename.

For the Greeks, Dionysus is known as the god of wine and fertile crops. Dissimilarly, in Egypt, Osiris is the supreme god and king of eternity, with other attributes: judge of the dead, ruler of the kingdom of the Other World, creator, god of the Nile. Historian John G. Jackson claims that Osiris is a member of the ancient African solar trinity. Along with Ra and Horus, the other two solar partners, they are emblems of the setting sun.[14] In another direction, Albert Churchward (1903, 1997) explains Osiris's architectural and metaphysical significance. He writes that Osiris sits "judging the dead upon the square that is imaged by the Masonic Square which was first employed in squaring the stones of the builders, and next in squaring the conduct in the sphere of morals of the Masonic Brotherhood, which in Egypt was as old as the brotherhood of the seven Khemmu or the seven Masons who assisted Ptah in building the heavens on the Square.... Ptah in Egyptian mythology, was the first great Architect of the Universe."[15]

Browder on Ausar says: "It has been written that at the time of his birth, a voice was heard to proclaim that the lord of creation was born."[16] Ausar is recognized as a great king who bought civilization to his people and established a law code and religion. In the African creations, Ausar/Osiris is a generative God. In the Greek and later Roman interpretations or reinterpretations as Dionysus, he sinks into orgiastic rites and debauchery. In the Roman text, Dionysus becomes Bacchus.

In Gates' above quote, he plays double-dutch with a Western and African image. Such verbal play extends confusion with a conflation that disturbs the purpose of Henderson's reach to interpret "blackness." The Black Arts in fact was the beginning step backward to reclaim and identify with an African heritage and lineage, as Malcolm had taught. Before those poets, the notion of "blackness" was both obscure and hurtful, with shame and pain as common descriptors. That version of "black" is more in line with "Hades." The Hades that Gates mentions is not a proper identification of the African Under or Other World. His claim of "our own Hades" is misleading because this too is a Greek identifier of hell. Thus, it is not really "ours" in Gates' employ of the collective pronoun for Blacks. Henderson has an articulation struggle because of his initial attempt to interpret new concepts, trying to puzzle out a Black aesthetic. In the above repetition that Gates mocks, Henderson resembles one of Ralph Ellison's narrators who preaches in the prologue of *Invisible Man*:

"Brothers and sisters, my text this morning is the 'Blackness of Blackness.'"
"In the beginning..."
"At the very start," they cried.
"...there was blackness..."
...
"I said black is..."
...
"...an' black ain't..."
...
"Black will git you..."
"...an' black won't..."[17]

The simultaneous absence and presence that denotes deconstruction characterizes the compacted modernity and postmodernity of Ellison's visual text. A criminally created, dispossessed people who are not a people (denied human rights) naturally struggled, and struggle, with language for clarification. What Gates calls a tautology is much more than that. The Black Arts poets and critics were swimming in unknown waters but intuitively experienced. They were like Claude McKay searching through a remote distance that yielded absence because of the lost songs, stories, narratives, and epics.

However, in *The Signifying Monkey*, Gates restores the lost epics and theology and spirituality in an opposite and densely African-centered course. He establishes an impressive interpreter of Black texts or texts by Blacks, selecting as the critic's muse Esu Elegbara, the god of the crossroads, the deity who converses among the gods and, with proper ritual, among humans. He is Papa Legba in Haiti. Dona Richards (Marimba Ani) (1980) argues that Negroes have expressed Africanisms (Henderson's blackness saturation) in spirituality and in other social patterns since their arrival in America. Sterling Stuckey (1987) also puts forward this position after studying the unique nationalism and culture among English speaking Blacks who came from myriad African ethnic groups. Madhubuti, projecting the music of his mentor Malcolm X, synthesizes the myriad African ethnic groups that turned into the "negro." In the following poem, from *Think Black*, he offers a compounding and complicated message.

> America calling.
> negroes.
> can you dance?
> play foot/baseball?
> nanny?
> cook?
> needed now. Negroes
> who can entertain
> ONLY
> others not
> wanted...[18]

The "not wanted" others are significant and integral to the *meaning* of the poem; in the neo-African realm, the malcolmian sphere, they *are* desired, and that desire marks the significance of this expression. Madhubuti disrespects the language when he lower-cases the Negro "n."[19] However, he is not imitating e.e. cummings. Rather, he demonstrates the new "day" that Garvey wished into being. In the *mode* in which the poem is expressed, it rejects what Ronald Takaki, one of the first teachers in Black Studies in California, calls the master narrative. It is not written to uphold White supremacy. Composed in 1966, a year after X's assassination, Madhubuti *forms* this versification as a warrior artist, showing his audience the *function* of unity with a *motif* that speaks directly to his people. "Negroes" is a symbol of the actual "not wanted." The lowercase "n" is his reviving X's re(re)naming argument.

Marcus Garvey, W.E.B. Du Bois and others had already fought for the capitalizing of the Negro "n." However, Madhubuti resumes the lowercase for reasons other than returning to racist orthography. He signifies, lowercasing to cast the term in a dubious, demeaning context. In signifying normally two or more people engage in a ritual of insults meant either to hurt, to triumph over, or to entertain; it is verbal play indigenous to Black people.[20] In poetry, Madhubuti jousts with White America, his *ethos* exuding the spirit of transformation and the threatening emotion and energy of Malcolm X. He double-voices with the pose of Ogun, lowercasing the Negro "n," clearing the way for the *mau mau* music of Malcolm. Deriding the subservient "negro" occupations, he displays the stage prior to the Garvey elevation where "Blacks are men, no longer cringing fools / they demand a place, not like weak tools." In the "others not wanted" line, the truth inverted, they are the new, revolutionary Black men and women: the nightmare of Whites and the Negro's ideal.

In June 1999, a White policeman admitted to sodomizing with a broomstick the Haitian Abner Louima. This horror speaks for too many White males who visualize from Western memory an image of the "black" and the negro creation as "thing." Sodomizing Abner Louima represents a subdivision of racism: integral to renaming and to dehumanizing this thing in the Western mind. A series of officers were involved in the sodomy that broke the internal organs of Louima. Yet, only one officer was charged and this offending policeman in court never apologized to the victim's family, only his own.

Too many Western Whites project their interior world onto the victim, failing and refusing to connect the Black to the idea of humanity. Marimba Ani explains and details this historical behavior in the following:

> In European ideology the cultural other is like the land — territory or space into which Europeans expand themselves. The cultural other is there for Europeans to define, to "make over." That is why they can describe their new awareness of objects, peoples, and territories as *their* "discovery." This idea is coherent for them because according to their world-view it is their role to impart definition to the world. People of other cultural traditions and "persuasions" are part of the world to be defined; it is a European world. And in this sense, the conception of the cultural other is that of the *nonhuman*. It is Europeans who define "humanness" in terms of their own self-image and with such intensity that the ethic and rules of behavior that apply to those who are like them do not apply to those who are not. The cultural other is, therefore, the person (object) who can be treated in any manner — *with an unlimited degree of hostility and brutality*[21] [my emphasis].

Ani in *Yurugu: An African-Centered Critique of European Cultural Thought and Behavior* (1995) argues that this European expansion and imperialism starts with Plato. His epistemology asserts that control accompanies power and that rationalism produces morality, a position that Ani disputes. In Madhubuti's poem, he prefigures the negative Negro image as worth entertainment "only." In contemporary television commercials this absence and presence is clearly paraded. Beginning in the late 20th century, television commercials feature all White actors with identifiably Black rhythm and blues music in the background. One also finds this reverse minstrelsy in Hollywood movies. Whites appropriate Blackness silhouetted in soul music. Thus, in entertainment and advertisement, the negro is absent and present.

Madhubuti addresses another aspect of absence and presence in the next poem where he uses the Lone Ranger and his sidekick Tonto as metaphor. He writes:

>have you ever
>heard tonto say:
>   "I'm part negro?"[22]

Madhubuti spotlights the common practice of Negroes adopting a real or imagined dual heritage. Such adoption allows him or her to elevate the subhuman status that the name "negro" indicates. It can also beautify the individual, even if only in the imagination. In the above, Madhubuti ironically signifies, pointing to the Indian Tonto who never swore he was anything else but Indian. His character is the subservient stereotype and sidekick of the dashing White cowboy. Among Blacks, since slavery as William Wells Brown shows in *Clotel* (1852), a Negro will strongly desire, welcome, and prefabricate dual ancestry.[23] This subtraction of the African continues in the present day, for example, when the heralded golfer Tiger Woods muffled his obvious African heritage. He caused discomfort among Blacks. In his line of thinking, which derives from sentiments Countee Cullen advocated during the Harlem Renaissance, he, like the "so-called Negro," leaps into a biracial status that diminishes the contribution or the effect of the African parent.

The criminal creation of the Negro caused the disdain of racial features and heritage. From early to modern American literature by Blacks, one sees the tension surrounding identity and the desire and glorification of White aesthetics. I offer three literary cases: *Iola Leroy* (1893), *Meridian* (1976) and *Brothers and Keepers* (1985).

In *Iola Leroy*, F.E.W. Harper's title character could pass for White. She is the character on which to dream, the controller of the story. In fact, this trend in 19th century Black women's literature inspired Houston Baker to incorrectly argue that these authors relished the rape of the Black female. He claims this provocative point because Black female authors consistently created quadroon or mulatto protagonists. However, in the 20th century, Alice Walker in *Meridian* does not glorify; she creates a White female character, a friend of the Black female protagonist of the title name, who captivates a 1960s Black male activist. The Black male prefers the White female instead of his comrade-in-arms and Black female counterpart. In *Brothers and Keepers* John Edgar Wideman explores honestly his preference for a White aesthetic and his discomfort in what he terms Black culture and behavior. Harper, Walker, and Wideman designed characters that expose the self who wanted very much to erase the heritage of the (re)named African because of the inherent anxiety of the image. Madhubuti, recognizing this tendency, projects poetry that urges the Negro to evaluate such American behavior and to countenance why he (or she) runs from an African relationship.

Madhubuti's *unity of occasion* prefigures Africa and himself as desirable. His *meaning* for creating art is to defend and to teach his people. The *form* of his artistry *eliminates the chaos* of racism because it challenges it, wrestles it to the ground, or holds a mirror up to it. Such unity could only result in *peace among disparate voices* because it enables a unique and harmonic trend. It is poetry that deliberately includes itself with an artistic wave started to ignite transformation between itself and its literary objects: its people. Prior to Malcolm and the Black Arts Movement the symbol power of White went unchallenged. Marimba Ani writes:

> A continual pressure exerts itself upon the psyche of a "nonwhite" person living within the ubiquitous confines of the West to "remold," "refashion," "paint," "refine" herself in conformity with this European aesthetical image of what a human being should be. The pressures begin at birth and outlive the person, often breaking her spirit long before her physical demise. This aspect of the European aesthetic is a deadly weapon at the service of the need to dominate and destroy. So deep is the wound it inflicts that in Senegal, West Africa, women, some of the most beautiful in the world, burn and disfigure their rich, smooth, melanic ebony skin with lye in the attempt to make it white.[24]

Malcolm X discusses this issue in the terminology of incarceration, a condition that he intimately experienced. He lectures:

> [Once] we hated ourselves. Our *color* became to us a *chain*—we felt that it was holding us back; our color became to us *like a prison* which we felt was keeping us confined, not letting us go this way or that way. We felt that all of these restrictions were based upon our color, and the *psychological reaction* to that would have to be that as long as we felt imprisoned or chained or *trapped by* those features and that *blood* holding us back automatically ... it becomes *hateful* to us[25] [my emphasis].

In the above, Malcolm recalls Countee Cullen's "Shroud of Color," which is vital today in the appearance and life of the King of Pop, Michael Jackson, now whiter than White people, his appearance like ghost dust, ghastly. In the above, X's oratorical *meaning* in relationship to his community is to unify the biological and societal causes of imprisonment. Like Cullen's "shroud," X's color, his chains, imprison and cause a demented psychological reaction within the (re)named negro. Using "blood" as a synonym for "color" this life source turns "hateful," compounding an already debilitating condition. Blood, a synecdoche for the human in X's rendition, restricts, limits and traps.

In its colloquial use, "blood" has another connotation. Young people in revolutionary organizations in the 1960s and 1970s called one another, along with "brother" or "sister," "Blood." It was common to hear "Yo, Blood, what it is?" However, despite its use denoting kinship, the twin facets of biology, blood and color, tormented the Negro to depths that language is incapable of explaining. This amorphous monolith persuaded Madhubuti to write forthrightly about his own unique light shade of color, his self-hatred. In the following poem from *Black Pride* (1968), in the confessional mode, he seeks both cure and self-forgiveness:

i
at one time,
loved
my
color—
it
opened sMall
doors of
tokensim
&
acceptance.
    (doors called, "the only one" & "*our negro*")[26] [my emphasis].

Sharing a moment of light-skinned privilege, Madhubuti prepares the stage for a pre-malcolmian issue. Where X talked about the collective color of Black, Madhubuti refers to his slim-shade, to paraphrase his lyric, as the color of an almond, inside. Since enslavement, Negroes have been categorized and rewarded according to personal pigmentation (Douglass, 184; Harper, 1893).[27] Abhorring this custom, Madhubuti first opens up to its contemporary advantage in "The Self-hatred of Don L. Lee," making the personal the political, a common practice of the period. His holding up a mirror to this personal advantage allows his audience to recognize his knowledge of color prejudice. This racism satellite often left the "token" or "our negro" surrounded by isolation. The physical aspects of biracialism, whether or not in the immediate parentage, inspired another kind of inner turmoil, which sometimes led to a Walter White, a Charles Chestnutt, or even a Malcolm X. These men penetrated the hypocrisy of slim-shade privilege and through writing and activism corrected the stratification of separation in the Negro aggregate. In Madhubuti's next stanza he therefore "escapes into sanity."

> i
> began
> to love
> only a
> part of
> me —
> my inner
> self which
> is all
> black —...

Madhubuti transforms his blood and his mind back to black. Of course this is not the traditional "black." It is the malcolmian, reconstructed ideology of "black." It is James Brown's song turned slogan "Say it Loud, I'm Black and I'm Proud," the Langston Hughes "The night is beautiful / So the faces of my people." The premiums that White America place on complexion explode here. As a malcolmian poet, he cuts the color hierarchy in the aesthetics of America, and indirectly encourages others to view the absurdity of color as well. Additionally, he slices himself in half and the opposites mirror Western bipolarism, not reconciled.

Also, one discovers the climb up to wholeness as "The Self-Hatred" builds. Madhubuti dislikes his external color, a natural reaction to the ravages of enslavement and the rape of the Black woman (Akbar, 1991; Nobles, 1986; Wright, 1984). In his effort to generate language that erases self-hatred he indirectly addresses the desire to adopt new behavior, the ethical component of inner and outer harmony. He like Malcolm provides answers to the challenges that limit the Negro's growth. He does this in a method of racial conflation where he writes:

> I
> seek
> integration
> of
> *negroes*
> with
> *black*
> people[28] [my emphasis].

This example of Pan-Africanism or Garvey integration shows a redefinition of "black" from negative to positive, one of the earliest Black aesthetic tenets. Begun by Langston Hughes and Marcus Garvey, Malcolm evolved it in Afrocentricity, but the transition was slippery, turbulent, and bumpy. That formidable negating imagery was entrenched in the American psyche. Almost two centuries prior, Wheatley had begun this evil when she pens, "Remember Negroes *black as Cain.*"

However, in the above poem, Madhubuti repeats and revises Wheatley's darkness, recognizing that the Negro is himself and his people. Gates writes that Black texts talk to one another, and through repetition, revise the previous concept or antecedent.[29] Therefore, Madhubuti through Garvey integration plunges the disappearing Negro into the upcoming and becoming "Black," no longer a symbol from Wheatley's lexicon. If I borrow Henderson's "saturation" and place it in a malcolmian construction, then saturation involves the following: to challenge and change White society; to separate from it; to redirect energy and purpose into Black communities; to reconnect with Africa, wholistically. The structure of Madhubuti's poem provides a fast or slow reading. Like change, whether slow or fast, "Don Haki"[30] is a guide to new possibilities and directions, reversing the previous Black image and meaning—double-voicing—like Esu Elegbara, clearing the way with the *ntu* of Ogun, the blacksmith.

Black Pre- and Post-Malcolm

Like Richard Wright in *Native Son*, Madhubuti wrote with a political agenda. Wright's masterpiece was to transform and enlighten readers about the psychological turmoil of the nonspeaking (at least to Whites), economically deprived Negro. Bigger Thomas's double-voice, the speech in his head, was certainly not the oration that he shared with his family, friends, and employers. However, Don Haki and the Black Arts poets extended the practice of protest literature, turning it into liberation literature, a poetry that located *nzuri*, "African" beauty. In contrast, in *Native Son* an image of "black" remembers Wheatley's rendition. The rat that Bigger kills, Bigger himself, his family members, and Bessie his girlfriend are all indistinguishably "black" with undertones of dirt, bleakness, and poverty. Madhubuti revisits that traditional image before lopping it in lyrics:

> like
> if he had da called me
> *black* seven years ago
> I wd've —

>   broke his right eye out
>   jumped into his chest...³¹ [my emphasis].

Madhubuti like Malcolm applies history, personal and public, for analysis and context. Above he recalls the pre-malcolmian meaning of black. It was an epithet, as degrading as publicly insulting someone's mother. His use of "like" is not in simile. Like, an adverb expressing a precondition, it prepares for a later act and action in the 'hood. It is hard spoken, like hitting a piano chord in bass clef. Returning to "black," the Don presents it prior to a malcolmian conversion.

> About my *blackness* and my early escape
> period, trying to be white.
> About the nights my mother would go out —
> without money — to get us something to eat,
> she always came back with food. Some people
> would call this prostitution but I call it —
> providing for her family...
> About negative images as a child — all *black*³² [my emphasis].

The closure signals a cluster of negativity: "all black." Similar to John Edgar Wideman's version in *Brothers and Keepers*, Madhubuti views bleakness as the source of obscurity in "blackness." Portraying his outlaw brother in this bleak/black nuance, Wideman illustrates why he left home. Presenting his brother Robby as an emblem of "blackness," he predates the X-factor inversion, although chronologically this event occurs after Malcolm's reformation. Speaking directly to his brother, Wideman explains:

> Because we were brothers, holidays, family celebrations, and troubles drew us to the same rooms at the same time, *but I felt uncomfortable around you.* Most of what I felt was guilt. I'd made choices. I was running away from Pittsburgh, from *poverty, from blackness*³³ [my emphasis].

Both Madhubuti and Wideman couple bleak/black tension that emphasizes the lingering torment that Ani portrays in those non-Whites who live in "ubiquitous" white-skinned privilege. As Madhubuti's family dysfunction jumbles, unlike Wideman, the obscure bleak/blackness transforms into hope, a malcolmian inspiration. When X constructs the chain of color, he prefigures and makes public the Negro's hidden truth. Following with the Negro's pre-American experience, he takes his audience to a crossroads and like Ogun and Esu, two warrior dieties, he routes them away from despair, guilt, and perplexity, saying: "So as the African nations gained their independence and the image of the African continent began to change, the things agreed as the image of Africa switched from *negative to positive.*

Subconsciously, the *Black* man throughout the Western Hemisphere, in his subconscious mind, began to identify with that emerging positive *African image*. And when he saw the *Black* man on the African continent taking a stand, it made him become filled with the desire also to *take a stand*"[34] [my emphasis].

Equating the American and African black as one, X pictures and stimulates the change in the *becoming* Black man. This historical unity although tenuous and unclear still awoke within the American Negro the rethinking of her racial name and American status, quietly developing a new level of nationhood. Similarly, Madhubuti writes:

> Swinging, Swinging,
> Into *blackness* away from
> Negroness to *Self* to
> *awareness* of basic color
> my color, I found it...[35] [my emphasis].

Don Haki breaks the Western chain of color, finding a "basic" collective racial color that X transformed. He explains the acceptance of Blackness through a dichotomous phrase. Malcolm X, from his spiritual teacher Elijah Muhammad, consistently spoke the oxymoronic phrase "lost/found" when referring to the complex, unstable identity of the Negro and those outside of Islam. Madhubuti, in the above poem, creates a metaphoric language "swinging" (lost) which psychologically suggests the drifting and dangling Negro mass produced in America. Furthermore, "swinging" has other reminders: (1) lynching, (2) Tarzan swinging tree to tree, and (3) a jazz band "getting down." In sum, it displays movement from one state to another. It is the blacksmith's swing of Ogun's hammer, until the object is right for the world. Madhubuti turns the locomotion into location because his "swing" has an Esu double-mouthed purpose. Not only does it land in the realm of "blackness," but also, it "swing[s]" away from "negroness." Madhubuti is *Found* in Blackness, in Africa, in *Self*. Found "blackness" is not the physical, but the metaphysical, his African mother who rebirths him.

In the neo-African world, this is an initiation poem in America, a rite of passage that celebrates abandoning youth and gaining maturity. The *meaning* is a direction to his audience to join him and reject subservience. The *ethos*, the emotion, is vital, distinguishing a joy, a revelation for living. The operative relationship between the Don and his audience *functions* as a personal and public roadmap. The poem's *motif* is Black language and symbols, most evident in the "swing." Now that blackness has caught and cradles him, he can sup from useable African culture and through his individual creativity replenish its local focus. His new birth is the internationalized man of Langston Hughes' poetry but he claims Marcus Garvey's Pan-Africanism. In his attempt to seamlessly link that African and the American, Madhubuti teaches. In "A Message All Blackpeople Can Dig: (& a few negroes too)," we sample an almost completely transformed image of Africa with X's revolutionary injection. This poem was written in 1969, four years following X's assassination:

> we are going to do it.
> Us: *blackpeople, beautiful* people; the sons and
> daughters of beautiful people...
> we'll move together
> *hands on weapons* and families
> blending into the sun,
> into each/other
> we'll love...[36] [my emphasis].

In the title, Madhubuti signifies but includes Negroes in his vision of revolutionary nation-building and the protection of that nation. His inclusion of "negroes" with "blackpeople" culminates the wish of his earlier poem where he sought to integrate the two concepts. The significance of his expression relative to him and his community, the *meaning*, is a harmonic prediction. He speaks the future in the present moment. And how does he figure the aesthetics in that future and present moment? They are of the *nzuri* model. They reflect a complimentary and complementary beauty beginning in neo "black" America and looking back to Africa, "sons and daughters." Madhubuti's *ethos* exudes that spiritual past and present energy. In Africa, folk protected their residences. The *motif* and symbols are of the Age of Malcolm, "hands on weapons" and of a long known metonym for Africa, "sun." This is the *function*, the blending of families, men, women, and children.

Such Garvey integration is Pan-African in both scope and imagery and it emerges from the malcolmian principle that suggests responsibility for lost members of the race. The above again speaks the oxymoronic concepts of the "lost/found," absence and presence, as it records the cultural nationalist organization US which reclaimed a direct African aesthetic during the 1960s. The image of "hands on weapons" signals self-defense, a Black Panther image, and a beauty motif in X's oratory and aesthetic. This *form* of the artistic product is another kind of defender poem. When X writes about living in a time of revolution in his speech "There's a Worldwide Revolution Going On," he signals his understanding of the possibility of revolt.

In that speech, Malcolm in secular language foreshadows global nationalism and in southern geography the Negro's connection. Similar to Langston

Hughes, Malcolm emphasizes "worldwide," placing the Negro in an international context, again extending boundaries for transformation. Earlier Hughes wrote "Black Seed" whereby "world-wide dusk / of dear dark faces / [were] driven before an alien wind." Malcolm likewise recognizes injustices abroad and at home, making it unquestionably clear that nonviolence is not his response to inequality.

Negro as adjective nullifies the potential of "revolution" according to Malcolm. He hints that with subservience, commodity, imitator, and beast imbedded in this synonym for slavery, the dominant culture disregards the civil rights movement. Malcolm's involvement with international revolutionaries and revolutionary movements enabled him to try to relocate the typical passivity of Negro leaders to the harsh realities of actual freedom fighters. He creates in the imagination the merging of Negroes to Black people, the conflation of subservience to independence, the adjustment of nonviolence to violence. His kind of "change" was more total than integration allowed. Revolutionary change can include bloodshed as well as the transformation and transference of ideas. Don Haki demonstrates the transference of ideas in a "change" refrain in the following poem:

> change.
> life if u were a match i wd light u into something
> beautiful. Change.
> change....
> change nigger...
> know the realenemy...
> change change your change change change.
> Your
> mind nigger.[37]

The beauty in black includes the theory and practice of change. When the "match" strikes, the once dull inflames. H. Rap Brown during this epoch created the repeated phrase "burn baby burn." The image and idea of "fire" and "flames" also recall and record the impact of the riots on the American landscape. In X's oratory where he differentiates between the house negro or nigger and the field negro or nigger, he also uses "fire" as a tool that the more aggressive field negro or nigger desired to fight his master. Ogun is the master of the forge and the flame. He fires everything that requires transformation and transcendence. In change, Madhubuti above refers to the "realenemy," a counterpart to Elijah Muhammad's "natural" enemy, with David Walker (1829) preceding each with "natural enemies." Natural and real connote a propensity for a particular behavior. All four men insist that Black and White harmony is not "natural." Madhubuti's repetition of "change" identifies the difficulty in persuading the Negroes to detach from McKay's "cultured hell." The repetition also indicates his urgency for and his persuasion of his followers to accept his controlling idea of transformation.

The way Madhubuti penned the poem, the word "nigger" snaps. This is a double-voice of tough love. In the "nigger" snap, he demands an Afrocentric difference, showing the multiple meanings of the N-word, and his unconcern for the inappropriateness of using the epithet "nigger." The snap is a rhythm of transformation. In the *meaning* Madhubuti guides his people bringing a message divine. As if receiving the oracle, his artistry is not the cryptogram but the revelation for what is to be. His *ethos*, the quality of expression is an attentive order, a demand, in a *form* of incantation.

In his *unity of occasion* he visualizes the need for change or transformation of the Negro or nigger to something else, beautiful like the faces in Langston Hughes' poem and revolutionary like the worker. Madhubuti *eliminates chaotic* racism because the poem urges a different kind of behavior to solve challenges, the separation from the parent who (re)named the race. In this separation, *the elevation of peace* is implied. Madhubuti's *meaning*, his significance of expression and its relationship to his listeners and readers, highlights the dramatic shift he desires to occur. Spirit, emotion, and energy exude in the *ethos* of this long poem excerpted above. The repetition of change is incantation like the Native American artist-healers who worded charms to make things happen. With the spirit of ancestral survival, the *ntu* (energy) reflects the rhythm of ancient and contemporary vibrations. The *mode* in which he expresses this poem is close to song.

The Issue of Re(re)naming

Madhubuti like Malcolm begins the tradition of manipulating racial designators to applaud or disparage behavior. Negro and Black become bipolar: bad* and good, negative and positive. Even well beyond the 1960s, this conflict continues with Negro as negative, a new addition in African American lingo. Consider the following poem first published in 1987 in *Killing Memory* entitled, "negro: an updated definition part 368 for clarence pendleton and diana ross, to be read to the popular song, 'born in the USA:'" It goes like this:

---

*It is important to differentiate between the African American's use of "bad" as good from the Western dictionary meaning. The word "bad" has been inverted in the African American lexicon since the modern era. Michael Jackson has a contemporary song entitled "I'm Bad" which means he is exciting, audacious, sensual, strong, etc. However, the "bad" in reference to the "negro" is the Western version of the word.

> negroes (negroes/knee grows)pc.,grows and
> devours itself; invented around 1619 in the
> americas by the british, french, spanish and
> portuguese ...
> They are Born In the USA
> negroes were reborn in such TV shows as webster,
> gimme a break, the jeffersons, different strokes,
> benson, amen, and miami vice. They have currently
> captured the imagination of the world/and
> hollywood in movies like soldier's story, the
> color purple and native son, love money...
> negroes, the people that gave the world
> billy dee williams and diahann carroll,
> wake up and go to sleep praying,
> 'Thank God for Slavery.'[38]

Engaging the malcolmian method of providing historical context, his verbal play narrates the saga of the mass-produced "negro." Inspired by Bruce Springsteen's popular song "Born in the USA," the poet when reciting sings a few lines in the pop song's melody. This postmodern montage is a scathing indictment of political figures, movie stars, and television, all intertextual contributors to the poet's malcolmian conception and replication of the Negro. In the first line with the homophone "knee grows" he implies the begging posture of the "so-called negro," as an introduction to the history of this commodity. The self-perpetual Negro is *not* out of Africa because it is "Born in the USA." Consumers cyclically devour the television and televised (re)birth of the Negro. As ambiguity and subtlety are not features of the Black Arts expression, the poet "names the names." He talks through poetry directly and clearly to his audience. In contemporary Black culture activists and speakers have a call and response linguistic play with the audience. They do a verbal interaction that "names the names." The speaker will first list unfair and hurtful practices perpetuated against Black people and when he pauses for breath the audience responds, with "name the names." Activist Steve Cokely encourages this indigenous rhetorical entertainment or "edutainment" that demands clarity. In the above poem, Madhubuti by exact naming alerts us to what he considers examples of injurious cultural consumption.

Madhubuti's *meaning* in relationship to his community is in his accentuating cultural poisons that are habitual and pervasive. His *motif*, manipulation of symbols, begins in the title and extends throughout the length of the poem. The symbolism here portrays the visions and the culture of the parent who (re)named the Negro. The *function* of this poem, then, is to emphasize the requirement to reject cultural projects that fail to solve relevant challenges within the collective. Of course the *mode* of the poem is similar to a Bruce Springsteen song.

Haki Madhubuti's collective themes are not far from the prominent subjects in Carter G. Woodson's *Mis-education of the Negro* (1930). Woodson brilliantly articulates the abstract thinking of Negro intellectuals as a spotlight and reflector of Western education. He argues that they, thinking as White men, fail to assist the Negro community. Most importantly, Woodson urges Negroes to bend their White education to serve the economic needs of their own communities, to forge it into something beautiful. In the reverse, Madhubuti's above listing illustrates imitation, absurdity, and stereotypes, not nation-builders or independent African theorists and practitioners. Like Marcus Garvey, Madhubuti desires a connection between culture and ethics; therefore, he mocks the television shows starring Negro media images. They are the "entertainers only" in his earlier poem. Webster is a child-midget, adopted by a White family. The Jeffersons are a family of comedians. Such isolation and employ of "negroes" causes his audience to contemplate the sitcoms' unreality, as it implicitly indicts movie stars who escape the problems of the aggregate. In the closure that welcomes slavery, Madhubuti repeats, reverses, and trumps Wheatley, who earlier wrote "Twas mercy brought me from my Pagan land."

His signifying trump spotlights the absurdity of "Twas mercy" and it reminds us of a birth into slavery. Therefore, his *unity of occasion* is the reforming of the Negro to demonstrate and categorize a pattern of dysfunctional behavior that masquerades and celebrates vulgar dependency on White America. It *eliminates the chaos* of racism because of its pattern of exposure through humor and culture. The biracialism of the poem, the Bruce Springsteen inclusion, provides *an elevation of peace*, a unique backdrop and harmony. Bruce Springsteen wrote a song entitled "41 Shots" about the Amadou Diallo murder. He is known for supporting projects and issues that benefit people of color.

In another poem, Madhubuti encourages re(re)naming using a different mix of racial terminology. By compressing words to illustrate several concurrent meanings, he creates a linguistic aesthetic that emits a malcolmian switch. In 1971, Don Haki writes:

> We're an *African*people
> hard-softnessburning*black*.
> the earth's magic color our veins.
> an *African*people are we;
> burning blackersoftly, softer[39] [my emphasis].

In *meaning* and *function* Madhubuti's first line reminds the "so-called negroes" that they are other than that. They are two concepts that have evaded the group psychology since enslavement: to be "African" and a "people." Negroes are seen as non-people and certainly not African as shown in earlier chapters. Here, Madhubuti reverses that trend, and in a soft *mode*, his manner of expression, and the *form* does not defend the "Africanpeople." Nor does it snap persuasion, like "change." Instead, it evokes a matter-of-fact spirit of an obvious yet obscure-for-centuries racial rejoining.

Reversing the subject and predicate in the fourth line dramatically underscores this new, linguistic notion, a global unification by non-separating "African" and "people." The "black" is the emerging consciousness and renaming of American negroes, the *unity of occasion*. Following, the oppositional adjectives "hard-soft" suggest the complexity of being human, that bipolarism, and absence-and-presence, but with something else. The "earth's magic color our veins" replaces the "hated blood" Malcolm previously explained, as it tropes and reverses Cullen's shroud, *eliminating the chaos* of racism. This is blood to live for, the earth pumping life and color into a people on the move, becoming. Seeking a unity within complexity, Madhubuti replicates the emotion and energy that urged Garvey to say "One Aim, One Destiny," and Bob Marley to sing "One Love" and Cheikh Anta Diop to discover one common culture. Madhubuti says "onepeople." Several tendencies emerge from burning and being black: the heat of transformation, the flame of anger, Ogun, and the night velvet beauty, in alliteration and repetition.

To be hard and soft simultaneously also speaks a traditional African ethos or shared belief, contrary to bipolar opposition. As Marimba Ani (Dona Richards) tells us in *Let the Circle Be Unbroken* (1980), life explanations are not neat either/or propositions. Western ideology points to contrasts without considering, as in the African world, the composite of opposites without tension, conflict, or separations, *an elevation of peace, harmony*. For example, in an African worldview, highly spiritual time is cyclical where all formations of space can combine in a shared area. The past, present, and future are a complex unit. Ani writes:

> Opposing pairs in the European view are "knowledge/opinion," "objective/subjective," "science/religion," "mind/body," "male/female," "man/boy," "white/black," and so forth. To the African, on the other hand, the universe is made up of *complementary* pairs. These "pairs" are forces, or principles of reality that are interdependent and necessary to each other, in a unified system. The Divine Essence, for instance, is both female and male and therefore able to reproduce itself. It does so in the form of male and female twins that then pair in order to continue the process. The determining mode of the African worldview is harmony. The goal is that of discovering the point of harmonious interaction, so that interferences become neutralized, allowing constructive energy to flow and to be received.[40]

This idea of twins and doubles intrinsically informs areas of traditional African thought where Esu is a prominent diviner. Statues of him are sometimes doubled with female characteristics such as breasts. It is understood that the notion of twoness or multiples of it composes the universe on which the society is based as it was in ancient Kemet. For example, the Fon of Dahomey match doubleness in society whereby the king is two in one. He may be one royal personage but he has two courts, two bodies of similar officials, and two series of rituals in honor of royal ancestors.[41]

In another type of duality in "Expectations," a cautionary poem, Madhubuti continues to racially identify and to explain the significance of aesthetics and culture. In 1983, eighteen years after X's assassination, he writes:

> PeopleBlack and stone
> be careful of that which is designated beautiful
> most of us have been taught from the basements
> of other people's minds.
> ...
> it is accepted in america that beauty is
> thin, long, & the color of bubblegum[42]

The "color of bubblegum" trivializes the persistent imitative tendencies of the people now "Black and stone." The operative relationship or *function* of "Expectations" blots the effect of ubiquitous European imagery. The parent who once owned the African remains the dominant teacher. In that respect, the Don's *meaning* is to remind, to teach, and to warn. In two dimensions, he incorporates symbols or develops a *motif*: (1) PeopleBlack and stone and (2) PeopleBlack and bubblegum. His *ethos* keeps current or brings back the spirit and energy of the Black Arts Movement, caring and concern for the racial collective.

He borrows the Spanish manner of noun and adjective placement in line one. In Spanish, the adjective follows the noun, Pueblo de negro, for example. Madhubuti's English "PeopleBlack" calls attention to the second capitalized noun. When he places a natural object, "stone," divinely made, close to "People," he transforms Africa, humanizing the negro or commodity aspects, *eliminating the chaos* of racism. Stone also indicates the resilience of a people. The capitalization of the Black "b" elevates the symbol, Afrocentrically. He is quite at home within the image, and so are his people. "Basement" and "bubble gum" signal "low," as in base or crude and childishness or triviality. Signifying sophisticatedly on White, for him the identity issue is no longer tense; therefore, it is unnecessary to convert the symbol's gradations. He then reroutes the poem:

> trust people
> one by one
> the *darker* they come [my emphasis].

As Madhubuti reconstructs "black" he does so for its derivative, dark. Now that he has adopted the malcolmian principle of black being beautiful, his job as writer is to invert and generate successful synonyms suggesting the Black-side of humanity. However, because he recognizes the snare in pigmentation being the only criteria of worth, he defuses essentialism by flexing the conflicts inherent in color encoding:

> even within the hue & hueless
> among them are those
> who have recently lost their
> ability to recall.
>
> they can hurt you
> drop you to your knees with words...

Those who can drop you to your knees lack historical memory, which, like Malcolm orates, Madhubuti writes to restore *the elevation of peace among disparate voices*. His previous employment of "knee" is a pun on phonetics and the begging posture. The above is one of defeat: knocked down, each a weakness. Without historical memory, a healthy relationship to Africa, one can easily stay at the "negro" stage, and as Madhubuti shows, either slim-shade or midnight black, those without what Kariamu Welsh-Asante calls epic memory suffer the arrogance and aggrandizement of White racial supremacy. Because as Ani writes in *Let the Circle Be Unbroken*:

> Our oppressors have emphasized the loss of language, dress, living patterns and other tangible and surface aspects of culture, just as they do in discussions of African culture on the continent. They emphasize differences in language, and customs — even physique — from one society to another. They do this with good reason. It is an emphasis that serves their objectives. Until we learn that it serves our objectives to emphasize the similarities, the ties, the unifying principles, the common threads and themes that bind and identify us all as "African," we will continue to be politically and ideologically confused.[43]

Madhubuti is not confused, as he consistently focuses on what he believes to be his people's best interest. From his earliest text *Think Black* (1966), he calls his people "African people." His African reach is not superficial. In his perspective and in his artistry, he penetrates all levels of awareness. He goes beyond "skin recognition" of Blackness, beyond "environmental recognition," beyond "personality awareness," beyond "interest-concern." Madhubuti has become "totally changed to a conscious level of involvement in the struggle for his ... own" liberation of the mind.[44] His rhetoric of resistance *is* an escape into African-centered sanity that he brings to his readers.

Keto believes that one must relate his or her core back to the African continent. Madhubuti, from his early years to the present, has done that. In fact, he wrote poetry to introduce Africans in America to the issues and the culture of continental Africans. In *Black Pride* (1968), for example, he refers to Africa as mother in "The Primitive," and also in "No More Marching." In *Don't Cry Scream* (1969), he calls for "Nigerian Unity." His regenerative image of Africa keeps Africans throughout the Diaspora acquainted with current events and history that interconnect and relate each to the other. For him, Africa has been rescuer, nurturer, inspiration, refuge, haven and point of origin. His literary imaginative African ideal follows in "A Poem for a Poet":

> read yr/exile
> i had a mother too,
> & her death will not be
> talked of around the world.
> Like you,
> i live/walk a strange land
> my smiles are real but seldom:
> our enemies eat the same bread
> and their waste
> (there is always waste)
> is given to pigs,
> and then they consume the pigs.[45]

Here, Madhubuti's *unity of occasion* revolves the continental African and himself as alter egos. They have much in common, and in a thoughtful, soft way, Madhubuti turns himself into the African geographically. This connection is in the exile of each in America, representing to Madhubuti the "strange" land in Hughes' poem or the "alien wind." The *function* similar to its *meaning* operates to unify three audiences. It explains commonality among the continental, the American African, and the individual poet. For all three audiences, the *ethos* is the backward looking bird going forward. The *motif* crafts a cycle of cannibalism where the common enemies eat their own waste, a reminder of a Muslim anti-pig diet. This digestion and regurgitation also lights up the cyclical power of the Africans' enemies. For example, Blacks worldwide have been fighting for freedom since the 16th century beginning of the Europeans' incursions into Africa. Therefore, the "struggle" has persisted despite shifting aspects of time and circumstance. The following lines of this same poem reroute into opposite imagery:

> Africa still has sun & moon,
> has clean grass & water u can see thru;
> Africa's people talk to u with their whole faces,
> and their speech comes like drumbeats. comes like drumbeats.

In this *unity of occasion* Africa has cosmic beauty, "sun & moon." Implicitly, he contrasts Africa with America, its *function* to show American Africans an African geographic beauty: "clean grass," "water u can see thru." The opposite is American smog and polluted water. This also replicates his *motif* of opposite symbols. The body language of the Africans maintains the distinctions between Africa and America. The body language of White America in particular comes to mind. For instance, the term "whole faces" is synecdoche, the link into someone's eyes or the gestures of the whole body as one communicates. Friendliness that emerges out of the entire countenance is not associated with Americans. This diverse behavior can also be categorized geographically in that folks from the South speak to and greet one another no matter how often they see one another throughout the day. This is unknown behavior in the North.

The social scientist Joy Leary says something similar when differentiating between Africans on the continent and those in America. About her recent trip to Africa, she lectures that Africans have a common greeting that goes: "we see you," *meaning* that they in joyful manner acknowledge your presence on the planet. However, young male African Americans reversed the concept. I or we "see you" in Black vernacular turns into the derogatory "what are you looking at?" Leary identifies this opposition as the disconnection from Africa, which X orated about, and the falseness and harshness of male-centered urban culture.[46] This complication also points to the deep and vast breach, despite the Africanisms, that occurred because of the importation of labor, people, from there to here.

Next, in the poem, the repetition of the line "comes like drumbeats" echoes back to Langston Hughes' leitmotif. In his poem titled "Drum" he uses the instrument as a metaphor for death, and the final line speaks "come" three times. Hughes' onomatopoetic "come" repetition has a thumping which drifts to dreaminess in Madhubuti's refrain, "comes like drumbeats." Hughes' drum personifies the male and deeply commands, while Madhubuti's simile is feminine and friendly. Dissimilarly, in "Juke Box Love Song," along with the drum, Hughes merges geography and humans. He gives Harlem a heart and a drumbeat, which come straight out of Africa, like Madhubuti interfacing the continental and the Diaspora (American). Both poets centrally position the drum to remind readers of its significance in Africa and in America. For instance, in African culture the drum factors expansively. Francis Bebey in *African Music: A People's Art* (1975) reports that among some groups, the drum is considered a "man." Women are not allowed to play the percussions because women are not supposed to "beat" a man. However, in the Upper Volta, women are allowed to play the waterdrum, and in neo-African American culture today, women, like men, are drummers. On the continent, however, special musicians are chosen to play certain percussion instruments. Bebey insists that the drum is the instrument that best expresses the inner feelings of Africa. It speaks and people imitate the instrument's voice-sound through handclaps, foot stomps, and onomatopoeia, which sends messages from this and the metaphysical world.[47] Native Americans similarly use the drum.

Some Africans carve drums to resemble family members because the family is central in traditional African life. Stuckey tells us of its communicative powers, the voice bringing forth vibrations from the gods. This is why dancers face and dance toward the percussion.[48] This is also why drum playing was outlawed in the Americas during enslavement. Since they could talk, they carried communication from one plantation to another. William Loren Katz tells us that to kill African culture, enslavers banned the drum from plantations.[49]

In *Flash of the Spirit* (1983) Robert Farris Thompson densely discusses the variations and important functions of this instrument throughout the Diaspora. For example, certainly drums could talk, but they could also be silent and their silence was a script ready for reading. For particular ceremonies, drums were painted with signs similarly painted on the skin of the Africans. In Cuba the *sese* drums are seen at funerals to be read and not heard. Even in literature, Toni Morrison in *Jazz* (1992) crafts a funeral in Harlem during the Garvey era where marchers carried an array of percussion. The grim-faced marchers filled the Harlem streets in solidarity against White violence that killed Black people. Although the drums were present, most were silent except for one that played a single, mournful beat. In Madhubuti's "drumbeats," he *elevates peace among disparate voices* when showcasing aesthetic and useful elements of African culture.

In the following poem, Madhubuti pays homage to the Senegalese Cheikh Anta Diop (1923–1986), one of the earliest Afrocentric thinkers who isolated and examined ancient classical African behavior. When other nationalities referred to Egyptians as White, Diop the physicist employed carbon dating to prove that the ancients were African. To praise him, Madhubuti writes:

we were raised on the lower east side of detroit,
close to harlem, new york, around the block from
watts,
next to the mississippi delta in north america.
unaware of source or history, unaware of reasons,
whys, or beginnings, accepting tarzan and she
woman,
accepting kong as king, accepting stanley—
livingstone and europocentric africa,
accepting british novels, french language
and portuguese folktales that devastated africa's
values and vision, people.

you helped restore memories,
gave us place and time,
positioned us within content and warnings,
centered us for the fire from the
first world...[50]

In the first world, the writings of Diop caused an intellectual reawakening among Black scholars. Diop compared African culture, particularly his Wolof language, to the language of ancient Kemet (Egypt) and found commonality. Most African-centered thinkers pay homage to Diop because of his providing physiological proof that refuted the White or Oriental ethnicity of the ancients. This is a praise poem, one of the earliest literary genres on the continent. The *meaning* expresses the significance of Diop's contribution to the world and the *function* awakens all readers to the knowledge of the scientist's scholarship. It opens in the geography of the Diaspora African in America, the "unaware[ness]" that welcomes McKay's ghost as well as his bend to alien gods, and the tormenting results. The repetition of "accepting" marks the behavior of being Negro, the *motif* collecting a montage from literature and cinema.

The poet also reconfigures "fire from the first world," but this is not the flame of malcolmian transcendence. Rather, it is the fire from McKay's "cultured hell," burning the "unaware" through time until Elijah Muhammad met his god, Master Fard. The *form* of the poem is similar to the one dedicated to Blacks and a few negroes too. It is a list of objects that influence the "necro" aspects of "Negro": "portuguese fairy tales," "french language," "british novels," "she woman." Such listing is a repeated structure in the rhetoric of X. Thus, the *ethos* of the poem, its spirit, emotion, and *ntu*, bring forward X's legacy, magnifying not only his key ideas, but the *mode*, the *manner* in which he introduced them. Madhubuti double-voices Malcolm introducing his hero to another generation, as Henry Louis Gates writes about the mystery of African-centered investigative implements:

For Esu is the dynamic of process, the dialectical element of the system. It is Esu whose role of messenger we must conceive of, not as delivery boy, but as "he who interrelates all the different and multiple parts which compose the system."[51]

Esu then is the way of the drum and the sound of the message, as well as the code or key for interpretation to gain textured resonance in Black artistry. Madhubuti's poetry is the dynamism of a process, the determination to defy injustices by creating a brand of art devoted to defining and defending a particular people. The "dialectical element" resulted in the spirit of being a malcolmian mouthpiece. Generating a new generation of spoken word imagery, *nommo*, Madhubuti by the 1980s assisted in the race name "negro" falling into Ogun's ashes, rejected by the new people burning softly. Something else was emerging.

>   ...
>   there is storm on the horizon
>   beneath calm & cold & killer death
>   there is vision approaching.
>   Beneath filth & fear & running asses
>   There is planning & hope & connecting trust.
>   Beneath traffic stops and sex crazed *negroes*
>   There are *new people* arising
>   clothed in love & work & a will to advance...[52] [my emphasis].

The storm in the first two lines is a metaphor that contains the dynamism of an emerging people. The answer spirals in the "storm" that in the third line becomes "vision." Such imagery harkens back to his earlier poem written in 1970 titled "A Nationhood Poem," which has the exciting line, "if u can't stop a hurricane, be one."[53] Each poem *prefigures* the African as powerful, boundless and vast.

In the above, his war language of the 1960s Black Arts aesthetic shifts in nuances to the turbulent power of nature. In this more sophisticated, contemporary verse, Madhubuti parallels faith and hope with overwhelming elements that in his view can and must be neutralized. His faith is the *function* of this poem, which *means* a people with insight and foresight fighting and winning. The wind is a variation of Ogun's smoke. Madhubuti's *meaning* in the above speaks to defenders of Blacks, people like him. Creating a *motif* of metonymy in the fourth line "filth," "fear," and "running asses" he parallels (his) faith overpowering adversity. The application of "negroes" indeed contrasts with the "new people arising." His *practical means of realization* in his own poetry suggests a correct read of malcolmian thought earth-bound and inspiring, a thing that does not die.

Yet, some have claimed the death of the Black Arts Movement. In contrast, my interpretation and explication of Haki Madhubuti's art reveals a spiritual continuation. The Don's focus never shifted; the diction and maturity enriched the versification, but it maintains the image of Black Power, Black Arts poetry. With time everything transforms, people, animals, plants, but the vibratory elements change hands like long distance runners passing the baton. Like Esu, Madhubuti predicts the future, walking the way of the ancient poets, the seers. Like Malcolm, the Don lives in and enlivens the present, struggles and relaxes with the past, works for and anticipates the future. Just as he insisted that the Panther leaders were "murder[ed]" long before the officials were forced to acknowledge that truth, he also predicted the Negro or Blacks' future race name.

Madhubuti wrote a lyric, two years after Malcolm X spoke the name, April 3, 1964. Malcolm said:

> Right now, in this country, if you and I, 22 million *African Americans*— that's what we are — Africans who are in America[54] [my emphasis].

In *Think Black* (1966), Madhubuti in the 12th line of "Mainstream of Society" writes "*African American*, blackman true."[55] Over twenty years later, the masses caught the smoke of the poet and his muse. Haki Madhubuti and Malcolm X effectively spoke a new people into being.

About Mothers and Music

Besides writing about prescient issues of collective racial identity, in his latest book, *YellowBlack*, Madhubuti traces the first twenty-one years of his life. Primarily he creates a series of word portraits of his mother, Maxine Graves Lee. Additionally, this text travels to the moment when X affected his young life. The idea of mothers, masculinity, maleness, and men is at an interesting juncture in this text. For one, Madhubuti is finally able to lyricize in stunning stanzas the private pain he truncates in an earlier poem from *Think Black* about his mother's prostitution. In *YellowBlack*, through his poignant personal story in poetry and essays, we experience a fuller visual and auditory feast that images how the Ralph Ellison's dispossessed manage in a capitalistic society. Yet, this is not a treatise on economics. It is a book of poetry, memorable in message and design. We experience young Don Luther Lee's heroic and heinous adventure of being an only son in a single parent home. In *YellowBlack*, he does not concentrate on defender poems. We already know him as our champion. Instead, we experience him as a son, a subject he often writes about, particularly in *Tough Notes*, but he speaks to other people's sons. Here, he is the subject of himself: quite a huge spiritual and personal move for him.

Malcolm X was never able to discuss his mother in the *Autobiography*. Her saga was too hurtful and personal for him to pursue in print. Yet, today, two prominent hip-hop artists, Nas and Tupac Shakur, like Madhubuti on a smaller scale, make lyrics about their mothers. In this area of artistry, they generate a relationship to the Don, Haki Madhubuti, a godfather of rap and hip hop culture. Nas in fact on his album *God's Son* (2002) features Pac, in a remix of "Thug Mansion,"[56] speaking from the grave to his Panther mother, Afeni Shakur. He tells her that he is all right, that he is kicking it with Malcolm, Billy Holiday. He is doing his thing in thug heaven. Conversely, Nas raps lyrics about his mother who died of cancer recently and he praises her for raising a ghetto brother in the 'hood, alone. His rap, "Dance," where he repeatedly asks for one more dance with his mother, is as tender as the skin-soft sensual songs that Madhubuti pens about Maxine. Don L. writes about his mother:

> She wanted to be a dancer
> She wanted to be warm weather year round
> She wanted to know the origin of walnuts and wealth
> She wanted to play the harmonica and sing like Billy Holiday

Billy Holiday spoke to Malcolm, Maxine, Madhubuti, Nas, and Tupac. She ties all of the artists together. But there is more with Tupac. My students in different universities have claimed Pac as an expression of Malcolm X. He is the X after X. Although I point out the differences, the similarities are most exciting, making the in-class discussion electric and a common denominator for students of multiple ethnicity. However, if Tupac is the X after X than he is an extension of Haki Madhubuti, who is currently unknown to most on college campuses. He is unknown because he is rare: an independent African man speaking and expressing Black Power through poetry in books. Pac, on the other hand, lives in music and Nas, the same thing. However, the hip-hop artists and the poet all spring from the mosaic of Malcolm.

Final Words

Malcolm X and Haki Madhubuti transformed American discourse to enable Negro people to re(re)name. By introducing the concept and notion of Africa as a continent with accomplishments that precede those of Europe, they made it attractive to a people linguistically labeled with derivatives of bondage, discrimination, and death. Neither Malcolm nor Madhubuti consistently employed the term African American throughout their careers.

However, each started the racial-name-change process, referring to Negroes or Blacks as "African" before other postmodern intellectuals. They charged the metaphysical space and the psychology of the Negro with reasons to adopt new racial terminology. It took a future generation to advance and close the action.

Julius E. Thompson (1992) tells us that Madhubuti has greatly excited the art of writing poetry and that he has captured the regard of younger generations for the past thirty years. I agree and add that Madhubuti made an impression on the art of poetry writing because he begins from an African center. The youth are aroused by his poetry because in manner and voice the Black Arts poets resemble contemporary rappers. Black Arts poets for example play verbal games when reciting. Madhubuti makes noises, whistles, sings, and emphasizes vowels and consonants for effect. Most significantly, he produces functional art, writing about issues relevant to the African American community Molefi. Asante tells us that "all African writing must retrace the steps to home."[57] Understanding history and White supremacy, Madhubuti points poetry and essays to improve the conditions of Blacks, taking them "home," to themselves and to what he considers right actions.

Hence, Madhubuti through his writing has organized people around specific imagery that has led to an appreciation of a more advanced collective identity. His body of work *eliminates much of the racism chaos* because it addresses the trauma of African people; it offers solutions to Black problems; and it exposes antagonists. Certainly his *unity of occasion* prefigures Africa as agreeable. His *elimination of racism* through poetry synthesizes the African experience in America bringing a new and old *harmony*. Nationalism is a unifier among diverse peoples.

Madhubuti's push to re(re)name unified the diverse units within dark America. This X-factor influence inspired his redefinition of terms and his public concern for the universal African. It persuaded him to keep the re(re)naming issue before the public by way of poetry once X was assassinated. He kept Malcolm's music alive, playing in language, oration, and institution building. Madhubuti himself says that Malcolm "influenced [his] life more than any other person dead or alive."[58]

In *Run Toward Fear* (2004) and *YellowBlack* (2005), the Malcolm swing continues. In *Run Toward Fear*, he portrays the dead and living X by celebrating his wife, Betty Shabazz, in the following poetic narrative where each stanza begins with a small "i."

> i a poet, a weaver of life, an unfinished soul in motion   still
> a closet dancer who greyhounded between
> detroit and chicago
> on the same roads

> that Malcolm Little, Malcolm X, El Hajj Malik El Shabazz
> traveled the identical highways...
>
> i, a poet whose voice was confirmed, layered & enlarged
> after hearing
> a "young shining prince," before we knew
> we had the sons of kings and queens among us whispering
> African truths that gutted the whiteness in our bellies & minds...[59]

Don Haki is an "unfinished soul in motion," still swinging in *Run Toward Fear*, still mirroring the Negro time prior to the "shining prince." This excellent poetry book and poetry handbook is important for the budding artist and the seasoned word sorcerer. In this text, he makes his connection to the Black Arts modern and meaningful. *YellowBlack* contrasts with *Run Toward Fear* in chronology because the poet creates a retrospective of his first twenty-one years in poetry and essays. More than a memoir, it parallels the urban raw-edged narratives audible in hip-hop. At a recent poetry reading, I listened to and watched young males give Don Haki "rhythm"* when he spoke and recited his life in poetry. They related to him because of similarity, walking "identical roads." Kariamu Welsh-Asante says that "rhythm" as a source for the seven *nzuri* senses has multiple layers and existences. "It is possible for people to respond to different layers, levels and planes and still be in harmony with the framework of the rhythms and with each other."[60] In the compression of spirit, space, and time, the young males responded to the rhythms of Madhubuti and indirectly, the vibrations of Malcolm X. He spoke his Black Arts issues in a contemporary frame of reference, still playing the message of Malcolm. In *YellowBlack* he says:

> Malcolm X was the first Black man who had a national reputation and following that I saw and heard speaking truth to his people and to power. Before I heard Malcolm X I was literally suffocating in a room full of "white" air. Malcolm X helped to shape my young voice. His voice was the immediate call, an S.O.S. to young Black men and women who felt deeply that we needed a Black leader that would push our agenda via direct action rather than always reacting to white world supremacy. Malcolm X had the voice, the walk, the nerve, the right education, the debating skills, the street smarts, the moral high ground, and a deep sense of urgency that we were all drawn to.... Above all ... his private and public lives were not a contradiction.[61]

---

*To give someone "rhythm" is a contemporary expression, which means to provide feedback and affirmation to the speaker or person. Used in this context, the word "rhythm" is a new addition to the lexicon of Black English.

Malcolm the non-contradiction took him "home" to Africa and the idea of an African-center in America and throughout the Diaspora. Madhubuti fired up this message singing and playing into the echoes of Black people, who were always on the alert, listening and searching for signs of liberation. With the emphasis on name change, X and Madhubuti helped make fertile the ground for the coming and now the new people, who discarded a racist name. They, we, are now African Americans.

Chapter Notes

Introduction

1. Magnus O. Bassey, *Malcolm X and African American Self-Consciousness* (Lewiston, New York: Edwin R. Mellen Press, 2005), 151.
2. Karl Evanzz, *The Judas Factor: The Plot to Kill Malcolm X* (New York: Thunder's Mouth Press, 1992), 28–31.
3. Molefi Kete Asante, *The Afrocentric Idea* (Philadelphia: Temple Unversity Press, 1987), 93.
4. Asante in *The Afrocentric Idea* says that *nommo* is "the generative and productive power of the spoken word" (17).
5. Sterling Stuckey, *Slave Culture: Nationalist Theory and the Foundations of Black America* (New York: Oxford University Press, 1987), 3–4.
6. Asante, *The Afrocentric Idea*, 99.
7. Michael Eric Dyson, *Making Malcolm: The Myth and Meaning of Malcolm X* (New York: Oxford University Press, 1995), 85.
8. Haley, *Autobiography*, 267.
9. William W. Sales, Jr., *From Civil Rights to Black Liberation: Malcolm X and the Organization of Afro-American Unity* (Boston: South End Press, 1994), 57–58.
10. Asante, *The Afrocentric Idea*, 64.
11. Talmadge Anderson, "Black Psychology and Psychological Concepts." In *African-Centered Psychology: Culture-Focusing for Multicultural Competence*. Ed. Daudi Azibo (Durham: Carolina Academic Press, 2003), 3–38.
12. Anderson, 12.
13. George Breitman, *The Last Year of Malcolm X: The Evolution of a Revolutionary* (New York: Pathfinder Press, 1984), 110–111.
14. Michael Schwartz, ed., *Visions of a Liberated Future: Black Arts Movement Writings by Larry Neal* (New York: Thunder's Mouth Press, 1989), 78.
15. Bobby Seale, personal interview, 16 April 2000.
16. Joe William Trotter, *The African-American Experience: Volume II. From Reconstruction* (Boston: Houghton Mifflin Company, 2001), 599.
17. Richard J. Powell, *Black Art and Culture in the 20th Century* (New York: Thames and Hudson, 1997), 17–18.
18. Alex Haley, *The Autobiography of Malcolm X* (New York: Ballantine Books, 1990), ix.
19. Schwartz, *Liberated Future*, 125.
20. Schwartz, 29.
21. Eugene B. Redmond, *The Mission of Afro-American Poetry: Drumvoices: A Critical History* (New York: Doubleday, 1976), 12.
22. Redmond, 19.
23. Amiri Baraka, *The Autobiography: Leroi Jones/Amiri Baraka* (New York: Freundlich Books, 1984), 185.
24. Mary L. Gogumil and Michael R. Molino, "Pretext, Context, Subtext: Textual Power in the Writing of Langston Hughes, Richard Wright, and Martin Luther King, Jr." *College English* 52 (1990): 800.
25. Haki R. Madhubuti, *Claiming Earth: Race, Rage, Rape, Redemption* (Chicago: Third World Press, 1994), 77.
26. Huey P. Newton, *Revolutionary Suicide*

(New York: Harcourt Brace Jovanovich, Inc., 1973), 71.
27. Kalamu Ya Salaam, *The Oxford Companion to African-American Literature* (New York, Oxford University Press, 1997). <aalbc.com/authors/blackartsmovement.htm>.
28. Schwartz, 63.
29. Jack Salzman, David Lionel Smith, and Cornel West, *Encyclopedia of African-American Culture and History*. Volume 5 (New York: Simon and Schuster and Prentice Hall International, 1996), 2695.
30. Kalamu Ya Salaam, *The Oxford Companion to African-American Literature*.
31. Nikki Giovanni, *Black Feeling Black Talk Black Judgement* (New York: William Morrow and Company, 1970), 19.
32. Leroi Jones and Larry Neal, *Black Fire: An Anthology of Afro-American Writing* (New York: William Morrow and Company, 1968), 302.
33. Geroge Breitman, ed., *Malcolm X Speaks* (New York: Grove Weidenfeld, 1990), 33–34.
34. Wilson Jeremiah Moses, *The Golden Age of Black Nationalism, 1850–1925* (New York: Oxford University Press, 1978), 9–28
35. Bruce Perry, ed., *Malcolm X: The Last Speeches* (New York: Pathfinder Press, 1989), 162.
36. Tricia Rose, *Black Noise: Rap Music and Culture in Contemporary America* (Middletown, Conn.: Wesleyan University Press, 1994), 106.
37. Chuck D with Yusuf Jan, *Fight the Power* (New York: Delta Trade Paperbacks, 1997), 26–27.
38. Dyson, 92.
39. Nas Nasir Jones, *God's Son* (New York: Sony Entertainment, 2002), compact disc.
40. Anderson, 31
41. Trotter, 598.
42. Patricia Liggins Hill, ed., *Call and Response: The Riverside Anthology of the African American Literary Tradition* (Boston: Houghton Mifflin Company, 2001), 1356.
43. John Henrik Clarke, *Malcolm X: The Man and His Times* (Canada: Macmillan Company, 1969), 322–23.
44. Benjamin Goodman, *The End of White World Supremacy* (New York: Merlin House, 1971), 24.
45. Stephen Henderson, *Understanding the New Black Poetry* (New York: Morrow Quill Paperbacks, 1973), 63–66.
46. Haki R. Madhubuti, *GroundWork: New and Selected Poems: Don L. Lee/Haki R. Madhubuti from 1966–1996* (Chicago: Third World Press, 1996), 17.
47. Giovanni, 18.
48. Henry Louis Gates, "Black Creativity: On the Cutting Edge," *Time*, Oct. 10, 1994, 74.
49. Stanley Crouch, "The Incomplete Turn of Larry Neal," in *Visions of a Liberated Future* (New York: Thunder's Mouth Press, 1989), 4.
50. Tricia Rose, 2.
51. Rose, 100.
52. *Russell Simmons Presents Def Poetry*, season I, episode III (New York, 2004).
53. John Shields, ed., *The Collected Works of Phillis Wheatley* (New York: Oxford University Press, 1988, 1773), 74.
54. Regina Jennings, *Pennsylvania English* 22 (Spring 2000): 69.
55. Maria Carmela Betro, *Hieroglyphics: The Writings of Ancient Egyptians* (New York: Abbeville Press, 1996), 122–123.

Chapter One

1. Haki Madhubuti, *GroundWork: New and Selected Poems: Don L. Lee/Haki R. Madhubuti from 1966–1996* (Chicago: Third World Press, 1996), 21.
2. Albert Memmi, *The Colonizer and the Colonized* (Boston: Beacon Press, 1965), ix.
3. Kenneth Stampp, *The Peculiar Institution: Slavery in the Ante-Bellum South* (New York: Vintage Books, 1956), vii.
4. Lorenzo Turner, *Africanisms in the Gullah Dialect* (Ann Arbor: University of Michigan Press, 1973), vi.
5. Kwame Appiah, *In My Father's House: Africa in the Psychology of Culture* (New York: Oxford University Press, 1992), 10–27.
6. Eric J. Sundquist, *The Oxford W.E.B. Du Bois Reader* (New York: Oxford University Press, 1996), 70.
7. Sundquist, 70–71.
8. Sundquist, 71.
9. Lorenzo Turner, *Africanisms in the Gullah Dialect* (Ann Arbor: The University of Michigan Press, 1973).
10. M.J. Herskovits, *The Myth of the Negro Past* (Boston: Beacon Press, 1990), xviii.
11. Richard Moore, *The Name "Negro": Its Origin and Evil Use* (Baltimore: Black Classic Press, 1992).
12. Winthrop Jordan, *White over Black: American Attitudes Towards the Negro 1550–1812* (New York: Norton, 1977), 37.
13. Jordan, 38.
14. Henry Louis Gates, *Figures in Black: Words, Signs, and the "Racial Self"* (New York: Oxford University Press, 1987), 14–20.
15. Jordan, 20–35.
16. Philip Butcher, ed., *The Minority Presence in American Literature: 1600–190*, vol. 1,

Morgan State Series in Afro-American Studies (Washington: Howard University, 1977), 142.
17. Molefi Kete Asante, *Kemet, Afrocentricity and Knowledge* (Trenton: African World Press, 1990), 132–133.
18. John Henrik Clarke, *Notes for an African World Revolution: Africans at the Crossroads* (Trenton: African World Press, 1991), 146.
19. Cheikh Anta Diop, *Civilization or Barbarism* (New York: Laurence Hill Books, 1991), 212.
20. Sterling Stuckey, *Slave Culture, Nationalist Theory and the Foundations of Black America* (New York: Oxford University Press, 1987), 1–97.
21. Paul Edwards, ed., *Equiano's Travels: His Autobiography. The Interesting Narrative of the Life of Olaudah Equiano or Gustavus Vassa the African* (London: Heinemann, 1977), 59.
22. Edwards, 60.
23. Edwards, 122.
24. Edwards, 87.
25. Jordan, 28.
26. Frances E.W. Harper, *Iola Leroy or Shadows Uplifted* (New York: Oxford University Press, 1988), 22.
27. Harper, 16.
28. Harper, 55.
29. Orlando Patterson, *Slavery and Social Death* (Cambridge: Harvard University Press, 1982), 2–18.
30. Karen Horney, M.D., *Our Inner Conflicts: A Constructive Theory of Neurosis* (New York: W.W. Norton and Company, 1992), 13.
31. *Oxford English Dictionary, The Compact Edition*, vol. 1, A–O (London: Oxford University Press, 1985), 1226.
32. John G. Jackson, *Introduction to African Civilizations* (New Jersey: Citadel Press, 1980), 215.
33. Gates, 19.
34. Edwards, 21.
35. Edwards, 129.
36. Molefi Kete Asante, "Locating a Text: Implications of Afrocentric theory," in Carol Aisha Blackshire Belay, ed., *Language and Literature in the African-American Imagination* (Westport: Grenwood Press, 1992), 15.
37. Sundquist, 71.
38. Horney, 14.
39. Harper, 64.
40. Harriet Jacobs, *Incidents in the Life of a Slave Girl: Written by Herself* (Cambridge: Harvard University Press, 1987), 13.
41. Jacobs, 197.
42. Mellen, 239.
43. Jacobs, 23.
44. V.P. Franklin, *Black Self-Determination: A Cultural History of African-American Resistance* (New York: Lawrence Hill Books, 1992), 67.
45. OED, 1924.
46. Kirkpatrick Sale, *The Conquest of Paradise: Christopher Columbus and the Columbian Legacy* (New York: Penguin Books, 1990), 86.
47. In the color hierarchy created and based on racism during slavery, the lighter the Negro the more valuable. Additionally, lighter enslaved individuals were often but not always given jobs closer to the master and mistress of the plantation. See William Wells Brown's *Clotel or the President's Daughter* (1852), *The Narrative of Frederick Douglass* (1845), and Linda Brent, *Incidents in the Life of a Slave Girl* (1861).
48. Randall Kennedy, *nigger: The Strange Career of a Troublesome Word* (New York: Pantheon Books, 2002), 54–55.
49. Gwendolyn Brooks, *Blacks* (Chicago: David Company, 1987), 489.
50. OED, 223.
51. Regina Jennings, "This Is Not a New Story: Jasper, Texas Is America," *The Black Suburban Journal*, July 1998, 3, 10.
52. OED, 1924.
53. Deborah Gray White, *Ar'n't I a Woman: Female Slaves in the Plantation South* (New York: W.W. Norton and Company, 1985), 27–61, 152–153, 164, 165. Chancellor Williams, *The Destruction of Black Civilizations* (Chicago: Third World Press, 1976), 269–270.
54. Deborah Gray White, 28–29.
55. White, 29.
56. White, 38.
57. John Hope Franklin and Loren Schweninger, *Runaway Slaves: Rebels on the Plantation* (New York: Oxford University Press, 1999), 2–4.
58. Robin D.G. Kelley, *Race Rebels: Culture, Politics, and the Black Working Class* (New York: Free Press, 1996), 34.
59. Charles Perdue Jr., et al., *Weevils in the Wheat* (Indiana: Indiana University Press, 1980), 115.
60. James Mellen, ed., *Bullwhip Days: The Slaves Remember: An Oral History* (New York: Weidenfeld and Nicolson, 1988), 451.
61. Mellen, 448.
62. Stratton D. Brooks, *English Composition: Book One — Enlarged* (New York: American Book Company, 1912), 242.
63. Amy Jacques Garvey, ed., *The Philosophy and Opinions of Marcus Garvey* (Dover, Massachusetts: Majority Press, 1986), 138.
64. Richard Moore, 43.
65. Moore, 46.
66. H.H. Fairchild, "Black, Negro, or Afro-American? The Differences are Crucial!" *The Journal of Black Studies*, 47–55.

67. Walter Rodney, *How Europe Underdeveloped Africa* (Washington D.C.: Howard University Press, 1982), 142–144.
68. Moore, 52.

Chapter Two

1. Larry Neal, "The Black Arts Movement," *Black Theatre: tdr* 12 (Nov. 4, 1968): 30.
2. Elijah Muhammad, *Message to the Black Man in America* (Chicago: Muhammad's Temple #2, 1965), 54–55.
3. John Henrik Clarke, ed., *Malcolm X: The Man and His Times* (Canada: Macmillan Company, 1969), 151.
4. For more information on this tradition read *Call and Response: The Riverside Anthology of the African American Literary Tradition*, general ed. Patricia Liggins Hill (New York: Houghton Mifflin Company, 1998), 540.
5. Andrew Hacker, *Two Nations: Black and White, Separate, Hostile, Unequal* (New York: Ballantine Books, 1992), 65.
6. *Survey Graphic: Harlem Mecca of the New Negro*, March 1925, 633.
7. Tony Martin, *Race First: The Ideological and Organizational Struggles of Marcus Garvey and the Universal Negro Improvement Association*, The New Marcus Garvey Library, no. 8 (Dover, Mass: Majority Press, 1976), 3.
8. Faith Berry, ed., *Langston Hughes, Good Morning Revolution: Collected Writings of Social Protest* (Westport: Laurence Hill and Company, 1973).
9. Haki Madhubuti, *Enemies: The Clash of Races* (Chicago: Third World Press, 1978), 9.
10. *Enemies*, ii–iii.

Chapter Three

1. Scholes, "A Fortunate Fall?" *Falling into Theory: Conflicting Views on Reading Literature* (Bedford: St. Martin's, 2000), 111.
2. Haki R. Madhubuti, *GroundWork: New and Selected Poems: Don L. Lee/Haki R. Madhubuti 1966–1996* (Chicago: Third World Press, 1996), 195.
3. Scholes, 116.
4. Molefi Kete Asante, *Kemet, Afrocentricity and Knowledge* (Trenton: Africa World Press, 1990), 98.
5. Donald Gibson et al., eds., *Encyclopedia of Black America* (New York: McGraw-Hill, 1981); J. Saunders Redding, *To Make a Poet Black* (Ithaca: Cornell University Press, 1988), 9–11.

6. Reginald Horsman, *Race and Manifest Destiny* (Cambridge: Harvard University Press, 1981), 22.
7. Howard Zinn, *A People's History of the United States* (New York: First Harper Perennial Edition, 1990), 1–175.
8. W.O. Blake, *History of Slavery and the Slave Trade* (Columbus, Ohio: H. Miller, 1860), 93–94.
9. Blake, 98.
10. John Hope Franklin, *From Slavery to Freedom* (New York: Knopf, 1974), 30.
11. Franklin, 30.
12. Basil Davidson, *The African Slave Trade: A Revised and Expanded Edition* (Atlantic Monthly Press Book, 1990), 101.
13. Davidson, 42.
14. Chancellor Williams, *The Destruction of Black Civilizations* (Chicago: Third World Press, 1976), 268.
15. Williams, 270.
16. Chapman Cohen, *Christianity, Slavery, and Labor*, 52–53, quoted in John G. Jackson, *Introduction to African Civilizations* (New Jersey: Citadel Press, 1980), 305.
17. Richard B. Moore, *The Name "Negro": Its Origin and Evil Use* (Baltimore: Black Classic Press, 1992), 36.
18. Blake, 95.
19. Blake, 95.
20. Horsman, 102–103.
21. Kirkpatrick Sale, *Conquest of Paradise: Christopher Columbus and the Columbian Legacy* (New York: Penguin, 1990), 326.
22. Toni Morrison, *Playing in the Dark: Whiteness and the Literary Imagination* (New York: Random House, 1992), 32–34.
23. Morrison, 38.
24. Horsman, 49.
25. Horsman, 50–51.
26. Morrison, 34–35.
27. Joanne M. Braxton and Andree Nicola McLaughlin, eds., *Wild Women in the Whirlwind: Afra-American Culture and the Contemporary Literary Renaissance* (New Jersey: Rutgers University Press, 1990), 22–34.
28. Vernon Loggins, *The Negro Author* (New York: Columbia University Press, 1931), 1.
29. John C. Shields, ed., *The Collected Works of Phillis Wheatley* (New York: Oxford University Press, 1988), 231.
30. Julian D. Mason, ed., *The Poems of Phillis Wheatley* (Chapel Hill: University of North Carolina Press), 53.
31. Asante, *Kemet, Afrocentricity, and Knowledge*, 21.
32. Winthrop Jordan, *White over Black: American Attitudes Toward the Negro, 1550–1812* (New York: W.W. Norton, 1977), 27–28.

33. Henry Louis Gates, *The Signifying Monkey* (New York: Oxford University Press, 1988), x.
34. Gates, *The Signifying Monkey*, x.
35. Philip Butcher, ed., *The Minority Presence in American Literature: 1600–1900* (Washington: Howard University Press, 1977), 144.
36. Zinn, 88.
37. Shields, 1988.
38. Henry Louis Gates, *Figures in Black: Words, Signs, and the Racial Self* (New York: Oxford University Press, 1987), 61–79.
39. W.E.B. Du Bois, *W.E.B. DuBois Writings: The Suppression of the African Slave Trade. The Souls of Black Folk. Dusk of Dawn Essays* (New York: Literary Classics of the United Sates, Inc., 1986), 364–365.
40. Shirley Graham Du Bois, *The Story of Phillis Wheatley: Poetess of the American Revolution* (Julian Mesner, 1949; 1972), 43.
41. Mason, 52.
42. Gates, *Figures in Black*, 18–20.
43. Yosef A.A. Ben-Jochannan, *Black Man of the Nile and his Family* (Baltimore: Black Classic Press, 1989), 277–83; Cheikh Anta Diop, *Civilization or Barbarism* (New York: Laurence Hill Books, 1991), 101–108; Gerald Massey, *Ancient Egypt, the Light of the World*, volumes 1 and 2 (Baltimore: Black Classic Press, 1907; 1992).
44. J. Saunders Redding, *To Make a Poet Black* (Ithaca: Cornell University, 1988), 8–11.
45. However, I do examine Phillis Wheatley's poetry that involves the "sun" in another direction in the following article: "The Afrocentric Sun Imagery in the Poetry of Phillis Wheatley," *Pennsylvania English*, Fall 2000.
46. Molefi Asante, "Locating a Text: Implications of Afrocentric Theory," in Carol Aisha Blackshire-Belay, ed., *Language and Literature in the African American Imagination* (Westport: Greenwood Press, 1992), 13.
47. Maxwell Whiteman, *Poems on Miscellaneous Subjects by Frances Ellen Watkins Harper* (Philadelphia: Historic Publications, 1857), introduction.
48. Redding, 38–44.
49. Frances Smith Foster, Ed., *A Brighter Coming Day: A Frances Ellen Watkins Harper Reader* (New York: Feminist Press), introduction endnote.
50. Whiteman, 45.
51. Whiteman, 9.
52. Whiteman, 39.
53. Whiteman, 7.
54. Whiteman, 21.
55. Whiteman, 29.
56. Houston Baker, *Workings of the Spirit: The Poetics of Afro-American Women's Writings* (Chicago: University of Chicago Press, 1991), 24–25.
57. Whiteman, 37.
58. F.E.W. Harper, *Idylls of the Bible* (100 Bainbridge Street, Philadelphia, 1901; New York: AMS, 1975), 8.
59. Harper, 18–19.
60. Dorothy Porter, ed., *Early Negro Writing 1760–1851* (Boston: Beacon Press, 1971), 3.
61. Maryemma Graham, ed., *Complete Poems of Frances E.W. Harper*, The Schomburg Library of Nineteenth Century Black Women Writers (New York: Oxford University Press, 1988), xxxiii.
62. Graham, 117.
63. Graham, 126.
64. Frances Ellen Watkins Harper, *Atlanta Offering Poems* (Miami, Florida: Mnemosyne Publishing Inc., 1885; 1969), 17–18.
65. Harper, *Atlanta Offering*, 51–53.
66. Foster, 123.
67. Asante, *Kemet, Afrocentricity, and Knowledge*, 98.
68. Richard Barksdale and Keneth Kinnamon, eds., *Black Writers of America: A Comprehensive Anthology* (New York: Macmillan Company, 1972), 467–479.
69. Barksdale and Kinnamon, 576.
70. W.E.B. Du Bois, *The Negro* (New York: Henry Holt and Company, 1915), 138–139.
71. Asante, *Kemet, Afrocentricity, and Knowledge*, 132–133.
72. Countee Cullen, ed., *Caroling Dusk: An Anthology of Verse by Negro Poets* (New York: Harper and Sons, 1927), forward, ix.
73. Haki Madhubuti, "Notes from a Black Journal," *Negro Digest*, 1970, 11.
74. Arna Bontemps, ed., *The Harlem Renaissance Remembered* (New York: Dodd, Mead, and Company, 1972), 83.
75. Nathan Irvin Huggins, *Harlem Renaissance* (New York: Oxford University Press, 1971), 81.
76. Akbar, 47.
77. Countee Cullen, *Cooper Sun* (New York: Harper and Bros., 1927), 20.
78. Cullen, *Copper Sun*, 33.
79. W.E.B. Du Bois, *W.E.B. Du Bois Writings: The Suppression of the African Slave Trade; The Souls of Black Folk; Dusk of Dawn Essays* (New York: Literary Classics of the United States, Inc., 1986), 364–365.
80. Arthur P. Davis, "The New Poetry of Black Hate," *CLA Journal*, June 1970, 81.
81. Gerald Early, ed., *My Soul's High Song: Collected Writings of Countee Cullen* (New York: Doubleday, 1991), 97.
82. Early, 90.
83. Early, 80.

84. Arthur P. Davis, *From the Dark Tower* (Washington: Howard University Press, 1981), 33.
85. Tyrone Tiller, *Claude McKay* (University of Massachusetts Press, 1992), 115, 181.
86. Tillery, 174–175.
87. Wayne Cooper, ed., *The Passions of Claude McKay: Selected Prose and Poetry 1912–1948* (New York: Schocken Books, 1973), 120.
88. Chancellor Williams, 53.
89. Tony Browder, *Nile Valley Contributions to Civilization* (Washington: Institute of Karmic Guidance, 1992), 141.
90. Browder, 141.
91. Cooper, 121.
92. Cooper, 121.
93. Akbar, 53.
94. Cooper, 121.
95. Bobby E. Wright, *The Psychopathic Racial Personality and Other Essays* (Chicago: Third World Press, 1984), 19.
96. Akbar, 51.
97. Cooper, 126.
98. Cooper, 126.
99. Franz Fanon, *Black Skin White Masks* (New York: Grove Press, 1967), 18.
100. J.E. Cirlot, *A Dictionary of Symbols* (New York: Philosophical Library, 1983), 76–77.
101. Cirlot, 227.
102. Akbar, 54.
103. Talmadge Anderson, "Black Psychology and Psychological Concepts," in *African-Centered Psychology: Culture-Focusing for Multicultural Competence*, ed. Daudi Ajani ya Azibo (Durham: Carolina Academic Press, 2003), 3–38.
104. Wright, 18.

Chapter Four

1. Kete Asante, *The Afrocentric Idea* (Philadelphia: Temple University Press, 1987), 169.
2. Arna Bontemps, ed., *The Harlem Renaissance Remembered* (New York: Dodd, Mead and Company, 1972); and Nathan Irvin Huggins, *Harlem Renaissance* (New York: Oxford University Press, 1971).
3. Faith Berry, ed., *Langston Hughes, Good Morning Revolution: Collected Writings of Social Protest* (Westport: Laurence Hill and Company, 1973), x–xiii.
4. Arnold Rampersad, *The Life of Langston Hughes*, vol. 2, *1941–1967: I Dream a World* (New York: Oxford University Press, 1988), 9.
5. Bontemps, 6.
6. Richard Barksdale and Keneth Kinnamon, eds., *Black Writers of America: A Comprehensive Anthology* (New York: Macmillan Company, 1972), 515.
7. Tony Martin, ed., *The Poetical Works of Marcus Garvey* (Dover, Massachusetts: Majority Press, 1983), 8.
8. Wilson Jeremiah Moses, *The Golden Age of Black Nationalism 1850–1925* (New York: Oxford University Press, 1978), 212–218.
9. H.H. Fairchild, "Black, Negro, or Afro-American? The Differences are Crucial! *Journal of Black Studies*, 53.
10. John Henrik Clarke, ed., *Notes for an African World Revolution: Africans at the Crossroads* (Trenton: Africa World Press, 1991), 89.
11. Langston Hughes, *Selected Poems: Langston Hughes* (New York: Vintage Books, 1974), 272.
12. Berry, 4–5.
13. Basil Davidson, *The African Slave Trade: A Revised and Expanded Edition* (Boston: Little, Brown and Company), 5. An Atlantic Monthly Press Book.
14. Davidson, 59.
15. Ian Lopez, *White by Law: The Legal Construction of Race* (New York: New York University Press, 1996), 41.
16. Berry, 6.
17. Tony Martin, *Race First: The Ideological and Organizational Struggles of Marcus Garvey and the Universal Negro Improvement Association*, The New Marcus Garvey Library, no. 8 (Dover, Mass: Majority Press, 1976), 59–62.
18. Berry, 12.
19. Berry, 97.
20. Berry, 117.
21. Berry, 36–37.
22. Na'im Akbar, *Chains and Images of Psychological Slavery* (New Jersey: New Mind Publications, 1991), 47–51.
23. Amy Jacques Garvey, ed., *The Philosophy and Opinions of Marcus Garvey* (Dover, Massachusetts: Majority Press, 1986), 11.
24. Martin, 60.
25. Wilson Jeremiah Moses, *The Golden Age of Black Nationalism 1850–1925* (New York: Oxford University Press, 1978), 214.
26. Martin, 44.
27. Martin, 59.
28. Susan Gubar, *Race Changes: White Skin, Black Face in American Culture* (New York: Oxford University Press, 1997), 111.
29. Martin 65.
30. Martin, 23.
31. John Henrik Clarke, *Notes for an African World Revolution: Africans at the Crossroads* (Trenton: Africa World Press, 1991), 112.
32. Lopez, 157.

33. Lopez, 158.
34. Martin, 24.

Chapter Five

1. Diop's biological investigations on the ancients are available in several works including the following two: "Pigmentation of the Ancient Egyptians: Test by Melanin Analysis," *Bulletin de L'institut fondamental D'Afrique Noire*, series B, Sciences Humaines, Tome XXXV, No. 3, Juillet (1973): 515–530; *Parente Genetique de L'Egyptien Pharaonique et des Langues Negro-Africaines* (Dakar: University of Dakar Press, 1976). Additionally, in his book *The African Origins of Civilization: Myth or Reality* (Westport: Lawrence Hill and Company, 1974), he addresses this issue in chapters 1–3 and 7. Other scholars who agree with his premise include Chancellor Williams, *The Destruction of African Civilization* (Chicago: Third World Press, 1976); John G. Jackson, *Introduction to African Civilizations* (Secaucus, New Jersey: Citadel Press, 1980); Ivan Van Sertima, *Egypt Revisited* (New Brunswick: Transaction Publishers, 1989); and Martin Bernal, *Black Athena*, vols. I and II (New Brunswick, New Jersey: Rutgers University Press, 1987 and 1990).
2. Ivan Van Sertima, ed., *Great African Thinkers: Cheikh Anta Diop* (New Brunswick: Transaction Books, 1987), 46.
3. James Spady, "The Cultural Unity of CheikhAnta Diop 1948–1964," in *Black Images: A Critical Quarterly on Black Arts and Culture* I, III–IV (1972): 14–22; 15.
4. James Spady, 17.
5. Cheikh Anta Diop, *Civilization or Barbarism* (New York: Lawrence Hill Books, 1991), 276–277.
6. Katherine Bankole, *You Left Your Mind in Africa: Journal Observations and Essays on African American Self-Hatred* (Dellsslow, West Virginia: Nation House Foundation, 2001), 17.
7. Quoted in Haki Madhubuti, *Yellow-Black: The First Twenty-One Years of a Poet's Life* (Chicago: Third World Press, 2005) 208.
8. Cheikh Anta Diop, *Civilization or Barbarism: An Authentic Anthropology* (New York: Lawrence Hill Books, 1991), 216–217.
9. *Civilization or Barbarism*, 217–218.
10. I deliberately lowercase the "n" in Negro to emphasize its presentation from American enslavement of the African to the 20th century when Marcus Garvey, W.E.B. Du Bois and others demanded the capitalization of the "n."
11. John Henrik Clarke, *Malcolm X: The Man and His Times* (Toronto, Ontario, Canada: Macmillan, 1969), 322–23.
12. Henry Louis Gates, Jr., *Figures in Black: Words, Signs, and the Racial Self* (New York: Oxford University Press, 1987), 18.
13. *Malcolm X on Afro-American History* (New York: Pathfinder Press, 1982), 20.
14. Graham Hancock and R. Bauval, *The Message of the Sphinx: A Quest for the Hidden Legacy of Mankind* (New York: Three Rivers, 1996), 42.
15. John Anthony West, *Serpent in the Sky: The High Wisdom of Ancient Egypt* (Wheaton, Ill.: Theosophical Publishing House, 1993), 21.
16. Quoted in Hancock and Bauval, 198.
17. Cheikh Anta Diop, *The African Origin of Civilization: Myth or Reality* (Westport, Conn.: Lawrence Hill Books, 1974), 111–113.
18. Robin D.G. Kelley, *Race Rebels: Culture, Politics, and the Black Working Class* (New York: Free Press, 1996), 161–182.
19. David Levering Lewis, *W.E.B. Du Bois: Biography of a Race* (New York: Henry Holt and Company, 1994), 27.
20. *YellowBlack*, 237.

Chapter Six

1. Regina Jennings, *The Encyclopedia of Black Studies* (London: Thousand Oaks, 2005), 142.
2. Sterling Stuckey, *Slave Culture: Nationalist Theory and the Foundations of Black America* (New York: Oxford, 1987), 172.
3. Alfreda M. Duster, ed., *Crusade for Justice: The Autobiography of Ida B. Wells* (University of Chicago Press, 1970), 62.
4. Sterling Stuckey, *Slave Culture: Nationalist Theory and the Foundations of Black America* (New York: Oxford, 1987), 292.
5. Chancellor Williams, *The Destruction of African Civilizations* (Chicago: Third World Press, 1987), 161–175.
6. Stuckey, 345–346.
7. Kariamu Welsh-Asante, *The African Aesthetic: Keeper of the Traditions* (Westport, Conn.: Praeger, 1994), 23.
8. Welsh-Asante, 24.
9. Welsh-Asante, 9.
10. Welsh-Asante, 9.
11. Carl Waldman, *Encyclopedia of Native American Tribes* (New York: Checkmark Books, 1999), 233–234.
12. Welsh-Asante, 19.
13. Welsh-Asante, 24.
14. "Slavery's Buried Past," producers Bill Kurtis and Molly Bedell, *60 Minutes* (The New York Explorers, Public Media Video, 1996), videocassette.
15. M. Brodrick and A.A. Morton, eds., *A*

Concise Dictionary of Egyptian Archaeology: A Handbook for Students and Travelers (Chicago: Ares Publishers, Inc., 1924), 101.

16. Molefi Kete Asante, *The Egyptian Philosophers: Ancient African Voices from Imhotep to Akhenaten* (Chicago: African American Images, 2000), 32–34.

17. Kariamu Welsh-Asante and Molefi Asante, eds., *African Culture: The Rhythms of Unity* (Westport: Greewood Press, 1985), 74.

18. Tony Bolden, *Afro-Blue: Improvisations in African American Poetry and Culture* (University of Illinois Press, 2004), 23.

19. Bolden, 24.

20. Bruce Perry, *Malcolm X: The Last Speeches* (New York: Pathfinder Press, 1989), 89.

21. *The American Heritage Dictionary of the English Language* (Boston: Houghton Mifflin Company, 1992), 1190, 2114.

22. Brodrick, 53; Maria Carmela Betrò, *Hieroglyphics: The Writings of Ancient Egypt* (New York: Abbeville Press Publishers, 1996), 71, 75.

23. Larry Neal, *Hoodoo Hollerin' Bebop Ghosts* (Washington: Howard University Press, 1974), 10.

24. Amiri Baraka, *The Autobiography of Leroi Jones/Amiri Baraka* (New York: Freundlich Books, 1984), 215.

25. John Henrik Clarke, *Notes of African World Revolution: Africans at the Crossroads* (Trenton: Africa World Press, 1991), 146.

26. George Breitman, *The Last Year of Malcolm X: Evolution of a Revolutionary* (New York: Pathfinder Press, 1989), 109.

27. Patrick T. Reardon, "Poetic Justice: Success Hasn't Diminished Haki Madhubuti's Passion for Struggle," *Chicago Tribune*, Thursday, 10 August 2000, sec. 5.

28. Haki Madhubuti, personal interview, Chicago, 28 October 2002.

29. Reardon, "Poetic Justice."

30. George Breitman, *Malcolm X Speaks: Selected Speeches and Statements* (New York: Pathfinder, 1989), 39.

31. Haki Madhubuti (Chicago: Third World Press, 2002).

32. George Breitman, *Malcolm X Speaks*, 21.

33. John Henrik Clarke, *Notes of an African*, 155.

34. *Malcolm X on Afro-American History* (New York: Pathfinder, 1991), 12.

35. Corey Hall, "African-Centered Charter School Displays Methods During Tour; Betty Shabazz International Charter School Toured During National Charter Schools Week," *Citizen Newspaper*, 2 May 2002 (Chicago, Illinois), 3.

36. Gary Rivlin, "Eye on the Prize: Over More Than Two Decades, Haki and Safisha Madhubuti Have Proved That African-Centered Education Can Amount to More Than a Black Version of History. It Can Also be a Springboard to a Bright Future," *The Chicago Reader* 26, no. 33, sec. 1 (23 May 1997).

37. Rivlin, "Eye on the Prize."

38. Welsh-Asante, *The African Aesthetic*, 8.

39. Elaine Moseley, personal interview, Chicago, 28 October 2002.

40. Ann Ward, personal interview, Chicago, 28 October 2002.

41. Rivlin, "Eye on the Prize."

42. *Malcolm X on Afro-American History*, 13.

43. Madhubuti has started two other enterprises, the Barbara Sizemore Campus (2005) and the DuSable Leadership Academy (2005).

Chapter Seven

1. Marimba Ani, *Yurugu: An African-Centered Critique of European Cultural Thought and Behavior* (Trenton: Africa World Press, 1995), 35.

2. Quoted in John Henrik Clarke, *Notes for an African World Revolution: Africans at the Crossroads* (Trenton: African World Press, 1991), 156.

3. Molefi Kete Asante, *Malcolm X As Cultural Hero and Other Afrocentric Essays* (Trenton: African World Press, 1993), 18.

4. William W. Sales, Jr., *From Civil Rights to Black Liberation: Malcolm X and the Organization of Afro-American Unity* (Boston: South End Press, 1994), 121–122.

5. Taylor Branch, *Pillar of Fire: America in the King Years 1963–65* (New York: A Touchstone Book, 1998), 392–395.

6. Sales, 122.

7. Sales, 121.

8. Gary Rivlin, "Eyes on the Prize: Over more than two decades, Haki and Safisha Madhubuti have proved that African-centered education can amount to more than a Black version of history. It can also be a springboard to a bright future," *The Chicago Reader* 26, no. 33, sec. 1 (23 May 1997): 1

9. Amos N. Wilson, *The Developmental Psychology of the Black Child* (New York: Africana Research Publications, 1980), 184.

10. Haki Madhubuti, *From Plan to Planet: Life-Studies: The Need for Afrikan Minds and Institutions* (Chicago: Third World Press, 1987), 45.

11. Madhubuti, *From Plan* 45.

12. Quoted in Saki Mafundikwa, *Afrikan*

Alphabets: The Story of Writing in Afrika (New York: Mark Batty Publisher, 2004), ix.
13. Joy Leary, *Post Traumatic Slave Syndrome* (New York: WBAI, 2004), compact disc.
14. "Race First" is a term coined by Marcus Garvey, head of the Universal Negro Improvement Association.
15. Manthia Diawara, *In Search of Africa* (Cambridge: Harvard University Press, 1998), 100.
16. Walter Rodney, *How Europe Underdeveloped Africa* (Washington, D.C.: Howard University Press, 1982), 33–38.
17. With the founding of the Betty Shabazz International Charter School in 1998, New Concept is now a preschool teaching children from two to six years old. Betty Shabazz International Charter School is a middle school, with ages from six to twelve.
18. Kariamu Welsh-Asante, ed., *The African Aesthetic: Keeper of the Traditions* (Westport, Conn.: Praeger Publishers, 1994), 17.
19. Haki Madhubuti, *Claiming Earth: Race, Rage, Rape, Redemption, Blacks Seeking a Culture of Enlightened Empowerment* (Chicago: Third World Press, 1994), 77.
20. Haki Madhubuti, personal interview, 22 July 2004.
21. George Breitman, *Malcolm X Speaks: Selected Speeches and Statements* (New York: Pathfinder, 1989), 72–73.
22. John Henrik Clarke, *Notes for an African World Revolution: Africans at the Crossroads* (Trenton: Africa World Press, 1991), 145.
23. George Breitman, *Malcolm X Speaks: Selected Speeches and Statements* (New York: Pathfinder Press, 1989), 79.
24. Breitman, 80.
25. Haki Madhubuti, *From Plan to Planet: Life-Studies: The Need for Afrikan Minds and Institutions* (Chicago: Third World Press, 1987), 25.
26. Haki Madhubuti, *Enemies: The Clash of Races* (Chicago: Third World Press), 69.
27. Asante and Welsh-Asante, *African Culture: Rhythms of Unity* (Westport, Conn.: Greenwood Press, 1985), 74.
28. Chancellor Williams, *The Destruction of Black Civilization* (Chicago: Third World Press, 1976), 165.
29. Haki Madhubuti, *From Plan to Planet*, 33.
30. Gary Rivlin, "Eyes on the Prize," 1
31. Gayle T. Tate, *Unknown Tongues* (Michigan State University Press, 2003), 40–59.
32. Komozi Woodard, *A Nation Within a Nation: Amiri Baraka (Leroi Jones) and Black Power Politics* (Chapel Hill: University of North Carolina Press, 1999), 34.
33. Stephanie Stokes Oliver, "Liberation Love," *Essence*, July 1991. 94.
34. Clenora Hudson-Weems, *Africana Womanism: Reclaiming Ourselves* (Troy, Michigan: Bedford Publishers, 1993), 51.
35. Haley, Alex, ed., *The Autobiography of Malcolm X* (New York: Ballantine Books, 1990), 232.
36. Benjamin Karim with Peter Skutches and David Gallen, *Remembering Malcolm* (New York: One World Ballantine Books, 1992), 95.
37. Karim, 95.
38. Haki Madhubuti, *From Plan to Planet: Life-Studies: The Need for Afrikan Minds and Institutions* (Chicago: Third World Press, 1987), 68–69.
39. Dr. Elaine C. Mosley, personal interview, 28 October 2000.
40. Corey Hall, "African-Centered Charter School Displays Methods During Tour," *Citizen Newspaper*, week of 2 May 2002, 3.
41. Corey Hall, 3.
42. Ann Ward, personal interview, 28 October 2000.
43. Haki Madhubuti, telephone interview, July 2004.

Chapter Eight

1. Vibert L. White, *Inside the Nation of Islam: A Historical and Personal Testimony by a Black Muslim* (University of Florida Press, 2001), 23.
2. White, 25.
3. White, 25.
4. White, 30–31; and Claude Andrew Clegg III, *An Original Man: The Life and Times of Elijah Muhammad* (New York: St. Martin's Press, 1997), 20–30.
5. Ernst Lewy, "Historical Charismatic Leaders and Mythical Heroes," *Journal of Psychohistory* 6 (1979).
6. Benjamin Karim, et al., *Remembering Malcolm* (New York: Ballantine, 1992), 90.
7. Haki Madhubuti, *YellowBlack: The First Twenty-One Years of a Poet's Life* (Chicago: Third World Press, 2005), 236.
8. Huey P. Newton, *Revolutionary Suicide* (New York: Harcourt Brace Jovanovich, 1973), 165.
9. The historian Ronald Takaki discusses the term "master narrative" in public lectures. It refers to school curriculums that are mostly composed of information that explains Americans as only of European descent. Takaki in *A Different Mirror: A History of Multicultural America* (1993) retells the nation's history

through perspectives of other cultures and peoples.
10. Newton, 135.
11. Haki Madhubuti, *From Plan to Planet: Life Studies: The Need for Afrikan Minds and Institutions* (Chicago: Third World Press, 1987), 87.
12. Sarah Bradford, *The Moses of Her People* (New York: Carol Publishing Company, 1994), 95.
13. Madhubuti, *From Plan to Planet*, 87.
14. Haki Madhubuti, *Enemies: The Clash of Races* (Chicago: Third World Press, 1978), 136.
15. Newton, 71.
16. Kariamu Welsh-Asante, ed., *The African Aesthetic: Keeper of the Traditions* (Westport, Conn.: Praeger), 15.
17. H. Rap Brown, *Die Nigger Die!* (New York: Dial Press, 1969), 99–128.
18. H. Rap Brown is today Jamil Al-Amin, an Iman of the Muslim faith once based in Atlanta. He is currently incarcerated for allegedly killing a policeman. He says he is innocent of the charges.
119. David Llorens, "Poet is acclaimed creator of black art, is writer-in-residence at Cornell University," *Ebony*, March 1969, 72.
20. Madhubuti, *From Plan to Planet*, 47.
21. Ethel Paris, personal interview, Washington, D.C., 23 February 2003.
22. Lary Platt, *Only the Strong Survive: The Odyssey of Allen Iverson* (New York: Harper Collins Publishers, 2002), 115–117.
23. Mark Stewart, *Basketball's New Wave* (Brookfield, Conn.: Millbrook Press, 2001), 14–15.
24. Platt, 115.
25. Rick Reilly, "Looks Aren't Everything," *Sports Illustrated*, 22 May 2001. <http://sportsillustrated.cnn.com/inside_game/magazine/life_of_reilly/news/2001/05/22/lifeof ...> (5 May 2001).
26. Reilly.
27. Mike Celizic, "Iverson — the great anti-hero," MSNBC Sports, 25 May 2001, <http://www.msnbc.com/news/569635.asp?cp1=1>.

Chapter Nine

1. Haki Madhubuti, *YellowBlack: The First Twenty-One Years of a Poet's Life* (Chicago: Third World Press, 2005), 6.
2. Madhubuti, *Claiming Earth*, 9.
3. Madhubuti, *Claiming Earth*, 10.

4. I am aware of Bruce Perry's rendition of X's father's death as one not necessarily related to murder in *Malcolm: The life of a Man Who Changed America*. However, the unevenness of that text and his circumstantial evidence cause me to question his findings around the circumstances of Earl Little's death. Therefore, I have deliberately decided to stay with the description of Little's death as written in the *Autobiography*. In either event, after the absence of the father, the family was divided and Malcolm's mother institutionalized.
5. Haki Madhubuti, *Claiming Earth*, 6.
6. George Kent, *Blackness and the Adventure of Western Culture* (Chicago: Third World Press, 1971), 205.
7. Haki Madhubuti, *YellowBlack* (Chicago: Third World Press, 2005), forthcoming.
8. Haki Madhubuti, *YellowBlack: The First Twenty-One Years of a Poet's Life: A Memoir* (Chicago: Third World Press, 2005), 61.
9. George Kent, *Blackness and the Adventure of Western Culture* (Chicago: Third World Press, 1971), 205–6.
10. Kristy Odelius, "Whole Culture, Whole People, Whole Book: Third World Press Opens Up a Continent," *ForeWord*, December 1998, 35.
11. Patrick T. Reardon, "Poetic Justice: Success Hasn't Diminished Haki Madhubuti's Passion for the Struggle," *Chicago Tribune*, Thursday, 10 August 2000, sec. 5, 1.
12. Reardon, 3.
13. Reardon, 3.
14. Rodnell Collins, *Seventh Child: A Family Memoir of Malcolm X* (Secaucus, New Jersey: Carol Publishing Group, 1998), 39.
15. Alex Haley, ed., *The Autobiography of Malcolm X* (New York: Ballantine Books, 1990), 40.
16. Gwendolyn Brooks, *Blacks* (Chicago: David Company, 1987), 501.
17. Dona Richards (Marimba Ani), "African-American Spirituality," in *African Culture: The Rhythms of Unity*, eds. Molefi Asante and Kariamu Welsh-Asante (Westport: Greenwood Press, 1985), 208.
18. Harold Courlander, ed., *A Treasury of African Folklore* (New York: Marlowe and Company, 1996), 188–189. I am specifically referring to the Yoruba Orisha whereby Olurun, the supreme orisha, has an eldest son. Orunmila and Obatala is either a second son or one adopted. This family structure of the Divine is also in the pantheon of Kemetic Divinity. In African spirituality the Divine can be married and sometimes have more than one wife.

Chapter Ten

1. "Negro, Black and African-American" (Jesse Jackson's preferred terminology), *New York Times*, 22 December 1988.
2. Patricia Hill Collins, "Learning to Think for Ourselves: Malcolm X's Black Nationalism Reconsidered," in *Malcolm X in Our Own Image*, ed. Joe Wood (New York: St. Martin's Press, 1992), 68.
3. Quoted in Kariamu Welsh-Asante, ed., *The African Aesthetic: Keeper of the Tradition* (Westport: Praeger, 1994), 13.
4. For more information on Madison Washington read George Hendrick and Willene Hendrick, *The Creole Mutiny: A Tale of Revolt Aboard a Slave Ship* (Chicago: Ivan R. Dee, 2003), and William L. Andrews, ed. *Three Classic African-American Novels: The Heroic Slave, Frederick Douglass, Clotel, William Wells Brown, Our Nig, Harriet E. Wilson* (New York: Penguin Group, 1990).
5. Sean Wilentz, introduction to *David Walker's Appeal: To the Coloured Citizens of the World, but in particular, and very expressly, to those of The United State of America* (New York: Hill and Wang, 1965, 1994). Walker's possible poisoning is in Patricia Liggins Hill, *Call and Response: The Riverside Anthology of the African American Literary Tradition* (New York: Houghton Mifflin Company, 1998), 245–248.
6. David Walker, 63.
7. Bruce Perry, *Malcolm X: The Last Speeches* (New York: Pathfinder Press, 1989), 56.
8. Welsh-Asante, 12.
9. Walker, 9.
10. Jerry W. Ward Jr., ed., *Trouble the Water: 250 Years of African-American Poetry* (New York: A Mentor Book, 1997), 3.
11. Walker, 17.
12. Other races purchased Blacks, but on a lesser degree, and there were some free Blacks who purchased slaves. My claim is that the function of American chattel slavery enabled legally all Whites as a division of manifest destiny to purchase Africans. Additionally, White people started the American trade.
13. Richard Barksdale and Keneth Kinnamon, eds., *Black Writers of America: A Comprehensive Anthology* (New York: Macmillan Company, 1972), 234.
14. Zora Neale Hurston, *The Sanctified Church: The Folklore Writings of Zora Neale Hurston* (Berkeley, Turtle Island, 1981), 69–78.
15. Walker, 8.
16. Louis E. Lomax, *When the Word Is Given* (New York: Signet Books, 1963), 114.
17. Benjamin Goodman, *The End of White World Supremacy* (New York: Merlin House, 1971), 12.
18. Robert Farris Thompson, *African Art in Motion* (Los Angeles: University of California Press, 1979), 218–219.
19. Goodman, 34.
20. Goodman, 65.
21. Goodman, 69.
22. Goodman, 68.
23. George Breitman, *Malcolm X: By Any Means Necessary* (New York: Pathfinder Press, 1982), 1–13.
24. Goodman, 133–134.
25. Goodman, 2–7.
26. C. Eric Lincoln, *The Black Muslims of America* (Boston: Beacon Press, 1961), 69.
27. Hakim Jamal, *From the Dead Level: Malcolm X and Me* (New York: Random House, 1972), 252.
28. Rodnell Collins, *Seventh Child: A Family Memoir of Malcolm X* (Secaucus, N.J.: A Birch Lane Book, 1998), 103–104.
29. Goodman, 91.
30. John Henrik Clarke, *Malcolm X: The Man and his Times* (Canada: Macmillan Company, 1969), 151.
31. George Breitman, *Malcolm X Speaks: Selected Speeches and Statements* (New York: Pathfinder Press, 1989), 33.
32. Goodman, 106–107.
33. Clarke, 275.
34. Malcolm during the final year of his life decided that a bloodless revolution was possible in America. See Karl Evanzz, *The Judas Factor: The Plot to Kill Malcolm X* (New York: Thunder Mouth's Press, 1992), 243.
35. Goodman, 24.
36. Justine Rector, *In Fear of African American Men: The Four Fears of White Men* (self-published: Merion Station, Penn., 1998), 1–18.
37. Clarke, 322–323.
38. Matthew Frye Jacobson, *Whiteness of a Different Color* (Massachusetts: Harvard University Press, 1999), 32.
39. Jacobson, 33.
40. Stephen Jay Gould, *The Mismeasure of Man* (New York: W.W. Norton and Co., 1996), 77.
41. Gould, 54.
42. Gould, 59.
43. Collins, 80–94.
44. *Malcolm X on Afro-American History* (New York: Pathfinder, Press, 1982), 73.
45. Elijah Muhammad, *Message to the Black Man in America* (Chicago: Muhammad's Temple #2, 1965), 125.
46. Goodman, 57.
47. Goodman, 79–80.
48. Geneva Smitherman, *Talking and Testi-*

fying: The Language of Black America (Detroit: Wayne University Press, 1977), 121.

49. Breitman, *By Any Means*, 110.

Chapter Eleven

1. Haki Madhubuti, personal interview, Chicago, October 2000.
2. Larry Neal, "The Black Arts Movement," *Black Theatre: tdr*, vol. 12, no. 4, T40.
3. C. Tsehloane Keto, *The Africa Centered Perspective of History: An Introduction* (Blackwood, New Jersey: K.A. Publications, 1991), 3.
4. This coinage is in Henry Louis Gates, *The Signifying Monkey: A Theory of African-American Literary Criticism* (New York: Oxford University Press, 1988), 9. He received it from Wole Soyinka.
5. Gates, 31.
6. Kariamu Welsh-Asante, ed., *The African Aesthetic: Keeper of the Traditions* (Westport, Conn.: Praeger Publishers, 1994), 11.
7. Leroi Jones and Larry Neal, eds., *Black Fire: An Anthology of Afro-American Writing* (New York: William Morrow and Company, 1968), 302
8. Haki Madhubuti, *Groundwork: New and Selected Poems: Don L. Lee/Haki R. Madhubuti from 1966–1996* (Chicago: Third World Press, 1996), 95. First published in Madhubuti, *We Walk the Way of the New World* (Detroit: Broadside Press, 1970).
9. Molefi Kete Asante, *The Afrocentric Idea* (Philadelphia: Temple University Press, 1987), 124.
10. Jill Nelson, ed., *Police Brutality* (New York: Norton, 2000); Jerome G. Miller, *Search and Destroy: African-American Males in the Criminal Justice System* (Cambridge: Cambridge University Press, 1996); Andrew Hacker, *Two Nations: Black and White, Separate, Hostile, Unequal* (New York: Ballantine, 1995).
11. Barbara Reynolds, "Our Sons Under Siege," *Essence*, November 1999, 139–140, 206, 208; Reverend Al Sharpton, "Making Local Police Misconduct a Federal Case," *Essence*, November 1999, 162.
12. Henry Louis Gates, *Figures in Black: Words, Signs, and the Racial Self* (New York: Oxford University Press, 1987), 35.
13. Cheikh Anta Diop, *Civilization or Barbarism* (New York: Laurence Hill Books, 1991), 21, 152.
14. Tony Browder, *Nile Valley Contributions to Civilization* (Washington: Institute of Karmic Guidance, 1992), 89.
15. John G. Jackson, *Introduction to African Civilizations* (New Jersey: Citadel Press, 1980), 124.
16. Albert Churchward, *Signs and Symbols of Primordial Man* (New York: A and B Publishers, 1903, 1993), 290–1.
17. Browder, 89.
18. Ralph Ellison, *Invisible Man* (New York: Vintage International Edition, 1990), 9–10.
19. Don L. Lee (Haki Madhubuti), *Groundwork: New and Selected Poems: Don L. Lee/Haki R. Madhubuti from 1966–1996* (Chicago: Third World Press, 1996), 5
20. D.H. Melhem, *Heroism in the New Black Poetry* (University of Kentucky Press, 1990), 101.
21. Geneva Smitherman, *Talking and Testifying: The Language of Black America* (Detroit: Wayne University Press, 1977), 82, 122–128.
22. Marimba Ani, *Yurugu: An African-Centered Critique of European Cultural Thought and Behavior* (New Jersey: Africa World Press, 1999), 403.
23. Don L. Lee, *Think Black* (Detroit: Broadside Press, 1967), 15.
24. William Wells Brown, *Clotel or the President's Daughter* (New York: Carol Publishing Group, 1853; 1995), 130–133.
25. Ani, 221.
26. *Malcolm X on Afro-American History*, 74.
27. Haki Madhubuti, *YellowBlack* (Chicago: Third World Press, 2005), 123. First published as *Black Pride* (Detroit: Broadside Press, 1968), 19.
28. Frederick Douglass, *Narrative of the Life of Frederick Douglass: An American Slave* (Belknap Press of Harvard University Press, 1845; 1982), 184; F.E.W. Harper, *Iola Leroy* (New York: Oxford University Press, 1893; 1988).
29. *Groundwork*, 21.
30. *The Signifying Monkey*, chapter three.
31. The term "Don Haki" is a borrowing from Dr. Eleanor Traylor, chair of English at Howard University, who read a public paper on Madhubuti's work on Heart's Day at Howard in February 2003.
32. Don L. Lee/Haki Madhubuti, *Think Black* (Detroit: Broadside Press, 1967), 19.
33. *Think Black*, 13.
34. John Edgar Wideman, *Brothers and Keepers* (New York: Penguin, 1984), 26–27.
35. Bruce Perry, ed., *Malcolm X: The Last Speeches* (New York: Pathfinder Press, 1989), 171.
36. Don L. Lee/Haki Madhubuti, *Black Pride* (Detroit: Broadside Press, 1968), 25.
37. Haki Madhubuti, *Don't Cry Scream* (Chicago: Third World Press, 1992), 63. First published by Broadside Press in 1969.
38. *Don't Cry Scream*, 36–37.

39. It is important to differentiate between the African-American's use of "bad" as good from the Western dictionary meaning. The word "bad" has been inverted in the African-American lexicon since the modern era. Michael Jackson has a contemporary song entitled "I'm Bad" which means he is exciting, audacious, sensual, strong, etc. However, the "bad" in reference to the "negro" is the Western version of the word.

40. *Groundwork*, 288.

41. Haki Madhubuti, *Groundwork: New and Selected Poems: Don L. Lee/Haki R. Madhubuti from 1966–1996* (Chicago: Third World Press, 1996), 87.

42. Marimba Ani (Dona Richards), "Let the Circle Be Unbroken: The Implications of African Spirituality in the Diaspora," *Presenceafricaine* no. 117/118 (1980): 5–6.

43. Gates, *The Signifying Monkey*, 29.

44. Haki Madhubuti, *Earthquakes and Sunrise Missions: Poetry and Essays of Black Renewal 1973–1983* (Chicago: Third World Press, 1984), 38.

45. Ani, *Let the Circle Be Unbroken*, 1.

46. The terms in parentheses are borrowed from Molefi Asante, *Afrocentricity: A Theory of Social Change* (Philadelphia: Temple University Press, 1980), 56.

47. Madhubuti, *Groundwork*, 88.

48. Joy Leary, *Post Traumatic Slave Syndrome* (New York: WBAI, 2004), Compact Disc.

49. Francis Bebey, *African Music: A People's Art*, trans. Josephine Bennett (New York: Lawrence Hill, 1975).

50. Sterling Stuckey, *Slave Culture: Nationalist Theory and the Foundations of Black America* (New York: Oxford University Press, 1987), 20.

51. William Loren Katz, *Breaking the Chains: African-American Slave Resistance* (New York: Atheneum, 1990), 68, 73.

52. Ivan Van Sertima, ed., *Great African Thinkers: Cheikh Anta Diop* (New Brunswick: Transaction Books, 1987), back cover.

53. Gates, *Signifying Monkey*, 38.

54. *Earthquakes*, 115.

55. Don L. Lee/Haki Madhubuti, "Notes from a Black Journal," *Negro Digest*, 1970, 69.

56. George Breitman, *Malcolm X Speaks: Selected Speeches and Statements* (New York: Pathfinder Press, 1989), 36.

57. *Groundwork*, 14.

58. Nas, *God's Son* (Sony Music Entertainment, 2002).

59. *The Afrocentric Idea*, 125.

60. Personal interview, 2000.

61. Haki Madhubuti, *Run Toward Fear* (Chicago: Third World Press, 2004), 22.

62. To give someone "rhythm" is a contemporary saying, which means to provide feedback and affirmation to the speaker or person. Used in this context, the word "rhythm" is a new addition to the lexicon of Black English.

63. Kariamu Welsh-Asante, ed., *The African Aesthetic: Keeper of the Traditions* (Westport, Conn.: Praeger Publishers, 1994), 12.

64. Haki Madhubuti, *YellowBlack* (Chicago: Third World Press, 2005), 120.

Works Cited

Abarry, Abu Shardow. 1992. "Afrocentric Aesthetics in Selected Harlem Renaissance Poetry." *Language and Literature in the African American Imagination.* Ed. Carol Aisha Blackshire-Belay. Westport: Greenwood Press.
Akbar, Na'im. 1991. *Chains and Images of Psychological Slavery.* New Jersey: New Mind Publications.
Allen, J. Hilton Als. 2000. *Without Sanctuary: Lynching Photography in America.* Santa Fe, New Mexico: Twin Palms Publishers.
Anderson, Talmadge. 2003. "Black Psychology and Psychological Concepts." *African-Centered Psychology: Culture-Focusing for Multicultural Competence.* Ed. Daudi Azibo. Durham: Carolina Academic Press.
Ani, Marimba, and Dona Richards. 1980. "Let the Circle Be Unbroken: The Implications of African Spirituality in the Diaspora." *Presence Africaine* 117/118.
____. 1995. *Yurugu: An African-Centered Critique of European Cultural Thought and Behavior.* New Jersey: Africa World Press.
Appiah, Kwame A. 1992. *In My Father's House: Africa in the Philosophy of Culture.* New York: Oxford University Press.
Asante, Molefi Kete. 1980. *Afrocentricity: A Theory of Social Change.* Buffalo, New York: Amulefi Publishing Company.
____. 1987. *The Afrocentric Idea.* Philadelphia: Temple University Press.
____. 1990. *Kemet, Afrocentricity and Knowledge.* Trenton: Africa World Press.
____. 1992. "Did He Ever Leave." Editorial. *The Philadelphia Inquirer,* 15 Nov.
____. 1992. "Locating a Text: Implications of Afrocentric Theory." *Language and Literature in the African American Imagination.* Ed. Carol Aisha Blackshire-Belay. Westport: Greenwood Press.
____. 1993. *Malcolm X as Cultural Hero and Other Afrocentric Essays.* Trenton: Africa World Press.
____. 2000. *The Egyptian Philosophers: Ancient African Voices from Imhotep to Akhenaton.* Chicago: African-American Images.
Azibo, Daudi Ajani. 2003. *African-Centered Psychology: Culture-Focusing for Multicultural Competence.* Durham, North Carolina: Carolina Academic Press.
Baker, Houston A. 1974. *A Many Colored Coat of Dreams.* Detroit: Broadside Press.

———. 1994. *Workings of the Spirit: The Poetics of Afro-American Women's Writings*. Chicago: University of Chicago Press.
Baraka, Amiri. 1984. *The Autobiography: Leroi Jones/Amiri Baraka*. New York: Freundlich Books.
Barksdale, Richard, and Keneth Kinnamon, eds. 1972. *Black Writers of America: A Comprehensive Anthology*. New York: Macmillan Company.
Bassey, Magnus O. 2005. *Malcolm X and African-American Self-Consciousness*. Lewiston, New York: Edwin Mellen Press.
Bebey, Francis. 1975. *African Music: A People's Art*. Josephine Bennett, trans. New York: Lawrence Hill.
Benjamin, Playthell. 1991. "Spike Lee: Bearing the Cross." *Emerge*, Nov.
Ben-Jochannan, Yosef A.A. 1989. *Black Man of the Nile and His Family*. Md.: Black Classic Press.
Benston, Kimberly. 1976. *Baraka: The Renegade and the Mask*. New Haven and London: Yale University Press.
Berry, Faith, ed. 1973. *Langston Hughes, Good Morning Revolution: Collected Writings of Social Protest*. Westport: Laurence Hill and Company.
Betró, Maria Carmela. 1996. *Hieroglyphics: The Writings of Ancient Egypt*. New York: Abbeville Press.
Blackshire-Belay, Carol Aisha. 1992. *Language and Literature in the African-American Imagination*. Westport: Greenwood Press.
Blake, W.O. 1860. *History of Slavery and the Slave Trade*. Columbus, Ohio: H. Miller.
Bolden, Tony. 2004. *Afro-Blue: Improvisations in African-American Poetry and Culture*. Champaign: University of Illinois Press.
Bontemps, Arna, ed. 1972. *The Harlem Renaissance Remembered*. New York: Dodd, Mead, and Company.
———. 1974. *American Negro Poetry*. American Century Series. New York: Hill and Wang.
Bradford, Sarah. 1994. *The Moses of Her People*. New York: Carol Publishing Company.
Branch, Taylor. 1998. *Pillar of Fire: America in the King Years, 1963–1965*. New York: Simon and Schuster.
———. 1988. *Parting the Waters: America in the King Years, 1954–1963*. New York: Simon and Schuster.
Braxton, Joanne M., and Andree Nicola McLaughlin, eds. 1990. *Wild Women in the Whirlwind: Afra-American Culture and the Contemporary Literary Renaissance*. New Jersey: Rutgers University Press.
Breitman, George. 1982. *Malcolm X: By Any Means Necessary*. New York: Pathfinder Press.
———. 1989. *Malcolm X Speaks: Selected Speeches and Statements*. New York: Pathfinder Press.
———. 1989. *The Last Year of Malcolm X: The Evolution of a Revolutionary*. New York: Pathfinder Press.
Brisbane, Robert. 1983. *Black Activism: Racial Revolution in the U.S. 1954–1970*. Valley Forge: Judson Press.
Brodrick, M., and A.A. Morton, eds. 1924. *A Concise Dictionary of Egyptian Archaeology: A Handbook for Students and Travelers*. Chicago: Ares Publishers, Inc.
Brooks, Gwendolyn. 1987. *Blacks*. Chicago: The David Company.
Brooks, Stratton D. 1912. *English Composition: Book One—Enlarged*. New York: American Book Company.
Browder, Tony. 1992. *Nile Valley Conributions to Civilization*. Washington: Institute of Karmic Guidance.

Brown, H. Rap. 1969. *Die Nigger Die*. New York: Dial Press.
Brown, William Wells. [1853] 1995. *Clotel or The President's Daughter*. New York: Carol Publishing Group.
Butcher, Philip, ed. 1977. *The Minority Presence in American Literature: 1600–1900*. Volume I. Morgan State Series in Afro-American Studies. Washington: Howard University Press.
Bynum, Edward Bruce. 1999. *The African Unconscious: Roots of Ancient Mysticism and Modern Psychology*. New York: Teacher's College Press.
Carson, Clayborne. 1991. *Malcolm X: FBI File*. New York: Carroll and Graf Publishers.
Celizic, Mike. 2001. "Iverson — the great anti-hero." *MSNBC Sports*, 25 May. <http://www.msnbc.com/news/569635.asp?cp1=1>.
Chernoff, John Miller. 1979. *African Rhythm and African Sensibility*. Chicago: University of Chicago Press.
Churchward, Albert. [1903] 1993. *Signs and Symbols of Primordial Man*. New York: A and B Publishers.
Cirlot, J.E. 1983. *A Dictionary of Symbols*. New York: Philosophical Library.
Clarke, John Henrik, ed. 1969. *Malcolm X: The Man and His Times*. Canada: Macmillan Company.
_____. 1991. *Notes for an African World Revolution: Africans at the Crossroads*. Trenton: Africa World Press.
Cleage, Albert. 1968. "Brother Malcolm." *The Black Messiah*. Kansas City: Sheed, Andrews and McMeel, Inc.
Clegg III, Claude Andrew. 1997. *An Original Man: The Life and Times of Elijah Muhammad*. New York: St. Martin's Press.
Collins, Rodnell P. 1998. *Seventh Child: A Family Memoir of Malcolm X*. Secaucus, N.J.: Carol Publishing Group.
Cooper, Wayne, ed. 1973. *The Passions of Claude McKay: Selected Prose and Poetry*. New York: Schocken Books.
Crouch, Stanley. 1989. "Introduction: The Complete Turn of Larry Neal." *Visions of a Liberated Future*. Ed. Michael Schwartz. New York: Thunder's Mouth Press.
Cullen, Countee. 1927. *Copper Sun*. New York: Harper and Bros.
_____. Ed. 1927. *Caroling Dusk: An Anthology of Verse by Negro Poets*. New York: Harper and Sons.
Davidson, Basil. 1990. *The African Slave Trade: A Revised and Expanded Edition*. An Atlantic Monthly Press Book. Boston: Little, Brown and Company.
Davis, Arthur P. 1970. "The New Poetry of Black Hate." *CLA Journal*, June.
_____. 1981. *From the Dark Tower*. Washington: Howard University Press.
Davis, Thulani. 1992. "He Made Me Understand Rage." *New York Times*, 15 Nov.
Diawara, Manthia. 1998. *In Search of Africa*. Cambridge: Harvard University Press.
Denham, Robert D., ed. 1990. *Myth and Metaphor: Northrup Frye Selected Essays 1974–1988*. Charlottesville: University of Virginia Press.
Diop, Cheikh Anta. 1974. *The African Origin of Civilization: Myth or Reality*. Westport: Laurence Hill and Co.
_____. 1991. *Civilization or Barbarism*. New York: Laurence Hill Books.
D, Chuck, and Yusef Jan. 1997. *Fight the Power*. New York: Delta Trade Paperbacks.
Douglass, Frederick. [1845] 1982. *Narrative of the Life of Frederick Douglass, an American Slave*. The Belknap Press of Harvard University Press.
Drake, St. Claire. 1987. *Black Folk Here and There*. Vol. 1. Los Angeles: University of California, CAAS.
Du Bois, Shirley Graham. [1949] 1972. *The Story of Phillis Wheatley: Poetess of the American Revolution*. Julian Messner.

Du Bois, W.E.B. 1915. *The Negro.* New York: Henry Holt and Company.
———. 1986. *W.E.B. Du Bois Writings: The Suppression of the African Slave Trade. The Souls of Black Folk. Dusk of Dawn Essays.* New York: Literary Classics of the United States, Inc.
Duster, Alfreda M., ed. 1970. *Crusade for Justice: The Autobiography of Ida B. Wells.* Chicago: University of Chicago Press.
Dyson, Michael. 1995. *Making Malcolm: The Myth and Meaning of Malcolm X.* New York: Oxford University Press.
Early, Gerald, ed. 1991. *My Soul's High Song: The Collected Writings of Countee Cullen.* New York: Doubleday.
Edwards, Paul, ed. 1977. *Equiano's Travels: His Autobiography. The Interesting Narrative of the Life of Olaudah Equiano or Gustavus Vassa the African.* London: Heinemann.
Ellison, Ralph. 1990. *Invisible Man.* New York: Vintage International Edition.
Evanzz, Karl. 1992. *The Judas Factor: The Plot to Kill Malcolm X.* New York: Thunder Mouth's Press.
Fairchild, H.H. 1985. "Black, Negro, or Afro-American? The Differences are Crucial! *Journal of Black Studies,* September, 47–55.
Fanon, Franz. 1967. *Black Skin, White Masks.* New York: Grove Press.
Fedo, Michael W. 1979. *They Was Just Niggers: An Account of One of the Nation's Least Known Racial Tragedies.* Ontario, California: Brasch and Brasch.
Flick, Hank. 1981. "Malcolm X: The Destroyer and Creator of Myths." *Journal of Black Studies* 12, no. 2 (Dec.).
Floro, Lewis. 1989. "Jackson as African-American." *New York Times,* 11 Jan.
Foster, Frances Smith, ed. 1990. *A Brighter Coming Day: A Frances Ellen Watkins Harper Reader.* New York: Feminist Press.
Franklin, John Hope. 1974. *From Slavery to Freedom.* New York: Knopf.
Franklin, John Hope, and Loren Schweninger. 1999. *Runaway Slaves: Rebels on the Plantation.* New York: Oxford University Press.
Fuller, Charles, ed. 1989. "Life and Work of Malcolm X." Temple University Handout, Spring.
Garvey, Amy Jacques, ed. 1986. *The Philosophy and Opinions of Marcus Garvey.* Dover, Mass.: Majority Press.
Gates, Henry Louis. 1987. *Figures in Black: Words, Signs, and the Racial Self.* New York: Oxford University Press.
———. 1988. Foreword. *Collected Works of Phillis Wheatley.* New York: Oxford University Press.
———. 1988. *The Signifying Monkey.* New York: Oxford University Press.
———. 1994. "Black Creativity: On the Cutting Edge." *Time* 144 (Oct. 10).
Gibson, Donald B., W.A. Low, and Virgil A. Clift, eds. 1981. *Encyclopedia of Black America.* New York: McGraw-Hill.
Giddings, Paula. 1971. "From a Black Perspective: The Poetry of Don L. Lee." In *Amistad.* Eds. John A. Williams and Charles P. Harris. New York: Random House.
Ginzburg, Ralph. 1992. *100 Years of Lynchings.* Baltimore: Black Classic Press.
Giovanni, Nikki. 1970. *Black Feeling, Black Talk, Black Judgment.* New York: William Morrow and Company.
Gitlin, Todd. 1987. *The Sixties: Years of Hope, Days of Rage.* New York: Bantam Books.
Gogumil, Mary L. and Michael R. Molino. 1990. "Pretext, Context, Subtext: Textual Power in the Writing of Langston Hughes, Richard Wright, and Martin Luther King Jr." *College English.* 52.
Goodman/2X Benjamin. 1971. *The End of White World Supremacy.* New York: Merlin House.

Gould, Stephen Jay. 1996. *The Mismeasure of Man.* New York: W.W. Norton and Company.
Graham, Maryemma, ed. 1988. *Complete Poems of Frances E.W. Harper.* The Schomburg Library of Nineteenth Century Black Women Writers. New York: Oxford University Press.
Gubar, Susan. 1997. *Race Changes: White Skin, Black Face in American Culture.* New York: Oxford University Press.
Hacker, Andrew. 1992. *Two Nations: Black and White, Separate, Hostile, Unequal.* New York: Ballantine Books.
Haley, Alex, ed. [1964] 1990. *The Autobiography of Malcolm X.* New York: Ballantine Books.
Hall, Corey. 2002. "African-centered Charter School Displays Methods During Tour: Betty Shabazz International Charter School Toured during National Charter Schools Week." *Citizen Newspaper,* 2 May. Chicago, Illinois. 3.
Hampton, Henry, creator and producer. 1990. *Eyes on the Prize.* Blackside, Inc.
Hancock, Graham, and Robert Bauval. 1996. *The Message of the Sphinx: A Quest for the Hidden Legacy of Mankind.* New York: Three Rivers Press.
Harding, Vincent. 1990. *Hope and History.* New York: Orbis Books.
"Harlem: Mecca of the New Negro." [1925] 1980. *Survey Graphic.* New York.
Harper, Frances Ellen Watkins. [1885] 1969. *Atlanta Offering Poems.* Miami, Florida: Mnemosyne Publishing, Inc.
———. [1893] 1988. *Iola Leroy.* New York: Oxford University Press.
———. [1901] 1975. *Idylls of the Bible.* 100 Bainbridge Street, Philadelphia, 1901. New York: AMS.
Harris, William J. 1979. "Militant Singers: Baraka Cultural Nationalism and Madhubuti." *Minority Voices: An Interdisciplinary Journal of Literature and the Arts.*
———. 1985. *The Poetry and Poetics of Amiri Baraka: The Jazz Aesthetic.* Columbia: University of Missouri Press.
Henderson, Stephen E., and Mercer Cook, eds. 1969. *The Militant Black Writer in Africa and the United States.* Madison: University of Wisconsin Press.
Henderson, Stephen E. 1973. *Understanding the New Black Poetry.* New York: Morrow Quill Paperbacks.
Hernandez, Roger. 1992. "Buchanan, Malcolm X, Both Ignited Hatred." *Philadelphia Inquirer,* 30 Nov.
Herskovits, M.J. 1990. *The Myth of the Negro Past.* Boston: Beacon Press.
Higginbotham, Leon A., Jr. 1980. *In the Matter of Color: Race and the American Legal Process: The Colonial Period.* New York: Oxford University Press.
Hill, Patricia Liggins, ed. 2001. *Call and Response: The Riverside Anthology of the African American Literary Tradition.* Boston: Houghton Mifflin Company.
Horsman, Reginald. 1981. *Race and Manifest Destiny.* Cambridge: Harvard University Press.
Huggins, Nathan Irvin. 1971. *Harlem Renaissance.* New York: Oxford University Press.
Hughes, Langston. 1974. *Selected Poems, Langston Hughes.* New York: Vintage Books.
Jackson, John G. 1980. *Introduction to African Civilizations.* New Jersey: Citadel Press.
Jacobs, Harriet. [1861] 1987. *Incidents in the Life of a Slave Girl; Written by Herself.* Cambridge: Harvard University Press.
Jacobson, Matthew Frye. 1998. *Whiteness of a Different Color: European Immigrants and the Alchemy of Race.* Cambridge: Harvard University Press.
Jamal, Hakim A. 1972. *From the Dead Level: Malcolm X and Me.* New York: Random House.

Jennings, Regina. 1998. "This Is Not a New Story: Jasper Texas Is America." *The Black Suburban Journal* (Philadelphia), July, 3, 10.
_____. 2000. "African Sun Imagery in the Poetry of Phillis Wheatley." NAME OF PERIODICAL 22 (Spring).
_____. 2003. "From Nigger to Negro: Dysfunctional Beginnings for New World Africans." In *African-Centered Psychology: Culture-Focusing for Multicultrual Competence.* Ed. Daudi Ajani ya Azibo. Durham: Carolina Academic Press.
_____. 2005. "Third World Press." "The Institute of Positive Education." *Encyclopedia of Black Studies.*
"Jesse Jackson Gains Backers (in movement to call American blacks African Americans)." 1989. *New York Times,* 12 Jan.
Johnson, Lemuel. 1979. "Aints, usens and Mother dear..." *Journal of Black Studies* 10, no. 2 (Dec.). Newbury Park, Cal., SAGE.
Jones, Leroi. 1963. *Blues People: Negro Music in White America.* New York: Morrow Quill Paperbacks.
Jones, Nasir, Nas. 2002. *God's Son.* Sony Entertainment. New York. Compact disc.
Jordan, June.1981. *Civil Wars.* Boston: Beacon Press.
_____. 1990. "The Difficult Miracle of Black Poetry in America or Something Like a Sonnet for Phillis Wheatley." In *Wild Women in the Whirlwind: Afra-American Culture and the Contemporary Literary Renaissance.* Eds. Joanne M.Braxton and Andree Nicola Mclaughlin. New Jersey: Rutgers University Press.
Jordan, Winthrop D. 1977. *White Over Black: American Attitudes Towards the Negro.* New York: Norton.
Karenga, M. 1979. "The Socio-Political Philosophy of Malcolm X." *The Western Journal of Black Studies* 3, no. 4 (Winter): 251–259.
Karim, Benjamin, et al. 1992. *Remembering Malcolm.* New York: Ballantine.
Katz, William Loren. 1990. *Breaking the Chains: African-American Slave Resistance.* New York: Atheneum.
Kelley, Robin D.G. 1996. *Race Rebels: Culture, Politics, and the Black Working Class.* New York: Free Press.
Kent, George. 1971. *Blackness and the Adventure of Western Culture.* Chicago: Third World Press.
Kessler, Jascha. 1973. "Trial and Error." *Poetry* 121 (February).
Kestleloot, Lilyan, ed. 1974. *Black Writers in French.* Philadelphia: Temple University Press.
Keto, C. Tsehloane. 1991. *The Africa Centered Perspective of History: An Introduction.* Blackwood, New Jersey: K.A. Publications.
King, Mary. 1987. *Freedom Song: A Personal Story of the 1960s Civil Rights Movement.* New York: Quill/William Morrow.
Kovel, Joel. 1984. *White Racism: A Psychohistory.* New York: Pantheon.
Lauter, Paul, et al. 1990. *The Health Anthology of American Literature.* Vol. 1. Lexington, Massachusetts, Toronto: D.C. Heath and Company.
Leary, Joy. 2004. *Post Traumatic Slave Syndrome.* WBAI. New York. Compact Disc.
Lee, Spike. 1992. "Some Say Malcolm Is Back." *Philadelphia Inquirer* (15 Nov.).
Lewy, Ernst. Missing year. "Historical Charismatic Leaders and Mythical Heroes." *Journal of Psychohistory* 6, no. 3 (Winter).
Lichtheim, Mariam. 1973. *Ancient Egyptian Literature: The Old and Middle Kingdoms.* I. Berkeley: University of California Press.
Lincoln, Eric C. 1961. *The Black Muslims of America.* Boston: Beacon Press.
Llorens, David. 1989. "Poet is acclaimed creator of black art, is writer-in-residence at Cornell University." *Ebony,* March.
Loggins, Vernon. 1931. *The Negro Author.* New York: Columbia University Press.

Lomax, Alan, and Raoul Abdul, eds. 1970. *3000 Years of Black Poetry*. New York: Dodd, Mead and Co.
Lomax, Louis. 1963. *When the Word Is Given*. New York: Signet Books.
Lopez, Ian. 1996. *White by Law: The Legal Construction of Race*. New York: New York University Press.
Madhubuti, Haki R. (Don L. Lee). 1967. *Think Black*. Detroit: Broadside Press.
_____. 1968. *Black Pride*. Detroit: Broadside Press.
_____. 1969. *Don't Cry Scream*. Detroit: Broadside Press.
_____. 1970. "Notes from a Black Journal." *Negro Digest*, Jan.
_____. 1970. *We Walk the Way of the New World*. Detroit: Broadside Press.
_____. 1984. *Earthquakes and Sunrise Missions: Poetry and Essays of Black Renewal 1973*. Chicago: Third World Press.
_____. 1987. *From Plan to Planet: Life Studies the Need for Afrikan Minds and Institutions*. Chicago: Third World Press.
_____. 1987. *Killing Memory, Seeking Ancestors*. Detroit: Lotus Press.
_____. 1992. *Don't Cry Scream*. Chicago: Third World Press.
_____. 1993. *Why LA Happened: Implications of the 92 Los Angeles Rebellion*. Chicago: Third World Press.
_____. 1994. *Claiming Earth: Race, Rage, Rape, and Redemption: Blacks Seeking a Culture of Enlightened Empowerment*. Chicago: Third World Press.
_____. 1996. *GroundWork: New and Selected Poems: Don L. Lee/Haki R. Madhubuti from 1966 to 1996*. Chicago: Third World Press.
_____. 1999. Telephone interview with author, July.
_____. 2002. Interview with author, 28 October.
_____. 2002. *Tough Notes: A Healing Call for Creating Exceptional Black Men*. Chicago: Third World Press.
_____. 2004. *Run Toward Fear*. Chicago: Third World Press.
_____. 2004. Telephone interview with author, 20 June.
_____. 2005. *YellowBlack*. Chicago: Third World Press.
Mafundikwa, Saki. 2004. *Afrikan Alphabets: The Story of Writing in Afrika*. New York: Mark Batty Publisher.
Malcolm X. 1982. *Malcolm X on Afro-American History*. New York: Pathfinder Press.
Martin, Tony. 1976. *Race First: The Ideological and Organizational Struggles of Marcus Garvey and the Universal Negro Improvement Association*. The New Marcus Garvey Library. No. 8. Dover, Mass.: Majority Press.
_____. Ed. 1983. *The Poetical Works of Marcus Garvey*. Dover, Massachusetts: Majority Press.
Mason, Julian D. Jr., ed. 1989. *The Poems of Phillis Wheatley*. Chapel Hill: University of North Carolina Press.
Massey, Gerald. [1907] 1992. *Ancient Egypt: The Light of the World*. Volumes 1 and 2. Baltimore: Black Classics Press.
Melhem, D.H. 1990. *Heroism in the New Black Poetry*. Lexington: University of Kentucky Press.
Mellen, James, ed. 1988. *Bullwhip Days: The Slaves Remember, an Oral History*. New York: Weidenfeld and Nicolson.
Miller, Jerome. 1996. *Search and Destroy: African-American Males in the Criminal Justice System*. Cambridge and New York: Cambridge University Press.
Miller, Ross. 1972. "Autobiography as Fact and Fiction: Franklin, Adams, Malcolm X." *The Centennial Review* 16 (Summer).
Montagu, Ashley. 1997. *Man's Most Dangerous Myth: The Fallacy of Race*. Cal.: Altamira Press.

Moore, Acel. 1992. "African American experience as seen in two powerful films." *Philadelphia Inquirer*, 17 Nov.
Moore, Richard. 1992. *The Name "Negro": Its Origin and Evil Use*. Baltimore: Black Classic Press.
Morrison, Toni. 1992. *Playing in the Dark: Whiteness and the Literary Imagination*. New York: Random House.
Moses, Wilson Jeremiah. 1978. *The Golden Age of Black Nationalism 1850–1925*. New York: Oxford University Press.
Moseley, Elaine C. 2002. Interview with author, 28 October, Chicago.
Muhammad, Elijah. 1965. *Message to the Black Man in America*. Chicago: Muhammad's Temple #2.
Murray, Albert. 1970. *The Omni-Americans*. New York: Outerbridge and Dienstfrey.
National Association for the Advancement of Colored People. 1919. *Burning at the Stake*.
Neal, Larry. 1968. "The Black Arts Movement." *Black Theatre: tdr*. Vol. 12, no. 4. T40.
———. 1974. *HooDoo Hollerin' BeBopGhosts*. Washington, D.C.: Howard University Press.
"Negro, Black and African-American (Jesse Jackson's preferred terminology)." 1988. Editorial. *New York Times*, 22 Dec.
Nelson, Jill, ed. 2000. *Police Brutality*. New York: Norton.
Newton, Huey P. 1973. *Revolutionary Suicide*. New York: Harcourt Brace Jovanovich.
Niane, D.T. 1994. *Sundiata: An Epic of Old Mali*. England: Longman.
Nobles, Wade W. 1986. *African Psychology: Toward Its Reclamation, Reascension and Revitalization*. Oakland, California: A Black Family Institute Publication.
Odelius, Kristy. 1998. "Whole Culture, Whole People, Whole Book: Third World Press Opens Up a Continent." *ForeWord*, Dec.
Ohmann, Carol. 1980. "The Autobiography of Malcolm X: A Revolutionary Use of the Franklin Tradition." *American Quarterly* 22, no. 2 (Summer).
Oliver, Stephanie Stokes. 1991. "Liberation Love." *Essence*, July.
O'Reilly, Kenneth. 1989. *Racial Matters: The FBI's Secret File on Black America 1960–1972*. New York: Free Press.
Oxford English Dictionary. 1985. Volume 1. Oxford University Press.
Paris, Ethel. 2003. Interview with author, 23 February, Philadelphia.
Patterson, Orlando. 1982. *Slavery and Social Death*. Cambridge: Harvard University Press.
Patterson, William L. 1971. *We Charge Genocide: The Crime of Government Against the Negro People*. New York: International Publishers.
Perdue, Charles L., et al. 1980. *Weevils in the Wheat*. Indiana: Indiana University Press.
Perry, Bruce, ed. 1989. *Malcolm X: The Last Speeches*. New York: Pathfinder Press.
———. 1991. *Malcolm: The Life of a Man Who Changed Black America*. New York: Station Hill Press.
Pete, Pistol. 1992. "A Souljah Story." *The Source: Magazine of Hiphop Music, Culture, and Politics* 36:16 (Sept.).
Platt, Larry. 2002. *Only the Strong Survive: The Odyssey of Allen Iverson*. New York: Harper Collins Publishers.
Porter, Dorothy, ed. 1971. *Early Negro Writing 1760–1851*. Boston: Beacon Press.
Powell, Richard. 1997. *Black Art and Culture in the 20th Century*. New York: Thames and Hudson.
Public Enemy. 1990. *Fear of a Black Planet*. New York: Columbia Records.
Rampersad, Arnold. 1988. *The Life of Langston Hughes: Volume 2, 1941–1967: I Dream a World*. New York: Oxford University Press.

Randall, Dudley, and Margaret Burroughs, eds. 1973. *For Malcolm: Poems on the Life and Death of Malcolm X*. Detroit: Broadside Press.
Raspberry, William. 1989. "When 'black' becomes 'African-American.' (Thoughts on Jesse Jackson's campaign to change an ethnic group's name)." *Washington Post*, 4 Jan.
Reardon, Patrick T. 2000. "Poetic Justice: Success hasn't diminished Haki Madhubuti's passion for the struggle." *Chicago Tribune*, Thursday, 10 August, sec. 5.
Redding, J. Saunders. [1939] 1988. *To Make a Poet Black*. Ithaca: Cornell University Press.
Redmond, Eugene B. 1976. *The Mission of Afro-American Poetry: Drumvoices: A Critical History*. New York: Doubleday.
Reilly, Rick. 2001. "Looks Aren't Everything." *Sports Illustrated*, 22 May. <http:\\ sports illustrated.cnn.com/inside_game/magazine/life_of_reilly/news/2001/05/22/life_of ...> (5 May 2001).
Richards, Dona. 1980. "Let the Circle Be Unbroken." *Presence Africaine* 117/118.
Richmond, M.A. 1974. *Bid the Vassal Soar: Interpretive Essays on the Life and Poetry of Phillis Wheatley and George Moses Horton*. Washington: Howard University Press.
Richter, David H. 2000. *Falling into Theory: Conflicting Views on Reading Literature*. Bedford: St. Martin's Press.
Rivlin, Gary. 1997. "Eyes on the Prize: Over more than two decades, Haki and Safisha Madhubuti have proved that African-centered education can amount to more than a black version of history. It can also be a springboard to a bright future." *The Chicago Reader* 26, no. 33, sec. 1 (23 May).
Rodney, Walter. 1982. *How Europe Underdeveloped Africa*. Washington, D.C.: Howard University Press.
Rose, Tricia. 1994. *Black Noise: Rap Music and Culture in Contemporary America*. Middletown, Connecticut: Wesleyan University Press.
Russell Simmons Presents Def Poetry. 2004. Season I. Episode III. New York.
Salaam, Kalamu Ya. 1997. *The Oxford Companion to African-American Literature*. New York: Oxford University Press. <aalbc.com/authors/blackartsmovement.htm>.
Sale, Kirkpatrick. 1990. *The Conquest of Paradise: Christopher Columbus and the Columbian Legacy*. New York: Penguin Books.
Sale, William W., Jr. 1994. *From Civil Rights to Black Liberation: Malcolm X and the Organization of Afro-American Unity*. Boston: South End Press.
Salzman, Jack, David Lionel Smith, and Cornel West. 1996. *Encyclopedia of African-American Culture and History*. Volume 5. NewYork: Simon and Schuster and Prentice Hall International.
Scholes, Robert. 2000. "A Fortunate Fall." *Falling into Theory: Conflicting Views on Reading Literature*. Bedford: St. Martin's.
Seale, Bobby. 1978. *A Lonely Rage*. New York: New York Times Book Company.
———. 2000. Interview with author, 16 April.
Shakur, Assata. 1987. *Assata*. Westport: Lawrence Hill and Company.
Shields, John C., ed. 1988. *The Collected Works of Phillis Wheatley*. New York: Oxford University Press.
Sistrunk, Alberta. 1982. "The Influence of Alexander Pope on the Writing Style of Phillis Wheatley." *Critical Essays on Phillis Wheatley*. Ed. William H. Robinson. Boston, Mass.: G.K. Hall and Company.
Slavery's Buried Past. 1996. Producers Bill Kurtis and Molly Bedell. 60 minutes. The New York Explorers. Public Media Video. Videocassette.
Small, James. 2000. "Who Killed Malcolm X." Personal interview. New York.
Smitherman, Geneva. 1977. *Talking and Testifying: The Language of Black America*. Detroit: Wayne University Press.

Stampp, K.M. 1956. *The Peculiar Institution: Slavery in the Ante-Bellum South*. New York: Vintage Books.
Stewart, Mark. 2001. *Basketball's New Wave*. Brookfield, Connecticut: Millbrook Press.
Stuckey, Sterling. 1987. *Slave Culture: Nationalist Theory and the Foundations of Black America*. New York: Oxford University.
Sundquist, Eric J. 1996. *The Oxford W.E.B. Du Bois Reader*. New York: Oxford University Press.
Tate, Gayle T. 2003. *Unknown Tongues: Black Women's Political Activism in the Antebellum Era, 1830–1860*. East Lansing: Michigan State University Press.
Thomas, Lizzie. 1984. "The Autobiography of Malcolm X: A Social Commentary on Black American Urban Society." *Afro-Americans in New York Life and History*, January.
Thompson, Julius E. 1992. "The Public Response to Haki R. Madhubuti, 1968–1988." *The Literary Griot* 4, nos. 1 and 2.
Thompson, Robert Farris. 1983. *Flash of the Spirit: African and Afro-American Art and Philosophy*. New York: Random House.
Tillery, Tyrone. 1992. *Claude McKay*. Amherst: University of Massachusetts Press.
Turner, Lorenzo. 1973. *Africanisms in the Gullah Dialect*. Ann Arbor: University of Michigan Press.
Trotter, William Joe. 2001. *The African-American Experience: Vol II: From Reconstruction*. Boston: Houghton Mifflin Company.
Van Sertima, Ivan, ed. 1987. *Great African Thinkers: Cheikh Anta Diop*. New Brunswick: Transaction Books.
Waldman, Carl. 1999. *Encyclopedia of Native American Tribes*. New York: Checkmark Books.
Walker, Alice. 1983. *In Search of Our Mothers' Gardens*. New York: Harcourt Brace Jovanovich.
Walker, David. [1829] 1991. *Appeal to the Coloured Citizens of the World, but in Particular and very expressly, to those of the United States of America*. New York: Hill and Wang.
Ward, Ann. 2002. Interview with author, Chicago, 28 October.
Ward, Jerry W., Jr. 1997. *Trouble the Water: 250 Years of African-American Poetry*. New York: Penguin Books.
Weems, Clenora Hudson. 1993. *Africana Womanism: Reclaiming Ourselves*. Troy: Bedford Publishers, Inc.
Welsh-Asante, Kariamu, and Molefi Kete Asante, eds. 1985. *African Culture: The Rhythms of Unity*. Westport: Greenwood Press.
Welsh, Kariamu, ed. 1994. *The African Aesthetic: Keeper of the Traditions*. Westport, Conn.: Praeger.
West, Cornel. 1993. *Race Matters*. New York: Vintage Books.
West, John Anthony. 1993. *Serpent in the Sky: The High Wisdom of Ancient Egypt*. Wheaton, Ill.: Quest Books.
White, Deborah Gray. 1985. *Ar'n't I a Woman?: Female Slaves in the Plantation South*. New York: W.W. Norton and Company.
White, Vibert L., Jr. 2001. *Inside the Nation of Islam: A Historical and Personal Testimony by a Black Muslim*. Gainesville: University of Florida Press.
Whitfield, Stephen. 1978. "Three Masters of Impression Management: Benjamin Franklin, Booker T. Washington, and Malcolm X as Autobiographers." *South Atlantic Quarterly* 77 (Autumn).
Whiteman, Maxwell. [1857] 1969. Introduction. *Poems on Miscellaneous Subjects by Frances Ellen Watkins Harper*. Philadelphia: Historic Publications.

Whitten, Norman E., and Arlene Torres. 1998. *Blackness in Latin America and the Caribbean.* Indiana University Press.
Wideman, John Edgar. 1984. *Brothers and Keepers.* New York: Penguin.
Williams, Chancellor. 1976. *The Destruction of Black Civilizations.* Chicago: Third World Press.
Wilson, Amos N. 1978. *The Developmental Psychology of the Black Child.* New York: Africana Research Publications.
Wood, Joe, ed. 1992. *Malcolm X in Our Own Image.* New York: St. Martin's Press.
Woodard, Komozi. 1999. *Nation Within a Nation: Amiri Baraka (Leroi Jones) and Black Power Politics.* Chapel Hill: University of North Carolina Press.
Wright, Bobby E. 1984. *The Psychopathic Racial Personality and Other Essay.* Chicago: Third World Press.
Yosef. A.A. Ben-Jochannan. 1989. *Black Man of the Nile and His Family.* Baltimore: Black Classic Press.
Zangrando, Robert L. 1980. *The NAACP Crusade Against Lynching, 1909–1950.* Philadelphia: Temple University Press.
Zinn, Howard. 1990. *A People's History of the United States.* New York: First Harper Perennial Edition.

Index

Abyssinian Baptist Church 144
Africa 5, 201, 208, 209, 210, 213, 215, 238, 245, 247, 252, 255
African-American 199–200, 218, 251, 255
African art 25–26, 55
African-centered 1, 2, 5, 7, 30, 37, 61, 88, 103, 116, 129, 131, 138, 142, 145, 149, 151, 153, 157, 162, 172, 177, 221, 224, 227, 239, 246, 249, 253, 255
African Music: A People's Art 248
African Origins of Civilization 141
African poetry 26
Africana: The Encyclopedia of the African and African-American Experience 204
Africanisms in the Gullah Dialect 31, 33
Afrika 161
Afro 19, 181, 182, 183, 186
Afrocentricity 7, 36, 55, 101, 124, 135, 138, 149, 158, 165, 168, 181, 202, 208, 226, 235, 240, 244
Agassiz, Louis 215
Age of Malcolm X 2, 5, 19, 104, 218, 238
age-set groups 167
Akbar, Na'im 91, 113
Ali, Muhammad 181
All Africans Peoples Party 11
Allen, Richard 205
American Hunger 107
Amini, Johari 148, 169
Anderson, Talmadge 10, 20, 102
Anglo aesthetics 73–77
Anglo-saxon 63
Ani, Marimba 135–136, 157, 197, 229, 230, 232, 236, 243, 245
Anxiety of Influence 136
Appiah, Kwame 31, 204
Arabs 65
art of war 2, 22, 142–143

Asante, Molefi 6, 8, 36, 41, 62, 80, 85, 86, 143, 144, 158, 165, 226, 253
Asantewa, Yaa 118
Asr 79, 145, 158, 227–228
Assata 79, 145
Ast 79, 145, 158
Atlanta Offering Poems 75
(A)tum-Ra 145
Audubon Ballroom 12, 209, 218
Aunt Chloe 80–82
Ausar 79
Auset 79
Autobiography of X 7, 12

badman tradition 203, 208, 213
Baker, Houston 77–78, 231
Baldwin, James 12
Bankole, Katherine 127
Baraka, Amiri 2, 12, 13, 14, 15, 16, 17, 56, 136; Malcolm as muse 144–145, 146, 156, 222–223
Barbara Ann Sizemore Campus 2, 133, 172, 173
Bearden, Romare 21
Bebey, Frances 248
Behn, Aphra 69
Beloved 23
Berry, Faith 105, 112
Betty Shabazz International Charter School 2, 133, 151–156, 159–160, 171, 173, 174
Betty X 170
Bigger Thomas 235
Biko, Stephen 139
Birth of a Nation 215
Bishop, Jimmy 167
black 145
Black American (newspaper) 12
black arts 1, 2, 6, 10, 12, 13, 25, 56, 136, 143, 144, 149, 163, 185, 193, 197, 202, 227, 244,

283

250, 254, 251; movement 5, 6, 10, 11, 13, 14–24, 26, 29, 220–224
Black Boy 132, 190, 191
Black Classic Press 149
Black Consciousness 139
Black Nationalism 1, 6, 7, 12, 14, 18, 24, 58, 75, 82, 83, 105, 106, 125, 158, 175, 176, 185, 186, 189, 191, 211, 253
Black Nations and Culture 126
Black Noise 19
The Black Panther (newspaper) 11, 179, 223
Black Panther Party 11, 12, 14, 16, 223, 238
Black Power 10, 14, 16, 20, 24, 54, 55, 136, 137–138, 146, 148, 152, 156, 163, 183, 184, 185, 194, 223, 225, 251, 252
Black Pride 231, 246
Black Skin, White Masks 101
Black Star Line 115
Black Studies 9, 36
black women 19
Blake, W.O. 63, 66
Blake or the Huts of America 24, 203
blank slate theory 33, 68
Bloom, Harold 100, 136
Bluest Eye 23
Blyden, Edward W. 31, 99
Bolden, Tony 142
Bontemps, Arna 106
Boyz to Men 120
braids 184
Broadside Press 149, 197
Brooks, Gwendolyn 15, 149, 156, 182, 185, 187, 188; and Haki 193–195, 196, 97, 198
Brothers and Keepers 231–232, 235
Browder, Anthony 98, 227–228
Brown, Elaine 11
Brown, H. Rap (Jamil Al-Amin) 10, 11, 55, 182, 239
Brown, James 234
Brown, Larry 184–185
Brown, Marion 15
Brown, Oscar, Jr. 193
Brown, Sterling 15, 181
Brown, William Wells 77, 231
Burroughs, Margaret 191, 193

Caesar, Julius 98
Cain 69
Campbell, James 159
Carmichael, Stokely (Kwame Tourè) 10, 11, 14, 137, 142, 156, 182, 225
Carter, Vince 184
Catlett, Elizabeth 12
Cèsaire, Aimè 128
Chase-Riboud, Barbara 12
Chestnutt, Charles 234
Christians and Christianity 65, 69, 70, 71, 74, 75, 76, 78, 79, 89, 96, 113, 114, 116, 146, 211
Chuck D 19–20, 23
Churchward, Albert 227
Civil Rights Movement 30, 135, 190

Civilization or Barbarism 127, 128
Claiming Earth 177
Clark, Mark 84, 183, 224
Clarke, John Henrik 36, 107, 121, 146, 150–151, 164, 178
Cleaver, Eldridge 179
Cleaver, Kathleen 10, 11, 14
Clotel 231
The Coasters 167
Coates, Paul 149
Cokely, Steve 241
Collins, Ella 132, 187, 188; and Malcolm 193–196, 198
Collins, Patricia Hill 202
Collins, Rodnell 195, 212
Colon, Cristobal 66
The Colonizer and the Colonized 30
The Color Purple 24
Columbus, Christopher 66
common 20, 23
Communism 111, 145, 159
Congress of Racial Equality 138
Constab Ballads 95
Copper Sun 91
cornrows 183, 184, 186,
Council of Independent Black Institutions 152
The Crisis 32, 85
Crisis of the Negro Intellectual 57, 111
Cross, W.E. 20
Crouch, Stanley 22
Crummell, Alexander 31, 147
Cruse, Harold 57, 111
Cullen, Countee 62, 85, 87–95, 96, 98, 101, 102, 106, 110, 210, 213, 225, 231, 233, 243
cultural revolution 10, 11, 17
cummings, e.e. 229

Darkwater 132
Davidson, Basil 64, 109
Davis, Angela 10, 11, 14
Davis, Arthur 93, 95
Davis, Ossie 144
De Camp, David 31
Decapitated art 92, 96, 98, 114
Delany, Martin 24, 26, 203, 213
Destruction of Black Civilizations 48, 138, 167
The Developmental Psychology of the Black Child 160
Devil 206–208
Diallo, Amadou 225, 242
Diawara, Manthia 162, 163
Dickinson, Emily 72
Diop, Cheikh Anta 36, 125–126, 128, 131, 133, 141, 202, 227, 243, 248, 249
dislocation 99, 204
Don't Cry Scream 147, 246
Douglass, Aaron 85
Douglass, Frederick 24, 26, 143, 203, 213
The Drifters 167
drumming and drums 166, 247–248, 247–249
Du Bois, Shirley Graham 71

Du Bois, W.E.B. 31, 32, 41, 44, 54, 55, 71, 82, 85, 92–93, 106, 125, 126, 127–128, 129, 131, 132, 133, 137, 138, 144, 146, 162, 189, 198, 202, 203–204, 229
Dunbar, Paul Lawrence 81
DuSable Leadership Academy 133
Dusk of Dawn 132
Dyson, Michael 9, 20

Early Negro Writing 79
ebonics 80, 113
Ebony 182
Egypt 72, 96–97, 98, 130, 208, 227
Eliot, T.S. 15
Ellison, Ralph 83, 145, 228, 251
Encyclopedia of African-American Culture and History 204
End of White World Supremacy 22
Enemies the Clash of Races 57, 180
Engels, Friedrich 138
The Enlightenment 67
Ennead 145
Equiano's Travels 37–41, 63, 73
Esu Elegbara 221, 229, 235, 236, 237, 244, 250, 251
Ethiopia 64, 109, 111
Ethiopianism 18
Eurocentric 1, 7, 31, 32, 34, 47, 55, 68, 76, 77, 89, 99, 135–136, 184, 185, 227
Evans, Mari 19
Eyes on the Prize 13, 224

Fairchild, H.H. 48
Fanon, Franz 101
Farrakhan, Louis 176, 179
Fauset, Jessie Redmon 85, 118
Flash of the Spirit 248
Franklin, John Hope 64
Freedom Schools 159
Freedom's Journal 205
From Civil Rights to Black Liberation 9
From Plan to Planet 160, 180

Garnet, Henry Highland 138
Garvey, Marcus 8, 30, 47, 54–57, 83, 85, 96, 103, 104–108; poetry of 115–124, 138, 166, 175, 199, 202, 204, 212, 213, 223, 229, 235, 238, 242, 248
Gates, Henry Louis 22, 67, 70, 129, 204, 221, 223, 226–229, 235, 249–250
Geb 145
Ghost Dance 139–140
Giovanni, Nikki 16–17, 19, 20, 22
Gladys Knight and the Pips 167
Goodman, Benjamin 22
gothic 72, 77, 101
Gould, Stephen Jay 215
Graham, Maryemma 80
Greek(s) 72, 97, 98, 208, 227, 228
Gubar, Susan 118, 226
Guinea 37–40, 82

Gwendolyn Brooks Center for Black Literature and Creative Writing 148, 153, 154–155, 180, 194–195

Hammon, Jupiter 70
Hampton, Fred 84, 183, 224
Hancock, Graham 130
Handler, M.S. 12
Harlem Renaissance 11, 14, 74, 85, 128
Harlem Renaissance 88, 95, 103, 105
Harlem Shadows 95, 96
Harper, Frances Ellen Watkins 25, 26, 62, 67, 73, 74–85, 90, 95, 97, 109, 116, 214, 224, 231
Hayden, Palmer 85
Hayden, Robert 13
Hegel, George W.F. 72
Helen of Troy 118
Henderson, Stephen 226, 235
Henry, Milton 165
Hernton, Calvin C. 15
The Heroic Slave 24, 203
Herskovits, Melville 33, 141
High John 207–208
History of Slavery 63, 66
Holiday, Billy 252
Horsman, Reginald 66
Horton, George Moses 70
Horus 227
How Europe Underdeveloped Africa 48, 63, 97, 163
How to Eat to Live 177, 180
Huckleberry Finn 69
Hudson-Weems, Clenora 169
Huggins, Nathan 88, 106
Hughes, Langston 15, 56, 74, 80, 81, 85, poetics of resistance 103–115, 116, 124, 146, 199, 211, 212, 214, 234, 235, 238, 239, 246, 247–248
Hume, David 72, 129
Hurston, Zora Neale 85, 105, 118, 153, 207

Idylls of the Bible 75, 79
Iola Leroy 38–39, 82, 231
image of Africa 60, 61, 72, 78, 81, 94, 95, 96, 100, 101, 104, 121, 238
Imhotep 141–142
In Montgomery 196
In Search of Africa 162
In the Mecca 193
Incidents in the Life of a Slave Girl 41–43, 84
Inside the Nation of Islam 175
Institute of Positive Education 2, 133, 148, 151, 153–154, 156, 172
Introduction to African Civilizations 48
Invisible Man 83, 107, 145, 228
Italy 109, 111
Iverson, Allen 174, 184–187, 213
Iverson, Ann 184

Jackson, Andrew, 141
Jackson, George 11
Jackson, Jesse 219
Jackson, John G. 63, 227

Jackson, Jonathan 11
Jackson, Michael 233
Jacobs, Harriet 37–43, 73
Jacobson, Matthew Frye 215
Jazz 248
Jefferson, Thomas 35, 36, 63, 70, 73, 77, 215
Jesus Christ 208, 210
Johnson, Jack 204
Jones, Leroi 10, 12, 13
Jordan June 68
Jubilee 107
The Judas Factor 8

Karenga, Maulana 16, 160
Karim, (Goodman) Benjamin 170, 176, 209, 211, 212
Katz, William Loren 248
Kawaida 160
Keats, John 93
Kelley, William Melvin 21
Kemet 97, 98, 104, 119, 126, 127, 131, 133, 145, 244, 249
Kemet, Afrocentricity, and Knowledge 62
Kemetic 61
Kendricks, Eddie 167
Keto, C. Tsehloane 221, 246
Killens, John Oliver 21
King, Martin Luther 1, 21, 31, 55, 183, 214
King, Rodney 225
King Shyyam 65
Knight, Etheridge 11
Kongo 64
KRS1, 20, 23
Kwanzaa 160

La Roche, Cheryl 141
Larsen, Nella 118
The Last Poets 23
Leary, Joy 162, 247
Lee, Don L. 1, 6, 10, 55, 61, 127, 128, 132, 133, 188
Lee, James 132, 189, 193
Lee, Maxine Graves 132, 189, 190–193, 198, 251
Lee, Spike 23
Let the Circle Be Unbroken 245
Library of Alexandria 98
Lipsitz, George 117
Little, Earl 115, 189, 190, 195
Little, Louise 189, 190
location theory 6, 235, 237
Locke, Alain 53–55, 58, 86, 105
Loggins, Vernon 68
A Lonely Rage 12
Louima, Abner 225, 230
L'Ouverture, Toussaint 180
Lumumba, Patrice 8
lynched art 92, 96, 98

Ma'at 61, 62, 104
Madhubuti, Haki 2, 3, 6, 7, 10, 12, 13, 14, 20, 22, 74, 83–84, 87, 103, 104, 114, 124, 125, 128, 132, 133, 135–136

Madhubuti, Safisha 133, 151–152, 153, 156, 157–158, 159, 168–173; Malcolm and renaming 220–255
Madison Square Garden 115
Mafunkikiwa, Saki 161–162
Make It Plain 178
Making Malcolm 9
Malcolm X 2, 3, 5, 6, 7, 9, 10, 11, 12, 14; on Africa 165–166, 170–173, 174, 177, 178, 179; African fusion 162–166; black arts influence 15, 16, 17, 18, 20, 23, 26, 36, 49, 29, 30, 49, 52–53, 56–58, 103, 113, 114, 121, 123, 124, 125, 127, 129, 131, 132, 133, 135, 136, 138; Brook's involvement 193–195, 196, 198, 199, 202; dietary influence 177–180; Ella Collin's involvement 193–196, 198, 199, 200–202, 204–205, 209; globalist 142–144, 200, 202, 216; muse 142, 144–146, 151, 155, 156, 157–158, 159, 164; oratory and Madhubuti's poetics 220–255; re(re)naming 210–214; and Safisha 169–173, 174; signifying 215–218; style influence on Newton and Madhubuti 183, 185, 186, 188, 189, 190, 191–192; third world press 148–151, 157, 159, 160, 161; uttering African-American 218
Malcolm X on Afro-American History 159
Malcolmian 2, 6, 24, 29, 56, 61, 103, 136, 174, 179, 219, 220, 223, 224, 229, 234, 236, 238, 241, 242, 245, 249, 250
Marley, Bob 243
Maroons 18, 138
Martin, Tony 105
The Marvelettes 167
Marx, Karl 138
Mary McLeod Bethune Teachers Training Center 154
Massachusetts General Colored Association 205
McKarthy, Joseph 112
McKay, Claude 62, 85, 87, 95–103, 106, 210, 213, 225, 228, 239–240, 249
McKee, Larry 141
Mdu/Ntr 98, 141
Meiners, Christoph 67, 77
Memmi, Albert 30
Menelik 109
Mentu 141
Meridian 24, 231–232
Mintz, Sidney 33
The Mis-education of the Negro 30, 242
Mnemosyne 144
Monster's Ball 215
Monument to Malcolm X 12
Moor 65–66
Moore, Richard B. 65, 200, 210
Morrison, Toni 23, 67, 77, 248
Mos Def 23
Mosley, Elaine 153, 171
Motown 149, 167
Muhammad, Clara 159
Muhammad, Elijah 7, 10, 12, 16, 18, 30, 49, 52–53, 57, 103, 114, 115, 123, 129, 132, 138,

143, 146, 147, 174–177, 179, 186, 190, 199, 207, 210, 215, 218, 249
Muhammad, Wallace Deen 176
Muhammad, Wallace Fard 175
Muhammad Speaks 179
multiculturalism 14
Muslim Mosque Inc. 132, 150
Muslims 52, 65, 176, 177, 178, 181
Mussolini, Benito 109, 116
The Myth of the Negro Past 33, 141

The Name "Negro": Its Origins and Evil Use 47, 65
Nas 20, 252
Nation of Islam 5, 7, 8, 9, 10, 18, 30, 159, 190, 201, 202, 212
Nation Within a Nation 169
National Association for the Advancement of Colored People/NAACP 32
nationalist 116, 123, 138, 143, 144
Native Americans 63, 66, 120–121, 139, 240, 248
Native Son 107, 235
Neal, Larry 10, 11, 12, 22, 52, 56, 136, 139; Malcolm as muse 144–145, 146, 156
Negro 2, 5, 7, 8, 10, 12, 19, 21, 23, 26, 29, 30, 32, 33, 34, 37, 38, 46; and Garvey 115–124, 127, 135, 137, 142, 146, 158, 161, 162, 176, 181, 185, 194, 200, 202, 208, 209, 210, 211, 218, 226, 231, 253; and Harper 75–85; and Hughes 108–115; and McKay 96, 100–101, 102, 103; old and new 51–58, 86; and Wheatley 61–74
Negro es Bello II 12
Nephthys 145
New Concept Development Center 151, 152–156, 157, 158, 159–160, 163, 167, 168, 169, 170, 171–172, 173
New Concept School 133, 174
Newton, Huey P. 10, 11, 12, 13, 14, 20, 55, 177, 178, 179; X influence on style 180–183, 186, 201
Nguzo Saba 160
Nigger 32, 37, 43–46
Nkrumah, Kwame 121
Nommo 8, 9, 17, 206, 217, 218, 219, 223, 250
Notes on the State of Virginia 35
Nṯr 141, 209
Nṯrw 209
ntu 205–209, 213, 222, 235, 249
Nyerere, Julius 166
Nzuri model 142, 222, 235

Oedipus 99, 100, 136
Ogun 141, 221, 230, 235, 236, 237, 239, 242, 250
Organization of Afro-American Unity 5, 8, 9, 132, 147, 158–159
Oroonoko 69
Osirus/Osiris 79, 145, 227–228
Othello 34, 45, 93

Pan-African 2, 18, 30, 61, 106, 107, 166, 235
Paris, Ethel 183
paterrollers 224–225
The Peculiar Institution 30, 33
Philadelphia 76rs 183
pigs and pork 177–179
Plato 230
Playing in the Dark 67
Poems on Miscellaneous Subjects 74, 75, 78
Poetical Works of Marcus Garvey 105
police brutality 223–225, 230
Pope, Alexander 68
Porter, Dorothy 79
The Possessive Investment in Whiteness 117
Post-Traumatic Slave Syndrome 162
Pound, Ezra 15
Powell, Adam Clayton 137, 143, 144, 148, 217
Pre-Colonial Black Africa 126
Pythagoras 130

Queen Nzingha 65

Ra 227
RaceChanges 226
Race Matters 200
racism 23, 24, 63, 70, 78, 95, 101, 102, 103, 104, 129, 132, 169, 175, 178, 180, 182, 184, 195, 201, 224, 233
Rampersad, Arnold 105
Randall, Dudley 149
rap and hip hop 9, 19, 23, 55, 201, 203, 209, 213, 252
Reed, Ishmael 14, 15
renaming 199–200, 212, 213, 218–219, 221, 229, 242, 252, 253
Republic of New Africa 223
Revolutionary Action Movement (RAM) 223
Revolutionary Suicide 12, 13, 178, 181, 201
rhythm and blues 166
Ricks, Willie 14
Robeson, Paul 8, 57, 125, 129, 133, 138, 139, 165, 189, 198
Robinson, Randall 164
Rockefeller 113
Rodgers, Carolyn 12, 148, 169, 172–173
Rodney, Walter 48, 63, 97, 163, 209
Rose, Tricia 19
Ruffin, David 167
Run Toward Fear 197, 253

Sales, William 9, 159
Sanchez, Sonia 2, 13, 19
Scholes, Richard 60
Scott, Dred 110
Seale, Bobby 10, 11, 12, 14, 23, 55, 177, 178, 179, 182, 186
Senghor, Leopold S. 128
set 145
Seventh Child 195, 212
Shabazz, Betty 253
Shakur, Afeni 252

Shakur, Tupac 252
Sharpton, Al 23
Shelley, Percy Bysshe 93, 96
Shepp, Archie 15
Shields, John 71
Shorty 195
Shu 145
signifying 206, 217, 225, 229–230, 231
Signifying Monkey 223, 228
Sistrunk, Albertha 68
slam poetry 23
Slave Culture 8, 37, 138
slave trade 63, 76
Slavery's Buried Past 141
Smokey Robinson and the Miracles 167
Snellings, Ronald (Askia Muhammad Toure) 12, 14
so-called negro 129, 143, 200, 201, 208, 209, 211, 212, 213, 217, 218, 221, 227, 241, 242
Songs of Jamaica 95
Southern Christian Leadership Council 138
spoken word 23
Sports Illustrated 184
Springsteen, Bruce 241
Spurr, David 215
Stagolee 181
Stampp, Kenneth 30, 33
Statement of Basic Aims and Objectives 5
Still, William 75
Stubbs, Levi 167
Stuckey, Sterling 8, 37, 138, 208, 229, 248
Student Non-Violent Coordinating Committee 11, 14, 182
Sun Ra 15
The Supremes 167

Tadadjeu, Maurice 161–162
Takaki, Ronald 229
Taney, Roger 110
Tanner, Henry O. 85
Tate, Gayle 75, 168
Taylor, Cecil 15
Tefnut 145
Temple, Shirley 226
The Temptations 167
Theodosius 98
Think Black 14
Third World 13
Third World Press 2, 133, 148–150, 151, 153, 169, 172, 196, 197
Thompson, Julius E. 253
Thompson, Robert Farris 248
Tillery, Tyrone 96
To Die for the People 183, 186
"to live for the people" 182, 186
Toomer, Jean 85, 87
Tourè, Sèkou 166
Training Day 215
Trotter, Joe William 21
Tsoi tsoi 139–140
Tubman, Harriet 9, 84, 138, 153, 158, 180

Turner, Lorenzo 31, 33
Twain, Mark 69

Umbra Workshop 15
Umfundalai 139, 145, 156
The Underground Railroad 75
Understanding the New Black Poetry 226
United States 223, 238
Universal Negro Improvement Association 8, 85, 159, 189, 191
Unknown Tongues 75, 168

vegetarianism 177, 180

Wade, Abdoulaye 164
Walker, Alice 24
Walker, David 30, 36, 76, 123, 138, 147, 151; compared to X 204–208
Walker, Margaret 107
war poetry 62, 103, 193–194, 223
Ward, Ann 153, 172
WARPLAND: A Journal of Black Literature and Ideas 155
Washington, Madison 204
Wasiri 79, 145
WDAS 167
Wells, Ida B. 123, 138, 143, 204
Welsh-Asante, Kariamu 99, 139–140, 151, 156, 181, 197
West, Cornell 200, 204, 206
Wheatley, Phillis 24, 25, 26, 61–74, 96, 98, 101, 113, 215, 235, 242
White, Vibert 175; *Whiteness of a Different Color* 215
White, Walter 234
white-face 74, 77, 78, 80, 85, 92
White Over Black 34
white supremacy 9, 55, 78, 95, 113, 114, 117, 160, 175, 179, 181, 185, 229, 225, 253
Wideman, John Edgar 236
Wilder, Douglas 184
Williams, Chancellor 48, 64–65, 97, 138, 167
Wilson, Amos 160
Wilson, Jackie 167
Winthrop, Jordan 34
Woodard, Komozi 169
Woods, Georgie 167
Woods, Tiger 231
Woodson, Carter G. 30, 242
World War I 85
World War II 105
Wright, Bobby 99, 102
Wright, Richard 14, 132, 133, 137, 189, 190, 198, 235

Ya Salaam, Kalamu 14, 16
YellowBlack 178, 188, 189, 220, 251, 253
Yoruba 141, 209, 210, 221
Yurugu: An African-Centered Critique of European Cultural Thought and Behavior 157, 230

Zeus 144

www.ingramcontent.com/pod-product-compliance
Lightning Source LLC
Chambersburg PA
CBHW051211300426
44116CB00006B/521